W9-CUZ-866

Professional
Practice 101

Also from Wiley:

The Survival Guide to Architectural Internship and Career Development
by Grace Kim

Becoming an Architect
by Lee Waldrep

Architect's Essentials of Professional Development
by Jean R. Valence

Architect's Essentials of Starting a Design Firm
by Peter Piven and Bradford Perkins

The Architect's Handbook of Professional Practice
by The American Institute of Architects

For these and other books for emerging architects, visit www.wiley.com/youngarchitect

Professional
Practice 101

Business Strategies
and Case Studies
in Architecture

Second Edition

Andrew Pressman, FAIA

WILEY

JOHN WILEY & SONS, INC.

This book is printed on acid-free paper.

Copyright © 2006 by Andrew Pressman. All rights reserved

Published by John Wiley & Sons, Inc., Hoboken, New Jersey
Published simultaneously in Canada

No part of this publication may be reproduced, stored in a retrieval system, or transmitted in any form or by any means, electronic, mechanical, photocopying, recording, scanning, or otherwise, except as permitted under Section 107 or 108 of the 1976 United States Copyright Act, without either the prior written permission of the Publisher, or authorization through payment of the appropriate per-copy fee to the Copyright Clearance Center, 222 Rosewood Drive, Danvers, MA 01923, (978) 750-8400, fax (978) 646-8600, or on the web at www.copyright.com. Requests to the Publisher for permission should be addressed to the Permissions Department, John Wiley & Sons, Inc., 111 River Street, Hoboken, NJ 07030, (201) 748-6011, fax (201) 748-6008, or online at http://www.wiley.com/go/permission.

Limit of Liability/Disclaimer of Warranty: While the Publisher and the author have used their best efforts in preparing this book, they make no representations or warranties with respect to the accuracy or completeness of the contents of this book and specifically disclaim any implied warranties of merchantability or fitness for a particular purpose. No warranty may be created or extended by sales representatives or written sales materials. The advice and strategies contained herein may not be suitable for your situation. You should consult with a professional where appropriate. Neither the Publisher nor the author shall be liable for any loss of profit or any other commercial damages, including but not limited to special, incidental, consequential, or other damages.

For general information about our other products and services, please contact our Customer Care Department within the United States at (800) 762-2974, outside the United States at (317) 572-3993 or fax (317) 572-4002.

Wiley also publishes its books in a variety of electronic formats. Some content that appears in print may not be available in electronic books. For more information about Wiley products, visit our web site at www.wiley.com.

Library of Congress Cataloging-in-Publication Data:
Pressman, Andrew.
    Professional practice 101 : business strategies and case studies in architecture /
Andrew Pressman.—2nd ed.
    Includes bibliographical references and index.
    ISBN-13 978-0471-68366-7
    ISBN-10 0471-68366-3
1. Architectural practice—United States—Management. 2. Architectural
services marketing—United States. I. Title: Professional practice one 'o'
one. II. Title: Professional practice one hundred and one. III. Title.

NA1996.P76 2005
720'.68—dc22
2005025150

Printed in the United States of America

10 9 8 7 6 5 4 3 2 1

This book is dedicated to the memory
of my father, Norman D. Pressman—
an individual with unsurpassed strength
of character, wisdom, vision, and humor.

"Man is not a farmer or a professor or an engineer, but he is all."
—Ralph Waldo Emerson

"With great power comes great responsibility."
—Spider-Man (by Stan Lee)

Contents

Chapter 4
Project Management | 129

Chapter 5
Making a (Financial) Statement | 171

Chapter 6
To Market, to Market | 199

Chapter 11
Social Responsibilities | 349

Foreword to the Second Edition

Design Practice

Many architectural students, and even some architects, seem to find practice boring, as if it involved simply following rules, applying formulas, and meeting standards, with none of the creative potential of design. Nothing could be further from the truth. Architectural practice has become one of the most dynamic parts of the profession, with change happening and opportunities arising faster than almost any other aspect of our field. The best firms understand that, applying the same level of creativity to their practices as they do to their buildings.

Think of this book, then, as a design primer, providing the basics you will need to create the practice you want. See the legal context of practice as the foundation on which the profession stands, with health, safety, and welfare as the practice equivalent of commodity, firmness, and delight. Consider fees, schedules, and budgets as the means and methods by which the work gets done in a firm, enabling it to work much as a set of contract documents allow a contractor to build. And look at the ethics of practice much as you do the aesthetics of architecture, as something fundamental and inescapable.

At the same time, think of this book as helping you give your practice a shape and form, as you do your buildings. Will your practice radiate from a central point—with a lead designer, a primary vision, a single service— or will it have a modular form, with different units that may change over time in response to shifts in the economic climate or context? Will your firm have a flat organization, with everyone on the same level to maximize interaction and accessibility, or will it have a hierarchical one, with many levels of responsibility and maximum efficiency? Will your office have clear and defensible boundaries between it and consultants and contractors, or will it have a permeable edge that allows for various associations and methods of delivery?

Such questions may seem obvious, but all too often they get overlooked in both school and in the field. Architects whose buildings show extraordinary leaps of imagination often run offices, paradoxically, with the most conservative structure and most unimaginative form. Likewise, firms that have innovated in the organization and operation of their practice often produce, unfortunately, less-than-stellar buildings. Although some of the case studies in this book belie the argument, it seems that too many of us see innovative practice and innovative design as incompatible with each other.

That perspective stems from the artificial division of practice courses from design studios in most architecture schools, leading to a disconnection between the environments we envision and the ways we might achieve them operationally, budgetarily, and politically. Overcoming that disconnect does not necessarily translate to the merger of practice courses and design studios; each has specific content that needs its own setting. However, design educators and reviewers could do a much better job asking not just what a student's design involves or what it means but also how the student might organize its delivery, sequence its construction, justify its cost, or explain its value to a community.

Not that the form of a firm's design and practice have to align: a firm that generates a lot of free-form buildings does not, necessarily, need a free-form office. Rather, a practice requires the same degree of consciousness and creativity that we put into our buildings, responding to the internal and external forces of a particular place and time. Different kinds of clients or building types often require different office organizations, whatever the final form of the buildings produced. And, with increasing frequency, a single office will have more than one way of operating in response to the needs of the different markets it serves.

Just as we would never assume that there exists one building form or organization plan that fits all needs, so too should we never assume that there exists one form of practice or way of organizing an office or delivery process. While a universal form might have worked in simpler times, when many viewed Beaux Arts Classicism or International-Style Modernism as universally valid, it no longer applies in a world where diverse perspectives and varied needs have become the norm. In such a world, design becomes more important than ever, especially when we apply it to our practices as much as to the environments we create.

Thomas Fisher, Professor and Dean
College of Architecture and Landscape Architecture
University of Minnesota

Preface

This book renders accessible the art and science of professional practice in architecture through narratives, essays, interviews, firm profiles, diagrams, and case studies. Both the pragmatics and intangibles are set forth to inspire readers toward outstanding practice, design excellence, and professional growth.

Case studies augment each chapter of this second edition to place material into real-world settings and make this book a powerful didactic tool for both student and professional development. Employing topic-specific case studies requires associated background reading so that the reader is equipped to critically analyze the cases and develop an informed opinion about the often complex and ambiguous situations depicted therein. The chapters in *Professional Practice 101* provide that essential background reading. Professor Christopher Bartlett of the Harvard Business School suggests, "Cases are not just illustrations; they're vehicles for learning. Students make real-life decisions about key management issues, and each decision should lead to a broader set of principles."[1]

Practical. Pragmatic. Nuts and bolts. The basics. A Primer. Fundamentals. "101." Is professional practice the most dull, boring, and inherently dry course you will ever be forced to sit through? *No way!* In fact, as Chuck Thomsen elaborates, the *process* of delivering architectural services should be just as creative, intellectually rigorous, and fun as wrestling with design problems.

Sure, it goes without saying that a certain amount of rather practical knowledge is required to achieve success in the real world, and this material is woven into the pages that follow (for example, project management, firm management and organization, legal and liability issues, marketing, risk management, licensing, internship, teamwork, client and contractor relations, financial management, design and information technology, project delivery, time management, communication and leadership skills, and ethics and professionalism). However, it is the thoughtful application of this knowledge in support of *design excellence* and *a true service ethic* that together define the best in professional practice. The major thrust of the book, then, is to capture the essence of *professional architecture* and to suggest what it takes to achieve this lofty goal. It is just not sufficient to be practical and complete projects on time and within budget.

Essays by renowned professionals supplement the text and include anecdotes from real situations involving staff, clients, contractors, and engineering consultants. The essays illuminate ideas of practice and provide object lessons from which students can begin to derive a theory of practice.

Whenever appropriate, practice issues are linked to *the process of design* to make this text relevant and intriguing. Associating practice and de-

---

[1]Harvard Business School publishing, *Teaching Materials Newsletter* (Winter 1996), p. 1.

sign in the curriculum represents state-of-the-art thinking by a large group of practice and design educators. Students can (and should) immediately apply some of the material in *Professional Practice 101* to design studio projects or related part-time or summer job activities.

Practice in the real world is often exciting and fascinating on many dimensions. My hope is to have translated these rewards into a textbook—to give life to the subject matter and to demonstrate that practice is central to architectural design. Design solutions *must* become more creative and innovative (in response to real-world constraints) to be considered architecture. Decisions are less arbitrary, and schemes are enriched (and get built) when guided by principles of architectural practice. There is indeed a blurring of the design and practice dichotomy.

Nontraditional careers in allied fields (or in professions not allied to architecture) are also addressed. Increasingly, the power of an architectural education is supporting endeavors in satisfying and lucrative areas outside the conventional definition of practice, and involve a broad spectrum of social, commercial, and economic problems.

You will not see standardized forms, checklists, rules of thumb, tables, or formulas in this professional practice text. Paraphrasing Somerset Maugham, there are three rules for successfully running an architectural firm. Unfortunately, no one knows what they are.

Acknowledgments

Much appreciation, respect, and gratitude are extended to John Czarnecki, Assoc. AIA, Acquisitions Editor, and Amanda Miller, Publisher, at John Wiley & Sons, Inc.

The contributors make this book compelling, distinctive, and relevant. Sincere appreciation and thanks are extended to all seventy of them for their generous participation.

The following individuals deserve special mention:

- Lisa Kauffman, MD
- Peter Pressman, MD, Eleanor Pressman, and Iris Slikerman
- John Maudlin-Jeronimo, FAIA, and Kate Schwennsen, FAIA

Andrew Pressman, FAIA
Washington, D.C.
February 2006

Chapter 1

Practice, Practice, Practice

These are incredibly crucial times for an exploration into the nature of professional practice in architecture. Dramatic changes in the way practice is conducted in the last decade alone require students and practitioners alike to develop a *survival* strategy. Some of these recent changes (which are discussed in subsequent chapters) include unstable and recessionary economic trends, innovations in design and information technology, globalization of architecture, a variety of project-delivery modes, diminished responsibility and authority of architects in the construction industry, and the rise of specialization.

Critical thinking and inquiry may well begin with a rediscovery of what it really means to be a professional architect—a concept easily eroded in the struggle to survive. This concept of "professional attitude" is an essential guide for formulating behavior in addressing the challenges architects now face in myriad practice situations.

What It Means to Be a Professional, or the Courage to Be a Misfit

The three essays that follow are intended to define the "professional attitude" alluded to above and to suggest ways to implement it. Since this attitude cannot be written into a contract or legislated, it falls upon our shoulders as professionals to reinvent ourselves and generate a *moral perspective*. The following essays show how this element is as important as the art and science that an architect or any professional brings to the client.

The essays overlap to the extent that each asserts, as Bernard Lown has noted, an "ancient sacred compact"[1] in which another human being is embraced. The importance of this assertion is again best captured by Lown, who has discussed how an allegiance to the tradition of morally embracing another is not only at the heart of being a professional but the source of

---

[1]Bernard Lown, MD, is Emeritus Professor of Cardiology, Harvard School of Public Health; senior physician, Brigham & Women's Hospital; and corecipient of the 1985 Nobel Peace Prize. The full text of Dr. Lown's remarks, quoted from here, appears in his book, *The Lost Art of Healing* (New York: Houghton Mifflin, 1996).

courage in dealing with the "pervasive uncertainties for which technical skill alone is inadequate."

The three short essays you are about to read fully and pragmatically explicate Lown's words and provide slightly different disciplinary viewpoints that dramatize virtually every facet of being a "professional."

PETER PRESSMAN, MD, is a graduate of Northwestern University Medical School. He practices, writes, and does research in Los Angeles and is on staff at Cedars-Sinai Medical Center.

I am a doctor. I think it is a great job, not simply because it involves the practice of medicine but because, at its *best,* being a doctor is *being a professional.* What then is a professional? The answer is difficult since we have come to use the term to describe anyone who does anything a little better than average, but, in fact, *not* everyone is a "real pro." Very few among us, even those who are credentialed members of the great professions—law, medicine, and of course architecture—are, in fact, real pros. So, *what is a professional?* To paraphrase Justice Potter Stewart (who was struggling to define pornography), "It's difficult to define, but I know it when I see it."

We can do a bit better than Justice Stewart, but with the caveat that a consideration of being a professional is ultimately a highly personal matter, and it is likely that the conception and the way of being will be constantly modified and perhaps reinvented over one's professional life. Having said all this, let us begin to get at the more universally accepted foundations of a profession and then work ahead to the beginning of the private and idiosyncratic elements.

First, the classical notions of profession always encompass some large but circumscribed body of specialized information and discipline. Mastery of this material and associated skills requires a relatively long and standardized period of education, training, and apprenticeship, all of which is regulated by an association of already accomplished members of the profession. Intrinsic to this classical material is the service ethic; the professional exists to serve others who do not have a similar extraordinary background and calling. These foundation notions are reasonable and, I suspect you will agree, not particularly provocative or illuminating. By the aforementioned description, it can be argued that most of us—not everyone but most of us—are "real pros."

To better articulate the meaning of being a "professional," it is necessary to dissect the potentials that are buried in the foundations and then project them upward in three dimensions. One element of professionalism has recently been described especially well as the "hard work of great teams" in the local setting; such teams of professionals are dedicated to ongoing, collaborative, disciplined, and practical learning, and they are committed both to educating the public on advances in their field and to drawing appropriate distinctions between what is merely intriguing or interesting and what constitutes meaningful progress (see references 1 and 2 on page 3). Thus professionals conduct research that improves the quality of their interventions, and they report their findings not only to their colleagues but also to the public.

Another dimension of being a "real" professional involves the character of the relationship between the professional and the client or patient being served. This relationship has been affected by waves of social change, by the stresses of the fiscal environment, by the impact of exploding technologies, and by a climate of legal and philosophical hypervigilance, yet great potential remains inherent in it. Despite the press to further stem the already diminishing authority of professionals, to preserve the autonomy of those being served, and to integrate third-party control of resources, a real professional never, ever forgets about the *caring* relationship he or she must develop with the one who receives professional service. This caring relationship can still exist and contain a core of altruism, trust, and virtue (3). It may be the combination of capacity to act in some highly expert and efficacious way in conjunction with caring that begins to properly complete our articulation of the meaning of "professional" (4).

I am suggesting that what distinguishes an "expert" from a "professional" is the sense of urgency about helping that the professional possesses and nurtures. This sense serves as a kind of antenna for receiving the call for assistance from our fellow human beings *who need help now* (5).

In sum, I highlight a little essay by W. E. Gutman that recently appeared in the *Wall Street Journal* (6). Gutman describes his father, a consummate professional, who happened to be a physician:

> He was incorruptible. He had no time for sophistry, no patience for equivocation, no room for shaded areas separating right and wrong. Compassion was his guide, his patients' health and welfare his sole mission and reward. . . . [He] devoted his career to deconstructing aphorisms. He was the magnificent misfit lesser men do not have the courage to be.

Physician, lawyer, or architect—let us all consciously set aside some energy so that we can strive to be a little courageous, a little misfit, and real pros.

REFERENCES

1. Berwick, D. M. "Harvesting Knowledge from Improvement." *Journal of the American Medical Association*. 1996; 275: 877–878.
2. O'Connor, G. T., S. K. Plume, E. M. Olmstead, J. R. Morton, et al. "A Regional Intervention to Improve the Hospital Mortality Associated with Coronary Artery Bypass Graft Surgery." *Journal of the American Medical Association*. 1996; 275: 841–846.
3. Brennan, T. A. "An Ethical Perspective on Health Care Insurance Reform." *American Journal of Law and Medicine*. 1993; 24: 28–41.
4. Balint, J. and W. Sheton. "Forging a New Model of the Patient–Physician Relationship." *Journal of the American Medical Association*. 1996; 275: 887–891.
5. Phrase attributed to geneticist W. French Anderson.
6. Gutman, W. E. "Magnificent Misfit." *Wall Street Journal*, January 31, 1996.

Professionalism and the Public Interest

CARL M. SAPERS is Adjunct Professor of Legal Practice in Design at the Harvard University Graduate School of Design. He was a member of the Boston law firm Hill and Barlow, and his clients included the National Council of Architectural Registration Boards and more than a hundred architectural and engineering firms. © Carl Sapers. Reprinted with permission of Carl M. Sapers.

In these days when the Orwellian vision of language as obfuscation rather than clarification has become a reality, the words *professional* and *professionalism* seem to have lost their hard edge. Once these terms connoted a vocation requiring considerable education, the development of specialized skills, a position of trust and high regard in our society, and usually more than average rewards for performance.[2]

The registration of persons qualified to practice a profession and enjoy the monopoly privilege, which the registration system assured, was based in large part on the notion that the high skills of the professional could be tested and should be tested to protect the public from persons who sought to enjoy the privileges of a professional calling without having endured the rigors of necessary training.

Now we live in an era in which embalmers, hairdressers, and (in the brave new world of California) babysitters require registration under professional licensing statutes.[3] Everything that, in our grandparents' era, was a trade or occupation now lays claim to being a profession: Dry cleaners, insurance agents, real estate brokers, automotive mechanics, all think of themselves as professionals. It is downright undemocratic to deny any American citizen the right to call him- or herself a professional.

Moreover, as we shall soon examine, the gap between what the law expects of tradespeople and of the traditional professional has narrowed. The tradition that the purchaser must beware in dealing with tradespeople has been replaced by consumer-oriented laws giving the purchaser additional rights and giving tradespeople duties of honesty and forthrightness. At the same time, some courts see the design professional (as well as the doctor, lawyer, and other members of the learned professions) as supplying a product much like

---

[2]Professor Walter Gellhorn, in his splendid article, "The Abuse of Occupational Licensing," appearing in the 1976 volume of the *University of Chicago Law Review,* raises serious questions about the mythology of "learned professions." He cites President Charles W. Eliot of Harvard, who remarked that in the last half of the nineteenth century anybody could "walk into a medical school from the street" and many of those who did walk in "could barely read and write." Gellhorn also noted that the earliest compilations of law in New England were based on inaccurately remembered legal principles rather than on any great learning: as is recorded that there was only one law book in Massachusetts in 1636 and seven in 1647, when six more arrived from England. Even in Abraham Lincoln's time, the great emancipator suggested in 1858 that any young man wishing to enter the learned profession of the law should have read five books that Lincoln named. As late as 1900, one could be admitted to practice law in every state in the United States without having earned a law degree or even an undergraduate college degree.

[3]In 1969, California led with 178 licensed occupations while Pennsylvania, close behind, licensed 165.

tradespeople, as opposed to the traditional notion that a professional is supplying advice based upon synthesizing a great body of learning.

Having observed the confusion in our times as to who is a professional and who is not, I propose in this note to declare those hallmarks of a professional and, in particular, those hallmarks characteristic of a design professional, and thereafter to deal with the terms "professional" and "professionalism" in the terms used to define them. Thus, with a sweep of the hand, I clear from the table the septic tank cleaners, beekeepers, and babysitters who, by effective lobbying of their local legislators, have had themselves declared "professionals." I consider only the traditional learned professions in what follows.

There are three important characteristics of design professionals. First, they are expected to have had substantial and specialized education and training in their professional work before they are permitted to practice it. Second, in their practice, they are expected to exercise discretion wisely. Third, they are expected to accept fiduciary responsibilities at a level well beyond the level expected of tradespeople in the marketplace.

The first of these characteristics, that professionals have special training, is obvious and need not be expanded upon here. We should note, however, that many critics of the design professions believe that the professional fraternity has overemphasized this aspect of professionalism and neglected the other two.

The point about exercising discretion is an essential characteristic of all of the learned professions. The auto mechanic may synthesize knowledge to remedy a defect in your motor. In most cases, however, there is one correct remedy and a series of incorrect remedies, and the good auto mechanic will always choose the correct remedy. For the design professional, the situation is different. First, the problem is multifaceted and light-years more complex than the problem the automotive mechanic faces. Even more important, there is never "one correct remedy" but a multitude of "remedies," and each selected solution carries with it ramifications affecting other aspects of the client's problem. (The same can be said for lawyers and doctors in their attempts to solve their clients' problems.) When a client selects a design professional, that client has the right to expect that the design professional will exercise wisely the broad discretion that has been assigned by virtue of the selection, rather than simply cataloging the choices the owner must make in connection with the project.[4]

A fiduciary duty is the duty that a trustee has to the beneficiaries of the trust. It is characterized by loyalty and good faith. It is the opposite of an arm's-length relationship. The beneficiary of a fiduciary duty expects the fiduciary to exercise skills and intelligence on the beneficiary's behalf at all times, without the necessity of skeptical oversight by the beneficiary. Such

---

[4]I have heard this proposition contested by an eminent female architect, who asserts this view of broad discretion wisely exercised is entirely the product of a millennium of male domination. Put in abbreviated form, her proposition is that the male architect or engineer believes, as part of his maleness, that he must bear the decision-making burden for the project. Why, the female architect asks, isn't it the role of the architect to synthesize the knowledge necessary to make each significant decision on a project and to ask the owner or client to make that decision, once educated by the architect, on his or her own?

a beneficiary need not watch the fiduciary as the prudent meat purchaser watches the scales to be sure that the heavy hand of the butcher is not nestled in next to the beefsteak when calculating the price of the meat, for it is the characteristic of the fiduciary to put his or her own self-interest to one side and consider the interest of the beneficiary paramount.[5]

It has been said that it is the design professional's obligation to prefer the client's interest over his or her own and, when the issues are clear, to prefer the public interest over both. That is one way of expressing the professional's fiduciary duty. As with so much in life, it is much easier to state a general proposition than to apply it to the specific circumstances confronting you in the real world. Here are three examples taken from the real world:

1. Under the terms of the contract documents, the architect is to be the judge of the performance of both the owner and the contractor. In the course of construction, the window channels, already installed, are retaining water. The contractor states that the channels should have had weep or vent holes but that none were shown on the drawings nor specified in the specifications. The contractor says that to remedy the situation will cost the owner $50,000. The owner is taking the position that an experienced contractor should have known that weep holes are required and put them in without regard to the absence of such a requirement in the plans and specifications. The architect is called upon to render a decision in the dispute. What does the architect do?

2. An architect has designed housing using poured-in-place concrete as the structural system for a developer and owner who is building the housing with his own subsidiary construction company. In the course of a weekly inspection, the architect discovers that the superintendent of construction has been cheating on the cement content of the concrete and that the concrete will not meet the strength required by the specifications and by the local building code. The architect tells the owner about the problem immediately. The owner says, "Don't worry about it. I'll talk to my construction superintendent." But the architect has reason to believe that the owner knew about the cheating from the very beginning and was pleased to enjoy the money savings. The architect, by the way, is required to certify the owner's and contractor's requisitions before the construction lender will make payment. A requisition including the month's concrete work is on the architect's desk. What does the architect do?

3. A structural engineer, responsible for the structural design of a major skyscraper in an important and densely populated American city, discovers a year after substantial completion that he made a basic error in his calculations with the result that the building will fail in a twenty-year re-

---

[5]While the notion that the architect and the engineer are each in a fiduciary relationship to their clients is widely held, there are very few legal cases that have turned on that point. Those cases chiefly arise out of the architect's or engineer's failure to keep clients fully informed of increased costs. See, for example, *Getzschman v. Miller Chemical Co., Inc.,* 443 N.W. 2d 260 Neb. (1989); *Kaufman v. Leard,* 356 Mass. 163, 248 N.E. 2d 480 (1969); and *Zannoth v. Booth Radio Stations,* 333 Mich. 233, 52 N.W. 2d 678 (1952).

turn wind. The hurricane season in that part of the country is two months off. The owner and chief occupant of the building is a major insurance corporation. If a twenty-year return wind should occur, there is a high probability that portions of the building will fly off and fall to the ground within six blocks of the structure. The structure and its calculations had been approved by the building department of the city. The remedial action will cost $2 million and take three months to complete if all parties cooperate in the work. What does the structural engineer do?

Persons connected with Ralph Nader's organization and their friends in government agencies like the Federal Trade Commission have, in recent years, tended to disparage the notion of professionalism. You will note that Judge John Sirica refers to architecture as a "business"; we can assume that that word was used consciously as a way of saying, "When push comes to shove, I know you're in it chiefly for money." Nader would observe that all this talk about professionalism is dandy, but the facts are that the profession, whenever given a chance, tightens the gate by which people are admitted to the franchise but enforces rules of professional conduct only when they are anticompetitive in effect. To Nader and his allies, the attempt of the American Institute of Architects to enforce Standard Nine is consistent with the attempts by the American Institute of Architects and the National Society of Professional Engineers to prevent their members from bidding for jobs on the basis of competitive fees. It is closely connected to the efforts of both organizations and similar professional organizations to establish fee schedules to which all members would adhere in seeking work.[6] How seldom, they comment, has a design professional been called on the carpet by the profession because he or she cheated a client, bribed a public official, or behaved in a way that violated the high standards of professionalism set forth earlier in this note.

This dispute rages at this very hour. The Justice Department, the FTC, and state sunset commissions across the country are devoting considerable energies to the deregulation of occupations and professions. Their view seems to be that since registration procedures do so very little to protect the public and so much to protect the income of professionals, it follows that the public will at least benefit from reduced costs for professional services if the franchise is broadened.

But there are professionals whose careers meet the standards discussed earlier. There are architects and engineers who flourish in that exacting relationship to their clients and the public described above. They have contributed honorably and significantly to our built environment. This commentator believes that, if Nader and the various government agencies have their way, professionalism may not survive in America.

---

[6]In 1975, the United States Supreme Court struck down professional fee schedules as violating the Sherman Act. *Goldfarb v. Virginia State Bar,* 421 U.S. 773 (1975) REH'G denied, 423 U.S. 886 (1975). In 1978, the Court struck down the National Society of Professional Engineers' ethical prohibition against bidding for work. *National Society of Professional Engineers v. United States,* 435 U.S. 679 (1978).

Professional Through and Through

ABBOT KOMINERS is an attorney and arbitrator based in Maryland. He holds an AB from Bowdoin College and a JD from George Washington University. Copyright 2005 by Abbot Kominers.

Professionalism is a continuous structure that exists outside and inside the natural person who is the professional. It is a phenomenon that theoretical mathematicians would label a möbius strip—a structure on which all points can be reached from every other point. Professionalism is the manner in which professionals deal with their colleagues and the public, and the spirit that professionals carry in their heads and their guts about what they do.[7]

The Route to Professionalism

To colleagues and the public, the professional is an expert in the specialized knowledge and mechanics of the field in which he or she practices. To obtain that expertise, the professional undergoes a formal training process, frequently academic in nature. From that base, however, the professional must build an inventory of practical skills based on the world as it actually is, not on a textbook or stylized version of reality. Practical experience assists the professional in traveling the uncertain regions of performance that fall between the points of fixed knowledge learned in formal training.

In addition to initial training, a professional understands that the specialized knowledge in his or her field is dynamic. Therefore, a professional engages in a continual learning process (both formal and informal) to increase substantive knowledge and to hone practical skills. Appreciating that no field exists in a vacuum, a professional also remains alert to events and information in the world beyond his or her specialized area of knowledge. The professional remembers that common sense must not be lost to professional doctrine and processes.

Outside the Professional

From this base of learning and skills, a professional operates in a world of people with whom he or she works (colleagues and other specialists) and people whom he or she serves (the clients or public). A professional is distinguished from other diligent and expert workers by the fact that these relationships with colleagues and clients are "consensual and fiduciary."[8]

---

[7]While the observations herein about professionals and professionalism apply in the military context, the topics of military professionals and professionalism should be treated separately. One of the best analyses of military professionalism is: Maj. C. A. Bach, "Know Your Men . . . Know Your Business . . . Know Yourself," *US Naval Institute Proceedings,* April 1974. For an interesting study of contrasting premises and methodologies, see: Pat C. Hoy, II. "Soldiers and Scholars," *Harvard Magazine,* May–June 1996.

[8]*Holloway v. Faw, Casson & Co.,* 319 Md. 324, 572 A. 2d 510, 516 (1990). In this case, Judge Lawrence F. Rodowsky also opined, "Accountants, like doctors and lawyers, are engaged in a profession which requires clients to reveal personal and confidential information to them in the course of the professional relationship."

As part of the "consensual and fiduciary" relationship, the professional owes clients both judgment and learning; the professional is, after all, the client's expert advisor. When objecting to the questions by a U.S. Senator to his client, Oliver North, attorney Brendan V. Sullivan Jr. once observed that his role was not to sit idly by while his client stumbled into serious legal difficulty.[9] Although there is a positive trend in codes of professional conduct to require that professionals provide clients with information and options so that clients have the opportunity to understand their situation and to make choices as to a course of action, professionals may not abandon their responsibility to give their clients the benefit of their learning and experience by way of their judgment as to the course of action selected. In the overly litigious atmosphere of today's professional practice, there is a strong economic incentive not to risk advising a course of action for fear that an unsatisfied client will blame the professional for any unsatisfactory result and sue for malpractice. This danger, however, does not relieve the professional from the obligation to voice his or her judgment.

The professional is further obliged to protect the public from his or her own profession. A lawyer, for instance, must be knowledgeable—or must become knowledgeable—about the substance of any matter undertaken. Likewise, a professional knows his or her limitations and admits that there are some matters that he or she does not have the expertise or the time to undertake. Staying with the earlier example, a lawyer must not put his or her interest in either further employment from a client or embarrassment at not knowing all the answers ahead of the client's interest in competent representation. Indeed, a lawyer must have no conflicts of interest with the client and must place the client's welfare before the lawyer's own. In addition, the lawyer must assess these, and all other questions, with integrity and honesty.

Allegations of substandard professional performance are measured against the sound judgment of similarly situated professionals as to the best interests of clients, the public at large, and the profession—that separate and distinct entity that is the collective history of all prior and current practitioners. Diligent self-policing of incompetence as well as of intentional misconduct and abuse is a hallmark of professionalism.[10] In many professions, including law, professional codes of conduct or ethical standards have grown up over many years with the intent of improving the standard of practice and policing the profession. These written standards have attempted to codify what was once considered simply good judgment and

---

[9]In response to Hawaii's Senator Daniel Inouye's demand that Mr. Sullivan's client, Oliver North, interpose his own—not Mr. Sullivan's—objection to the Senator's question, Mr. Sullivan stated, "Well, sir, I'm not a potted plant. I am here as the lawyer. That's my job" (*The Washington Post*, July 10, 1987). Compare Sullivan's response to Edmund Burke's comment: "Your representative owes you, not his industry only, but his judgment; and he betrays, instead of serving you, if he sacrifices it to your opinion" (Edmund Burke, "Speech to the Electors of Bristol," November 3, 1774.)

[10]The practical necessity of cost containment has spurred the increasing use of paraprofessionals in many fields. This trend raises troubling questions of how diligent will be the policing of the performance of these individuals and by whom will it be accomplished. See Robert L. Ostertag, "Nonlawyers Should Not Practice," *ABA Journal*, May 1996.

fair dealing. Too frequently, however, compliance with the written standards has been substituted for ethics or professionalism. Sadly, there is a danger that the measure of ethical performance has become whether or not an action fit into approved ethical guidelines or rules rather than whether it was the manifestation of good judgment and fair dealing to the client, the public, and the profession.[11]

The result of the professional's fulfilling these myriad obligations is the simple respect of clients, the public, and the profession for the professional's workmanlike performance, abilities, and spirit. Respect is not arrogance-inspired fear nor demigodlike awe. It is not about overpaid megacelebrities who shamelessly mug for cameras or perform feats well within the capacities of trained circus animals yet contribute nothing to clients or society. Neither is respect the corrupt notion now popular with street gangs and political rabble-rousers that mere existence rather than achievement and merit entitles a person or group to credit, reverence, or acceptance by the community. Respect is the understanding of the skills, drive, and right conduct that the professional practices and exhibits publicly and privately. To understand the difference between genuine and counterfeit respect is to begin to understand the workings of the head and guts of the professional.

Inside the Professional

The professional must possess an understanding of the history of his or her profession.[12] Understanding the path and process of doctrinal evolution aids in understanding the doctrine, because the changes come about through refinements of the specialized knowledge. Likewise, the history of the profession's philosophy illuminates the profession's relation to society so that the professional knows his or her role in society and what society demands of the professional. A profession's history also serves as the professional's inspiration. An understanding of the profession's past performance educates the professional as to what is the aspirational pinnacle of professional action and where the profession needs to improve its behavior.

Professionals also must have a driving energy that compels their attention to a task. Professionals exhibit grit and zeal. They vigorously pursue their obligations. They act. They set the bar high. Although stymied or defeated, in the words of my Grandfather Koplow, "[A professional] gets dressed each day like he's going downtown." He knows that one cannot always be right (or as my Grandfather Kominers said, "They put rubber mats under cuspidors because men make mistakes"), but a professional still drives him- or herself toward that impossible *and impractical* goal. The professional knows that professionalism is understanding that the penalty for being wrong is not necessarily some explicit statutory or regulatory sanction but his or her own sense of failing the client and the profession.

The professional must season this drive with optimism, good humor, courtesy, and human warmth. Not only are they the right behavior, but also they serve a practical purpose as well: These are the fertile media in which

---

[11]Meg Greenfield. "Right and Wrong in Washington," *The Washington Post,* February 6, 1995.
[12]Edwin H. Simmons, "Why *You* Should Study Military History," *Fortitudine,* Fall 1995.

flourish positive working relationships with colleagues and clients. The professional's vigor and persistence would be as ineffective as a world-class sprinter's running on ice without the motivation, loyalty, and peace that these characteristics help to establish.

Professionalism is characterized by an earnestness and gravity that often include a nearly obsessive attention to detail. As an example, I recall the sergeant major in my college ROTC (Reserve Officers' Training Corps) unit. He was a wiry, bantamweight soldier with at least a quarter-century in his country's uniform. Without any comment or fanfare, he wore several decorations for valor and the Combat Infantryman's Badge, which evidenced the honor and dedication with which he had served his fellow Americans. Yet on one occasion, when pressing an ROTC cadet's ink-covered fingertips onto a blank Army identification form, he was moved to observe, "Fingerprinting is very serious business."

Professionalism. Very serious business indeed.

Linking Design and Practice

One of the factors that distinguishes architects from other participants in the construction world is the conception and production of high quality *design*. And one of the main issues of *practice* is the full realization and delivery of that design. Thus it should be evident that design and practice can and should be—*must be*—inextricably linked. This is such a crucial linkage that I decided to go "straight to the top" and address it in the following way:

I asked four individuals, each of whom is a world-renowned educator *and* a practitioner, to write an open letter to students and young architects, responding to the following questions:

1. What are the most significant practice issues that influence the design process? How should students view or address these issues to support or perhaps enrich design solutions?
2. What should students be thinking and doing while engaging projects in the design studio to better prepare for professional practice?
3. What advice would you give to a student or an emerging architect to promote the transition from design excellence in school to achieving design excellence in practice?

CHARLES GWATHMEY

The Importance of Design

1. The most significant practice issue that influences the design process is your commitment to the idea of discovery within the context and constraints of the problem. Preconception and replication are the curse of an uncreative process that will ultimately produce solutions that are known and unprovocative.

It is essential to view constraints as a positive reference for interrogation and invention rather than as a limitation.

I believe the design discovery process must be holistic and composite, that one must objectively analyze and prioritize the various elements that will impact the solution. The design process is not a linear diagram but a composite overlay, where formal strategies, circulation, structure, sequence, plan and section, site and orientation, and schedule and budget are all investigated, tested, and refined concurrently. Only then is the essential creative editing process meaningful or possible.

2. Students should objectively assess their passion for making the art of architecture. This passion cannot be about money, efficiency, or expediency. It can only be about a kind of commitment to creating vital and enduring, memorable and aspiring works that affect the perceptual and intellectual speculation of the experiencer. Design is an insidiously conflicting process, because unlike a painter or sculptor, who is the creator and the executor of a private vision, the architect relies on the client/patron who is speculating on an as-yet-unseen or unrealized vision. Therefore, the role of the architect invariably becomes both pedagogic and psychoanalytic, as well as creative, causing continual contradictions and conflicts between the ideal/idea and the reality.

Commitment to one's ideals is a prerequisite. Compromise is an unresolvable alternative. Thus the student to become architect, the architect to be always student, must commit to the idea that the creative process is as gratifying and rewarding as the manifestation and the moments of recognition. Otherwise the rationale and the justification are problematic.

3. My advice is to work for an architect whose work you admire and to realize that the time invested, though somewhat different from the school experience, is critical to the continuity of your growth and maturation.

Also, if a design opportunity arises, no matter how small or "insignificant," no matter your "lack of experience," take it, relish it, commit to it, and most importantly take the risk. Without fulfilling the obligation of risk, you will neither grow nor learn. There is no failure in a continuous process of discovery. There is failure only in accommodation and compromise.

Charles Gwathmey

Mr. Gwathmey paints in broad strokes a picture of just how design and practice are not only closely linked but at best driven by each other; they are mutually interdependent, one unable to exist without the other. Gwathmey's piece also makes it almost poetically clear that creativity is demanded in all phases of professional practice and not limited to design. When done right, design and practice may even be synergistic; that is, together they yield a product greater than the sum of the forces that led to its development.

On a personal note, I especially appreciated Gwathmey's caveat about seizing every opportunity no matter how small and no matter how ill-prepared one may feel. Gwathmey calls upon us to seize the day and make the most of it. This clearly is not only a philosophy of professional practice but also a philosophy of life that seems to have stood the test of time.

JOHN HARTRAY
The Studio and the Real World

The cathedrals were products of an age that included the Hundred Years' War, and bubonic plague. We should remember that even without earthquakes, hurricanes, and floods, the environment in which architects practice is very unstable. Our clients keep changing as we attempt to fit them into permanent structures. Institutions often turn to architecture to ward off impending trouble. The AT&T Building was barely topped out when the corporation was broken up. As it searches for its place in a specialized market, Sears, Roebuck and Co. continues to fortify itself in new locations. Failing marriages also often employ architects prior to resorting to lawyers.

The academic studio contrasts with the real world because of its deadly stability. Studio critics often cling to the same aesthetic preferences for years. They call this consistency and are proud of it. Their project programs and sites are pretested to assure that most of the class will succeed. Real clients are more volatile and less compassionate.

The following techniques can introduce a sense of mischievous reality to studio projects:

- Design three alternate site plans, building plans, and elevation systems, and at each stage in the design process choose between them by rolling dice. (This was a requirement in IBM architectural contracts that worked well in getting past the designer's preconceptions.)
- Change the site from flat to a hill, or from Vermont to Arizona, halfway through the project.
- Roll dice to see who has to use steel frame, reinforced concrete, and masonry bearing walls.
- Draw straws to see who has to adapt their design to the Georgian, Art Deco, Collegiate Gothic, or International styles.
- Make a publishable rendering during the first hour of the project. Then try to fit the program and plan into your preconception during the remaining time.

In making the transition from school to work, stay away from architects for at least a couple of years. Work for a contractor.

Learn how details are built rather than drawn. You will also learn a great deal from mechanical engineers, and even more from civil engineers. If you understand the land, the buildings take care of themselves.

Every architect should build a boat.

Jack Hartray gives us a measured reality check. He warns us that *practice* in the real world bears little similarity to *practice* in the academic studio. This warning is balanced with an implicit promise of much greater creative potentials in the real world, a scary and less predictable place but one rich with opportunity and adrenalin. I would add that occasional use of Hartray's practical suggestions could be of enormous value . . . except maybe the one about the boat.

MARIO SALVADORI
A Daring Piece of Advice to Young Architects (from a Nonarchitect)

You have just obtained, after years of hard work, a degree in architecture; whether an undergraduate or a graduate degree makes little difference either financially or professionally. You have entered *the most difficult profession in the world.* And you are looking for a job, possibly in the greatest architectural office in your town or a few miles from it.

I am not an architect but just an engineer (and a professor of architecture) who gave most of his time to design architectural structures all over the world with some of the greatest architects in the world. On the basis of this fifty years experience, I dare to speak to you so that you might realize what you have achieved and what you are going to meet in your career.

First, let me emphasize that, since the entire world is a shamble and since architecture has to do with the people alive today, your training was not, nor could it have been, both great and sensitive. All the schools of architecture are in a state of confusion, mirroring the state of society. You have been told some great truths by some great teachers and as soon as you enter an architectural office, you will find that some of these great truths do not apply to reality.

Second, let me overemphasize, if I can, that, depending on the kind of training you have received, you may believe that architecture belongs to the field of art and are unaware that, out of a hundred of you, only seven will have a chance at designing an entire building, while the other ninety three will have minor responsibilities for the infinite number of demands required by a building.

Third, I want you to realize that architects have to be tough because they have to fight against the other twenty or so professionals who have something to say about architecture: owners, mechanical engineers, electrical engineers, the other ten varieties of engineers, and then the banks, the renting specialists, the environmentalists, and so on.

Fourth, I must alert you to the fact that structural engineers will make it hard if not impossible for you to realize your dreams and that, if you only knew a little more about structures than what you have learned in school, you might have a chance of fighting them. Actually the only solid piece of advice I can give you would be to get a degree in civil engineering with a major in structures, but I am sure that after four to six years in a school of architecture, you will not cherish my suggestion.

Last, I wish to suggest that you should ignore all the advice I have given you and should give all your enthusiasm, your belief in your dreams and your patience to design architecture the way you believe architecture should be designed. Remember that the greatest architecture has always been built by daring rebels and has been recognized a number of years after their death.

Was all your work and pain worth it? You bet it was, because the only way to be successful in life is to believe in a dream and refuse to bow to the negative pressure that comes against you from all corners. If you give yourself to what you believe in, you will work for love and not for money, and when you work for love, you do not feel you are working, you are just having a great time. If this is true for you, believe it or not, you are bound to be successful.

It worked for me; why shouldn't it work for you?

Mario Salvadori

The late Professor Salvadori gives us another kind of provocative reality-check, but one wedded to a more romantic vision. He observes that the challenges to architecture have never been tougher and more complex, and that, in fact, the entire globe faces sobering and unprecedented struggles—none of which we are ever really prepared to face in the course of any training. Salvadori seems to regard this condition as a badge of honor, perhaps even nobility. He implores us to possess a clear vision of the world, but *not* to be shy about nobly and boldly assaulting the rock face with our dreams. Convention may well be something to be questioned and defied in the pursuit of solutions and expression of passion.

GEORGE ANSELEVICIUS

"I don't want to be interesting; I want to be good."

There are a number of reasons why young people decide to become architects and undertake lengthy studies lasting from three-and-a-half to six years. It could be due to an interest in making and constructing things, an interest in art and drawing, a wish to make a better and more beautiful world, a response to the urging of parents, and possibly because being an architect sounds intriguing and glamorous and may even be lucrative.

Education is not just the province of schools but a continuing life-long attitude linking school and practice. Architecture is not merely a nine-to-five chore but an avocation that must become an architect's lover as well as spouse.

While architects do become involved in research and in teaching, a majority will join or establish architectural practices. These may vary greatly, from the offices of famous signature architects to more anonymous ones (whose work is seldom published by the elitist architectural press), as well as everything in between. Yet it is likely that all of these offices, whatever their critics may say, pride themselves on the design of their buildings, which is also true of most students creating designs in their studios at schools of architecture.

VALUES. *The design process is the heart of making architecture, professionally as well as academically.* The design of buildings is informed by values affirmed by architect or student, by the demands of client or instructor, values within the sociocultural ambiance of community, society, or school of architecture. While architects owe their best design efforts to their clients, who pay the bills for their services, as professionals (an honorable word) they also owe allegiance to the users of their buildings, to the surrounding community, and one hopes, to the highest aspirations of society. It is well to remember that architecture and the physical planning of places and spaces are not just private acts but exist within the public domain. This poses a number of ethical demands on architects, as the users of their buildings are often unknown or seldom have major input into the final design. There may even be conflicts between client demands and user needs. (Clients are users only when it comes to the design of their own houses.) Thus architects relying on a creative force must resolve a variety of needs, hopes, dreams as well as contradictions. Students, on the other hand, have the luxury to respond purely to theories, as to what they and their instructors see as "good," be it social, ethical, or aesthetic, and can avoid some of the inherent complexities of practice.

This brings us to the purpose of the design studio in architecture schools. While its prescribed task is to prepare students for professional practice, it inevitably raises a number of questions. Do studios, or should they, simulate the design activities of professional offices? Do instructors, or should they, stand in for real-world clients? The answers are equivocal, and as a consequence, students are often torn between reality and theory. They must decide whether their studio projects should respond to the "real" world or purely to academic, hypothetical theories, a dichotomy that may not have been clarified by their instructors. It is my view that studio projects should be a set of rigorous and conceptual finger exercises to prepare, inspire, and toughen students for future full-blown performances in actual practice (apologies for a musical metaphor).

GAPS. *Obviously, there are gaps and differences between practice and school.* Whether some of them are inherent may be debatable. In practice, the cost of buildings and the cost of providing professional services demand a hard discipline that is generally missing or avoided in school design studios. This is generally based on the argument that such considerations would inhibit a student's creativity, although some instructors introduce these issues into the studio, as they believe that realistic constraints demand more creative solutions.

Another difference is the implied demand in design studios that a student's project be "creative," a force that should assert an individual, artistic expression. While this is also true in offices, especially those controlled by strong designers, their efforts are the result of teamwork, which a young professional probably has not experienced in school. Not all buildings need to dazzle; in many cases reticence may be appropriate.

THE STUDIO. *Yet despite the problems and challenges, or perhaps because of them, the design studio is one of the most exemplary teaching methods, full of emotional rewards as well as letdowns.* Student and teacher are related on a "one-to-one" basis, and most importantly the studio demands integration and creation. This is missing in many educational methods, where issues are never integrated but isolated within specific courses, avoiding ethical, social, and political considerations. Closest in concept to the design studio is the case study method, but that approach is essentially analytical, after the fact (although it may lead to creative alternatives). The word "studio" itself brings with it a message of freedom and creativity, and it is even used by larger offices when establishing smaller integrated groups that are then identified as studios.

The environment or "culture" of a design studio in school is rather special. It is somewhat messy, an ordered disorder, yet essentially creative. Study models, sketches, diagrams, and computer drawings abound at various levels of completion, and students create their own personal space within the confines of the studio by whatever means available. There is no hierarchy, and studios are open day and night, frantic efforts during very late evenings and nights being quite fashionable. Offices, on the other hand, must be organized for group action, and an efficient flow of work, although sudden spurts before deadlines continue an architecture tradition.

On the one hand, students are dreaming of joining offices that will offer them creative opportunities rather than have them detail toilet partitions (someone has to do this), while on the other hand, some offices fault the schools for not preparing students to be immediately useful and find that they have to be retrained for the cooperative and more specialized discipline of offices. While there are many kinds of offices, I believe that the more creative ones will look more like studios in school rather than an environment where the only models are highly finished public relations models in the receptionist's entrance and where absolute neatness reigns in rigorous aligned desks inhabited by neatly groomed draftspeople.

Time is valued differently in offices than in schools. In offices, time is equated with money, a necessary discipline. Not so in schools, where personal discipline demands from students a control of their time to design, study, sleep, and perhaps work and also socialize within a twenty-four hour day.

TRANSITION. *Clearly there has to be a transition between school and office; both are different worlds, and both are quite real.* Many students have worked in offices while going to school, and for them the transition is easier. The Intern Development Program (IDP) is a useful system that has been introduced to continue the education of young architects in offices while they are preparing for the professional registration examination. While I support such a program, I do not like the word "intern" for graduates of architecture schools, as I believe such a designation lowers their compensation. The transition between school and practice can be helped by students spending their summers working for architects or contractors and by keeping a sketchbook or diary handy to document buildings and constructions.

EXCELLENCE. *Schools and offices pay homage to the "search for design excellence."* This has become a motherhood statement and a cliché, but like all clichés, it is partially true. Still it is not clear what it signifies. Designing is problem-solving of a specific kind and could be described as a plan of action to change a situation for the better. In architecture, it is too often simply seen as a response to the visual appearance, the form of the building as it expresses the latest fashion or the specific visual bias of student, instructor, or professional. While architects pride themselves on having an "educated" eye, beauty will always remain in the eye of the beholder, and there is a deep cleft between elitist and populist perceptions.

It is much more difficult to provide a balanced evaluation as to what beauty and design excellence in architecture mean. This is of course easier in a building that has become reality, that can be visited, and that has users who can be interviewed. In the school studio, one has to rely solely on drawings and models, which are more difficult to evaluate as beautiful techniques can cloud critical evaluation. This also holds true in the design efforts of offices, which must use special presentation techniques to persuade their clients as to their designs. It takes special talent to see within drawings and models the actual buildings as they may appear and fulfill human needs.

Design excellence cannot be skin deep; it must broadly relate to context, user needs, technical considerations, and cost, and to the important spatial and aesthetic quality of interior and exterior. While some architectural publications make attempts to view design excellence in a comprehensive manner, all too often it is the glitzy productions of talented photographers found in architectural publications that signify design excellence, and magazines have as much influence, if not more, on students' design efforts as their instructors.

An old-fashioned and perhaps useful bit of advice for potential architects who enter offices with their fresh BArch. or MArch. degrees are two words not heard too often among the architectural establishment: *modesty* and *competence*. These should be watchwords for much of architecture as practiced as well as for one's personal behavior, yet they are usually forgotten in the design studio and in many offices, now part of a world that values entertainment and novelty per se, and where strong egos dominate. To be different is not a value in itself. I understand that the great architect Mies Van der Rohe once said, "I don't want to be interesting; I want to be good." Even if this statement is apocryphal, it is appropriate.

George Anselevicius

Dean Anselevicius responds to the basic questions with a thoughtful rendition and contrasting of the worlds of studio and practice. His timely and persuasive essay brings to mind qualities such as moderation, discipline, integrity, openness, awareness, and ability to collaborate. Together with "modesty and competence," these form a common denominator for "success" with all that the term implies. This denominator is built from diligent commitment to academic and spirtual excellence; this is what makes "design excellence" and professional practice possible.

For Whom Should You Design?

In an ongoing exploration of what professional practice is about, Duo Dickinson takes us on his version of the journey by addressing the transition from school to practice. He points out a series of rather common and particularly malignant pitfalls and misconceptions that can be especially dangerous for the young ambitious architect. Most importantly, Dickinson offers his accumulated wisdom on how to "build well."

DUO DICKINSON, a Cornell University graduate, is principal of his own office in Madison, Connecticut. He is the author of six books and over thirty articles in more than a dozen national publications. Duo Dickinson has taught at Yale College and Roger Williams University. His award-winning work has been featured in over forty venues, including the *New York Times, Architectural Record,* and *House Beautiful.*

After you have been out of school and practiced or taught for a while, it is clear that there are two ways architects design.

1. You Can Design for Other Architects

In truth, that is what architecture students do in school. There are no clients, no budgets. The only rules are aesthetic rules; there are only your critics (who are usually architects) to deal with. It is probably impossible to learn how to design a building *without* this level of abstraction.

Unfortunately, the lessons of school are often hard to unlearn when it comes to getting buildings built. The values and goals of young architects when they leave school often gravitate toward the *product* they design, and they have nothing to do with the *process* of how they are made. What criteria do these architects use to judge their success?

Getting Published

Treating architecture primarily as a product encourages its presentation in a two-dimensional format—in other words, publication. More often than not, those architects who strive to be innovative begin their careers attempting to get published by designing their projects around preexisting architectural notions that may or may not have any real meaning to the actual project at hand.

In effect, these young architects, and sometimes those who are not so young, design for other architects. Due to this attitude, clients can become viewed as a necessary evil, providing a bankroll for the architect's ideas. Getting print exposure for a project, built or unbuilt, *validates* the work done by the architect. Utility, functional fit, or affordability are seldom addressed in magazines and therefore not always viewed as important by these architects.

Projects with the hidden agenda of future publication can cost the unsuspecting client thousands of dollars in fees and often hundreds of thousands of dollars in construction costs for final results that they may or may not find either useful or delightful.

In truth, the bitter lesson learned by those who aspire to be published is that publication has more to do with how you fit a magazine's editorial stance than with the brilliance of your work.

Entering Competitions

Other architects spend unending hours entering open-ended competitions. It is a lot like the lottery—you have to play to win, but there are so many players and so many losers that the payoff, more often than not, is a sense of futility. You often compete against those who have either more ability or more time to put into killer presentations that catch a jurist's eye. To these architects, premiation means justification.

But who does the premiating? Other architects. Do personalities and small group dynamics enter into the criteria for selection? Absolutely.

Getting Academic Exposure

Another subset of architects designing for architects are those who make exquisite drawings or models that will find their way into academic magazines or onto the walls of local galleries. This "paper architecture" is a valuable conceptual enterprise and in fact is more noble than the duplicitous nature of real projects being designed for real people based on a hidden agenda of preconceived notions. "Paper projects" have no victims. They are intended for the exploration of new ideas. The validation of the work comes via academic lectures and articles in journals or in design theory classes where abstract notions can be presented with the sanction of "the academy."

But who selects the writings or projects that will be presented? Professors of architecture who are often architects. Can small-scale politics play a role in this exercise? Ask any academician.

The three vehicles for validation—publication, competitions, and academia—have the common ground of designing for your peer group. This closed loop has inherent distorting effects. The alternative can also be problematic.

2. You Can Design for Clients

The vast majority of those who work in the profession are the architects who design for their clients. There is a derisive tone when architects get together and talk about other architects who are building spec projects or doing large-scale, low cost commercial or institutional work. The ongoing sense is that those who actually get a large number of projects built must "sell-out," and become "hacks." The same fervor of the architect-oriented designer can be found in Vincent Kling's unforgettable "three rules of architecture": (1) get the job, (2) get the job, and (3) get the job.

There *are* "plan mills"—offices that pump out projects like so much sausage, projects extruded through the die of extreme low cost and client preconception. The function of this type of office is simply to get it done on time and on budget; if there are aesthetic issues, they are often found in the signage. The validation of the work is seen in financial terms—making money by maximizing efficiency and good firm organization. But how are architects chosen for such work? Often by the "networking" that allows for a *familiar* choice—not necessarily the *best* choice for the work at hand.

Although almost all architects fall into one of the two categories in general, in practice most of us fall somewhere between the two extremes of self-serving "artist" and compromising "whore." In truth, each and every job we execute has a floating ratio of "whore" versus "artist" concerns.

"Artists" disregard their clients' needs, the local ambiance, cost, and the weatherability of their designs in favor of a "higher truth." "Whores" do whatever others (clients, builders, building inspectors) tell them to, without regard to the consequences.

But what are the *real* aesthetic issues when buildings are designed for other architects and, alternatively, when buildings are designed for clients? These issues all involve interchangeable sets of values between client and architect. It occurs to me that the basic element involved is faith—or the lack of it.

If an architect has faith in his or her ability then a client's bias is not a threat. If a client has faith in him- or herself, then there is no danger in listening to an outsider, in this case the architect.

What aesthetic consequences does a lack of faith have? Typically fear (what I consider to be the opposite of faith) forces us to look to the past for answers. Architects who have little faith in themselves and fear failure often use the Xerox machine to create buildings by mimicry. Clients who fear looking foolish look to existing buildings or magazine features to ensure that their project will not have to justify itself but sit on the firm footing of a graspable precedent.

If an architect fears losing control of a project, he or she can use design presentations to "sell" ideas—often to the point of deception. Often the hidden agenda of publication causes architects without faith in the latent integrity of their ideas to use exaggerations and cheap thrills window dressing to push style over substance.

Perhaps there is a coastal distinction as well. I know the East looks to antique stylizing for solace, and I suspect the West uses a futurist or nihilist outlook for distraction. In the East, Colonialoid buildings give comfort because they touch something familiar. The West Coast seems to have a different perspective. Could it be that a futurist building gives comfort because it changes the channel of our perspective? Either way, we are taken *out* of our present day and time.

Faith in the truths of the present day makes buildings that do not need captions or footnotes to be understood. Faith in the motivations of your client or architect allows for the exchange of perspectives. When people can share their perspectives and make a building, the world is enriched.

I validate myself as an architect by letting the client see what I have to offer, warts and all, up front. If hired, my goal is always to get the project built. I charge more than most but gear contracts to the owner's ability to pay. I will work for *anyone*—I *am* a whore. But I will only work for someone who knows what I have to offer—I am an *artist*.

Ultimately, my bias is to build. My office builds over 70 percent of the commissions we get. My own research tells me the average office like mine ultimately builds about 30 to 50 percent of what they start to design. It is too easy to play in the sandbox of my own mind. If I do not work with builders and clients and Andersen Window reps, I am not in the world at large. And if my buildings do not exist in *this* world, *now*, then they cannot stand on their own merit.

Generally speaking, projects built with trust between client and designer evidence the sort of integrity and spirit that ultimately leads to the publication, premiation, and academic validation so fervently sought by so many who design for other architects.

There is no free lunch. If you do not build well, you are simply chasing fame. If your work is *product* oriented, the *process* will be skewed. If you judge yourself by the paper of the printing press or the balance sheet, you are missing the point.

If I cannot be judged by what I build, then I am at the mercy of those who deal *only* in the world of ideas. I find that open-ended world too confining for my craft.

The Cephas housing site (Figures 1-1 and 1-2) was a classic "leftover" piece of land, a quarter acre that had once been the site of a parochial school that had burned down in the early 1970s, a site that had become an informal garbage dump. The adjacent Catholic church purchased the property from the city for back taxes and through a crusading priest, John Duffell, proceeded to determine within the context of the neighborhood what was needed in terms of housing and how that housing should be built.

It was via this client's deep convictions that my office proceeded to make this building, one that not only responds to all the relevant codes but also facilitates dignity and a sense of ownership and pride for these rental units. Some of the input from our client included making units that were larger than normal (mostly three bedrooms) but including no common corridors, no central lobbies, no separate laundries, no central mail room—in short, no common areas that could become the staging areas for the urban guerilla warfare that has plagued public housing projects throughout the country. The by-product of all these design criteria were units that had natural light on all four sides, front doors that opened to individual stoops, and massing that complemented the townhouses across the street.

It may be said that client-based design criteria can mitigate the aesthetic impact of projects, while playing it "safe" and pandering to the lowest common denominator of aesthetic familiarity. However, this particular project has been selected for national publication in several books and for a traveling exhibit of the National Endowment of the Arts, as well as receiving local AIA (American Institute of Architects) awards and publication in several national trade magazines. This project's essential core organization is due to a client's vision, integrated and applied in architecture in a way that is fresh but rooted in its context.

The bottom-line lesson is that you do not need to sell out to include a client, and by including a client in the design process, the project's utility is enhanced to the point where it becomes virtually aesthetic in its final realization.

Figure 1-1 Cephas housing in downtown Yonkers, New York. Duo Dickinson, architect. Photo © Mick Hales.

Figure 1-2 Drawing of Cephas housing. Courtesy of Duo Dickinson, architect.

Are You an Artist or an Architect?

Roger Yee extends our investigation into the flavor of professional practice with his incisive and hard look at today's economic incentives, which have resulted in the substitution of cost-efficient technologies for time spent with clients. Yee reminds us that the cornerstone of professional practice is still the client and that practice is still a very nontechnologic enterprise, requiring much dialogue, real relationships, and great teamwork to achieve successful outcomes.

Appropriate utilization of technologies and judgment about balancing form and function remain uniquely people-centered tasks and cannot be hastened by reductionist notions.

Roger Yee is a journalist specializing in architecture and is former editor-in-chief of *Contract,* a magazine of commercial and institutional interior design and architecture.

True or false? An Audemar-Piguet watch tells time better than a Swatch. A Mercedes-Benz sedan rides better than a Toyota. A Brioni suit fits better than a Jos. A. Bank. Answer? True, true, and true—if you think so.

Contemporary society has become so adept at producing goods and services that satisfy very specific utilitarian and symbolic needs that we are all obliged to choose our purchases with care. How much status do we want for how much utility? If telling time is less important a function than telling net worth, a gold-encased, jewel-studded Audemar-Piguet could be well worth 100 to 1,000 times the cost of a plastic Swatch, even if the two share similar quartz mechanisms. Architecture has certainly been differentiated in this manner for centuries, even before the rise of our market-driven economy. Some facilities have been so strictly utilitarian that anyone could take credit for the generic results. Others have been so symbolic that their functions seem almost secondary to their visual impact.

What complicates the dual role of the architect as artist and technician is that society increasingly expects more of the technician and less of the artist, despite the fact that what generally prompts a person to become an architect is the desire to create beauty. The client's changing point of view is not hard to understand. Technology is enabling us to expand our control over the environment, making every aspect of manufactured space—from heating, ventilating, and air-conditioning (HVAC), lighting, acoustics, security, safety, internal transportation, and other devices physically integrated into the building's structure to telephones, computers, facsimiles, photocopiers, information networks, and other devices brought into a building to work in close collaboration with its occupants—more machinelike. Hence, we expect more of the physical environment created by architects and interior designers and are less tolerant of its shortcomings. Architecture, unlike fine art, must always *do* something to justify its existence.

Yet architecture is still about *form* as well as function. Le Corbusier expressed the dual nature of the profession in writing *Vers une architecture* in 1923. He proclaimed that "Architecture is the masterly, correct and magnificent play of volumes brought together in light" and then described a house as "a machine for living in."

How today's architects perceive themselves goes well beyond whether they think they are artists conversant with technology or technicians who are facile with art. Yet every project begins with the same question: What does the client want? Commissioning an aesthetic monument will take us through much the same process as developing a utilitarian facility. The differences can be found in what opportunities are allowed to propel a project forward and what constraints are permitted to hold it back.

Consider the program, for example, the foundation of any design project that sets forth the client's needs in terms of function, cost, and time. Every design project must function in some way. However, the more the client can define the activity in a space as a precise operation, the more closely the space must correspond to the activity. Thus a factory leaves little room for error or interpretation, while a concert hall has broad latitude for getting things "right." The client of the aesthetic monument will propose to combine an objective function, such as a setting for hearing chamber music, with a subjective one, such as a glorification of his or her family. Where is the precise balance between acoustics and glory? This is for the architect to decide.

Everything Must Function Properly— Including Monuments to Client Ego

No architect should make the mistake of thinking that the client of an aesthetic monument cares little about the objective function. In 1975 audio equipment tycoon Avery Fisher commissioned acoustician Cyril Harris and architect Philip Johnson to redesign what was originally Philharmonic Hall, designed by architect Max Abramovitz, at New York City's Lincoln Center for the Performing Arts. Two acousticians, Robert Newman and Heinrich Kielholz, had already failed to civilize the building's dreadful sound. Fisher left no doubt in anyone's mind that the redesign would have to succeed in its acoustics—magnificently.

Still, the architect of an aesthetic monument will enjoy considerable liberty in establishing the boundaries of the subjective function. Who knows when a design becomes "too beautiful," "too original," or "too personal?" This becomes particularly apparent in the way the client deals with cost and time. Even the ostensibly straightforward business facility that serves as a corporation's headquarters can go disastrously off track in its cost and time when a self-indulgent CEO (chief executive officer) revels in the role of master builder.

Exhilarating as a commission for an aesthetic monument undoubtedly is, it can all too readily lead to a relatively unhealthy relationship between client and architect. Today's client and a growing array of consultants typically have as much to teach a designer as vice versa, and the final design fulfills its program better when the dialogue goes both ways, when all contributors to the project work concurrently as a team and when cost and time are realistically set and conscientiously honored. When the client of an aesthetic monument fails to engage the designer in an informed evaluation of function, cost, and time, possibly out of respect for the architect or perhaps due to overreaching social ambition, the project courts trouble. Such was the case of the magnificent Opera House in Sydney, Australia, designed by architect Jørn Utzon, which took sixteen years, from 1957 to 1973, to be completed.

Can our society continue to support architecture projects that stand somewhere between the extremes of aesthetic monument and utilitarian facility? Fortunately, most contemporary design commissions have some measure of symbolic function—thus room for artistry—because our visually oriented society is starting to realize how powerful design aesthetics can be. In the global competition for customers, businesses and institutions have found that design sends palpable signals that are picked up by customers of goods and services.

This revelation has made unaccustomed heroes of industrial designers, whose work is subjected to customer opinion every day when accountants tally what does or does not sell. Widgets such as an Apple PowerBook laptop, a Gillette Sensor razor, or a Federal Express postal service tend to sell when their attractive appearance is matched by their equally attractive performance and price. Suddenly names such as Ideo, Ziba Design, Ion, Fitch, and frogdesign are taken seriously on Wall Street and Main Street.

Architects have their pantheon too, of course. We need the work of such masters as Philip Johnson, Ieoh Ming Pei, Kevin Roche, Richard Rogers, Kenzo Tange, Aldo Rossi, Richard Meier, Gottfried Boehm, Fumihiko Maki, Norman Foster, and Renzo Piano to encourage us to reach for new means of expressive power. However, nurturing the artist within the architect—natural and inspiring as this may be—must not blind us to the dominant reality of the twenty-first century. Successful design in modern life must jump through the hoops of function, cost, and time to be built. Architecture that fails to be built, or is built poorly, confronts us with what is either accidental art or bad architecture.

Voodoo and Hearsay

The following is one of those passages filled with truth, passion, and insight that is incredibly illuminating about the terms in which one views the practice of architecture. Reconciling language with built form is liberating in both designing and analyzing architecture. Sharon Matthew's eloquent and magical words have the power to open readers' minds.

SHARON CARTER MATTHEWS, AIA is the Executive Director of the National Architectural Accrediting Board (NAAB). She was previously the Head of the Department of Architecture at the Wentworth Institute of Technology and Head of the Division of Architecture and Art at Norwich University. Her research has been focused on relationships between the technologies of construction and building design. She holds a BA from Columbia University and an MArch. from Yale University.

Of all the books you can buy about architecture, *Architectural Graphic Standards** seemed to this beginning student of the subject both the most straightforward and, at the same time, the most mysterious. It did not have a story;

---

*(Current edition) *Architectural Graphic Standards.* John Hoke, ed. Ramsey/Sleeper Architectural Graphic Standards. New York: John Wiley & Sons, 2000.

there was no beginning, no middle, and no end. When I tried to use it, the information did not fit anywhere. It felt like random pieces of a puzzle. Each piece made sense—like entries in an encyclopedia—but there were no instructions on how and when to use the material. If you asked studio instructors why students bought this big, expensive book, their answers were vague and impatient. I gave up on it pretty quickly. Other strategies for figuring out what to do in studio design classes might be more productive.

One possibility was to look around for students whose work was praised by critics and copy what they were doing. Another was to find a "better" book. There were books that described the life and ideas of successful architects. There were history books that told the stories of cultures and styles. There were theory books that explored ideas about buildings. There were books full of the manifestos of famous men. I wanted there to be a book that would have how-to instructions for doing the magic trick. The trick of putting down some lines on paper or building a little chipboard model that would galvanize my classmates and instructors. If I could find that book, then I thought I could make buildings that would startle and delight people in the professional world. As I remember those days now, it seems as if I had been looking in a book for an answer to a useless question.

In my understanding at the time, that was the way people used books. If you wanted answers to the mysteries of life and death, you read religious books. If you wanted to cook a complicated meal, you looked in cookbooks. If you wanted to know the meaning of a word, you looked it up in a dictionary. If you wanted to be a building magician, you needed a book of architectural magic spells. Books on architectural theory seemed most likely to be helpful. All my professors read them, some even wrote them. Nowadays, reading books on theories of architecture seems slightly less effective in the design of buildings than buying and using voodoo dolls from New Orleans.

Many of my instructors tried to explain these various books to me. When they talked among themselves about the books, they took each other very seriously and listened attentively. Their words flew around in my head but seldom stuck anywhere. Their words about my drawings and models also seemed less than relevant. If I could just find the right ideas—in words that I could translate into images—my projects would speak to them. They would see my great ideas in the lines and in the paper. Even as I searched for the right book, I knew there was something wrong with using a studio project as a way to illustrate a theory about buildings, but what would the alternative be?

The history books, the theory books, the manifestos, and the professor-speak are all about ideas about buildings. They are written and spoken in the language of ideas. Buildings have their own language and it is not made up of words. You don't speak it and you don't read it, you *see* it.

Only when I began to teach, and to struggle to find words to share with students, did I begin to understand what it might mean to see a building in its own language. Along with teaching, I was working in an architect's office and one day a client said to me as we walked through his project, "I wish I could see this building the way you do." Explaining what I could see in words seemed pointless. It felt humbling. I had to admit to myself that I had learned somehow, in school and during my internship, to see a building. The only words I had read that came back to me at that moment were from Louis Kahn—to "draw with a trowel." These words I had once deemed merely poetic, I now understood as explicit instruction. My first real magic spell.

And then I went back to *Architectural Graphic Standards*, the book that gave me information about a building in the language of a building. It includes information on the proportions of materials and on systems of proportional relationships, it describes materials and how they go together, and it shows subassemblies of buildings in ways that make the designers' choices clear. It is made up of many drawings and diagrams that speak the language of building. You can see how the pieces go together. You can see what *must* be there, and you can find the places where there is room for variety. If you have drawn what you know and need an answer about what happens in the gaps of your understanding, you can ask this book . . . a very useful question.

If you draw and model a building with a trowel and if you can see a building as a complicated thought with its own vocabulary and rules of grammar, you can arrange the parts to make the thought that is the building profound—or silly. It's *your* choice. There is a book full of the spells you need to make this happen. It's big, it's old, it's arcane, it's full of information, it's expensive . . . it's everything I always imagined a book of magic would be. I was just looking in the wrong language.

Almost All About IDP, ARE, AIA, NCARB, NAAB, and ACSA[13]

Until you are formally recognized as a professional—an architect—by a governmental jurisdiction, discussions about professionalism are in danger of being moot. You must first demonstrate competence to independently practice architecture while protecting the "health, safety, and welfare" of the public. Minimal competence (as defined by the regulatory bodies) does not, however, include anything about the artful qualities of design or the values associated with being a true professional. As a foundation for providing architectural services, it is absolutely essential to be well versed in the architect's codified responsibilities to the public on the regulatory dimension that ensures the well-being of building inhabitants. This dimension is not separate from the other dimensions of providing architectural services; it is an integral and essential component of shaping the design process and the built outcome.

In the following section, Don Schlegel describes the formal process of becoming an architect. More important, he details the rationale underlying the seemingly arbitrary obstacles leading to registration. It will be clear that there is indeed appropriate thought and logic behind the process of running through the hoops of an accredited degree, the Intern Development Program (IDP), and the licensing exam. Standards for education, training, and the exam are continuously scrutinized by a variety of organizations (to which Schlegel refers), and they evolve largely for the better with the changing nature of professional practice and society.

---

[13]The information in this section is current as of this writing. Since there is ongoing change and evolution in the regulatory environment, however, there must be a continuing vigilance about checking with the applicable agency or jurisdiction to verify relevant facts. Special thanks to Stephen Nutt, Rob Rosenfeld, and Mike Bourdrez.

DON SCHLEGEL, FAIA, has had a distinguished forty-year career as an architect and a professor of architecture at the University of New Mexico where he also served as Dean and Chairman. Among his many accomplishments (that imbue this essay with special meaning and perspective) are the following: he was President and member of the Board of Directors for both the National Architectural Accrediting Board (NAAB) and the Association of Collegiate Schools of Architecture (ACSA), and he was on the Examination Committee of the National Council of Architectural Registration Boards (NCARB). Schlegel holds an MArch from the Massachusetts Institute of Technology.

An individual using the title "architect," or practicing architecture (that is, providing architectural services for buildings of public habitation), in any jurisdiction of the United States and Canada is required by law to be registered as an architect in that jurisdiction. Individual states, provinces, and territories are empowered to establish architectural licensing laws, administered by a registration board, to safeguard public health, safety, and welfare. The basic laws of each jurisdiction are quite similar since each jurisdiction's registration board is a member of either the National Council of Architectural Registration Boards or the Committee of Canadian Architectural Councils (CCAC).

Though the basic registration requirements are similar, there are some differences, the most significant of which are the eligibility requirements to sit for the NCARB Architect Registration Examination (ARE). This examination has been adopted by all jurisdictions.

NCARB, the national federation of registration boards, has established educational, training, and examination standards for NCARB certification. Member boards in the United States grant NCARB certificate holders registration upon application and submittal of an NCARB Council Record. This procedure allows registrants to practice in jurisdictions other than their initial place of registration. The Canadian Council (CCAC) has approved NCARB certification for international reciprocity (mutual exchange of privileges) between the two countries, which has been accepted by most jurisdictions.

NCARB Certification

The standards established by NCARB for certification are education, training, and examination.

- *Education.* A first professional architectural degree from a program accredited by the National Architectural Accrediting Board (NAAB) or its equivalent.
- *Training.* Compliance with the Intern Development Program (IDP) training requirements.
- *Examination.* Successfully passing all divisions of the NCARB Architect Registration Exam (ARE).

These standards for NCARB certification meet the major requirements for registration in all jurisdictions in the United States. However, there are other requirements that are often added by the individual registration boards, such as minimum age, good character and repute, and an oral examination.

When the requirements of a registration board do not meet the standards for NCARB certification (for registration in a jurisdiction other than the individual's initial jurisdiction), then obtaining NCARB certification becomes very difficult or impossible. Here is a case in point:

An architect initially registered under California licensing laws applied for registration in another jurisdiction through reciprocity. The applicant was informed by the registration board that according to their reciprocity laws for registration, "The applicant must hold a valid NCARB Certificate before his or her application could be considered." The applicant then requested from NCARB an application for certification. This was denied on the grounds that the individual did not meet the NCARB education standard for certification. (It is salient to note the Broadly Experienced Architect (BEA) process. It is described in the NCARB Education Standard. See www.ncarb.org/Forms/educstand.pdf. Although the BEA is a rigorous process, many architects have successfully used it to obtain certification.)

California's requirements to sit for the Architect Registration Exam were: "The completion of 5 years of architectural education or work *or* an approved combination of education and work based on a table of equivalents established by the Board."

Since the applicant had received two years of credit in an architectural program at a junior college, he did not meet the NCARB's education standard, which had been adopted by the jurisdiction to which he had applied for reciprocity.

The NCARB lists two other options, however, to meet their education standard:

1. Completion of acceptable courses in a recognized foreign academic institution in five described subject areas and an evaluation of postsecondary education by the National Architectural Accrediting Board.
2. Broadly Experienced Architect—as noted above—is one "who can demonstrate that the NCARB education standard has been met through a combination of education and comprehensive architectural experience."

In the case of the applicant for reciprocity from California, if he pursued option 1, it would take three or more years to receive an accredited degree or complete acceptable courses. He may pursue option 2, which requires the preparation of a comprehensive education dossier and an interview.

The reality of not being able to be licensed in another jurisdiction (other than that of initial registration) may prevent the individual from meeting the changing circumstances of the architectural marketplace required in this mobile society. *Therefore, meeting the most stringent standards—established by either NCARB for certification or a particular jurisdiction for registration—is basic to your future well-being and job security.*

The NCARB certification requirements are established by the registration boards, which consist primarily of architects. The NCARB requirements track the Member Board requirements. For example, in the late 1970s, when a critical mass of states passed laws to require the NAAB accredited professional degree, a resolution was brought before the Council at the 1980 Annual Meeting that would have required a minimum of a four-year preprofessional degree for certification. The resolution was amended from the floor to require an accredited BArch or MArch, and the resolution passed as amended, with the proviso that the new requirement would not go into effect until July 1, 1984. This four-year waiting period was intended to give individuals sufficient time to adjust to the new reality.

The Collateral Organizations

There are collateral organizations affiliated with the process of entry into the profession of architecture. They are jointly interlocked through membership and committee structures that establish criteria, develop procedures, and provide the means for licensure of architects.

- *ACSA (Association of Collegiate Schools of Architecture), www.acsa-arch.org.* Member schools of higher education in the United States and Canada that offer architectural education.
- *NAAB (National Architectural Accrediting Board), www.naab.org.* The board that establishes criteria and procedures for accrediting architectural programs, consisting of members from each collateral organization.
- *NCARB (National Council of Architectural Registration Boards), www.ncarb.org.* A federation of member registration boards in the United States and its territories established to safeguard health, safety, and welfare of the public; to assist member boards in carrying out their duties; to develop and recommend standards required of an applicant for architectural registration; and to provide a process of certification to member boards for the qualification of an architect for registration.
- *CCAC (Committee of Canadian Architectural Councils), 55 Murray Street, Suite 330 Ottawa, ON K1N 5M3 Canada, (613) 241-8341.* The Canadian counterpart of the NCARB.
- *AIA (American Institute of Architects), www.aia.org.* "The objects of the AIA shall be to organize and unite in fellowship the members of the architectural profession; to promote the aesthetic, scientific, and practical efficiency of the profession; to advance the science and art of planning and building by advancing the standards of architectural education, training, and practice; to coordinate the building industry and the profession of architecture to ensure the advancement of the living standards of people through their improved environment; and to make the profession of ever-increasing service to society."
- *AIAS (American Institute of Architecture Students), www.aias.org.* AIAS chapters are involved in organizing professional development seminars, community action projects, curriculum advisory committees, guest speaker programs, local newsletters, regional conferences, and many other programs.

Education

As the practice of architecture becomes more comprehensive through new technology and is concerned with addressing broader environmental issues, registration boards have responded by increasing their educational requirements. As you may no longer simply read law for admission to the legal profession, you may no longer, in most jurisdictions, sit for the ARE or become licensed to practice architecture without a professional degree from a NAAB-accredited program.

The NAAB accreditation verifies that the program has been evaluated according to established achievement-oriented performance criteria. The NAAB Board of Directors serves both as a decision-making and policy-generating body reviewing and accrediting architectural programs. It consists of twelve members. The ACSA, AIA, and NCARB each nominate three individuals to three-year terms; there are two public members (an academic generalist and a noneducator who is also a nonarchitect) who also serve three-year terms; and the AIAS nominates one individual for a one-year term. The members' roles are to develop and use reliable, valid criteria and procedures for the assessment of professional programs in architecture and to encourage the enrichment of such programs.

When an accreditation is scheduled, the NAAB reviews the school's Architectural Program Report. Upon its acceptance, a team is selected consisting of a chairperson and a member from each collateral organization: ACSA, AIA, AIAS, NCARB, and generally a public member. During the three-day visit, the team has access to the school's facilities, faculty, students, and programs, examining student work and course content as evidence of fulfillment of the achievement-oriented performance criteria. The visiting team submits a report to the board conveying the team's impressions of the program's educational quality in terms of student performance and recommends the term of accreditation. The possible terms of accreditation include:

- *Six-year term.* Deficiencies, if any, are minor.
- *Three-year term.* Deficiencies are serious and have an impact on the quality of the program.
- *Two-year term.* Deficiencies are major and are eroding the quality of the program. There is no indication that the school has the intent or capability to correct these deficiencies. The status is probationary.

Programs judged not to be in compliance with the rules of accreditation do not receive a term of accreditation.

Dealing with Change

Architectural practice and education have drastically changed since the end of World War II to meet the demands of a changing society; new building technology and communications systems, computerized design and delivery, the Americans with Disabilities Act, environmental pollution, and energy consumption are just a few of the influences. Changes and demands will continue during the twenty-first century. Architectural education is always in a state of flux as it too reacts to these new and broader issues that are now part of the practice of architecture.

Accrediting agencies also must react to these changes. The NAAB responds by reevaluating its criteria and procedures for accrediting architectural programs during validation conferences held every three years. Educators react by adding new course content, introducing new courses, and dropping others. There is only so much time and money that can be allocated to a first professional architectural degree. Expanding the time period for formal learning appears to have reached its limit. Education of an architect is a continuing process, a lifelong learning experience. Society is well aware of the need for professionals to stay abreast of the times—new laws and regulations are appearing in many jurisdictions, requiring continuing education (i.e., professional development) to renew one's license to practice, and the AIA requires continuing education for membership. Formal architectural education is just the first step in the ongoing process of learning in order to practice.

Training

All architectural licensing boards require architectural work experience, generally a minimum of three years, in conjunction with a professional degree in architecture. If an individual's education doesn't meet this standard, the work experience requirement for eligibility to sit for the exam may be increased in accordance with specific board policy.

Work experience was historically characterized by apprentices trained by mentors. A daily working relationship allowed experienced practitioners to transfer knowledge and skill to the apprentice. However, with the decline of this apprenticeship model, interns lacked a structured transition between formal education and architectural registration. The Intern Development Program (IDP) was created to remedy this deficiency. The IDP consists of a systematic, comprehensive series of training activities. The IDP applies the knowledge and technical skills acquired through education in the architectural workplace. The goals are:

- Define areas of architectural practice in which interns should acquire basic knowledge and skills.
- Encourage additional training in the broad aspects of architectural practice.
- Provide the highest quality information and advice about educational, internship, and professional issues and opportunities.
- Provide a uniform system for documentation and periodic assessment of internship activities.
- Provide greater access to educational opportunities to enrich training.

The IDP training requirement for certification was adopted by the NCARB in 1996. It became part of the model law that is the Council's recommendation for registration to practice in any jurisdiction through reciprocity.

The program is based on verification of completing 700 training units [a training unit (tu) is equivalent to 8 working hours] in four different categories as follows:

- *Design and Construction Documents.* 350 tu or 2,800 hours.
- *Construction Administration.* 70 tu or 560 hours.
- *Management.* 35 tu or 280 hours.
- *Professional and Community Service.* 10 tu or 80 hours.

Each category is divided into subsections with respective required training units. The sum of these required training units is equivalent to 5,600 hours of work experience. If one works a 40-hour week, 50 weeks per year, the length of the training period approaches three years of internship.

Forty-nine out of the 50 states require IDP training for initial registration.

Interns are responsible for documenting their training and meeting with their employers and mentors. The employer supervises daily work experience, assesses the quality of the work, and certifies the intern's training record. The mentor provides broad guidance from an independent perspective.

The Committee of Canadian Architectural Councils (CCAC) has adopted a similar system for evaluating training that is considered equivalent by NCARB.

Establishing a record of training activities can be initiated by applying to the NCARB and paying a fee. The NCARB maintains your record throughout the IDP process. Upon completion of the IDP training requirements, the record is then forwarded to a registration board by the NCARB.

Examination

The Architect Registration Examination (ARE) has been adopted by all United States jurisdictions and all Canadian Provincial Associations (and is required for NCARB certification). The exam concentrates on those areas of knowledge, skill, and services that most affect public health, safety, and welfare.

The intent of this registration examination is to evaluate a candidate's competence to protect the public by providing the architectural services of predesign, site design, building design, building systems, and construction documents and services as they relate to social, cultural, natural, and physical forces and to other related external constraints.

Beginning in 1997, the ARE was administered exclusively on computers through a network of test centers across the United States and Canada. An applicant for the exam first contacts the registration board where he or she seeks initial registration. The candidate must meet that jurisdiction's eligibility requirements, then submit the application with a processing fee. Upon board approval, the applicant may choose any location with a certified test center. Test centers are located in each jurisdiction and most metropolitan areas. (There are over 350 centers in the United States and Canada.)

You may schedule any division in any order on any day a center is open. This is now possible for the first time because of the nature of the computerized exam mode. This procedure allows the examinee to schedule the time away from work, study particular divisions, and spread out the cost (you can even pay by credit card).

The exam was developed by the NCARB exam committee whose members include architectural practitioners, educators, and engineers from the United States and Canada working with the NCARB staff and employees of Thomson-Prometric, a national leader in test development and consulting.

The exam content is developed through a survey of practicing architects who respond to and suggest criteria, qualifying the relative importance of each to the practice of architecture. The intent is to ensure that the content is based on the kinds of knowledge, skills, and abilities required to practice architecture and protect the public interest. A *Practice Analysis Survey*, done by the Chauncey Group International, Princeton, New Jersey, was completed in 2001. The survey included over 1,700 participants and identified 82 tasks and 86 knowledge-skills critical for the independent practitioner. This information provides the basis for the specifications used by item writers to develop the questions (and vignettes for the graphic divisions) used in the ARE. Subcommittees appointed by the NCARB president-elect write these items or questions.

There are nine divisions in the exam, each testing different facets of the architectural process. Six divisions are multiple choice. Three divisions include graphic vignettes. Candidates may download software, free of charge, from the NCARB website to practice responding to the graphic vignettes. For more information, see *ARE Guidelines* published by the NCARB (www.ncarb.org). They provide a general overview of the exam and the application, administration, and score reporting procedures.

Conclusion

A licensed architect, once registered in a jurisdiction, may perform architectural services for any building type and scope. There are no limits to practice based on time and experience as there are in some foreign jurisdictions. The licensee, upon registration, is placed in a role of public responsibility and is expected to behave with moral integrity. This role and its codification is one very important means of demystifying and defining just what it means to be a professional.

Timing of the Architect Registration Examination

I asked Roger Schluntz, FAIA, Dean of the School of Architecture and Planning at the University of New Mexico, to respond to the following question:

Should architectural graduates be allowed to take the ARE immediately upon graduation? [This decision, of course, is up to each state—the entity that is empowered to control licensing. As of this writing, active debate continues. It is indeed possible to take parts of the exam—right after graduation—in Texas.]

I believe that those receiving professional degrees in architecture should have immediate access to the ARE and that this action would be in the best interests of our profession. The obvious precedent, of course, for examination upon fulfillment of the degree requirement is law. Strategies that will reduce the eight- or nine-year *minimum* time span that currently separates high school graduates from recognized entry into the architecture profession should be welcomed. This is one.

For eighteen-year-olds considering career choices, the duration (perceived as "half a life-time") necessary for formal education and internship requirements is probably a stark deterrent to many, particularly when coupled with the published salaries for entry-level positions in architecture. High school graduates have choices, and I fear that we inadvertently lose many talented individuals who are critical to our future ranks. To address the monumental challenges posed by escalating human populations, continued environmental degradation, and diminishing natural resources, we very much need to attract the best and the brightest for the coming century.

If the ARE could be taken immediately upon graduation, one could speculate that the immediacy of this activity might also have as a consequence a number of revisions in architectural curriculums and instruction. Some educators might view this as a negative outcome, while I suspect that most practitioners (as well as other faculty members) would argue that this juxtaposition will help clarify the relationship between formal education and the profession.

Examination need not be the final step for licensure. Registration could still be deferred for a requisite number of years of directed experience. We should, however, be able to find a more inspiring terminology than "internship" to describe this time frame and responsibility.

Designing Your Career

The objective of the following essay and accompanying case study, both articulately presented by Suzanna Wight, AIA, is to speak specifically to emerging architects and advanced students about career opportunities and issues.

From an employee's perspective, intern architect Tamara Iwaseczko states, in a New Mexico Board of Examiners article ("A Philosophy of Architecture vis à vis Internship," www.nmbea.org), "If one approaches the intern experience as a time of gestation, as well as a time for fueling one's interests, following one's passions, nurturing the true spirit that brought one to the threshold of this profession, and extending out and sharing the excitement, then the time can be incredibly enriching and can set the tenor for a profound career." In the material below, Suzanna Wight suggests approaches that operationalize the sentiment expressed so well by Iwaseczko.

SUZANNA WIGHT, AIA, is the Emerging Professionals Director at the American Institute of Architects in Washington, D.C. She served on the AIA Board of Directors in 2002 as the Associate Director. In 2001 she was the Regional Associates Director for the Mid-Atlantic Region and the National Associates Committee Chair. Suzanna most recently worked for Gensler in Washington, D.C. She has a BArch with a minor in Architectural History from Carnegie Mellon University.

Building Your Career: Tools for Success

Internship, apprenticeship, (on-the-job) training . . . whatever you call it, this is the time in your life when you have many options to explore. After five or more years in architecture school, graduates are well-poised for careers in various fields because design education encourages complex problem solving—looking at a problem from many different angles and considering multiple options, until you find the one that is best suited for the requirements set before you. You should apply these same techniques not just to design projects but also to your career. Consider your strengths, interests, and goals. Don't forget to think about your weaknesses, dislikes, and possible barriers to success.

Early in your career, the profession of architecture can seem overwhelming. Remember that sometimes knowing what you *don't* want to do is better than nothing. There are many things to consider before you graduate through life as a young architect. The most important thing is to realize that your career is yours to shape in a unique way that will ensure success in reaching your personal goals. Below are a few tips that I have learned through experience and observation that might help you along the way.

Congratulations. . . . Now What?

Getting your first job after school can be a daunting process. It usually helps to get your foot in the door with a firm if you have had relevant work experience prior to graduation. I always encourage students to take advantage of their summer vacations to get a resume-building job. An architecture firm is the obvious choice, but if that option is not viable because of the economy or location, related fields like construction, landscape architecture, and engineering are all excellent alternatives. If you have an interest in historic preservation, seek work with the local historical society. If you are interested in sustainability, sign on with an environmental advocate group.

Before graduation day, you should have an idea of what factors (i.e., work culture, location, firm size, practice areas, etc.) are important to you in your first job. You will need to do some research on your own about firms before you even sit down to write your cover letters. Truly, the interview is where you will gather the most information to assist you in making your decision. You should think of this not only as the firm's opportunity to get to know you but also your opportunity to get to know the firm. The portfolio will be your instrument to drive the discussion. It will be important to come prepared to ask questions about what it is like to work there, what role you will play, do they pay overtime and other issues that are important to you.

Traveling the Road to Licensure

Once you have chosen a firm, it will be important for you to find the right pace for your internship. Some interns will take the scenic route, bopping from one project to another without a real plan for how they are going to fulfill their Intern Development Program requirements (see IDP discussion on page 34). Others will be on the expressway to licensure, submitting completed forms every three months like clockwork. The IDP has a bad reputation. I believe, if used properly, it can be one of the most essential tools in your career toolbox. Most importantly, the IDP can help you to maintain your momentum and monitor your progress for at least the first three years of your career. I used my IDP reports for benchmarking in my professional development reviews each year. I was able to show myself and my firm exactly where I was getting experience and exactly where I was deficient. This helped me to maintain my speed on the expressway and provided the added bonus of showcasing my progress with the firm, leadership marking increased responsibility in projects and in the firm through those years.

There are a few keys that will make your IDP experience the best that it can be. First, find a "mentor" who cares and who will stick with you through the process, at least three years, to keep you on track; if at first a relationship does not work out for you, try again. Do not give up your search for a good fit. Second, teach your supervisor, if he or she does not already know (which is likely) about what it is like to be an intern today. They do not have to know all of the details, but some perspective on the program will not only help you to communicate in progress meetings but other interns with whom that person interacts will reap the benefits as well. Last but not least, find a support group of interns who are working through the IDP as well. Work together on supplementary education projects for IDP credit, encourage one another in getting credit in those more challenging training areas, and celebrate successes like passing exams along the way.

Distinguishing Yourself in Your Firm and in Your Life

As you grow through the stages of your internship, you will find that the most success comes when your contributions to the firm are unique. Whether you are at a large or small firm, you will need to emphasize your strengths and what you bring to the team. If you are interested in technology, management, marketing or design, seek opportunities to hone those skills. Be sure to showcase your successes on projects, and make note of the accomplishments in writing through your resume and orally in your annual review. Finally, always seek to improve upon your weak areas. Seek a coach who can help you progress in your professional development.

As a young professional, it is important to start your career with the right attitude about a work-life balance. Chances are you learned some bad habits in architecture school: using caffeine to keep you going unbelievable hours in the studio, procrastinating until the ultimate last minute, and, perhaps worst, neglecting important relationships with family and friends. It is important to be a well-rounded individual, and an internship can be an opportunity to learn how to direct your time and energy in more effective ways.

One of the hardest lessons for me to learn as a young professional was how to balance my work and life. Eventually, with great self-discipline, I have learned how to come to work and give 100 percent each day. Remember, if you manage your time well, then it is okay to leave after a good, productive eight-hour work day. Then, you will still have energy to put toward other projects that are important to you outside of the office. It is not easy—and, frankly, I work at it every day—but the benefits are extraordinary.

The NCARB requires 10 training units in professional and community service for a reason. Opportunities for growth outside the office can include the potential for leadership you may not have in your firm because you are the junior member of the team. Take the example of a local gallery show organized for young designers in your city. If you are interested in design, you can volunteer to prepare the floor plan of pieces to be displayed or even to develop the promotional materials. If you are interested in marketing, you could take on the task of facilitating the sponsors for the event. The lessons you learn by doing these "extracurricular" activities can be brought back to the office and applied to your projects. Professional and community service opportunities are key to advancing the skills that can help you in your practice.

Getting Ready to Take the Plunge

Completing the IDP can be the biggest challenge of your internship. Many interns have difficulty getting credit in areas like building-cost analysis, bidding and contract negotiation, and construction administration because they are junior, and the firm leadership does not believe that they can handle the responsibility. The key is to show your capability and understanding through complementary activities. Take the initiative and read up on the topic, develop a case study on a project in your office or, if your firm does not focus in that area, look at resources, like the *Emerging Professional's Companion* (AIA and NCARB, 2004), that have scenarios where you can role-play to get comfortable with different situations. Many of these things will count for IDP credit, but practice experience is critical to completing the minimum IDP requirements. Tell your IDP supervisor that you will meet him or her halfway. You will get the first half of your credit with these complementary activities, proving your understanding and competence, if they will give you the opportunity to work on real projects for the second half of your term of internship. You have to be willing to compromise and get creative.

Once you have completed the IDP, take a moment to congratulate yourself but then get right into studying for the exam. Many candidates stall in their careers because they tell themselves that they do not have time to study. Guess what? There will never be more than 24 hours in the day! This is the time to really put that work-life balance to the test. A few things will help you to stay on track. First, work with your IDP mentor to get the encouragement you need to get over the fears of studying and failure. Second, set a schedule outlining the areas when you will need to be studying and taking time off for testing; then share it with your supervisor. And perhaps most importantly, find a support group of peers who are also taking the exam. Whether you study together or just share stories about the testing center, you will be more motivated to keep on your schedule if you have peers to keep you honest.

Paying Dues?

Internship is only the beginning of a lifetime of learning in the architecture profession. I contend that "paying dues" is highly overrated. Internship is your time to make it what you want, to develop into the professional you intend to be. Remember that architectural licensing is only one milestone on your career path. There will be other important markers in your future. Whether you eventually decide to focus on technology, design, or management or focus on healthcare, interiors, or retail, the internship is a great time to sample different opportunities and hone in on your unique contribution to the profession. Get prepared, stay on course, and take full advantage of every opportunity to position yourself for greatness in your career, wherever the license to practice architecture may take you.

Case Study | Designing Your Career

SUZANNA WIGHT elaborates on her discussion about optimizing internship experiences with the following provocative case study.

Abby graduated from XYZ University, a small east coast school, in May 2001 with a professional BArch degree. Following graduation, she told her friends, "I want to move to California. The weather is so beautiful out there everyday, and people are so much more laid back than they are on the East Coast." Even though she had work experience in small- and medium-sized firms while she was in school, Abby found that the economy was not great in California and worried about moving without a secure position, particularly so far away from her family and friends. Having focused all of her efforts on finding a job in California and coming up completely dry, Abby moved back in with her parents who lived in the rural Pennsylvania, about one hour north of Philadelphia.

"You'd better find something soon," Abby's dad told her about a month after graduation. "Your mother and I don't want you living in your old room forever."

Disappointed that a job in California probably would not happen, Abby began to research firms where she knew some XYZ alumni had landed, in Philadelphia, after graduation. "I want to get a broad range of experience as an intern. I did my thesis on innovative building technology, but I don't mind what type of projects I work on," she told Sam, who had been out of school for two years and was now working at one of the largest firms in Philly—WPAM Architects. WPAM had over 750 people in 15 offices, Philly was their largest office with 175 staff.

"Do you find that the firm leaders care about you as an individual and support your goals?" she asked. Sam told her that the firm had recently helped him by paying for the LEED (Leadership in Energy and Environmental Design) exam, even giving him paid time off to take the test. "Our focus on sustainability is really growing and the clients seem to want 'greener' designs, so getting LEED accredited has really made me a wanted man on projects."

Abby had done her homework about intern salaries by checking out resources available online at various Web sites, particularly studying the AIA compensation survey. She also felt, with some advice from her dad, that she had a good idea of what she expected from a benefits package. After interviewing with five medium and large firms and receiving offers from three of them, she carefully weighed the different options, placing value on the different benefits they offered. One firm was nearly all production of construction documents and offered her so little that she was not sure she would be able to move out of her old room, which was one of her goals. Abby felt strongly that she was a professional now and deserved to be compensated appropriately for the services she would provide the firm. A second firm offered her the most money; but in the interview when she asked about what projects were in the firm pipeline, it sounded like the work might dry up after four to six months. She was afraid that if she took the high-paying job, she would be the first to be laid off if there was a slow down in work. Finally, Abby chose WPAM architects, the firm in which her friend, Sam, was doing so well. They offered her a fair salary and some exciting training opportunities for the duration of her internship.

Year 1: Getting Started and Making a Place for Yourself

It was now November, six months after she walked on the stage with her friends from XYZ University. While unpacking boxes at her new apartment in the city, Abby found the IDP packet that her IDP coordinator had given her last year. She realized that she had missed the deadline for a student discount, but she decided to approach her new studio director about paying for the fees so that she could get started as soon as possible. "Abby, I'm happy to reimburse you for those costs," her studio director explained. Licensure is important to this firm. You know, we used to have a pretty active intern

group here in the office. I wonder what ever happened with that. You should see if Sam will work with you to get that started again." Abby thanked him and considered the offer to reinvigorate the intern group. It would be a great way to meet the interns in other studios. Just by the looks of it, it seemed like a young office.

Abby resolved to fill out her NCARB forms every three months on schedule. But, there were two firms she worked for during school with whom she had never logged her time. Luckily, she had saved her timesheets and was able to tally up the numbers. In January 2002, she filled out the NCARB forms for each firm and mailed them to her old bosses with a pleasant cover letter telling them all about her new job in the city. One firm sent the forms back signed just two weeks later. "Good Luck to you, Abby," the note said. "You are a smart young woman with a bright future ahead of you. WPAM Architects is lucky to have you!" However, the employer from the other firm did not respond and after about a month, she called the firm to make sure that she received the package she had sent. Abby left a message for her old supervisor, but she did not have a lot of confidence that this would get resolved quickly.

Year 2: Work-Life Balance and Continuing Development

By the summer 2002, the WPAM intern group had been completely reorganized under the direction of Abby and Sam. With thirty people in the office who were either recent graduates of the IDP or ARE candidates, there was great diversity of activities for these young professionals. The group organized special lunch-time sessions focused on IDP training areas. Interns served as project managers responsible for shaping the topic and bringing together experts in the office to teach the seminar. Those who had completed IDP and were ready to study for the exam broke into a smaller group to study and set a schedule of monthly exam dates to keep everybody on track. The best part was the happy hour that had now become regular every Friday after work at the restaurant downstairs from the office. Abby never thought her social life could be so busy.

Abby was beginning to take on more responsibility on her projects as well. She had begun to take a more serious interest in building technology, showing talent for researching innovative building materials for projects in her studio. She had just been assigned to be on the team for an expansion to Philadelphia's largest public television station. This would give her a lot of experience in working with various consultants, giving her the IDP credit in engineering systems coordination that she had been lacking so far in her internship. Counting up the hours, she was more than half way done with the IDP requirements.

Luckily, when she was back for homecoming that year, she was able to stop by her old firm and personally hand a copy of the NCARB form she needed signed to verify work she had done with them. Ms. Watts, sole proprietor of the small architecture firm, said: "You know, Abby. I don't know how I am supposed to know you really did this work. It was three years ago. I can't even remember what I had for lunch yesterday." Abby agreed that she had been irresponsible in not starting her record file sooner, but she thought (to herself) that she had sent the firm the forms nearly a year ago without response. Not wanting to press the issue and risk that Ms. Watts would not sign the forms at all, Abby said, "Well, you can take a look at these copies of my timesheets, if you like, to help you refresh your memory." "Forget it. Just give me that pen," Ms. Watts responded.

Back at WPAM, the broadcast studio project, KAMZ, was really getting intense. Abby had to spend more and more time, even some Saturdays, to make her deadlines. Her project manager had a horrible reputation in the office for not allowing for enough staff time or fees to get the job done. What was worse, the designer was constantly coming to her with new ideas for the program that impacted the work of the consultants. Abby was having a hard time balancing her desire to be successful at work but also to have a social life. WPAM did not pay overtime either, though she had heard that if you put in extra hours now, your Christmas bonus would reflect that hard work.

Year 3: IDP Wrap-Up, Exam Prep, and Career Opportunities

Abby had been at her firm for two and a half years. With her work experience during school now logged with NCARB, she should be done with the IDP, but she has not been able to get enough credits in all the required training areas. The broadcast studio project was put on hold for about three months because of some issues with funding but was now back on track and into the construction-documents phase. At her annual review, Abby brought a copy of her latest report from the NCARB. "As you can see," she said to her studio directors, Anna and David, "I have fulfilled all of the credit I need in areas like schematic design and specifications. Working on the KAMZ job has given me the opportunity to get lots of engineering systems coordination credit, which I really appreciate. I know that I'll be able to fill out construction documents within the next month or so, too. It's really construction administration and project management that I need to complete this program. I'm anxious to get started on my exams right away, because I know I can only expect more project responsibility when I have my license."

"We'll talk to John, your project manager, about allowing you to shadow him more now to learn about project management and get you prepared to work with him," David said in response. Although Abby was not thrilled about learning project management from the worst project manager in the office, she was hopeful that her studio directors were committed to getting her to the exam as soon as possible.

Just six weeks after her review, at the monthly staff meeting, there was a big announcement. The CEO announced that the firm had received a huge commission to design a new studio for a movie producer in Hollywood, California. They were looking for volunteers from the junior and intermediate staff who would be willing to move to the Los Angeles office for at least six months to work on this high-profile project. Programming was already getting underway, and they needed to assemble a team quickly.

Abby went out for drinks with her old friend, Sam, that evening. "So what do you think about this LA job?" she asked. "Why, are you thinking about it? If you are willing to make the move, I mean, it will be great for you. It's a small office out there, so you'll have lots of responsibility. Besides, it's easy since you're single. Now that I am married with a baby on the way, it's a lot harder to consider something like that." Abby remembered how badly she had wanted to move to the West Coast after graduation. But now, she was settled in Philadelphia. She had a great network of friends and respect in her firm. Most importantly to her, she was so close to completing IDP. If she left now, that would be delayed. "Yeah, you're right. It is a great opportunity. I'm just not sure if it is the right time for me," said Abby.

QUESTIONS FOR CONSIDERATION

1. Should Abby's desire to see the West Coast trump her desire to get licensed as soon as possible?
2. Since Abby has enjoyed her social circle in Philly, how might that affect her happiness in Los Angeles where she knows no one?
3. How can Abby be most proactive in her career? Will the license or the high profile experience give her the currency she needs to take her career to the next level?
4. What other decisions might you have made differently if you were Abby?

Chapter 2

Do the Right Thing

Webster's defines "ethics" as a system of moral principles or values. By this time, it should be abundantly clear that a system of moral principles formalized as rules or standards of personal and professional conduct is a centerpiece of architectural practice. Why, then, do we need to dwell further on the topic and devote a separate chapter to it?

The answer to that question is: because it should be part of the architect's job to dwell on ethics. This new emphasis is defined against a backdrop of changes in society and the law that require a sophisticated and knowledgeable understanding of ethical issues that may not be intuitively obvious. And, again, let us not forget that the basic mission of a professional is to provide a service that is value-laden. Unlike the artist, who creates beauty and emotion, and unlike the scientist, who discovers and explains, the architect also has to do good. It is not easy to "do good" in a complex world.

Henry Cobb has written that good is a difficult goal because "the numerous constituencies whom we as a matter of professional responsibility see ourselves as serving—the client institution, the building's users, its neighbors, and so on—are often fiercely committed to widely divergent and deeply conflicting principles of human duty."

Moreover, there are difficult ethical issues associated with the design of different building types. William Saunders has pointed out that prisons may raise questions about the nature of punishment and rehabilitation, but he notes that equally troubling questions may be raised by office towers, malls, hospitals, schools, highways, and by the monumental public square.

If there is one thing in the field of ethics as it pertains to architecture that I am at all confident about, it is that generalizations and noble language, however germane and on-target, take us only so far. What is needed is careful, case-by-case analysis. We must all cultivate the habit of blending our personal sense of right and wrong with our professional canons of ethics. And then, we must apply this merger to each project we undertake.

It is in this spirit that this chapter presents a remarkably comprehensive yet comparatively brief primer on architects and ethics, in conjunction with an illustrative and absorbing case history.

Architects and Ethics

GEORGE WRIGHT, FAIA, is Dean Emeritus, School of Architecture, University of Texas at Arlington. He has had his own practice and has taught for over 40 years. Dean Wright has numerous design honor awards from the New Mexico Society of Architects and the American Association of School Administrators. His publications include a contribution to *The Instructor's Guide for the AIA Professional Practice Handbook* (1988), and design work in *Architectural Record, Life,* and *Time.* He received an MArch degree from the Harvard University Graduate School of Design.

An architect who writes, or attempts to write, about ethics is like an architect walking through a minefield: There are explosive issues with every step into the territory of philosophers (a philosopher who would write about architectural practice would be equally in trouble). An architect-educator who meets with students about to enter practice should endeavor, however, to alert students to the moral and ethical obligations architects owe to the public when they offer their services.

Ethics and the Practice of Architecture

A number of years ago, Derek Bok, then President of Harvard University (and husband of Sissela Bok, noted philosopher and author), in a State-of-the-University presentation regretted students' lack of exposure to standards of normative ethics. His remarks were directed particularly to the Business School, but other professional schools and colleges of the University were similarly neglectful. Bok could be said to have underscored the belief that academe has an obligation to make its students aware that society expects graduates entering the professions to have high moral and ethical standards.

For architects his concerns were, and remain, appropriate. Architects, in undertaking commissions for their services, enter into what may be called a "social compact" with their clients. Not only are architects assumed to be talented in the design and construction of buildings, they are thought to be of the highest ethical caliber. A recent public opinion poll revealed that architects were rated superior in ethical behavior to lawyers, to some medical doctors, and to almost all businesspeople. (The clergy was ranked highest.)

There are those who say that the teaching of ethics is "useless," for ethical behavior is a trait acquired in maturation from childhood to adulthood; it is not a science to be taught, at any level, in the classroom. The naysayers hold that "moral behavior" is a product of training, not "reflection," and that "abstract knowledge of right and wrong . . . does not contribute to character" (from Michael Levin in a recent op-ed piece in the *New York Times*). These points of contention may be arguable, but what is not arguable is the need for architectural students to know what ethical standards are expected of professional architects. The moral and ethical standards of the profession may be called an essential part of the "ground rules" for practice. Architects must zealously guard their reputation for integrity, and a review of some of the basic principles of ethics, personal and professional, is vital to one's career, especially as one enters practice. Such a review is valuable, not "useless."

A Brief Introduction to Several Ethical Concepts

A discussion of ethics that attempts to explain terms, meanings, and the nature of ethics is better left to philosophers. There is a need, however, to understand the origins of professional ethics and to note what some respected ethicists have written on the subject, although the material presented may raise more questions than can be answered. For our purposes ethics can be described as a set of moral values that define which actions we take are "right" and what are the principles for defining the "good." Right, or "rightness," are qualities that we separate from the "wrong" and the "good" or the "supreme good" (summum bonum). The meaning of "right" may relate to a number of concepts, most of which are too diverse in their nature to be considered here and are thus left to philosophers to debate.

The fundamental criteria for the meaning of the "right" and the "good" have been argued for centuries. The Greek philosophers, notably Plato and Aristotle, were among the forerunners of our present day ethicists, and much of their erudition remains in the discourse of our times. At the turn of the twentieth century, there was a major revival of the debate on definition of ethics and their significance for society. G. E. Moore, a philosopher at Cambridge, published in 1903, "Principia Ethica," which raised the question of metaethics and the meaning of ethical terms (i.e., what is the meaning of the "right" and the "good"). Other prominent ethicists writing about metaethics, along with Moore, were John Dewey, H. A. Prichard, W. D. Ross, A. C. Ewing, P. H. Nowell-Smith, and the existentialist, Jean-Paul Sartre. Debate over ethical issues is spirited and continues to expand in academe with no signs of abatement.

Opinion on what is meaning of "right" is agreed upon more readily than a meaning of the term the "good," which some philosophers claim defies acceptable interpretation. This is essentially the case in a discussion of professional ethics. Actions we take as architects, when of our own volition and of consequence, can be classified as right or wrong from a professional standpoint. It is right to perform our services as expertly as possible; it is not right to do otherwise. We have an obligation to do what is "right," not only because of the consequences but because, in a sense, we promise to do so when we proffer our professional services.

A former leading ethicist, W. D. Ross, one-time Vice Chancellor of Oxford University, wrote that "right" is that action that most people would approve of if that action were to do the most good. One theory to test that premise, perhaps over the objections of some philosophers, who would prefer to debate the issue, might come under a theory of obligation: What would be the consequences if every one performed the action in question? In a mundane sense, if in our cars we all "ran red lights," what would be the consequences? It might be for some a likely thing to do, but it would not be the action that would do the most good. Exaggerating credentials on a résumé, or qualifications for a commission are obviously not "right" in an ethical sense, and we may assume that Ross would agree to that, however prevalent that may be. Ross wrote at length on the question, "What makes right acts right?" He concluded, after much reflection, that in the end and in most instances: "We ought to do what will produce the most good," and "acts to promote the general good [are] one of the main factors in determining whether they are right."[1]

Closely allied to the concept of the "right" are theories of obligation. A. C. Ewing, a one-time Reader in Ethics at Cambridge University, and also a metaethicist, outlined a series of concerns for obligatory actions. He classified theories of obligations in four categories: Actions are obligatory by the actions they produce, by universal law independent of the good they produce, by what we do by intuition, and by the "prima facie duties" (i.e., a duty that holds unless it is overruled "by a superior moral obligation").

What most ethicists debate is the problem of the meaning of the term the "good." What is most desirable in our lives: Is it pleasure? Is it happiness, perfection, virtue? Is it a quality of intrinsic value? Pleasure seems to reflect hedonism, happiness is difficult to define, and perfection and virtue have many different interpretations. We can accept G. E. Moore's dicta that there has to be an intrinsic value in an action or object to realize the "good." Intrinsic is defined as the essential nature or character of the thing, action, object, and so on. The continuing argument over the term, the "good," probably never will be settled to the satisfaction of all ethicists and philosophers. Ethics is not a true science such as chemistry, nor a discipline where there is a fundamental agreement on most major concepts. One has only to look at a recent text on ethics to realize the diversity of opinions on such issues as utilitarian ethics, relevant ethics, material ethics, and so on. Pluralism in the study of ethics is the rule, not the exception.

Normative ethics, including practical ethics—uncodified ethics—may at times be confronted by professional codes of ethics to which we subscribe. Professional ethics are established to codify those standards of ethical behavior for which adherence is mandatory for membership in a professional organization. The standards and canons of these codes are explicitly related to the ethical behavior expected of the membership in their area of expertise.

The principal conflict in ethical behavior comes when self-interest, guided or not by practical ethics, differs from our professional ethics. First, one should understand the definition of a professional person. Architects are professionals by the nature of their specialized education, specialized training, and demonstrated expertise by examination for licensure and specialized experience. As professionals, we are presumed by the public to maintain high moral and ethical standards as exemplified by the AIA Code of Ethics and Personal Conduct, a document that has set, for the most part, the criteria for the ethical behavior of practicing architects. Pragmatic and self-interested concerns are ever present in practice, but if not overridden by some greater obligation, our manifest obligation is to our clients and ul-

---

[1]W. D. Ross, *The Right and the Good* (Oxford: Oxford University Press, 1930), Chapter 2.

timately to society. Architecture is a service profession, and we design and build structures for society. It is our overarching duty to serve our clients and as well the users of our buildings, the general public. Architecture is a noble profession with noble obligations, the foremost of which is service. Our actions are for "right" and for the "good." The AIA Code of Ethics (see page 50) makes this clear.

There remains, however, the issue of practical ethics. Codes of ethics are not, nor can they expect to be, perfect in the sense that they are all things to all persons at all times. An architect who must choose between strict observance of the AIA Code of Ethics and a violation of the Code is not necessarily at fault. In a situation where the architect faces financial ruin and the loss of the firm, practical ethics would mitigate a requirement of strict observance to a standard of a code of ethics. Codes must be established on the basis of reason: What would a reasonable person do in a given circumstance. The imperfectibility of the practice of architecture is a fact we are forced to acknowledge. This does not exonerate violations of standards of ethics but may explain them. In addition to the matter of practical ethics, architects owe obligations to society in obedience to the law.

The Code of Ethics of the AIA calls for its members to obey the law. A violation of the law is a violation of the Code of Ethics. Codes of ethics are not the law, however, and some violations of the codes may not be unlawful. Furthermore, an action against the law may be morally right in some circumstances, as the philosopher Dabney Townsend points out, as in "civil rights" actions in violation of the law. Codes of ethics often note legal requirements that presuppose ethical requirements but are fundamentally not the same. There may be no law against an architect acting in an unprofessional manner by ignoring national safety codes where such codes are not in force, but such an action would be morally and ethically wrong. Practical ethics do not justify breaking the law or violating codified behavior; the issue remains that obedience to the law transcends codes of ethics.

What then are professional ethics, as they may differ from intuitive or practical ethics? Do we pause to think of a possible action as "right," or for the "good," or do we act by intuition? A review of codified ethics for architects does not answer the latter question but does indicate what is expected ethically and what is obligatory for members of the Institute. Students who intend to practice architecture will find further study in ethics beneficial and of value for their future practice. Architects associating daily with clients, builders, and the general public regularly encounter situations where normative ethics are involved in actions required to be taken.

The material in this section is introductory and intended to serve as a lead to a short analysis of the Code of Ethics and Personal Conduct that follows. For a more lucid presentation on the issues, A. C. Ewing writes brilliantly on the "right" and theories of obligation. Moore does likewise for questions relating to the "good"; he writes more clearly for the uninitiated than many present-day philosophers. Students should avoid less respected authors and not equate moral values to knowledge.

The essential point is to be able to recognize which actions are "right" and which values are expected of architects in their professional practice.

Codes of Ethics for Practicing Architects

Codified ethical standards may seem, at first reading, not to relate directly to issues of "right" and the "good." While these terms may not appear verbatim, the American Institute of Architects canons of ethical standards have been conceived with these aspects of ethics as fundamental bases for concern. The intent of professional codes of ethics is to "distinguish professional practice from nonprofessional enterprise," quoting a phrase from an AIA document from many years ago. Not all registered architects are members of the AIA, but the codes that the Institute has formulated have served as the standards, moral and ethical, for the profession. The present Code of Ethics and Professional Conduct has evolved from a number of like documents prepared over the years and has been voted upon and approved by the membership. Lawyers, medical doctors, and other professionals have similar documents, although none so well known, perhaps, as the Hippocratic oath, a virtual symbol in the public mind for the medical profession.

The changes that have been made in ethical codes for architects in the last half of the twentieth century are radical at first glance. But change is endemic to the profession, and most architects have welcomed the move to improve the code and make it more responsive to the realities of practice at this time. As a key to understand better the development of the standards for professional behavior, and how change has come about, a comparison of two versions of ethical standards is useful.

In 1947 the Institute published Document Number 330 entitled "Standards of Professional Practice." It was divided into two sections—the first, "Responsibilities of the Profession, Advisory," and the second (in part), "Standards of Behavior . . . Mandatory for Membership." The two important words are advisory and mandatory. Looking ahead to the present set of canons, this format has been altered to outline goals that architects should aspire to (as opposed to responsibilities) and rules of conduct that are obligatory (as opposed to mandatory).

Document Number 330, in the second paragraph, states that to maintain a "high standard of conduct [the Institute] . . . formulates the following basic principles." These principles are in Part One, and some more noteworthy ones are: The profession of architecture calls for men of the highest integrity; the architect's honesty of purpose must be above suspicion; he has moral responsibilities to his associates and subordinates; he must act with entire impartiality (between all parties in a project); and other similar principles. Part One closed with the sentence, "He should respect punctiliously the hallmarks that distinguish professional practice from non-professional enterprise."

The second part of the 1947 Standards of Practice contains the mandatory standards for membership, different in tone and intent from the principles that were advisory for behavior. The eight mandatory standards, in paraphrase, were:

1. The Architect can only be compensated by his fee for work done on the project.
2. There shall be no services rendered without compensation (no free sketches except for an established client).

3. The Architect shall not compete for a project on a fee basis. (There shall be no competitive bidding for a commission.)
4. The Architect shall not "injure the professional reputation, prospects or business of a fellow Architect. He shall not attempt to supplant another Architect . . . nor undertake a commission for which another has been previously employed until he has determined that the original employment has been terminated."
5. An Architect cannot be employed for a project for which he has been the advisor even if the project has been abandoned.
6. An Architect shall avoid paid publicity (no advertising).
7. An Architect shall not guarantee the cost of a project.
8. The final article called for the mandatory adherence to these standards, noting "the obligation of every member" and establishing provisions for enforcement.

The 1993 Canon of Ethics, published almost fifty years later, is a very different document. The masthead notes that it is "from the Office of the General Counsel," which tells us that the lawyers are in charge and everything is strictly legal, even at the price of pragmatic ethics. Gone is the no-supplanting rule (see the *P/A* Ethics Poll, page 52); gone is the requirement for a fixed fee (no bidding for commissions); gone is the ban against advertising (paid publicity); gone is the stricture against free sketches; these and more all replaced by five canons of obligation. There is provision for enforcement and a proviso for penalties contained in Article III of the Rules of Enactment, ranging from admonition to termination of membership.

In the Preamble of the 1993 set of standards is the "Statement in Compliance with the 1990 Consent Decree." It says in precise legal language that the following actions or practices are no longer unethical: submitting competitive bids, providing discounts, and providing free services. (The Consent Decree was an action brought by the Justice Department against the AIA, the issues in which were agreed to by the Institute.) In this instance, the AIA ethical standards yielded to Federal laws that take precedence, based upon the concept that the common good is "right," over matters not based on laws, such as ethical standards.

The five obligatory canons in the 1993 document include the titles: General Obligations (and they are very general), Obligations to the Public, Obligations to the Client, Obligations to the Profession, and Obligations to Colleagues. All are based upon an ethical concept of "right." The Code of Ethics and Professional Conduct, as it is known, is formed by a series of paragraphs marked with an "ES" or "R." The ES denotes an Ethical Standard and signifies a goal or aspiration for members; an R indicates a mandatory rule of conduct, a violation of which is a ground for disciplinary action. An example of an R rule is related to undertaking a commission wherein "competence is substantially impaired by physical or mental disabilities." Such an action is in violation of Canon I, General Obligations.

Another R rule states in brief: "Members shall demonstrate a consistent pattern of reasonable care and competence." Other obligatory rules in the five canons are similar in nature. Canon Five does have a much needed rule that employers "recognize the professional contributions of their employees," as in naming the designer of a project when it is not the architect under whose name the project has been commissioned. Some architects consider that, in general, the new Code has been written not only to enumerate ethical principles but to avoid possible litigation such as might arise in setting a fixed fee and so on. Other professional architects feel that there is a marked shift in emphasis in the canons toward qualifications in practice, as opposed to adherence to pragmatic canons of ethical behavior. This may overstate the case, but it is difficult to reconcile the 1993 standards of ethics as equal to the rigor of the 1947 ethical standards. Many architects, however, welcome the 1993 Code as more appropriate to the mores of the time. The older document, they feel, with all its male pronouns and conservative standards, is no longer fitting for the world of today. Whatever the position one might take as to the relative ethical values of the two codes, personal ethical behavior of the highest standards is obligatory for architects.

In 1987, the magazine *Progressive Architecture* appended to one of its monthly issues, "The *P/A* Reader Poll on Ethics." The first question in the poll had twenty-five parts, marked from A to Y, and all were actions to be marked right or wrong from an ethical standpoint. Questions Two through Nine included much more narrow issues such as, "What percentage of architects do you believe engage in unethical behavior?" The questions assumed that all respondents largely agreed upon definitions in ethics of the "right" and the "good" and that the respondents were familiar with the then-current edition of the AIA Code of Ethics and Professional Conduct.

The *P/A* questionnaire serves to emphasize the importance of ethics for practicing architects. How truthful the answers were is not as important as that the questions were asked. The most significant, perhaps, was the query, to be responded to with a yes or no, made in the form of a statement: "The AIA Code of Ethics is too weak to influence actual practice." That statement could not be readily applied to the 1947 code, AIA Document Number 330. And by its introduction, the pollsters could be said to have underlined the lack of pragmatic rigor in the revised code. There have been many changes in AIA documents in recent years, and almost all changes have been made to lessen the exposure of architects to potential litigation. The revisions in the codes of ethics have been made chiefly for that reason. One ponders the question of whether these changes have lowered professional ethical standards.

The results of the *P/A* Poll were published in the February 1988 issue of the magazine. There seemed to be, in the responses, a hard core of support for high standards of professional ethical behavior. Over one-third, a startlingly high percentage, of the answering professionals indicated that they considered that other architects engaged in unethical behavior. Among the leading causes of unethical behavior were the perceived practices of concealing construction errors and sealing someone else's drawings. Other unethical actions reported were "altering credentials" and "padding of expenses." The former refers to exaggerating experience and academic achievements in resumes and applications for commissions. The padding of expenses is the all-too-common practice of charging clients for work not done, costs not incurred or overstated, and like matters. The younger respondents sharply criticized, as unethical, false promises of advancement as practiced by some employers. One positive response was that most architects felt that efforts to supplant another architect for a project (when another architect had been selected, or under contract, for a commission) were, and remain highly unethical, despite the "non-supplanting rule" having been deleted from the codes of ethics.

Most architects replying answered that the AIA would be reluctant to enforce the new code even though it was weaker, in their opinion, than earlier codes such as the 1947 document. They faulted the Justice Department's rulings for the failings of the newer codes and indicated that the principal reasons for unethical behavior are intense competition, pressures for money, and the tendency to please clients "at any cost."

Professional codified ethics intend to formulate for members high expectations for behavior. They are created to benefit society at large by stressing the "rightness" of obligatory actions by professionals for those persons and institutions they serve. In the end, ethical behavior is a personal matter, but codes of ethics establish principles of moral behavior that clearly establish the criteria for those who practice as professionals, in our case as architects.

It is of interest to review briefly a law suit against the AIA and its code of ethics. It had a significant effect on the existing code of ethics and is largely responsible for the form of the present Code of Ethics and Professional Conduct. A study of "Decisions" and "Advisory Actions" published by the AIA National Judicial Council (the Council) since the adoption of the revised code (post 1979) provides an insight into the more prevalent contemporary offenses of AIA members. There have been three major areas of violations, the most common of which are exaggerating achievements and making false claims of credentials, both academic and professional. Next is failure to give credit to associates or partners for work performed, followed by misleading clients in project management and, tied with that, involvement in conflicts of interest.

There was a case, reviewed by the Council, concerning the "supplanting" rule outlawed in its original form in 1979 (see page 54). The Council, in an advisory opinion, noted that many states have laws that protect contracts from forms of supplanting and that the new canons of obligation forbid violations of the law. And, most significantly, the Council felt that the issue of supplanting remains one of "serious ethical" concern. The *P/A* Poll on Ethics showed a similar concern.

The intent of the new code (the 1993 edition) is an issue for further study. Are the obligatory standards (R) and the ethical standards (ES) considered to apply separately to one of the following three categories of ethical concern: moral, legal, or practical? Or are there elements of all three of these concerns in many of the canons and their individual numbered standards? It appears to be the intention of the document to embrace all the categories: the standards demand high moral behavior, obedience to the law, and a reasonable acceptance of practical ethics. The resultant code of ethics becomes a highly pragmatic professional code and, some may argue, more representative of evolving morality at the close of the twentieth century as compared to the standards of the code at midcentury (the 1947 edition noted above). There are those who would not agree to this premise and prefer the earlier document, which remains an issue for debate.

A Case Study in Ethics and the Practice of Architecture

The judge's decision, handed down June 25, 1979, in the case of *Aram H. Mardirosian, AIA, vs. The American Institute of Architects and Seymour Auerbach, AIA*, resulted in a major change in codified ethics for architects. The case is well known in the profession and in some law schools, for it was a successful challenge by a member of the Institute of the then mandatory AIA standards for ethical behavior. Mardirosian charged that the actions taken against him for alleged code violations were unlawful in accordance with the Sherman Act. The AIA, the principal defendant, in losing the case, was forced to reinstate Mardirosian and pay treble damages. Furthermore, the Institute was forced to rewrite its code of ethics, deleting much of the strict verbiage of the document then in force, which was similar to Document Number 330 of 1947 discussed above. To be effective, a code of ethics must be lawful, and the code of ethics in 1977 was not.

The facts of the case have been reported in journals and, most explicitly, in the findings of Judge John Sirica (of Watergate fame), which were published in the Federal Register Number 474. Auerbach had been hired by the railroad owners of Union Station, with the stipulation that the National Park Service of the Department of the Interior would have the right to accept or reject the work, to remodel the existing Union Station in Washington, D.C., to serve as a National Visitor Center. He was also retained by the railroads to design a parking garage and a new railroad station. Congress allocated funds for the Visitor Center, which was to be housed in the remodeled Union Station, a much admired building designed by Daniel Burnham and opened in 1908. The Park Service retained Aram Mardirosian, a former employee, to act as consultant on the project, and to serve as a liaison with Auerbach. In 1973, in order to expedite the work, the Park Service assumed, by an amendment to the original contract, the role of owner for the Visitor Center; Auerbach remained as architect, in the employ of the railroads, for the parking garage and the new rail station.

Following completion of the design work for the Visitor Center, the contractor's bids far exceeded the monies allocated. According to news reports, Mardirosian, as consultant, had been highly critical of the work of Auerbach's firm and recommended his termination from the project; Auerbach, however, agreed to modify the documents to meet the budget and rebid the project.

Rather than allow Auerbach to continue with the commission, the Park Service acted to hire Mardirosian, and his firm Potomac Architects, to revise the documents for the design of the Visitor Center and complete the project. Mardirosian was instructed by the Park Service not to notify Auerbach of this proposed change, and the Government paid Auerbach his full fee through the bid phase of the work. Mardirosian did not advise Auerbach that he had been selected to supplant Auerbach as architect for the Visitor's Center, and Auerbach, in a complaint to the National Judicial Council of the AIA, claimed that this action, or lack of it, by Mardirosian was in violation of the code of ethics concerning supplanting. Article Nine of the extant code of ethics strictly forbade a failure to notify the architect to be replaced by the supplanting architect. Auerbach had learned of the Park Service's contemplated action but was not officially notified of his termination until July 3, 1975. Mardirosian's contract was dated July 27, 1975, but the negotiations, Auerbach contended, long preceded that date.

The National Judicial Council of the AIA held a series of hearings and then presented their recommendation to the Board of Directors, after which the Board responded to Auerbach's charges by suspending Mardirosian's membership for one year. Upon review, this action was modified to a ruling whereby Mardirosian was forbidden to use the designation AIA after his name but could retain his membership; furthermore (adding injury to insult), he was to pay his full dues for that year. Mardirosian subsequently brought suit against the AIA and Auerbach for damages for a probable loss of revenue resulting from not being allowed to use the AIA designation. His claim was that the Institute was in violation of the Sherman Act, which forbids actions in restraint of trade, and that he was deprived of his right to practice freely, using the designation AIA, which was an obvious benefit to his practice. Judge Sirica, while acknowledging the importance of ethical standards for professional organizations, found the law takes precedence despite any argument that Mardirosian had agreed to abide by the ethical standards of the AIA, whether this was an issue or not. The award of treble damages was justified by the Clayton Act, which "provides a cause of action . . . to persons injured in their business or property by reason of violation of the anti-trust laws" (i.e., the Sherman Act).

The code of ethics of the AIA extant in 1977 was found, by Judge Sirica, to be anticompetitive, which made it unlawful. This was the basis for Mardirosian's complaint under the Sherman Act. Sirica referred "to the rule of reason," which would include, not exclude, professional organizations as being required, under the Sherman Act, to permit competition. In a previous case in Federal Court, the Professional Engineers were found guilty of violating the Sherman Act in their prohibition of competitive bidding for commissions. That case established a precedent that foredoomed any defense by the AIA of its standard-fee schedule, as well as the nonsupplanting article in the then current code of ethics.

The merits of Mardirosian's case, as a matter of law, cannot be argued further. Its effect on the code of ethics of the AIA was immediate, and the present code reflects that. As to the issue of professional ethics, however, there is debate.

First, was Mardirosian obligated to adhere to the nonsupplanting rule and to refuse the commission offered to his firm by the Park Service? The National Judicial Council of the AIA ruled that he should have done so. This raises the second question: When Mardirosian joined the AIA did he agree to abide by the Code of Ethics at that instance and by any future revisions approved by the membership? Canon Nine required, at the time of the alleged supplanting, that he notify Auerbach of his intent to undertake the commission, an action he did not take. Third, should Mardirosian have protested the Park Service's order not to notify Auerbach, an act that put him in jeopardy under Article Nine? Fourth, was Mardirosian unethical in using portions of Auerbach's documents, sealed by Auerbach, as charged by the AIA? These and other questions come to mind. Was there ethical, practical, or intuitive justification for Mardirosian's behavior? Were his actions for the "right," regardless of the canons of professional ethics?

Mardirosian has claimed that he did not violate the nonsupplanting rule as the original contract was no longer in force when Auerbach was terminated. Therefore, he was not, in his mind and by the advice of his lawyers, obligated to notify Auerbach. These issues were not a matter for the courts so they remain moot, and the latest code includes only generalities on the subject. In the 1993 Canon of Ethics and Personal Conduct, there are no explicit bars to such actions as Mardirosian took. The issue, then, for many ethicists and some practicing architects becomes: Are the new standards of the same rigor and integrity as the earlier codes, such as the 1947 code, Document 330? Which better serves the individual, the profession, the client, the community, and the "common good": The old or the new code? 1947 or 1993?

Summary: Ethics and Practice

Philosophers suffer much the same fate as poets; their efforts often have only transitory success. Few contemporary philosophers, including ethicists, remain popular or fashionable over long periods of time, a state not unknown to architects. It can be expected that codes of ethics, designed to promote concepts of professional ethical behavior, will not have unlimited acceptance as societal mores, particularly in the twenty-first century, seem to change almost from decade to decade. Changes in ethical codes may not always be for the better but will, in most instances, be more truly contemporaneous. What is acceptable behavior in one generation may not have been acceptable in a previous generation, whether it is the height of fashion or the excesses of deconstruction. Codes of ethics will also need to be modified, or greatly changed, by new interpretations of existing laws and new legislation that may, of necessity, bring about a reworking of ethical canons.

In a little more than the last ten years, there has been a major revision in the approach to ethical standards for architects. Many architects consider the new canons more idealistic and less pragmatic than previous codes. They interpret the obligatory standards of the latest canons as less harsh in nature; at least, they stress reasonably obligatory actions and reasonable behavior. In the 1947 code, there were eight mandatory regulations in contrast to the five obligatory canons in the 1993 code; the latter five canons were composed with less rigor, perhaps, but were more humane in their understanding of the imperfectibility of the practice of architecture.

Students about to enter the profession of architecture should know that high moral and ethical standards are expected of them. An architect's personal reputation for integrity is one of his or her most valuable assets. That is the reason to reiterate that a study of ethics, however brief, is valuable. The works listed in the bibliography below would be a good beginning.

BIBLIOGRAPHY
1. Adler, Mortimer. *Ten Philosophical Mistakes.* New York: MacMillan, 1985.
2. Adler, Mortimer. *Six Great Ideas.* New York: Collier, 1981.

3. American Institute of Architects. *Standards of Professional Practice.* Document No. 330. Washington, D.C.: American Institute of Architects, 1947.
4. American Institute of Architects. *1993 Code of Ethics and Professional Conduct.* Washington, D.C.: American Institute of Architects, 1993.
5. Aristotle. *Nichomachean Ethics.* Translated by Terence Irwin. Indianapolis, Ind.: Hackett Publishing, 1985.
6. Behrman, Jack N., ed. *Essays on Ethics in Business and the Professions.* Englewood Cliffs, N.J.: Prentice-Hall, 1988.
7. Ewing, A. C. *The Definition of the Good.* New York: MacMillan, 1947.
8. Ewing, A. C. "Ethics." In *Encyclopaedia Britannica,* 14th ed. London: The Encyclopaedia Britannica Company, Ltd. 1957; 8: 757–761.
9. Guthrie, W. K. C. *Socrates.* Cambridge, U.K.: Cambridge University Press, 1971.
10. Johnson, Oliver, ed. *Ethics, Collections from Classical and Contemporary Writers.* 5th ed. New York: Holt, 1984.
11. Klemke, E. D., et al. *Philosophy, the Basic Issue.* 3rd ed. New York: St. Martin's Press, 1990.
12. "*P/A* Reader Poll, Ethics." *Progressive Architecture.* February 1988: 13–17.
13. US Government. *Aram H. Mardirosian, Plaintiff v. The American Institute of Architects, and Seymour Auerbach, Defendants.* Federal Register, Federal Supplement No. 474, pp. 628–651, Washington, D.C., 1979.

Postscript on Ethical Behavior

The dominant view *today* is that, no matter what, *tell the truth in real time.* This is an absolute ethical principle in the current social and legal climate. It is indefensible to actively mislead the public—that is unethical and illegal.

Twenty or thirty years ago, the social, ethical, and legal climate, across all professions, not only supported but called for a paternalistic approach relative to exercise of professional judgment. It is important, however, to recognize that there are shifts in the way "right" is viewed from one age or era to another. The paternalistic approach disappeared in the 1980s and 1990s, i.e., it is not the professional's job to be the "daddy" to the public but, rather, an honest collaborator.

The professional must step up and be a leader, take responsibility for the public good, and act on information. Remaining silent is simply not an option today.

There is also a communication issue. It is not sufficient to merely inform. The professional must actively inform *and* set forth educated and expert alternatives or a series of effective responses. Professionals must learn to communicate in ways that avoid panic and to tell the truth in a manner that mitigates or eliminates mass hysteria. The best ethical action is not about choosing one way or another. Rather, it is about the way in which bad news or mistakes are delivered, for example: "The situation is not ideal; there is an uphill battle; if everyone works together, we can beat the odds and make it right in a timely fashion."

The answers to just about any ethical scenario are rigid and prescribed. There is only one acceptable course of action in today's world. We are in a time now in which an ethical standard may not necessarily be in the best interest of the public. In effect, professional judgment really is prescribed—and that may not reflect the best *tradition* of professional judgment. Codifying professional judgment removes authority from the professional. This is what is acceptable today; there is just too much risk otherwise. Are the platinum ethical standards of the moment consistent with the professional who wants to call an "audible" as a function of a specific set of unique circumstances? No. So there is a tradeoff . . . prescribed standards erode the ability of the professional to do what he or she ideally should be educated, trained, and experienced to do best, that is, adjust an approach or tailor a decision to a particular set of circumstances.

The professional cannot comment on specific situations without all the evidence if he or she is not centrally involved. However, the professional can make guarded, qualified public comments based on what is known, as long as there is care in qualifying that the comments are based on limited knowledge. Comments should be restricted to what the professional does know or to very general principles. *Comments must be based on the evidence.* Professionals should not withhold any information of value from the public; however, assumptions about what professionals do not know specifically, should not be made.

As long as the information is known to the professional as accurate and specific to the situation under discussion, then it should be shared. Avoid any speculation! The professional must be informed by real data and evidence. It is ethically indefensible in today's ethical and legal climate to speculate. The culture of ethics and law today is to place absolute priority on truth-telling. There is no better public relations than telling the truth.

Clients and the public require autonomy in decision making. Autonomy is the ability to control one's own destiny. The ability for individuals to control their lives by making their own choices is paramount. This has become a preeminent ethical mandate and legal standard. It is the most important of the principles in ethical decision making. And that autonomy depends upon the professional telling the truth as soon as it is known. Autonomy supercedes all else; telling the truth is necessary for autonomy. This is the ethical hierarchy. Professionals must respect individuals' capacity to control his or her own destiny, which requires having all the information at his or her disposal. This is a political and ethical fact of life today. Politicians can be contrite—or destroy their careers by not fully disclosing the truth.

What is taught has to be black and white because, ultimately, the issues are legal. Ultimately, the law creeps into ethics and directs decisions.

Case Study | The Fifty-Nine-Story Crisis*

What's an engineer's worst nightmare? To realize that the supports he designed for a skyscraper like Citicorp Center (in New York City) are flawed—and hurricane season is approaching.

The following tale is a true and stunning example of good ethics in action. Structural engineer William J. LeMessurier demonstrates that doing the "right" thing—placing society's interests ahead of self-interest and even the client's interest—is an obligation of design professionals. This case also suggests how the side effects of ethical conduct enhance our reputa-

*Originally published in *The New Yorker,* May 29, 1995, pp. 45–53.

tions and the respect and trust given us by the public.

JOE MORGENSTERN is the *Wall Street Journal's* film critic. In addition to contributing to the *New Yorker,* where this piece first appeared, he has been a foreign correspondent for the *New York Times,* and has written for the *New York Times Magazine, The Los Angeles Times Magazine,* and many other national publications. His television writing includes episodes of *Law and Order* and the movie *The Boy In the Plastic Bubble.* Formerly the film critic for *Newsweek,* he is a founding member of the National Society of Film Critics.

On a warm June day in 1978, William J. LeMessurier, one of the nation's leading structural engineers, received a phone call at his headquarters, in Cambridge, Massachusetts, from an engineering student in New Jersey. The young man, whose name has been lost in the swirl of subsequent events, said that his professor had assigned him to write a paper on the Citicorp tower, the slash-topped silver skyscraper that had become, on its completion in Manhattan the year before, the seventh-tallest building in the world.

LeMessurier found the subject hard to resist, even though the call caught him in the middle of a meeting. As a structural consultant to the architect Hugh Stubbins, Jr., he had designed the 25,000-ton steel skeleton beneath the tower's sleek aluminum skin. And, in a field where architects usually get all the credit, the engineer, then 52, had won his own share of praise for the tower's technical elegance and singular grace; indeed, earlier that year he had been elected to the National Academy of Engineering, the highest honor his profession bestows. Excusing himself from the meeting, LeMessurier asked his caller how he could help.

The student wondered about the columns—there are four—that held the building up. According to his professor, LeMessurier had put them in the wrong place.

"I was very nice to this young man," LeMessurier recalls. "But I said, 'Listen, I want you to tell your teacher that he doesn't know what the hell he's talking about, because he doesn't know the problem that had to be solved.' I promised to call back after my meeting and explain the whole thing."

The problem had been posed by a church. When planning for Citicorp Center began, in the early 1970s, the site of choice was on the east side of Lexington Avenue, between 53rd and 54th Streets, directly across the street from Citicorp's headquarters. But the northwest corner of that block was occupied by St. Peter's Church, a decaying Gothic structure built in 1905. Since St. Peter's owned the corner, and one of the world's biggest banking corporations wanted the whole block, the church was able to strike a deal that seemed heaven-sent: Its old building would be demolished and a new one built as a freestanding part of Citicorp Center.

To clear space for the new church, Hugh Stubbins and Bill LeMessurier (he pronounces his name "LeMeasure") set their 59-story tower on four massive, 9-story-high stilts, and positioned them at the center of each side, rather than at each corner. This daring scheme allowed the designers to cantilever the building's corners 72 feet out over the church, on the northwest, and over a plaza on the southwest. The columns also produced high visual drama: A 914-foot monolith that seemed all but weightless as it hovered above the street.

When LeMessurier called the student back, he related this with the pride of a master builder and the elaborate patience of a pedagogue; he, too, taught a structural engineering class, to architecture students at Harvard. Then he explained how the peculiar geometry of the building, far from constituting a mistake, put the columns in the strongest position to resist what sailors call quartering winds—those which come from a diagonal and, by flowing across two sides of a building at once, increase the forces on both. For further enlightenment on the matter, he referred the student to a technical article written by LeMessurier's partner in New York, an engineer named Stanley Goldstein. LeMessurier recalls, "I gave him a lot of information, and I said,

Figure 2-1 Citicorp Center in midtown Manhattan, New York. High quality public spaces at the base are revealed and underscored by nine-story-high columns, dramatically positioned at the center of each elevation. Illustration, courtesy of Howard Associates, Architectural Renderings, Sylvania, Ohio.

'Now you really have something on your professor, because you can explain all of this to him yourself.' "

Later that day, LeMessurier decided that the information would interest his own students; like sailors, designers of tall buildings must know the wind and respect its power. And the columns were only part of the tower's defense against swaying in severe winds. A classroom lecture would also look at the tower's unusual system of wind braces, which LeMessurier had first sketched out, in a burst of almost ecstatic invention, on a napkin in a Greek restaurant in Cambridge: 48 braces, in 6 tiers of 8, arrayed like giant chevrons behind the building's curtain of aluminum and glass. ("I'm very vain," LeMessurier says. "I would have liked my stuff to be expressed on the outside of the building, but Stubbins wouldn't have it. In the end, I told myself I didn't give a damn—the structure was there, it'd be seen by God.")

LeMessurier had long since established the strength of those braces in perpendicular winds—the only calculation required by New York City's building code. Now, in the spirit of intellectual play, he wanted to see if they were just as strong in winds hitting from 45 degrees. His new calculations surprised him. In four of the eight chevrons in each tier, a quartering wind increased the strain by 40 percent. Under normal circumstances, the wind braces would have absorbed the extra load without so much as a tremor. But the circumstances were not normal. A few weeks before, during a meeting in his office, LeMessurier had learned of a crucial change in the way the braces were joined.

The meeting had been called, during the month of May, to review plans for two new skyscrapers in Pittsburgh, Pennsylvania. Those towers, too, were designed by Hugh Stubbins with LeMessurier as structural consultant, and the plans called for wind braces similar to those used in Citicorp Center, with the same specifications for welded joints. This was top-of-the-line engineering; two structural members joined by a skilled welder become as strong as one. But welded joints, which are labor-intensive and therefore expensive, can be needlessly strong; in most cases, bolted joints are more practical and equally safe. That was the position taken at the May meeting by a man from U.S. Steel, a potential bidder on the contract to erect the Pittsburgh towers. If welded joints were a condition, the project might be too expensive and his firm might not want to take it on.

To reassure him, LeMessurier put in a call to his office in New York. "I spoke to Stanley Goldstein and said, 'Tell me about your success with those welded joints in Citicorp.' And Stanley said, 'Oh, didn't you know? They were changed—they were never welded at all, because

Bethlehem Steel came to us and said they didn't think we needed to do it.' " Bethlehem, which built the Citicorp tower, had made the same objection—welds were stronger than necessary, bolts were the right way to do the job. On August 1, 1974, LeMessurier's New York office—actually a venture in conjunction with an old-line Manhattan firm called the Office of James Ruderman—had accepted Bethlehem's proposal.

This news gave LeMessurier no cause for concern in the days immediately following the meeting. The choice of bolted joints was technically sound and professionally correct. Even the failure of his associates to flag him on the design change was justifiable; had every decision on the site in Manhattan waited for approval from Cambridge, the building would never have been finished. Most important, modern skyscrapers are so strong that catastrophic collapse is not considered a realistic prospect; when engineers seek to limit a building's sway, they do so for the tenant's comfort.

Yet now, a month after the May meeting, the substitution of bolted joints raised a troubling question. If the bracing system was unusually sensitive to quartering winds, as LeMessurier had just discovered, so were the joints that held it together. The question was whether the Manhattan team had considered such winds when it designed the bolts. "I didn't go into a panic over it," LeMessurier says. "But I was haunted by a hunch that it was something I'd better look into."

On July 24th, he flew to New York, where his hunch was soon confirmed: His people had taken only perpendicular winds into account. And he discovered another "subtle conceptual error," as he calls it now—one that threatened to make the situation much worse.

To understand why, one must look at the interplay of opposing forces in a windblown building. The wind causes tension in the structural members—that is, it tries to blow the building down. At the same time, some of that tension, measured in thousands, or even millions, of pounds, is offset by the force of gravity, which, by pressing the members together, tends to hold the building in place. The joints must be strong enough to resist the differential between these forces—the amount of wind tension minus the amount of compression.

Within this seemingly simple computation, however, lurks a powerful multiplier. At any given level of the building, the compression figure remains constant; the wind may blow harder, but the structure doesn't get any heavier. Thus, immense leverage can result from higher wind forces. In the Citicorp tower, the 40 percent increase in tension produced by a quartering wind became a 160 percent increase on the building's bolts.

Precisely because of that leverage, a margin of safety is built into the standard formulas for calculating how strong a joint must be; these formulas are contained in an American Institute of Steel Construction specification that deals with joints in structural columns. What LeMessurier found in New York, however, was that the people on his team had disregarded the standard. They had chosen to define the diagonal wind braces not as columns but as trusses, which are exempt from the safety factor. As a result, the bolts holding the joints together were perilously few. "By then," LeMessurier says, "I was getting pretty shaky."

He later detailed these mistakes in a 30-page document called "Project SERENE"; the acronym, both rueful and apt, stands for "Special Engineering Review of Events Nobody Envisioned." What emerges from this document, which has been confidential until now, and from interviews with LeMessurier and other principals in the events, is not malfeasance, or even negligence, but a series of miscalculations that flowed from a specific mind-set. In the case of the Citicorp tower, the first event that nobody envisioned had taken place when LeMessurier sketched, on a restaurant napkin, a bracing system with an inherent sensitivity to quartering winds. None of his associates identified this as a problem, let alone understood that they were compounding it with their fuzzy semantics. In the stiff, angular language of "Project SERENE," "consideration of wind from nonperpendicular directions on ordinary rectangular buildings is generally not discussed in the literature or in the classroom."

LeMessurier tried to take comfort from another element of Citicorp's advanced design:

The building's tuned mass damper. This machine, built at his behest and perched where the bells would have been if the Citicorp tower had been a cathedral, was essentially a 410-ton block of concrete, attached to huge springs and floating on a film of oil. When the building swayed, the block's inertia worked to damp the movement and calm tenants' queasy stomachs. Reducing sway was of special importance, because the Citicorp tower was an unusually lightweight building; the 25,000 tons of steel in its skeleton contrasted with the Empire State Building's 60,000 ton superstructure. Yet the damper, the first of its kind in a large building, was never meant to be a safety device. At best, the machine might reduce the danger, not dispel it.

Before making a final judgment on how dangerous the bolted joints were, LeMessurier turned to a Canadian engineer named Alan Davenport, the director of the Boundary Layer Wind Tunnel Laboratory, at the University of Western Ontario, and a world authority on the behavior of buildings in high winds. During the Citicorp tower's design, Davenport had run extensive tests on scale models of the structure. Now LeMessurier asked him and his deputy to retrieve the relevant files and magnetic tapes. "If we were going to think about such things as the possibility of failure," LeMessurier says—the word "failure" being a euphemism for the Citicorp tower's falling down—"we would think about it in terms of the best knowledge that the state of the art can produce, which is what these guys could provide for me."

On July 26th, he flew to London, Ontario, and met with Davenport. Presenting his new calculations, LeMessurier asked the Canadians to evaluate them in the light of the original data. "And you have to tell me the truth," he added. "Don't go easy if it doesn't come out the right way."

It didn't, and they didn't. The tale told by the wind-tunnel experts was more alarming than LeMessurier had expected. His assumption of a 40 percent increase in stress from diagonal winds was theoretically correct, but it could go higher in the real world, when storms lashed at the building and set it vibrating like a tuning fork. "Oh, my God," he thought, "now we've got that on top of an error from the bolts being under-designed." Refining their data further, the Canadians teased out wind-tunnel forces for each structural member in the building, with and without the tuned mass damper in operation; it remained for LeMessurier to interpret the numbers' meaning.

First, he went to Cambridge, where he talked to a trusted associate, and then he called his wife at their summerhouse in Maine. "Dorothy knew what I was up to," he says. "I told her, 'I think we've got a problem here, and I'm going to sit down and try to think about it.'" On July 28th, he drove to the northern shore of Sebago Lake, took an outboard motorboat a quarter of a mile across the water to his house on a 12-acre private island, and worked through the wind-tunnel numbers, joint by joint and floor by floor.

The weakest joint, he discovered, was at the building's 30th floor; if that one gave way, catastrophic failure of the whole structure would follow. Next, he took New York City weather records provided by Alan Davenport and calculated the probability of a storm severe enough to tear that joint apart. His figures told him that such an event had a statistical probability of occurring as often as once every 16 years—what meteorologists call a 16-year storm.

"That was very low, awesomely low," LeMessurier said, his voice hushed as if the horror of discovery were still fresh. "To put it another way, there was one chance in sixteen in any year, including that one." When the steadying influence of the tuned mass damper was factored in, the probability dwindled to one in fifty-five—a fifty-five-year storm. But the machine required electric current, which might fail as soon as a major storm hit.

As an experienced engineer, LeMessurier liked to think he could solve most structural problems, and the Citicorp tower was no exception. The bolted joints were readily accessible, thanks to Hugh Stubbins' insistence on putting the chevrons inside the building's skin rather than displaying them outside. With money and materials, the joints could be reinforced by welding heavy steel plates over them, like giant Band-Aids. But time was short; this was the end of July, and the height of the hurricane season was approaching. To avert disaster, LeMessurier would have to blow the whistle quickly—on himself. That meant facing the pain of possible protracted litigation, probable bankruptcy, and professional disgrace. It also meant shock and dismay for Citicorp's officers and shareholders when they learned that the bank's proud new corporate symbol, built at a cost of 175 million dollars, was threatened with collapse.

On the island, LeMessurier considered his options. Silence was one of them; only Davenport knew the full implications of what he had found, and he would not disclose them on his own. Suicide was another; if LeMessurier drove along the Maine Turnpike at a hundred miles an hour and steered into a bridge abutment, that would be that. But keeping silent required betting other people's lives against the odds, while suicide struck him as a coward's way out and—although he was passionate about nineteenth century classical music—unconvincingly melodramatic. What seized him an instant later was entirely convincing, because it was so unexpected—an almost giddy sense of power. "I had information that nobody else in the world had," LeMessurier recalls. "I had power in my hands to effect extraordinary events that only I could initiate. I mean, 16 years to failure—that was very simple, very clear-cut. I almost said, 'Thank you, dear Lord, for making this problem so sharply defined that there's no choice to make.'"

At his office in Cambridge on the morning of Monday, July 31st, LeMessurier tried to reach Hugh Stubbins, whose firm was upstairs in the same building, but Stubbins was in California and unavailable by phone. Then he called Stubbins' lawyer, Carl Sapers [see Sapers' on professionalism in Chapter 1, page 4], and outlined the emergency over lunch. Sapers advised him against telling Citicorp until he had consulted with his own company's liability insurers, the Northbrook Insurance Company, in Northbrook, Illinois. When LeMessurier called Northbrook, which represented the Office of James Ruderman as well, someone there referred him to the company's attorneys in New York and warned him not to discuss the matter with anyone else.

At 9 A. M. on Tuesday, in New York, LeMessurier faced a battery of lawyers who, he says, "wanted to meet me to find out if I was nutty." Being lawyers, not engineers, they were hard put to reconcile his dispassionate tone with the apocalyptic thrust of his prophecy. They also bridled at his carefully qualified answers to seemingly simple questions. When they asked how big a storm it would take to blow the building down, LeMessurier confined himself to statistical probabilities—a storm that might occur once in 16 years.

When they pressed him for specific wind velocities—would the wind have to be at 80 miles per hour, or 90, or 95?—he insisted that such figures were not significant in themselves, since every structure was uniquely sensitive to certain winds; an 85 mile-per-hour wind that blew for 16 minutes from the northwest might pose less of a threat to a particular building than an 80 mile-per-hour wind that blew for 14 minutes from the southwest.

But the lawyers certainly understood they had a crisis on their hands, so they sent for an expert adviser they trusted: Leslie Robertson, an engineer who had been a structural consultant for the World Trade Center. "I got a phone call out of the blue from some lawyer summoning me to a meeting," Robertson says. " 'What's it about?' 'You'll find out when you get there.' 'Sorry, I have other things to do—I don't attend meetings on that basis.' A few minutes later, I got another call, from another lawyer, who said there'd been a problem with Citicorp Center. I went to the meeting that morning, and I didn't know anybody there but Bill. He stood up and explained what he perceived were the difficulties with the building, and everyone, of course, was very concerned. Then they turned to me and said, 'Well?' I said, 'Look, if this is in fact the case, you have a very serious problem.' "

The two structural engineers were peers, but not friends. LeMessurier was a visionary with a fondness for heroic designs, though he was also an energetic manager. Robertson was a stickler for technical detail, a man fascinated by how things fit together. LeMessurier, older by two years, was voluble and intense, with a courtly rhetorical style. Robertson was tall, trim, brisk, and edgily funny, but he made no effort to hide his impatience with things that didn't interest him.

In addition to his engineering expertise, Robertson brought to the table a background in disaster management. He had worked with such groups as the National Science Foundation and the National Research Council on teams that studied the aftermaths of earthquakes, hurricanes, and floods. (In 1993, he worked with the F. B. I. on the World Trade Center bombing.) For the liability lawyers, this special perspective enhanced his stature as a consultant, but it unsettled LeMessurier from the start. As he remembers it, "Robertson predicted to everybody present that within hours of the time Citicorp heard about this the whole building would be evacuated. I almost fainted. I didn't want that to happen." (For his part, Robertson recalls making no such dire prediction.)

LeMessurier didn't think an evacuation would be necessary. He believed that the building was safe for occupancy in all but the most violent weather, thanks to the tuned mass damper, and he insisted that the damper's reliability in a storm could be assured by installing emergency generators. Robertson conceded the importance of keeping the damper running—it had performed flawlessly since it became operational earlier that year—but, because, in his view, its value as a safety device was unproved, he flatly refused to consider it as a mitigating factor. (In a conversation shortly after the World Trade Center bombing, Robertson noted dryly that the twin towers' emergency generators "lasted for 15 minutes.")

One point on which everyone agreed was that LeMessurier, together with Stubbins, needed to inform Citicorp as soon as possible. Only Stubbins had ever dealt directly with Citicorp's chairman, Walter B. Wriston, and he was flying home that same day from California and still didn't know his building was flawed. That evening, LeMessurier took the shuttle to Boston, went to Stubbins' house in Cambridge, and broke the news. "He winced, I must admit—here was his masterpiece," LeMessurier says. "But he's a man of enormous resilience, a very grown man, and fortunately we had a lifelong relationship of trust."

The next morning, August 2nd, Stubbins and LeMessurier flew to New York, went to LeMessurier's office at 515 Madison Avenue, put in a call to Wriston, but failed to penetrate the layers of secretaries and assistants that insulated Citicorp's chairman from the outside world. They were no more successful in reaching the bank's president, William I. Spencer, but Stubbins finally managed to get an appointment with Citicorp's executive vice president, John S. Reed, the man who has now succeeded Wriston as chairman. LeMessurier and Stubbins went to see Reed at the bank's ornate executive offices, in an older building on Lexington Avenue, across the street from Citicorp Center. LeMessurier began by saying, "I have a real problem for you, sir."

Reed was well equipped to understand the problem. He had an engineering background, and he had been involved in the design and construction of Citicorp Center; the company had called him in when it was considering the tuned mass damper. Reed listened impassively as LeMessurier detailed the structural defect and how he thought it could be fixed. LeMessurier says, "I'd already conceived that you could build a little plywood house around each of the connections that were critical, and a welder could work inside it without damaging the tenants' space. You might have to take up the carpet, take down the Sheetrock, and work at night, but all this could be done. But the real message I conveyed to him was 'I need your help—at once.'"

When Reed asked how much the repairs would cost, LeMessurier offered an estimate of a million dollars. At the end of the meeting, which lasted half an hour, Reed thanked the two men courteously, though noncommittally, and told them to go back to their office and await further instructions. They did so, but after waiting for more than an hour they decided to go out to lunch. As they were finishing their meal, a secretary from LeMessurier's office called to say that John Reed would be in the office in ten minutes with Walter Wriston.

In the late 1970s, when Citicorp began its expansion into global banking, Wriston was one of the most influential bankers in the country. A tall man of piercing intelligence, he was not known for effusiveness in the best of circum-

stances, and LeMessurier expected none now, what with Citicorp Center—and his own career— literally hanging in the balance. But the bank's chairman was genuinely proud of the building, and he offered his full support in getting it fixed.

"Wriston was fantastic," LeMessurier says. "He said, 'I guess my job is to handle the public relations of this, so I'll have to start drafting a press release.'" But he didn't have anything to write on, so someone handed him a yellow pad. That made him laugh. According to LeMessurier, Wriston said, "All wars are won by generals writing on yellow pads." In fact, Wriston simply took notes; the press release would not go out for six days. But his laughter put the others at ease. Citicorp's general was on their side.

Within hours of Wriston's visit, LeMessurier's office arranged for emergency generators for the tower's tuned mass damper. The bank issued beepers to LeMessurier and his key engineers, assuring them that Reed and other top managers could be reached by phone at any hour of the day or night. Citicorp also assigned two vice presidents, Henry DeFord III and Robert Dexter, to manage the repairs; both had overseen the building's construction and knew it well.

The next morning, Thursday, August 3rd, LeMessurier, Robertson, and four of LeMessurier's associates met with DeFord and Dexter in a conference room on the 30th floor of Citicorp Center. (The decision to hold the initial meeting near the structure's weakest point was purely coincidental.) LeMessurier outlined his plan to fix the wind braces by welding two-inch-thick steel plates over each of more than 200 bolted joints. The plan was tentatively approved, pending actual examination of a typical joint, but putting it into effect depended on the availability of a contractor and on an adequate supply of steel plate. Since Bethlehem Steel had dropped out of the business of fabricating and erecting skyscraper structures, Robertson suggested Karl Koch Erecting, a New Jersey-based firm that had put up the World Trade Center.

"I called them," Robertson says, "and got, 'Well, we're a little busy right now,' and I said, 'Hey, you don't understand what we're talking about here.'" A few hours later, two Koch engi-

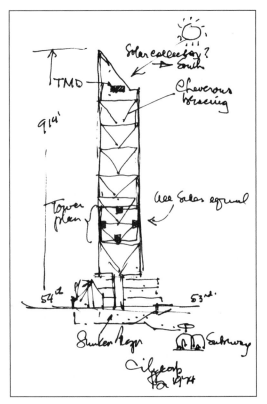

Figure 2-2 Original sketch by architect Hugh Stubbins. © The Stubbins Associates, Inc.

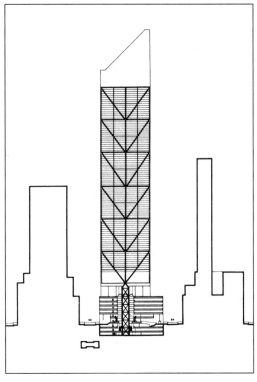

Figure 2-3 Diagram of the structural frame designed by engineer William LeMessurier. © The Stubbins Associates, Inc.

neers joined the meeting. LeMessurier and Robertson took them to an unoccupied floor of the building, and there workmen tore apart enough Sheetrock to expose a diagonal connection. Comparing the original drawings of the joints with the nuts-and-bolts reality before their eyes, the engineers concluded that LeMessurier's plan was indeed feasible. Koch also happened to have all the necessary steel plate on hand, so Citicorp negotiated a contract for welding to begin as soon as LeMessurier's office could issue new drawings.

Two more contracts were drawn up before the end of the following day. One of them went out to MTS Systems Corporation, the Minneapolis firm that had manufactured the tuned mass damper. MTS was asked to provide full-time technical support—in effect, around-the-clock nurses—to keep its machine in perfect health. The company flew one of its technicians

to New York that night. Four days later, in a letter of agreement, MTS asked Citicorp to provide a long list of materials and spare parts, which included three buckets, a grease gun, rags, cleaning solvent, and "1 Radio with weather band."

The other contract engaged a California firm, also recommended by Robertson, to fit the building with a number of instruments called strain gauges—pieces of tape with zigzag wires running through them. The gauges would be affixed to individual structural members, and electrical impulses from them would be funneled to an improvised communications center in Robertson's office, eight blocks away, at 230 Park Avenue; like a patient in intensive care, the tower would have every shiver and twitch monitored. But this required new telephone lines, and the phone company refused to budge on its leisurely installation schedule. When Robertson voiced his frustration about this during a late-night meeting in Walter Wriston's office, Wriston picked up the phone on his desk and called his friend Charles Brown, the president and chief operating officer of AT&T. The new lines went in the next morning.

A different problem-solving approach was taken by Robertson during another nighttime meeting in Citicorp's executive suite. Wriston wanted copies of some documents that Robertson had shown him, but all the secretaries had gone home—the only people on the floor were Wriston, Robertson, and John Reed—and every copying machine was locked. "I'm an engineer," Robertson says, "so I kneeled down, ripped the door off one of the machines, and we made our copies. I looked up at them a little apologetically, but, what the hell—fixing the door was a few hundred bucks, and these guys had a 175-million-dollar building in trouble across the street."

Robertson also assembled an advisory group of weather experts from academia and the government's Brookhaven National Laboratory, Long Island, New York, and hired two independent weather forecasters to provide wind predictions four times a day. "What worried us more than hurricanes, which give you hours and days to anticipate, were unpredictable events," Robertson says. "From time to time, we've had small tornadoes in this area, and there was a worry that a much bigger one would come down and take hold." Then Robertson raised an issue that LeMessurier had dreaded discussing. In a meeting on Friday that included LeMessurier, Robertson told Citicorp's representatives, DeFord and Dexter, that they needed to plan for evacuating Citicorp Center and a large area around it in the event of a high-wind alert.

During the first week of August, discussions had involved only a small circle of company officials and engineers. But the circle widened on Monday, August 7th, when final drawings for the steel plates went out to Arthur Nusbaum, the veteran project manager of HRH Construction, which was the original contractor for Citicorp Center, and Nusbaum, in turn, provided them to Koch Erecting. And it would widen again, because work could not go forward, as Robertson reminded the officials, without consulting the city's Department of Buildings. Citicorp faced a

public-relations debacle unless it came up with a plausible explanation of why its brand-new skyscraper needed fixing.

That night, DeFord and Dexter, following Robertson's advice, met with Mike Reilly, the American Red Cross's director of disaster services for the New York metropolitan area. "They laid out the dilemma, and it was clearly an ominous event," Reilly recalls. From that first meeting, which was attended by Robertson but not by LeMessurier, and from half a dozen subsequent working sessions with other disaster agencies, came plans for joint action by the police and the mayor's Office of Emergency Management, along with the Red Cross. In the event of a wind alert, the police and the mayor's emergency forces would evacuate the building and the surrounding neighborhood, and the Red Cross would mobilize between 1,200 and 2,000 workers to provide food and temporary shelter. "Hal DeFord was the bank's point man for all this," Reilly says. "The anxiety was so heavy on him that we wondered if he was going to make it."

On Tuesday morning, August 8th, the public-affairs department of Citibank, Citicorp's chief subsidiary, put out the long-delayed press release. In language as bland as a loan officer's wardrobe, the three-paragraph document said unnamed "engineers who designed the building" had recommended that "certain of the connections in Citicorp Center's wind bracing system be strengthened through additional welding." The engineers, the press release added, "have assured us that there is no danger." When DeFord expanded on the handout in interviews, he portrayed the bank as a corporate citizen of exemplary caution—"We wear both belts and suspenders here," he told a reporter for the *News*—that had decided on the welds as soon as it learned of new data based on dynamic-wind tests conducted at the University of Western Ontario.

There was some truth in all this. During LeMessurier's recent trip to Canada, one of Alan Davenport's assistants had mentioned to him that probable wind velocities might be slightly higher, on a statistical basis, than predicted in 1973, during the original tests for Citicorp Center. At the time, LeMessurier viewed this piece of information as one more nail in the coffin of his career, but later, recognizing it as a blessing in disguise, he passed it on to Citicorp as the possible basis of a cover story for the press and for tenants in the building.

On Tuesday afternoon, at a meeting in Robertson's office, LeMessurier told the whole truth to New York City's Acting Building Commissioner and nine other senior city officials. For more than an hour, he spoke about the effect of diagonal winds on the Citicorp tower, about the failure of his own office to perceive and communicate the danger, and about the intended repairs.

In the discussion that followed, the city officials asked a few technical questions, and Arthur Nusbaum expressed concern over a shortage of certified welders who had passed the city's structural-welding test. That would not be a problem, the representatives from the Department of Buildings replied; one of the area's most trusted steel inspectors, Neil Moreton, would have the power to test and immediately certify any welder that Citicorp's repair project required. Nusbaum recalls, "once they said that, I knew we were O.K., because there were steam-fitter welders all over the place who could do a fantastic job."

Before the city officials left, they commended LeMessurier for his courage and candor and expressed a desire to be kept informed as the repair work progressed. Given the urgency of the situation, that was all they could reasonably do. "It wasn't a case of 'We caught you, you skunk,' " Nusbaum says. "It started with a guy who stood up and said, 'I got a problem, I made the problem, let's fix the problem.' If you're gonna kill a guy like LeMessurier, why should anybody ever talk?"

Meanwhile, Robertson's switchboard was besieged by calls. "Every reporter in town wanted to know how come all these people were in our office," Robertson says. Once the meeting ended, the Building Commissioner returned the reporters' calls and, hewing to Citicorp's line, reassured them that the structural work was only a prudent response to new meteorological data.

As a result, press coverage in New York City the next day was as uninformative as the handout: a short piece in the *Wall Street Journal,* which raised no questions about the nature of the new data, and one in the *Daily News,* which dutifully quoted DeFord's remark about belts and suspenders. But when LeMessurier went back to his hotel room, at about 5 P.M. on Wednesday, he learned from his wife, who had come down from Cambridge to join him, that a reporter from the *New York Times* had been trying to reach him all afternoon. That worried him greatly; being candid with city officials was one thing, but being interrogated by the *Times* was another. Before returning the call, LeMessurier phoned his friend Carl Sapers, the Boston attorney who represented Hugh Stubbins, and mixed himself a martini. Sapers understood the need for secrecy, but he saw no real choice; talk to them, he said, and do the best you can. Two minutes after six o'clock, LeMessurier called the *Times* switchboard. As he braced himself for an unpleasant conversation, he heard a recording. The *Times,* along with all the other major papers in the city, had just been shut down by a strike.

Welders started work almost immediately, their torches a dazzlement in the night sky. The weather was sticky, as it had been since the beginning of the month—New Jersey's tomato crop was rotting from too much rain—and forecasts called for temperatures in the mid-80s the next day, with no wind; in other words, a perfect day for Citicorp Center.

Yet tropical storms were already churning the Caribbean. Citicorp pushed for repair work around the clock, but Nusbaum refused to allow welding during office hours, for fear that clouds of acrid smoke would cause panic among the tenants and set off every smoke detector in the building. Instead, he brought in drywall crews and carpenters to work from 5 P.M. to 8 P.M., putting up plywood enclosures around the chevrons and tearing down Sheetrock; welders to weld from 8 P.M. to until 4 A.M., with the building's fire alarm system shut off; and then laborers to clean up the epic mess before the first workers arrived.

The welders worked seven days a week. Sometimes they worked on unoccupied floors;

sometimes they invaded lavish offices. But décor, or the lack of it, had no bearing on their priorities, which were set by LeMessurier. "It was a tense time for the whole month," he says. "I was constantly calculating which joint to fix next, which level of the building was more critical, and I developed charts and graphs of all the consequences: If you fix this, then the rarity of the storm that will cause any trouble lengthens to that."

At Robertson's office, a steady stream of data poured in from the weather forecasters and from the building itself. Occasionally, the strain-gauge readings jumped, like spikes on an electrocardiogram, when the technicians from MTS Systems exercised their tuned mass damper to make sure it was working properly. One time, the readings went off the chart, then stopped. This provoked more bafflement than fear, since it seemed unlikely that a hurricane raging on Lexington and 53rd Street would go otherwise unnoticed at 46th and Park. The cause proved to be straightforward enough: When the instrumentation experts from California installed their strain gauges, they had neglected to hire union electricians. "Someone heard about it," LeMessurier says, "went up there in the middle of the night, and snipped all the wires."

For most of August, the weather smiled on Citicorp, or at least held its breath, and the welders made steady progress. LeMessurier felt confident enough to fly off with his wife for a weekend in Maine. As their return flight was coming in for a landing at LaGuardia Airport Sunday night, they looked out across the East River and saw a pillar of fire on the Manhattan skyline. "The welders were working up and down the building, fixing the joints," LeMessurier recalls. "It was an absolutely marvelous thing to see. I said to Dorothy, 'Isn't this wonderful? Nobody knows what's going on, but we know and we can see it right there in the sky.' "

A great deal of work remained. Robertson was insisting on a complete reevaluation of the Citicorp tower: Not just the sensitivity of the chevrons to quartering winds but the strength of other skeletal members, the adequacy of braces that kept the supporting columns in plumb, and the rigidity of the building's corrugated metal-and-concrete floors, which Robertson feared might be compromised by trenches carrying electrical connections.

His insistence was proper—settling for less would have compromised Robertson's own position. It amounted to a postconstruction autopsy by teams of forensic engineers. For LeMessurier, the reevaluation was harrowing in the extreme; every new doubt about his design for Citicorp Center reflected on him.

In one instance, Robertson's fears were unwarranted: Tests showed that the tower floors were entirely sound—the trenches were not a source of weakness. In another, Robertson, assuming the worst about construction tolerances, decided that the columns might be slightly, even though undetectably, out of plumb, and therefore he ordered the installation of supplemental bracing above the 14th floor.

Shortly before dawn on Friday, September 1st, weather services carried the news that everyone had been dreading—a major storm, Hurricane Ella, was off Cape Hatteras and heading for New York. At 6:30 A.M., an emergency-planning group convened at the command center in Robertson's office. "Nobody said, 'We're probably going to press the panic button,' " LeMessurier recalls. "Nobody dared say that. But everybody was sweating blood."

As the storm bore down on the city, the bank's representatives, DeFord and Dexter, asked LeMessurier for a report on the status of repairs. He told them that the most critical joints had already been fixed and that the building, with its tuned mass damper operating, could now withstand a 200-year storm. It did not have to, however. A few hours later, Hurricane Ella veered from its northwesterly course and began moving out to sea.

LeMessurier spent the following night in Manhattan, having canceled plans to spend the Labor Day weekend with his family in Maine. But the hurricane kept moving eastward, and daybreak dispelled any lingering thoughts of evacuation. "Saturday was the most beautiful day that the world's ever seen," LeMessurier says, "with all the humidity drawn away and the skies sunny and crystal clear." Alone in the city, he gave himself a treat he'd been thinking about for years—his first visit to the Cloisters, where he basked in an ineffable calm.

The weather watch ended on September 13th. That same day, Robertson recommended terminating the evacuation plans, too. Welding was completed in October, several weeks before most of the city's newspapers resumed publication. No further stories on the subject appeared in the wake of the strike. The building, in fact, was now strong enough to withstand a 700-year storm even without the damper, which made it one of the safest structures ever built—and rebuilt—by the hand of man.

Throughout the summer, Citicorp's top management team had concentrated on facilitating repairs, while keeping the lawyers on the sidelines. That changed on September 13th when Citicorp served notice on LeMessurier and Hugh Stubbins, whose firm held the primary contract, of its intention to seek indemnification for all costs. Their estimate of the costs, according to LeMessurier, amounted to $4.3 million, including management fees. A much higher total was suggested by Arthur Nusbaum, who recalled that his firm, HRH Construction, spent 8 million dollars on structural repairs alone. Citicorp has declined to provide its own figure.

Whatever the actual cost, Citicorp's effort to recoup it was remarkably free of the punitive impulse that often poisons such negotiations. When the terms of a settlement were first discussed—without lawyers—by LeMessurier, on one side, and DeFord and Dexter, on the other, LeMessurier spoke of 2 million dollars, which was the amount that his liability insurer, the Northbrook Insurance Company, had agreed to pay. "DeFord and Dexter said, 'Well, we've been deeply wounded here,' and they tried to play hardball," LeMessurier says. "But they didn't do it with much conviction." After a second meeting, which included a Northbrook lawyer, the bank agreed to hold Stubbins' firm harmless and to accept the 2 million dollar payment from LeMessurier and his joint-venture partners; no litigation ever ensued. Citicorp subsequently turned the building into a condominium, retaining the land and the shops, but selling all the office space to Japanese buyers at a handsome profit.

The crisis at Citicorp Center was noteworthy in another respect. It produced heroes, but no villains; everyone connected with the repairs behaved in exemplary fashion, from Walter Wriston and his Citicorp management team to the officials at the city's Department of Buildings. The most striking example, of course, was set by LeMessurier, who emerged with his reputation not merely unscathed but enhanced. When Robertson speaks of him, he says, "I have a lot of admiration for Bill, because he was very forthcoming. While we say that all engineers would behave as he did, I carry in my mind some skepticism about that."

In the last few years, LeMessurier has been talking about the summer of 1978 to his classes at Harvard. The tale, as he tells it, is by turns painful, self-deprecating, and self-dramatizing—an engineer who did the right thing. But it also speaks to the larger question of how professional people should behave. "You have a social obligation," LeMessurier reminds his students. "In return for getting a license and being regarded with respect, you're supposed to be self-sacrificing and look beyond the interests of yourself and your client to society as a whole. And the most wonderful part of my story is that when I did it nothing bad happened."

Chapter 3

The Firm: Commodity and Delight

The purpose of having a structure or organization—a firm for the practice of architecture—no matter what size, is to support the execution of projects while ensuring the firm's own long-term health. How the firm is structured will depend upon the personality and goals of the principals and the nature of the clients.

Specific management of projects should be suggested by the character of the projects themselves. For example, small versus large projects implies two different methodologies; similarly, different building and client types (i.e., public or private sector) will require a different focus on design, documentation, and service delivery. Areas of expertise and interest of principals and staff and details of project requirements and constraints will all have an impact on management. Peter Piven, FAIA, of The Coxe Group has written, "There is no 'right' way to organize and schedule projects . . . The trick is to consider each project situation as unique within the context of a process that is flexible enough to be applied differently to different project situations."

The message is that firm structure must be customized and periodically evaluated to maintain relevance, to effectively utilize all the firm's resources, and ultimately to provide a satisfying environment that promotes the best possible work in the most efficient manner.

"To accomplish great things one must not only act, but also dream, not only plan, but also believe." This quote is from a strategic plan of the architectural firm Russell Gibson von Dohlen.[1] Here's another quote from a vision statement from the website of Bohlin Cywinski Jackson (www.bcj.com): "Belief in the sensuality of place, the emotive qualities of materials, and the ability to give pleasure and insight, to comfort, and to transport, can produce humane and spirited architecture. It is our belief that exceptional architecture comes from the search for solutions which respond to the particular circumstances inherent in each situation." It is not a bad idea to introduce a strategic planning effort or vision statement with some poetry. It is a stirring way to begin conceptualizing the "*design* of a practice." Ellen Flynn-Heapes, a management consultant, invokes a more pragmatic style; she stated that strategic planning "involves appraising the firm's current situation; defining a vision for the future; charting a path toward these goals; and setting the plan in motion." It is important to have a framework that frees you to focus on doing

---

[1] This appeared in the March/April 1986 issue of *Architectural Technology*.

the projects and that ensures you will indeed have projects to be free to work on, that you'll be able to pay the rent and meet payroll, avoid litigation, and eventually pass the practice on to your kids.

So, there is much variability in the way firms operate and manage projects. This chapter includes a case study (ABC/Prieto Haskell) that illustrates how messy the business side of practice can be and how clashes of personalities and missions within the firm must be recognized and reconciled. Three very different firms are profiled as a basis for reflecting on how it is that issues of practice are interrelated and what it can mean firsthand to operate a firm.

For more information on issues of firm culture, refer to Chapter 11 for discussions on leadership and mentorship and Chapter 4 for working in groups and collaborative processes. For an excellent and comprehensive discussion on legal aspects of firm organization—proprietorship, partnership, and corporations—refer to *The Architect's Handbook of Professional Practice* (any recent edition).

Design Firm Typologies

I asked Peter Piven, FAIA, to describe the nature of the professional practice course he has taught at Rensselaer Polytechnic Institute and at the University of Pennsylvania. The course is especially intriguing since Piven applies the "SuperPositioning Model" from a book he coauthored, *Success Strategies for Design Professionals* (McGraw-Hill, 1987), to ways in which students can "design" their own careers and future firms.

Armed with information on how to recognize different typologies in firms, students and graduate architects can then tailor their job search to maximize what they want to learn (and from whom) during internship. The message is to take control of your future: Conduct a thorough investigation of what's out there, recognize the advantages and disadvantages of different types of practice, and do some sole searching to determine what firm characteristics are most consistent with your goals. Piven gives a structure to the process of this exploration, explaining how to do it and what to look for.

PETER PIVEN, FAIA, is the Philadelphia-based Principal Consultant of The Coxe Group, Inc., the oldest and largest multidiscipline firm providing management consulting services exclusively to design professionals. Mr. Piven instructs the Seminar in Architectural Practice at Rensselaer Polytechnic Institute and Starting a Design Firm at Harvard University's Graduate School of Design summer program. He has taught The Design of Design Organizations at the University of Pennsylvania and the Management Seminar at Drexel University. © Peter Piven, FAIA. Peter Piven, FAIA, Principal Consultant, The Coxe Group, Inc.

In the Autumn of 1993, Donald Watson, then Dean of the School of Architecture at Rensselaer Polytechnic Institute in Troy, New York, invited Weld Coxe and me to assume responsibility for what was then called the Seminar in Architectural Practice. We agreed to do it on the condition that we could restructure the course to address the important matter of career planning.

Three noteworthy premises underlay our thinking, our proposal to change the thrust of the course to focus on career planning and the curriculum we developed:

1. Students in and graduates of architectural programs need to be able to better plan their posteducation apprenticeships and careers.
2. To plan, they must recognize the differences in design organizations and determine for themselves the right fit for their talents and goals.
3. To make such determinations, they must learn that, ultimately, they must take responsibility for their own learning.

Our proposal having been accepted, the following course objectives were developed:

- Expose students to the diversity of paths, roles, and opportunities available to them.
- Provide students with the understanding and perspective to make appropriate career choices and the apprenticeship plans to achieve them.
- Provide a foundation for understanding the nature and substance of practice to provide a framework for ongoing self-learning to complement other academic and office experiences.

The pedagogical "design" balanced assigned readings, class discussion based on the readings, class lectures to expound and amplify, field trips, student reports and in-class presentations, and papers. The teaching plan incorporated an important idea—that although there would be recommended, and sometimes required, readings, *the students would become responsible for identifying what they wanted and needed to learn by learning to ask appropriate questions, not only in class but also in the firms they would be visiting on field trips.*

Alternative Archetypes

In *Success Strategies for Design Professionals,* (McGraw-Hill, 1987), the authors presented a model to better describe the relationship between the delivery system used by firms to execute projects and how the organization itself is structured and run. This "SuperPositioning Model" derives from an understanding of the two driving forces that shape the operation, management, and organization of any design firm: (1) its choice of technology, the particular operating system or process employed by the firm to do its work, and (2) the collective values of the firm's principals.

Design Technologies

Architectural firms exist to respond to three essentially different sectors of the marketplace, which we define as *Strong Idea, Strong Service,* and *Strong Delivery.* (See the case study "ABC/Prieto Haskell," pages 109–117, and its analysis, pages 117–123, for another discussion of these types of organizations.) "Strong Idea" firms are organized to deliver singular expertise or innovation on unique projects. The design technology of Strong Idea firms frequently depends on one or a few outstanding experts, or gurus.

"Strong Service" firms are organized to deliver experience and reliability, especially on complex assignments. Their delivery technology is designed to provide comprehensive services to clients who want to be closely involved in the process.

"Strong Delivery" firms are organized to provide highly efficient service on similar or routine assignments, often to clients who seek more of a product than a service. The project technology of a delivery firm is designed to repeat previous solutions over and over again with highly reliable technical, cost, and schedule compliance.

The essential design technologies of architectural firms, practiced in response to clients' needs and the firms' abilities and interests, influence:

- Choice of project process
- Project decision making
- Staffing at the middle of the firm and below
- Identification of the firm's best markets
- What the firm sells
- What the firm can charge
- Best management style

Organizational Values

The second driving force that shapes architectural firms is the values of the professionals leading the firm. These values are reflections of the essential upbringing and personas of the individuals who hold them. The choice of values is a personal, largely self-serving one, derived from how individual architects view their missions in life and what they hope to get out of their lives in return for working. The choice can be understood as a spectrum with practice-centered firms at one end and business-centered firms at the other.

Professionals with strong practice values see their calling as a way of life and typically have as their major goal the opportunity to serve others and produce examples of the disciplines they represent. They evaluate their success qualitatively. The questions, "How do we feel about what we are doing?" and "How did the job come out?" are elemental for them. Business-centered professionals do what they do more as a means of livelihood and are more likely to evaluate their success quantitatively. For those with strong business values, the elemental question would more likely relate to the tangible rewards of their efforts—"How did we do?"

The dominant value systems of those that lead the firm, and therefore the firm's values, whether practice-centered or business-centered, influence:

- Organizational structure
- Organizational decision making
- Staffing at the top
- Marketing strategies
- Identification of the firm's best clients
- Marketing organization
- Profit strategy
- Rewards
- Management style

When the axes of the two key driving forces—technology and values—are looked at in combination and the axes are displayed perpendicularly, they form a matrix within which it is possible to identify six essentially different types of firms:

Practice-centered Strong Delivery	Business-centered Strong Delivery
Practice-centered Strong Service	Business-centered Strong Service
Practice-centered Strong Idea	Business-centered Strong Idea

Based on their technologies and values, these different firms will have essentially different characters and characteristics in every area of practice. They will look and act differently with respect to their:

- Project process and decision making
- Organizational structure and decision making
- Staff recruitment and development
- Sales message and type of client
- Marketing approach and marketing organization
- Pricing and rewards
- Leadership and management

The article "Charting Your Course,"[2] by Weld Coxe et al., was required reading in the seminar; those interested in a more complete exposition of the subject read *Success Strategies for Design Professionals.* After extensive class discussion, the students visited architecture firms; their assignment was to ask the questions that would, at a minimum, allow them to identify what kind of firm it was, for example, its values and technologies, without asking the obvious question, "Where are you in the Model?" However, in almost every case, the students went beyond the questions that would reveal type and asked questions about recruitment policies, intern roles and responsibilities, professional growth, and compensation.

The result of the readings, discussions, visits, and questions was a clear understanding that:

- The profession is broader than the students knew.
- Firms are different.
- The differences are significant and visible.

---

[2]Weld Coxe, Nina F. Hartung, Hugh H. Hoehberg, Brian J. Lewis, David H. Maister, Robert F. Mattox, and Peter A. Piven, "Charting Your Course," *Architectural Technology* May/June (1986): pp. 52–58.

- There is no one definition of success.
- They have the ability to make choices.
- The choices are personal.
- Perhaps most important, they themselves are different and capable of contributing in different ways.

Firm Start-Ups

Many architecture students (and practitioners) aspire to run their own firms, and this is surely one manifestation of the American dream. Is it still possible in today's economy? Jill Weber addresses this question below and describes what it takes to launch a practice.

Being your own boss has great rewards, but it requires an entrepreneurial spirit, which is perhaps even more important than capital. Four differences between employees and entrepreneurs have been cited by industrial psychologist Craig Schneier. Where do you fit?

1. *Risk tolerance.* Entrepreneurs must be able to handle a good deal of risk.
2. *Need for interaction.* The loneliness of the sole proprietor is not for everyone.
3. *Ego.* Strokes are few and far between away from a more corporate environment.
4. *Control.* Achieving this is probably the single most important reason architects choose to go out on their own.

JILL WEBER is the founder of the Boston Society of Architects Marketing Service and Jill Weber Associates. She is a marketing consultant to the design industry and has helped over seventy firms manage and market their professional practices in creative, entrepreneurial, and proactive ways. Ms. Weber has developed and led professional development courses for the Harvard University Graduate School of Design, the American Marketing Association, The Coxe Group, Inc., and the Society for Marketing Professional Services.

Hundreds of architectural firms are founded each year and anecdotal data indicates that firm formation is growing at an increased rate. What does it take to get started, what is the business outlook, and what do firms need to do to get work and to be successful? To get a snapshot of start-up firms in the last decade, we recently interviewed principals of several young architectural firms.

All provided insights and perspectives about choices, flexibility, entrepreneurship, and values that may be useful to the countless others contemplating such a move.

Most of the firms with whom we spoke are young and small, but there is a distinction to be made. While firms started within the past five to eight years are generally considered "young" in the chronological sense, many have been started by principals with many years of experience and hundreds of strong contacts between them. This distinction can give firms an advantage in collective business and marketing acumen, often making their success trajectories shorter and faster.

Where To Begin?

Regardless of age, experience, or the amount of capital behind them, principals of new firms have far greater success when they have some sense of the framework in which they will live and conduct their practices, the clients for whom they wish to work, and the kinds of services they wish to provide. Formally or informally, it helps them to create a picture in their minds of who they want to be and the steps they'll take to get there. In other words, they must form a vision and create a plan.

"We wanted to experiment with new ways to respond to changes in the society and the profession," says Sherry Kaplan, one of the founding principals of Architecture International. Like many others with years of experience in large, established firms, Kaplan and her cofounders had a clear vision for their bicoastal start-up. "We recognized and wanted to make a contribution to a global society in general and urban environments in particular," she says.

Paul Lukez, who left his teaching position at Roger Williams College at the lowest point of the deep New England recession and never looked back, recalls: "I wanted to produce work of the highest quality. . . . To me it's an artistic endeavor as much as a business . . . and I needed to find clients who would appreciate it." Lukez exemplifies a characteristic we find in many of today's successful young firms—an understanding of their own value and a willingness and determination to articulate and persuade clients of that value in terms that clients recognize and want.

Not all the firms had written plans at the outset. However, whether they were starting from a position of strength or as a matter of survival, all of them had some form of written plan within the first two years. "I wish we had been more aware of what running a firm was all about," says David Hudson a founding principal of Artech Design Group. "My advice to start-up firms is to do a business plan or a strategic plan—the important thing is to know what you want the firm to be and how you're going to get there. And make sure to develop relationships with a bank, a lawyer, and an accountant!"

The reasons given for starting firms are, of course, endlessly varied. Some are classic: "We found ourselves in dead-end careers," "We can service clients and treat employees better," and "I knew I would be in the next round of lay-offs and wanted more control over my destiny."

Peter Piven, FAIA, a principal of The Coxe Group, a management consulting firm specializing in the design professions, suggests that designers considering a start-up ask themselves a few of the straightforward questions he uses with his class, "Starting a Design Firm," at Harvard's Graduate School of Design:

- Why do it? Is this what you really want?
- What will it do for your life?
- What do you hope to achieve?
- What personal values do you bring?

What Does It Cost?

Young design firms are like any other young service business in their struggle to maintain a balance between creating a firm reflecting their vision and economic survival.

Capitalization costs range from $500 to $30,000. Of those who have tried, none of the principals we spoke to for this essay were able to get a bank loan at the very start—not even with a signed contract in hand. Like any other small business, they called upon their families to help, depleted their savings accounts, and used ingenious combinations of home-equity loans and credit cards, until the cash flow began and lines of credit were established.

Most young businesses try to keep their overhead costs down. Major variations are a consequence of office location—downtown offices (usually on the modest side but well located near clients) versus the extra-bedroom mode—and investments in technology and equipment. Firms generally had professional liability insurance from day one.

Not surprisingly, young firm principals are convinced that their commitment to technology allows them to become competitive and maintain their edge. "We can compete with anybody now and put together the best team to do any job," says Dean Kahremanis of Dean Kahremanis & Associates. For those involved in overseas work, like Kahremanis and Kaplan, laptops and advanced communications technology allow them to be immediately responsive to clients and minimize the effects of time-zone changes.

Who Are the Clients? Where Are the Jobs?

Young firms often find work among client organizations that in some ways resemble them: entrepreneurial firms whose values correspond with those of the young design firm and where the potential for developing relationships is strong. In entrepreneurial organizations, those who are responsible for making selections and doing the hiring are more readily accessible to design firm principals. Trusting relationships are more easily established between principals of young organizations—and that often counts for more than years of experience.

Young—and often unknown—firms are less likely to win commissions from large corporations and government agencies, who look for extensive track records to reduce their risks. The key for the young firm is the connection—the relationship—whether it comes through a previous client, consultant, agency, family, or community contact. The importance of the relationship is paramount.

Like their corporate counterparts, young design firms have learned the value of keeping their overhead down by bringing in the expertise they need "just in time"—some by developing a core group of specialists brought in as needed, others by assembling teams of the best consultants around the country via fax and modem.

Drastic changes in organizational structures have created opportunities for design firms of all sizes. Knowing and understanding the client's world, their business, and their issues helps young firms position them-selves with the right service at the right time. Looking for work appropri-ate to the size of the firm makes sense, too. "We try to fly under the radar of the large nets," says Colin Flavin of Flavin Architects. "Much of the work we do is simply not work that a large firm would be able to do economically—large firms usually aren't set up to do small projects." Flavin credits this strategy to his successful entree into "that hot little bubble market, casinos."

Young firms whose principals have some marketing experience and much client contact in their previous firms tend to develop work more quickly than those who have been exclusively involved in production. How-ever, once made aware of the importance of building relationships, even production-experienced principals become successful in their business de-velopment efforts. Dean Kahremanis, who started out with little or no mar-keting experience, credits Peter Piven's advice, "Don't market projects . . . build networks," for the growth of his practice. He was advised to call po-tential clients and say that he would like an opportunity to "see what they are looking for." Armed with a list of questions, Kahremanis doggedly built closer relationships with a number of former clients. After a year he asked for work—and got the first of several ongoing jobs!

Getting the Word Out, Keeping in Touch

Hand in hand with relationship-building is the ongoing marketing, posi-tioning, and public relations strategies employed by all savvy young firms. Many learned the value of communicating with the press, clients, prospects, and referrals by closely observing their previous employers' successful strategies.

Fundamental to these efforts are the clear self-understanding and ar-ticulation of a firm's distinctive competence and the value it brings to clients. Coupled with graphically compelling, well-produced drawings and photographs, start-up firms have the essential ingredients to launch a fledg-ling communications program.

The key is to regularly communicate information about the firm's proj-ects, people, and ideas to its various audiences. More and more, firms are finding inexpensive ways to keep their names in front of their publics. They commonly use mailings, including well-designed inexpensively produced postcards, announcements, and reprints to keep in touch and to keep their names "on the clients' screen." More personal efforts are being used too—joint opening parties with clients are a favorite of Colin Flavin, while an of-fice open-house in their building, tenanted by artists, filmmakers, and pho-tographers, proves a good draw for Paul Lukez. "We do all kinds of little things on a regular basis," says David Hudson, who has developed good re-lations with the local press and whose firm frequently issues press releases.

With the use of in-house publishing software, start-up firms are as-sembling credible, professional-looking materials by scouring the better of-fice supply and stationery stores for high quality off-the-shelf folders and papers. (Often, principals with more experienced firms will invest in pro-fessionally produced marketing materials.) Firms generally find that hiring consultants for graphics and public relations is a good investment. While there are still firms handling all their graphics and writing in-house, many are farming out the work to consultants. Leslie Saul of Leslie Saul Associates has used eye-catching materials designed for her firm by a graphic designer to announce the firm opening, to send Valentine greetings, and to keep her wide network informed about her firm and its work. She observes: "Maturity brings the knowledge that you don't have to do everything better than everyone else—you can find others who can do it for you."

No matter their age, years of experience, or track record, designers would do well to keep the following ten essentials in mind:

1. Have a clear vision and create a plan.
2. Use your network.
3. Build relationships.
4. Control overhead.
5. Make a commitment to technology.
6. Get the best advice you can from those experienced in the field.
7. Find a way to differentiate yourself.
8. Understand your clients' values.
9. Keep your audiences informed about your firm and its work.
10. Keep your life in balance.

Two Start-Up Profiles: Young, Digital, and Good

The specific start-up profiles of the two firms selected by Michelle Negrette in the Supplement below reveal universal issues that are faced by start-up and seasoned firms alike.

MICHELLE NEGRETTE holds a Bachelor of Architecture from the University of Southern California, a Masters of Community and Regional Planning, and a Masters of Landscape Architecture from the University of New Mexico. She divides her time between a small multidisciplinary design consulting practice in Albuquerque and teaching design studio at the University of New Mexico.

Many aspiring architects muse upon the idea of starting their own firm. After years of architecture classes, with someone else always critiquing the design and constraining projects, the idea of having autonomy is definitely appealing. Or maybe you are working in an architectural office and are tired of the daily grunt work, questioning whether what you are doing is really architecture or perhaps thinking you would handle the design of projects differently.

To find out what it is really like to start your own firm in the new millennium, I interviewed two young start-up architecture firms in Albuquerque, New Mexico: Environmental Dynamics and E_vok Interactive. These two firms consist of young architects, recently out of school, who know first-hand what it is like to be out on your own.

Environmental Dynamics began in 2000 as a joint venture between two partners while in the final semester of graduate school. Four years later, the firm has grown to ten people, with four partners and a staff of six. Their typical projects include commercial and residential with an annual project load of around 50. The firm's focus is on green technologies and sustainable resources stressing design excellence.

E_vok Interactive is the recent brainchild of four young partners, two still in the final phases of graduate school. Conceived in spring of 2003, the firm consists of the four founding partners and six part-time employees. The past year's projects have included residential, commercial, and institutional work in several states. The firm is rooted in information-based technologies and relies on interactive digital tools for research, design development, and document production as well as office management.

Experience

While the idea of having your own firm may seem appealing, actually starting the firm can be daunting. Sure, you have taken the classes, you can put together a tight set of construction documents, and you know all the tricks of the building code, but are you ready to do it on your own? I asked Mike Ryan of Environmental Dynamics (ED) and the team of four principals of E_vok Interactive (EI) to speak about preparing for the new responsibilities as principals of an architectural office.

What type of architectural or business experience did you and your partners have prior to starting a firm?

ED: We all had many years of experience at different levels prior to attending graduate school. Two of our partners have architect parents and grew up in the environment, getting a sense of the business end of things in addition to the production end. One of us had seven years of construction experience as well as six years of employment in architecture firms prior to graduate school and graduation, and one specialized in veterinary clinics during graduate school.

EI: I had worked for several small architecture firms on a part-time or full-time basis since completing high school 15 years ago. All four of us have had construction experience in conjunction with the typical architecture and design jobs. Both Derrick and Matt have had experience with a "high-design" architecture firm, and Jimmy worked for several years within a large, corporate firm. Our combined work experience has provided a solid design foundation, but our business experience has been more of a crash course over the past year.

What did you do to prepare for creating a new business?

ED: One strategy that seems to work very well for start-up firms is to set up the business near an established architectural firm. The large firm can use your labor and talents to supplement their fluctuating work load, and you can use their resources and have some predictable income. This gets tricky if you grow too much and start competing for the same projects as the larger firm you are associating with, and you also run the risk of sharing some of the reputation (good or bad) of that larger firm.

EI: I think it's a continual process of getting ready. It's a similar process to a professional athlete with practice in competition. Learning the new technology, pushing yourself to take care of the business part of it, and constant correspondence become your routine. And everything you do becomes preparation for future work.

What parts of your architectural education versus practicing architecture were helpful to starting a business?

ED: The required professional practice course and an elective real estate development course were the only classes that addressed business issues. I believe that if at least one third-year studio, for example, had been devoted to designing a project that was at least partially subject to the realities of the business end of the profession, many of the lessons in the professional practice course would have had more impact.

EI: I found starting an architectural business to be really difficult because what you are told in school about practicing architecture is very much based on an old school way of practicing architecture. The business model is not as designed as it could be. Our business model is based on a lot of management theories and intelligence models that haven't yet been introduced to a typical architecture firm. Since we are trying to do something new in architecture, there really isn't a precedent for how it is supposed to work, so we have to base it on other professions or just forge ahead. Most people look at you and think, "You are too young for this, what are you trying to do, WHY are you doing *that?!* You should just be doing drawings for someone else." I feel that this attitude, and the lack of cross-pollination, is why the business side of architecture is not really touched upon in school, at least not in any way to give someone the ability to design their business as they can design a building.

In what areas did you feel unprepared? Did you take any additional classes or seminars or seek outside counsel?

ED: We did not take any additional classes in business but sought as much outside counsel as would tolerate us! The pitfall here is that start-up companies rarely have lots of extra capital and cannot afford the best legal and accounting services. Early on, we hired a fresh face in the accounting world. Unfortunately, this person gave us some bad advice and a false sense of security when it came to taxes and payroll. Luckily we discovered most of our errors upon hiring a more established accounting firm, but we are still feeling the effects of our initial actions.

EI: I was most unprepared for the polarized attitude toward youth. I thought that if you just did the work to the best of your ability and performed above expectations then you would be universally respected. As it turns out, you get out there and learn that the game is about a lot of other things first—and then it's about the work. I was completely unprepared for that. Sometimes being young, innovative, and experimental can be an asset, other times a liability. There seems to be no middle ground.

What experience or knowledge would you have liked to have before starting a firm?

ED: I think greater experience and knowledge of client relations, time and money management, payroll and taxes, specifications, and marketing. I realize that most of these things would have come with a lengthy stay at an established firm, but these things are not readily available in architecture school or during the internship period.

EI: Start the business before you're ready. One year before you decide to start a firm on your own, get a business license, get a bank account, start getting your ducks in a row, putting money away. I wish we had done that.

Productivity and Money

Many architecture students may be surprised to discover that there is more to practicing architecture than designing buildings. Designing buildings of course includes the building structure, the mechanical and electrical systems, code requirements, and dealing with all of the other entities that are required for a project to be permitted, bid, and constructed. Practicing architecture includes other very important nondesign activities primarily related to the acquisition and managing of finances. Here are Environmental Dynamics' and E_vok Interactive's experiences.

What is the biggest difference between practicing architecture and operating the business side of architecture?

ED: The business side is relentless while the architectural side can fluctuate with workload. What I mean by this is that payroll must be met and taxes paid even if the office is experiencing a slow period. The business side needs to inform the architecture without making architecture a slave to business. It is, however, difficult and time-consuming to track and control time and expenses on a project as well as do all those things required to make the project a success.

EI: With regard to the business side, I felt most unprepared for procuring finances. And I feel that has been our biggest challenge. What designers need to understand about running a business is that, unless you get clients to pay you up-front and wait for the service, you are going to have to front all of the costs of developing their projects. Contractors, developers, and other business people understand this keenly. They know how to maneuver around the system, while architects are only their tools. I don't see any of us at E_vok having any problems with completing any of the projects we have come across. Our client relationships have always been good too, it's just getting that bank to look at us and say, "Hey, we can lend some money to these people." We are beginning to redesign how we procure finances and look at nontraditional methods to support us.

Have you found it difficult to compete against more established firms?

ED: Yes, it is very difficult to compete against the more established firms, and almost impossible to land large projects because a start-up firm does not have the project experience required to earn enough points to be awarded the project.

EI: Absolutely, however, that competition gives us an opportunity. In our process we incorporate all the technology pertinent to the project that we can muster, so we have the opportunity to expand the parameters of architecture. If we were only drawing with the pencil we would be limited to what we could produce. Presently, we are virtually limitless in our possibilities because of our methodologies. For example, wider references, deeper investigations, in shorter periods of time, allow us to redefine what the public realizes as architecture through the languages of meaning, reference, and systemic information. In truth, these expansions take us out of the realm of direct competition with more established architecture firms because what we engage in may or may not be traditionally considered in the realm of "architecture."

What are some methods you have used to demonstrate competence and success as a "young" firm?

ED: Our firm uses a slightly different model from the traditional firm in that all of our principals are "working partners," capable of, and expected to, produce all levels of the construction documents on AutoCAD in addition to their other office responsibilities. We have found that this approach reduces the number of errors in a set of drawings and can result in more efficiency in production. Clients also seem to appreciate that their project gets that kind of attention from a principal. I believe the energy we have as

Figure 3-1 Offices of the Southern Sandoval County Arroyo Flood Control Authority, Rio Rancho, New Mexico. Courtesy of Environmental Dynamics, Inc., architects.

a start-up firm is appreciated by some clients who believe we will put our hearts and souls into their project. Some clients know that a young firm will work extra hard to prove themselves and are willing to trade diligence, energy, and new ideas for experience.

EI: We capitalize on the fact that we are young and digital and good. We move forward really fast, turn projects around for clients, and get done what they need to get done. The big selling point is that we are young, just out of school, and they can expect something fresh and nontraditional from us.

The Office

These two young firms have shared their architectural background and their experiences in production and financial matters, but what about general office dynamics? Who is going to solicit work (unfortunately and contrary to popular belief, people do not typically walk in on a daily basis and ask you to design their dream home)? Who is going to take care of the legal aspects of the business (such as preparing and negotiating the contracts for work, the billing, and the insurance)? There is also the technological side—keeping up on the latest code requirements, the newest building materials, systems, and consumer products. And what about the employees? Someone has to make sure that the interns, the CAD people, and the project managers have clear instructions on how to keep projects moving everyday. These tasks and many more are imperative to the successful operation of an architectural firm. Here are some thoughts from our two firms:

How have you selected the roles needed to make your office function and produce?

ED: Our roles for the partners are based on interest and ability—and of course the roles will continually morph and overlap. We have one partner in charge of marketing in the established architectural arenas, one who works to find new market niches, one in charge of human resources and information technology, and one who maintains compliance with the corporation regulations and keeps the office updated on building codes.

EI: We started by trying to figure out where we all were in terms of design philosophy. Other than Christi, whose role was more apparent and established (as a licensed architect), we had to figure everything else out. We determined our representative roles as digital, "documental," and technological. I am primarily responsible for all things comprising digital domains from the ether to computer-based design, to prestidigitation. Jimmy is responsible for all things documental, from site reconnaissance, to drafting organization, to financial statements. Matt is responsible for all things technological—meaning production and how things are produced. And finally, we have always maintained that Christi brings verification and validation to our studio, our work, and our design ethic. Although these responsibilities overlap, we realize that without overlap there would be no interactivity, which is at the core of our functional operations.

What are some advantages and disadvantages of starting your own firm versus working for others?

ED: There is more risk and responsibility in running your own firm. The freedom you get from calling your own shots comes with the price tag of being ultimately responsible for calling them wrong. When you work for someone else, an error made might make you one of the unemployed, when you are your own boss, it can make you bankrupt. When you work for yourself, your schedule is more your own in that no person tells you when to be at work; instead your schedule is dictated by the workload and demands of the business—it becomes your master and slave.

EI: Rather than a predictable job with a firm, I now go to work not always knowing what the day will bring. There is a sense of freedom and independence that is gained, but with this comes a sense of responsibility for myself and others. By becoming more connected with each and every job, work has become more satisfying. The choice to jump into this firm has frustrated me at times, but more than anything the experience has been invigorating and positive.

What are some myths you had about owning your own firm prior to actually experiencing it?

ED: I believed that work would be easier to come by, that if we completed one or two good projects, we would no longer have to worry about hunting down new work, it would just come to us. I believed that collecting money would not be one of the hardest parts of the business.

EI: I did have an idealized concept of what this would be, and that's gone out the window. I felt happier once I let go of it. When you are working for someone and you are watching them make mistakes every day, or at least so you think, you feel that you'd just do them differently when you own your business. Then you end up making the same mistakes because you are in the same situation, and you realize that you were unaware of the context as to why those other people made that decision.

What are some advantages and disadvantages of starting your own firm early in your career versus after many years of experience?

ED: Young firms are susceptible to overdesigning projects. This could be a result of the principals' experiences in studio, experiences that do not place limits on time and money. The down side to this is the potential of establishing an early reputation as a firm that cannot design a project on budget. This can be detrimental in securing future work, because most RFPs (Requests for Proposals) require a list of previous work that includes information on budget for the project and actual cost of the project.

EI: One of the biggest disadvantages of starting young is credibility with other architects, financial institutions, etc. Without twenty years of experience, it is really hard to get other people to believe in you. You don't have the track record to let them know that they can trust you.

What would you like to share with current students about starting a firm and working in the architectural profession in the twenty-first century?

ED: If you have talent and drive, good intuition, some business acumen, a little capital, some potential clients, and some good luck, starting early is not a disadvantage at all! It can be stressful at times, but it can also be very exciting and open up limitless possibilities; it can teach you things about business, clients, personnel management, architecture, and construction that you may never get as an employee at another firm.

EI: The most important thing for any architect in the twenty-first century, or anyone else who does business for that matter, is the concept of information. Information has always been a high priority, but right now we have a confluence of information from myriad sources, and any good architect must survey that to understand how clients' structures fit into their lives and fit into the landscape. To accomplish that well, you have to be apprised of all the salient information available and make use of it. The world is a much smaller place.

QUESTIONS FOR DISCUSSION

1. Based on your own experiences and these interviews, do you think it is important for architecture schools to provide more focused coursework on the business-side of architecture? If so, how and in what context?
2. What might be some ways that young architects who wish to start a firm can learn from the knowledge and experience of established architecture firms?
3. What are some challenges in starting a new firm that these principals may not have discussed?
4. How do you think the role of information technology has influenced the traditional model of the architectural firm? What are the advantages and disadvantages of technology for a young architectural firm?

Profiles in Courage: Three Firms

Why might you be interested in learning something about the following three firms? They have been selected for their representativeness and diversity—in size, philosophy of design, location of projects, profitability, and character of staff and principals. For all the differences, the firms depicted here share a common mission and are enormously successful at achieving it: Excellence in producing the product, excellence in providing the service, and enjoyment of what they do.

As you read through the sketches of the three practices, ask yourself these questions: What is good and bad about each? Would you want to intern in one of them, and why? Would you want to model your own practice after one of them—which one and why? Do the principals profiled motivate you to reflect on the impact of practice on architectural design in a positive or negative light? Is architecture really a commodity—does it have to be business? Can it be truly delightful in today's economy—as if the freedom and excitement of school studio never ended? Are the answers clear at all? This section, perhaps more than any other in the book, invites a very personal reaction.

1. Andrew Pressman, FAIA, Architect, Albuquerque, New Mexico, and Washington, D.C.

Be Somebody, Do Something Important, Advance the Profession

It happened following a competition win (for housing design ideas sponsored by Misawa Homes and the Building Centre of Japan). I felt that I should be opportunistic about the publicity surrounding this event. I had just become licensed, and after four years of internship, I was very anxious to be my own boss and have an impact in the profession. Buoyed by 1.5 million yen from the competition, I felt the time was right to take the plunge.

The Beginning and End

Another motivation to start my own practice was that I only wanted to do what I enjoyed doing: dealing with clients, schematic design, and construction contract administration—particularly the site visits (essentially the beginning and end of projects). Moreover, I wanted the flexibility to explore the teaching of design and to write about design, both of which would supplement income and fulfill my mission of attempting to make a difference.

I didn't want to be involved in production tasks, primarily because I wasn't very skilled, efficient, or interested in performing them. Developing construction documents is just as important as the conceptual design and requires experience, talent, and passion—they are an integral part of the design only with focus on a different scale. However, since I excelled at design in school, I was tracked into it early during my internship, and success kept those assignments coming. I didn't have the most well-rounded job experience, hence my lack of ability in the details and the desire to work on preliminary designs.

So who does the working drawings and specs? My intent was to associate or joint venture with colleagues who have this complementary strength. And it works extremely well. I am involved in all phases of projects since I maintain an ongoing dialogue with the clients. This ensures a continuity in the project's development and detailing consistent with the original design themes and prepares me for handling any circumstance that may arise during construction.

I spend an extraordinary amount of time with clients in the beginning of projects. This facilitates a thorough definition and understanding of the problems and all key personalities involved. I have found this strategy to be most efficient in the long run, since very few changes are requested during the course of projects. Clients are satisfied, happy from all the attention, and personally involved in helping to shape projects. The design direction is usually quite clear since there is so much information. The client should be regarded as a collaborator (not a necessary evil), who can inform and even enrich designs. On the other hand, simply responding to client needs and preferences is not sufficient to create architecture and should never be an excuse for poor design.

Stayin' Alive

Perhaps the thing that fascinates me the most about maintaining a practice is maintaining a practice. It is absolutely essential to apply every drop of creativity you have to find ways to generate income and get clients. It is another type of *design* problem. Bill Gates has succinctly articulated the old cliché: "When you're failing you're forced to be creative, to dig deep and think hard, night and day. Every company needs people who have made mistakes—and then made the most of them."

Certainly writing about my mistakes in professional practice has helped me to make the most of them, particularly in the area of client relations. Client relations is an aspect of practice and a subject in school that is underrated and understudied. This is a curious phenomenon since it is so fundamental to providing appropriate service and *getting more work* through referrals and repeat commissions. The point is that communication and leadership skills go hand in hand with designing good buildings, so whether you want to become a firm principal or not, make sure that your immersion in design studio is balanced with development of writing, speaking, and graphic skills—either formally in classes or on your own. (See Jerry Shea's essay on writing in Chapter 11 pages 361–366.)

The project in Figure 3-2, a gymnasium in Princeton, New Jersey, is an example of a commission acquired by "repeat work." The owners were favorably predisposed to hire my firm as a direct result of the relationship established during a residential addition and renovation I designed for them several years earlier.

Typical Projects

I've been fortunate to have had a diversity of projects in a diversity of locations around the country. I'm always intrigued by how practice issues affect the course

Figure 3-2 Gymnasium in Princeton, New Jersey. Andrew Pressman, FAIA, with Siegel Design, Architects. Photo © Norman McGrath.

Figure 3-3 Procession is a major aspect of the design of the Mottahedeh showroom in New York City: An angled arcade organizes the space into intimate display zones that change in scale and character as one walks down the long axis. Light beams align with columns, accentuating the rhythm of the arcade, and provide indirect ambient illumination. Photo © Norman McGrath.

of a project. For example, in the case of Mottahedeh's New York City show-room, the new owners believed it was time to establish an updated presence for this venerable company. Mottahedeh is world-renowned for its antique porcelain reproductions and its dinnerware collection. In the spirit of timeless quality, the display areas were to be reinterpreted as museumlike galleries.

The interesting complication was that the owner selected her own sub-contractor for all the custom casework, which was a significant portion of the job. Coordination with the various trades then became a problem be-cause the cabinetmaker was (1) not permitted to enter the building to in-stall the cabinets since he was from out of town and not a union member and (2) not really setup to produce shop drawings (it would have taken him longer to do the drawings than build the cabinets!). Predictably, the general contractor took advantage of the situation . . . what the client saved in dol-lars (which was impressive) was paid for by the architect in blood, sweat, and tears, and there was less than perfect installation. The project, though, was a great design success, and upon reflection, given the circumstances, we probably wouldn't do anything differently. Nevertheless, the message may be that unless the client is sophisticated about, and experienced in, con-struction, avoid awarding multiple construction contracts for relatively small-scale projects with a traditional design-bid-build delivery method.

A recently completed built project is a new 2,300-square-foot vacation house in New England. The site has been a revered summer destination for the owner since childhood.

Construction was extended over a two-year period. The contractor was a cousin of the owner and a perfectionist who wanted to do most of the

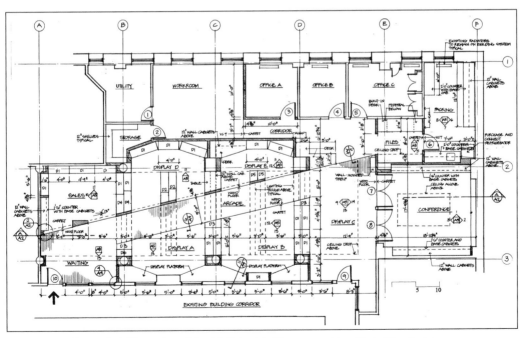

Figure 3-4 Floor plan of the Mottahedeh Showroom, New York City. Andrew Pressman, FAIA, Architect.

Figure 3-5 A sequence of shed roofs pitched in alternate directions facilitates the framing of special views and the capture of natural light and breezes. The almost serrated roof line creates a massing that is animated but easy to construct. Gray-stained clapboard siding and white trim harmonize with the coastal, rural surroundings and tie the bolder forms to the context. Photo © Steve Rosenthal.

work himself (rather than subcontract). So, understandably, tension developed between the owner and her contractor-cousin. One of my roles, then, was to mediate between these family members. At times, I had to defend the contractor, who was invested in the project and wanted to build it in his own personal manner. At other times, I had to defend the owner, who legitimately wanted to use the house after a year.

The project was about to start construction when the owner wanted a major design change. After construction documents were completed, the owner called me and said she felt that the street elevation was too severe, and could I make it a gable instead of a shed roof? I told her I would study it, knowing instantly that the change would destroy the whole concept and require major redesign. I prepared a rather lengthy rationale for making no changes, and this was agreed upon—it was a battle worth fighting.

A battle not worth fighting was for the removal of a new maple tree that was placed in the front of the house. The owner's aunt, who is also the mother of the contractor (architecture can indeed be soap opera), lives three blocks away and hates the house. As it was nearing completion, the aunt went to the local nursery and had them put in the largest tree they had, to block as much of the house as possible from the street view. (At this point in my site visits, I had been dreaming of the perfect magazine cover photo, which would, of course, be the street elevation.) The owner, who by this time had also decided this was the best elevation of the house, said she did not want to get into any more family squabbles . . . so the tree stayed. My conception of the ideal photo had to change, but there was family equilibrium, and my stock remained high. The moral of the story is that it is important to engage only those battles that may result in damage to the design concept. Do not waste time and energy on relatively trivial matters. But fight passionately to preserve design quality.

Figure 3-6 The double-height ceiling above the living room slopes down to the one-story dining area, simultaneously providing a focus and unifying the interior composition. Ceilings in second-floor bedrooms follow the pitch of scissor trusses, allowing clerestories and lots of daylight. Photo © Steve Rosenthal. Andrew Pressman, FAIA, Architect.

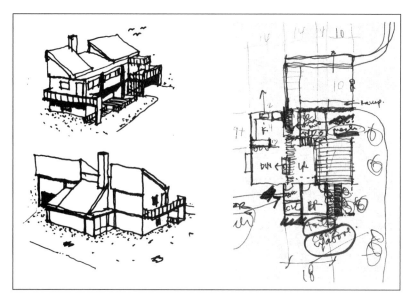

Figure 3-7 Process sketches. These demonstrate that there is at least one similarity between school and practice. Andrew Pressman, FAIA, Architect.

It should be noted that preserving the essence of a good design should (and usually does) correspond with the client's best interests (even if he or she doesn't know it yet). But just what does it mean to "fight passionately?" it does *not* mean one should beat up the client, and it does not mean one should strive to be the self-righteous and insulting Howard Roark. It *does* mean and demand impassioned and patient explanation, teaching, and a carefully cultivated diplomacy adapted for the particular client.

2. Ross Barney + Jankowski, Inc., Chicago, Illinois

Innovative Architecture for Public and Institutional Clients

Ross Barney + Jankowski, Inc. (RB+J) was organized in 1981 as Carol Ross Barney Architects, a sole proprietorship. That same year, Carol Barney was joined by her college classmate, James Jankowski, first as an employee and later in 1982, as her partner. The firm name was changed in 1985 to reflect Jim's contributions. For the first five years, the firm grew steadily to an average size of twenty-five employees. Since then, staff size has been relatively stable.

RB+J has a national reputation for design of institutional and public buildings, such as libraries, public utilities, government and transportation facilities, and elementary schools. Their projects have received numerous awards and recognition for design excellence, including several national AIA honor awards. Among the firm's notable buildings are César Chávez Multicultural Academic Center for the Chicago Public Schools, Mabel Manning Branch Library for the Chicago Public Library, Glendale Heights Post Office, and Remote Switching Units for Illinois Bell.

The firm regularly offers pro bono services to community organizations, including the Children's Home and Aid Society, Hubbard Street Dance Company, and the YWCA of Metropolitan Chicago.

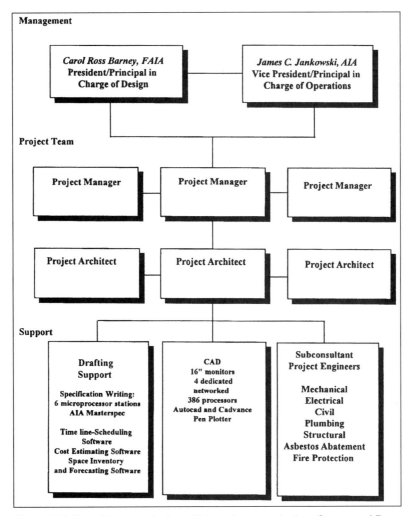

Figure 3-8 Ross Barney + Jankowski, Inc., firm organization. Courtesy of Ross Barney + Jankowski, Inc.

The composition of RB+J's staff reflects their belief that diversity is a desirable element in the design studio. Fifty percent of employees are women, approximately 30 percent are ethnic minorities, and the remainder (according to Carol Barney) are very sensitive modern males.

The following round table discussion with Carol Ross Barney (CRB) and James Jankowski (JCJ) was moderated by Alice Sinkevitch (AS), Executive Director of the AIA Chicago.

AS: What were your experiences as employees of other firms that inspired or compelled you to establish your own firm?

CRB: I never really thought that I would start my own architectural firm. I was perfectly happy working for someone else. When my job evaporated in a merger, two of my clients called me and suggested I work for them. I agreed, and two weeks later I went to the bank, opened a checking account, and that was the beginning of my company. Two important things happened to me during my stint as an employee. I worked for one company where I only worked on drawings; I never saw an invoice, never participated in construction administration, so I knew very little of the business of running a company. Then I worked for another office where the most important things were the bottom line and marketing. From these diverse experiences, I was ready to start a company even though I didn't know it.

JCJ: I have been involved with a couple of small companies. I was part of the start-up of an alternate kind of architectural firm including graphic designers, painters, and sculptors, which was not very business oriented. The other company I worked for had a staff of three, so I saw how all the pieces fit together. There was little firm management; the focus was on management of individual projects, and at that scale we had full responsibility for our own projects. If I was doing it again, I don't know that I'd start my own firm—it's a lot of work, and for me, I'm not sure the rewards are there. I came to Chicago in 1981 looking to work for a big firm since I never had that experience. Then Carol asked me to help with a few projects, and the rest is history!

AS: Are you a partnership now?

CRB: We are a corporation, mainly for tax purposes, but we operate like a partnership. Jim and I are the sole owners. We are now discussing extending ownership to some of our employees.

AS: Could you characterize the experience of your staff and make-up of project teams?

CRB: In a firm our size—twenty-five to thirty people—it is imperative to have maximum flexibility, so most of our people are not interns. We have thirteen registered architects. We do everything, we aren't specialists. People who are just out of school simply do not have the breadth of knowledge and experience to work independently on a diversity of projects. Our projects are in the 1 to 4 million dollar range. The project teams tend to be very small, and the schedules are very demanding.

JCJ: We have found that it is important to have continuity from the first day of a project—from the interview stage through postconstruction evaluation—so that people are aware of the rationale behind all decisions. Therefore, we organize our teams to have continuity. For example, we have a good project architect on our Maywood Library project, but his job will be transferred full-time to the field, so he is lost to our other teams. Even though he would be a valuable asset to these other teams, it is important that he stay at the job site to maintain continuity.

One of the advantages of small firms is that if you are early in your career and you have good instincts and learn well, you can gain responsibility quickly. We promote this sort of education by assigning our younger people to smaller projects as project architects, with a senior person looking over their shoulder. They get exposure and experience.

CRB: When we send a team chart to clients (see Figure 3-8), it looks fairly conventional but the truth is that we modify the team structure for every project. Another truth is that there are very few working titles in our company. Our teams have only two titles, Principal-in-Charge and Project Manager, everyone else is a team member, which gives us a relatively flat organization. The benefit is the opportunity to do something very creative. Our firm often works like a collaborative; everyone is encouraged to bring forth their ideas, and we sort them out as a team. The flat team organization promotes that kind of activity.

AS: How do you give staff the sense that they are making progress and are ascending through the ranks? Are there ranks to move up through, and if not, how do you keep people?

CRB: There aren't many ranks to move up through, and we have lost people because they can't stand not having a title. It was disturbing to have good people leave because they disliked the unstructured atmosphere of our company. On the other hand, the only thing that we ever wanted to do is make and design buildings. The people who are successful in our firm share that dedication. We do have people that have been rewarded. We've been in business for sixteen years and some of our employees have been with us a long time, eight or nine years out of the sixteen. The future partners that we're considering will come from that group. People can work their way up in the firm, but it is not structured, not like a corporate ladder, and it is not immediately visible to those who have just started.

JCJ: Most people desire a specific role in a project. We try to address those preferences, and we do have a loose management structure. Every other Thursday, a small group, including our three senior people, have lunch and discuss particular topics, or we may just chat about projects in general. We talk to these senior people about dealing with problems in motivation, team structures, or how we are handling projects and procedures. On alternate Thursdays, we conduct meetings with a larger group—the project managers. We discuss project schedules, assignment of personnel, deadlines, and positive and negative things that are happening. That is about as organized as we get.

AS: As an example of one of your representative projects, please talk about the César Chávez school. Where did the lead for this job come from?

CRB: There was a story about it in the newspaper. Chicago Public Schools were going to build seven new schools. After we inquired, they sent us a Request for Proposal, then they evaluated the submittals, and a week after that we received a letter saying thank you for the qualifications, however, other firms are more suited for what we need. That was okay, I get a couple of letters like that every day! I called the school architect looking for a debriefing as to why we weren't well suited. He told me that for these particular schools they wanted a firm with high design potential. These words made me so mad—they were fighting words! I also knew that the board had affirmative action set-aside goals. The short-listed firms were all good architects: mostly white male, a few minorities, and no women. So I wrote

Figure 3-9 César Chávez Elementary School. A narrow site and tight budget demanded an innovative architectural solution. Architect: Ross Barney + Jankowski, Inc. Photo: Steve Hall, Hedrich-Blessing; courtesy of Ross Barney + Jankowski, Inc.

a letter stating that I didn't think that the list was quite right because there were no women. (I didn't relate the design story, why I was upset.) Dr. Vernon Feiock, head of facilities, who was very influential, called and told me I was right and gave us an interview. We were awarded the commission. It was a big one for us, but we knew that we could handle it. It was about $5 million in construction, and 50,000 square feet.

AS: Did you have previous experience with schools?

CRB: I had a lot of school experience. The firm that I had been with prior to starting my own company only designed schools. I had no insecurity about getting the job done, just getting the commission. Dr. Feiock continued to mentor our company. He was amazing through the whole thing. He challenged us; he kept us going. He told us that the hardest thing about working with our firm was that we gave him too many good ideas from which to choose. The job took a long time to build because state funding was not approved for a year, and then they had to find a new site since the original site was a toxic waste dump.

AS: Who was on the client team? How many players were on their end, and who did they represent?

CRB: The Chávez school had a relatively small team compared to the ones we have worked with on subsequent public school projects. There was Dr.

Feiock and his right-hand man, Les Benscics. Because the project was funded by the State of Illinois, there was a Capital Development Board (CBD) project manager. One of the things I always regret about working for the Chicago Public Schools is that you don't meet their staff or teachers. It would be nice to bring them in at some point. The Chávez school principal is a very creative woman, and we have had good relations with her since the school opened.

Dr. Feiock was the most important person when it came to realizing the design potential and overall success of the project. He was probably one of the first of several good clients we have had who were willing to take a chance or recognize opportunity. The second site was very small, which required a very different concept just to get the building on the lot. We have had client personnel in similar positions on other projects who have either been road blocks from the start or who have gotten cold feet partway through the process and have had us redesign. I think the essential ingredient to do a good building for any client is trust in the architect. This probably is the key to good architect-client relationships; people don't have to be involved; they just have to trust the process.

AS: Who negotiated the fee and scope of services?

JCJ: Since it was a state-funded project, the Capital Development Board has a fee schedule that is used to pay for architectural services. They consulted their chart and determined our fee, which was reasonable for what we were providing. When the project restarted after it was delayed because of site conditions, our client's new project manager determined that we weren't as far in our documentation as we had been paid, and she subtracted money from our current contract. We had much negotiation and eventually the fees were fair by the end of the project.

AS: Who were the consultants on the job, and how were they selected?

CRB: At the time we were using the same mechanical, electrical, and plumbing (MEP) consulting firm for several of our projects. We selected them based on their school experience, but it ended up being a bad selection. The local office with whom we were working went through some turmoil. There were six different electrical engineers through the life of the project, and a couple of mechanical engineers that didn't know what they were doing. It was a disaster, and the mechanical bids were 60 percent over budget. The architectural work was right on, but the entire project was rebid. It was time consuming and expensive, and we ended up in a dispute with the consulting firm.

AS: What methods did you use for monitoring time and fee for this project?

CRB: We are pretty conventional about that. We are above average in terms of financial monitoring, and that's to Jim's credit. He is in charge of that stuff.

JCJ: A budget is established for each project before it starts, and that budget is coordinated with the schedule so we know how much manpower is re-

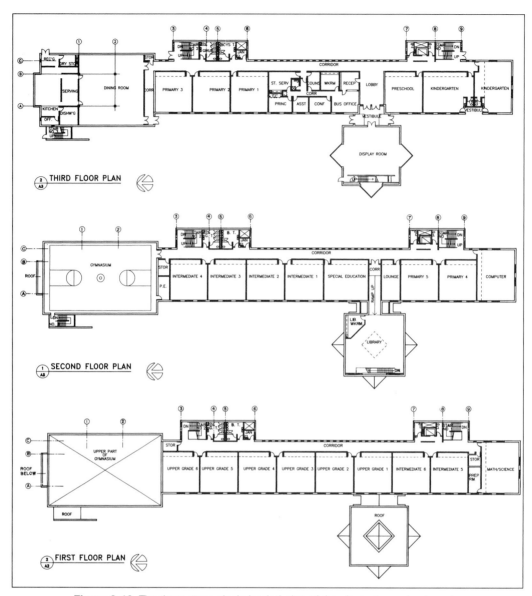

Figure 3-10 The three-story, single-loaded plan of the elementary school maximizes outdoor play space on the narrow lot. Classrooms face the yard, facilitating supervision of the outdoor area—an important consideration in this "gang-plagued" Chicago neighborhood. Architects: Ross Barney + Jankowski, Inc. Drawings courtesy of Ross Barney + Jankowski, Inc.

quired. In the last year we have become particularly efficient at tracking our time and expenses so that we can review project budgets the day and even hour that time cards are submitted. We weren't doing that as well when we were designing the César Chávez School, because we weren't fully automated. However, the basic principles still hold whether or not you automate the process. (See Chapter 5, pages 171–198, on financial management.)

Figure 3-11 César Chávez Elementary School. Exuberant forms, textures, and colors are intended to convey excitement about education, and distinguish the building in the community. Photo: Steve Hall, Hedrich-Blessing; courtesy of Ross Barney + Jankowski, Inc., architects.

The most difficult problem occurred with our mechanical engineer on the Chávez school, who severely underestimated the MEP construction budget, which required redesign and rebidding. At that point we were clearly off our schedule and project budget. The effort of rebidding the school cost $70,000 of our time and expense (printing alone cost $11,000). This was not covered in our fee.

How do you keep a job from hemorrhaging your company to death? That aspect of a project is still a problem. We are continually battling to control the time we spend on a day-to-day basis. It's one thing to get the reports and another to maintain control of the project. The more current the reports the better because we can then see what was spent and take corrective action as soon as problems are manifested.

AS: How do you know if you are making good progress?

JCJ: We are still trying to develop effective tools with our staff to measure progress. If you divide it all out, you figure you can spend 70 hours on this sheet or 60 hours on another. We are still battling with that; sometimes it works well, and sometimes it doesn't. There may be conflicts between project managers who are schedule- and budget-oriented and designers who say we don't have a good solution yet, but we may have one in a week. We're very efficient at coming up with many good ideas so those schedule- and budget-oriented folks sometimes just must have faith in the process and our people, so that by the deadline, we will indeed have the answer.

AS: Any trouble sending out invoices or getting paid?

CRB: We have had problems, but we are now getting them out on time. Anyone starting a firm needs to remember—*get the bills out!* You won't get paid until you do. We have a staff position with primary responsibility for accounting, including invoicing. We have become more sophisticated over the years since many of our clients are public clients who can take forever to pay.

AS: Is it the accounting person's responsibility to track invoices?

CRB: We have divided it up. Jim is ultimately in charge of that; however, we have broken it down to more reasonable tasks. First, the project manager calls the client to make sure they received the bill, that it didn't get lost in the mail, or lost on their desk, and to get their first blush as to its accuracy. We have clients that will kick back an invoice for a small item, which sets us back a month. For example, you may have a $60,000 invoice and you are missing a $3.00 cab receipt, so they will return it and request the cab receipt. The project manager files a report, and then it is the accounting person's job to follow it up. We have principals go after chronically past due bills. You have to be vigilant about invoicing. You would think people would just pay their bills, but they don't, and we have to keep on them.

JCJ: As we grew and as the number of invoices grew, it became easy for the billing to fall behind because there were so many other things to do on a daily basis. Our current accounting position has instituted set procedures on reviewing and issuing invoices. To speed up invoicing, we divided our projects into two batches; one is billed at midmonth and the other is billed at the end of the month. The draft invoices are issued by accounting and given to the project managers to review. They are given 24 hours to approve and pass it to the principal-in-charge. The principal then has 24 hours to approve and pass it back to accounting. If the invoice isn't returned to accounting, it is forwarded to the client without changes.

We have not hesitated to call clients at home to collect an invoice; after you do the work, you should get paid. I won't be polite about that.

AS: How do you maintain a client base?

CRB: Most of our projects are in a public institutional market, and so the job of getting jobs is really keeping up with the people who make decisions for those clients. Even our repeat clients generally require a complete selection process each time because they are public entities. It takes forever to develop a relationship with that type of client. For example, we just received a commission from my alma mater, the University of Illinois at Urbana–Champaign. We pursued them for over twelve years and were interviewed seven times for various jobs without success, until now.

The most important thing to remember is that marketing is a numbers game. If you do not make the contacts, calls, or proposals, you are not going to get the commissions. We don't worry about the end result of any particular contact. There is a point where marketing becomes sales and you go out to win. But marketing is essentially making enough good contacts. We meet periodically to talk about our markets, to see what has changed and who is building. In the United States, for the last few years, most of the building has been public work. Schools and libraries are important to us. We develop a strategy for each group of owners. It changes: school districts are different from libraries; libraries are different from the City of Chicago. We keep a database file on organizations with client potential by their major characteristics. For example, a few years ago we decided we wanted to work for the Girl Scouts, and we are now working for three of the seven councils in the Chicago area. We found out who they were, and it turned out our services matched their goals.

When you are marketing on a daily basis, it is a little discouraging. In the last few years we have been fortunate because people sometimes call us instead of us calling them. It wasn't until 1992 or 1993 that people knew who we were. Occasionally, prospective clients just call and say we want you to do this job. It's a new thing for us, and I hope it doesn't go away.

AS: How do you meet prospective clients? And how do you stay in touch with them and keep them informed about what you are doing? Do you socialize with them?

CRB: We do so little entertaining—if you put us on the scale of architects who entertain, we are on the extremely low end. Our client base is not the kind that you can wine and dine, and it doesn't suit my background and aspirations, or Jim's. However, you do need to know your clients well, and meeting them in social situations could further the relationship. But we don't go out of our way or spend much money to do that. We have a group of clients that we regularly see for lunch.

AS: Do you network with various groups in the city? Is there an old girls' network that you have formed or tapped into?

CRB: I spend a lot of time working on issues that I am interested in. I'm on a number of boards and give many speeches. After sixteen years of practice in this city, if I want to find something out about almost any client, I have someone I can call for an answer, as a friend or an acquaintance.

There is probably the beginnings of an old girls' network, but they don't play by the rules that the old boys' network does. You hear all the stories about the old Mayor Daley—he would call his old high school classmate, architect Charlie Murphy, and say, "Design this for me," and that would be it. I'm not sure there are many women in the position to do that. But in fact I can call on a high school classmate of mine who is a state government official, for all kinds of information. But I do not think that the old girls' network will ever approximate the legendary old boys' network.

I belong to a golf network that has some really good golfers and some very important women. My golf partner last year was a woman who also happened to be the Deputy Commissioner of General Services for the City of Chicago, one of the main buyers of architectural services. When you're out there golfing, you get a lot of information, sort of a captive audience.

I'm on the board of several organizations including Children's Home and Aid Society of Illinois, which is a very powerful board, and some of those contacts are very helpful to me. I'm on the board of Cliff Dwellers, a social club, and I'm on the council of one of the Girl Scout Councils in the area. I chair the Appearance Review Commission in my town, and I meet a lot of people that way. In the past I belonged to CREW (Chicago Real Estate Women). One of the largest commissions we've had was through a connection in this group—we were part of the McCormick Place Expansion project team, and our fee was quite large.

Making a contribution is an important part of building up a network, and I think that is often overlooked. I don't join boards because I want to meet people. I am genuinely interested in what they are doing.

AS: What's the best thing about running your own practice versus working for somebody else or in a large partnership?

CRB: The best thing about this is I do what I believe in. I suppose any small business owner would say that. There are still no women partners in the major Chicago firms so being part of a large partnership wasn't very likely for me.

AS: What's the terrible part of running you own small, closely held company?

CRB: Stress—I am supposed to have all the answers. That and maybe doing things that you may not be interested in doing but that need to be done. Our size helps because we can start to pull in other people to handle some of those unpleasant tasks.

AS: What's the effect on staff and your marketing efforts of receiving all those prestigious design awards?

CRB: Our staff loves it. Since 1993, we've had people approaching and wanting to work for us. We've picked up some good people who were willing to leave major firms to come here, because they liked the kind of work we do. Many people are interested in being involved in design that's not the normal everyday brick boxes. The awards haven't helped marketing all that much. However, media exposure helps. We have been lucky in terms of exposure. And I want to say that we don't employ a public relations company.

There are a group of clients who are suspicious of architects who win awards, because they think their projects must be more expensive. It's ironic because award-winning buildings are generally less expensive and function better—that is part of the criteria to win the awards. But that's a leap of faith for some potential clients. They are afraid that you are trying to make a design statement with their problems rather than solving them.

We have won awards for some surprising building types; post offices and schools aren't generally regarded as being at the cutting edge. Those projects were successful because the client trusted us to understand and balance their needs to produce a good building. I would like to reiterate that trust is more important than any other ingredient. The client can be hands on or watch from a distance, but trust is essential.

3. Norman Rosenfeld Architects, New York, New York

The Anatomy of a Specialized Firm

Making the Break. Our specialty has been in health care. In some sense it may have been easier to start the practice because of this specialization, although getting the first project in this field is not easy. I was an associate for eight years with a firm that focused on health-care work. I did not think that health care was an area that interested me at all, and that firm also had housing projects; I worked on senior housing for about half the time, and when they ran out of housing it was my decision whether to leave the firm or work on a health-care project. I had a lot of responsibility and liked the firm, so I decided to stay there and work on a health-care project.

I became enthralled with the challenges of health-care architecture. I immersed myself in the technology and the literature and began developing a strong background in health-care design. This was an investment that I made in education. I was interested in becoming a partner in the firm, but they were not interested in making that available to me; I decided that I'd rather have my own candy store than stay.

By good fortune, my private physician was affiliated with a hospital that needed a small-scale intensive care unit. He put me in touch with the powers-that-be in the hospital, and I was selected for the commission. I decided it was probably the right time to take that very small project and make the leap to my own practice even though I had a wife and two children. I said if I'm going to do it, I might as well do it now, because it seemed like the right opportunity.

The first project may well be the easiest one to land because you invariably get it through a friend, a relative, or some connection. It is getting the second and third projects that are not so easy. That requires entrepreneurial attributes and a sense of marketing. We all know that you should be selling the next project the day you get the first one—you do not wait until you finish the first! It takes a very long time. So, I had the first project, I left the office but remained as a consultant to provide me with some income on an ongoing basis, and then I went out divining ways of getting the next project.

I joined and became active on the health committee of the AIA. I met people who became future clients because they were working for other hospitals. My first project was finished and photographed; it was then published; and I circulated the reprints. I treated the planning and design for this high-tech project in some unique ways. Good design in hospitals, in the early 1970s, was not as prevalent then as it is today. This project caught the attention of potential clients. I then began to build one project on the next in similar fashion.

I started the office in the back area of an old friend and colleague's office. I did some consulting with him, and we marketed health care together, which provided me with entrée to new clients and income, but by and large I was developing my reputation through the one project that I completed. Then this hospital had a sister hospital for whom I did a project, and so on.

The most important attributes are not only having particular skills and capabilities as an architect but you also need entrepreneurial skills. You must be able to take risks, to recognize that you're not going to have the same paycheck every week that you may be accustomed to having. Accept a degree of uncertainty for the freedom and fun of launching your own practice, developing your own client contacts, and having the independence to make decisions that *you* think make sense. Often you work in an office and think that all sorts of wrong-minded decisions are being made, and you have no power to influence them—and you are sometimes a beneficiary but often a victim of what you think are dumb decisions. And you'd rather make your own dumb decisions!

In the health-care market, in particular, one has to make some quantum leaps of presence because the client is a corporate institution. It's a very conservative client, and they're looking for people with stature, and gray hair, and portfolios—and young architects don't have that. Consequently, I associated with someone who was just a little bit older than me, but he had a big head of gray hair and a beard—he looked like a grown-up, and I looked like a little kid. I did find resistance in some institutions where I was the lead person in the firm while I had other senior people in the office. They said, "What happens if you get hit by a bus?" I said, "What happens if *you* get hit by a bus? The hospital's not going to have a leader? Things carry forward." But lots of institutions want to know that they're dealing with a large, established organization that has continuity, although in fact we all know that good work is done by individuals or two or three people. You don't need a team of ten to fifteen people. Still, institutions seem to have an affinity for large teams, even though few of the members actually do substantive work.

I started in 1969. I was thirty-three years old, and it has been a wonderful ride since then. The firm has grown, the size of our commissions has grown, our reputation has grown. While we've had peaks and valleys, the curve has generally gone up. We're very fortunate in having had several sufficiently large projects to sustain us through the various recessions in architecture.

Health-care clients are typically not decisive, and the most urgent decisions to select architects to move forward with projects can take a year, while the least urgent could take five years. Therefore, firms need a large portfolio of prospects, of proposals out there, in order to have a flow of work to support an office.

Firm Organization. At this point, I have one associate who is a principal, my second-in-command. I am a sole proprietor. I have tried to interest people in partnerships, and I suppose they're the wrong people; they don't have the entrepreneurial spirit and yet want to become partners. Partnerships imply sharing the success and some of the downside. I think it's difficult to find those people. *If they don't start out with you, they rarely feel equal.* If you start an individual practice to bring partners in at a later date, after you've gone through all the growing pains, I think it becomes difficult to find those people. Finding the next generation of architects to take over the firm, I have found, is difficult. And I think this is characteristic of architectural practice—there are few firms that carry forward past the founding partners; they restructure themselves in some manner or form.

The best example of a firm carrying into a third generation is Skidmore, Owings and Merrill, but a lot of firms just disappear. Some very fine architects, either because of their personalities or their decision-making process, can't seem to attract or hold onto people to whom they could pass on the baton.

There's another person in my firm who is a principal and functions at a very high level, but he's not a partner. Then we have two associates at the moment, project architects and managers who provide support to the office. I just recently established these two associate positions—one is a director of technical services and the other is director of design—who *may* be the next generation of this firm. I'm evaluating giving them greater responsibilities, involving them more in the business and contractual aspects of the firm so that they will get a full flavor of running a professional practice, which is really a business that has to be sustained. You have to establish the right fee levels and spend the right amount of time on projects to keep the office afloat, to maintain quality staff and to maintain a physical environment in which you can do work and present the right image to clients (who want to know you're in business and not working off your kitchen table).

The business aspects of architecture are extraordinarily important. If you're not running a fiscally sound practice, you are likely not to be in practice to take care of the next client. This is particularly true in the healthcare field, or in institutional work where, if you have a client and do the job well and politics doesn't interfere, you're likely to have projects with that client for ten, fifteen, or twenty years. Some of our client relationships go back over twenty years. Sometimes there is a hiatus, but then you'll be invited back to work on other projects for them. If you're in for the long haul, you need to set a certain continuity of organization, image, place of business—so clients know that you are a solid individual in a solid practice and that people who are with the firm have background with that particular client. That's one of the reasons they'll continue to want our firm to do work for them over a long period of time.

Another interesting characteristic is that the office has had many people who have come through the firm who, because of their particular brilliance and capabilities, chose to go out on their own or leave. Lots of people have come through the office, and I think it's not by accident that they were in this office because I personally did most of the interviewing and hiring. I was probably seeking certain individuals who were smart, strong, competent self-starters, mature at their level. And these are the people who are edgy and itchy and want to do something else. So we've been a wonderful training ground, and I view that as a compliment—that the environment was right to attract these people in the first place, and right to hold them for two, three, and five years, for as long as they were professionally challenged and didn't want to go on and do something else. Our work benefited from those very fine professionals who contributed to it, and then they went off and did something else. While, on the one hand, it's disruptive to lose people where there's this enormous investment in training, on the other hand, they were terrific and we got really good work accomplished because of their special qualities. I think there is an interesting analysis here (maybe even a dissertation): The psychology of architectural firm recruitment and staffing—how they carry forward into the next generation and whether the firm that carries forward is really the same firm that the founders had in mind.

I think that architecture, in contrast to any of the other professions, is uniquely different in that there are so many aspects to being an architect from the creative to the technical to the business side. Moreover, it is something that has to be done in teams. Architects require all of these talents to be successful. One individual cannot be strong in all of those areas, but at least there has to be some unique strengths; sometimes people are stronger designers, stronger technically or in business, but to be an "architect" you at least need to have a sensitivity and appreciation of all the constituent areas. This may contrast to law, where an individual lawyer can function within a firm and in a sense that individual is a firm unto him- or herself; an individual can service clients, with an associate and a secretary for assistance. An individual lawyer doesn't often need the kind of team relationships that architects have, doesn't necessarily need the breadth of skills, the creativity, the technical and business acumen, because what a lawyer is doing is typically less complicated. Similarly, physicians are sole practitioners; even if they practice in groups, they're individuals who just do what they do. To do architecture on a large scale, you need to bring together lots of talents and lots of skills. Being a film director or an orchestra conductor is very much akin to being an architect—you have disparate talents that must be brought together and managed to produce the vision that you have in your mind. That's not easy.

The mix of people within an office and how an office is organized varies. I consider my practice to be small to medium size; it is loosely organized on a project team basis. There is a project architect, a partner-in-charge (myself or the other individual who is a principal). We have mature project architects (the associates) who are responsible for the job on a day-to-day basis and pull together the disparate talent within the office—whether it's in design or technical areas—to bring the project to fruition.

Advice to Students. I believe that students who are about to enter practice should select an office that feels good to them regardless of the kind of work that's happening there, select an office that will respect them as individuals and performers. Once there, they should seek to do everything and anything that the office has available to them. They shouldn't shy away from any task as a young architect—it's all a wonderful learning experience. Architects' offices are very complicated places, and there are dozens of jobs that need doing. Young architects shouldn't find themselves pigeonholed in any one area. They should seek to perform many different tasks, whether it's drafting toilet details or doing marketing material or writing. Design is not the only thing in an architect's office. And while all architects think they're designers and say that's what they're going to do, they also have to learn a lot of other things. Not that they should give up and not do design, but they should take on all the other tasks and see that they get put into all the other slots. They should learn about specifications, they should sit down and read Sweets Catalogs, take whatever time they can to look at all the books and read all the magazines that come through the office (on their own time, not on the boss' time!). They should view this as the most important part of their education—the jobs they get right out of school.

While in school, I recommend that students try to interest practicing architects (not necessarily faculty) in what they're doing in studio. Try to commandeer people that they may know, to communicate with them about what they're doing on design projects and to cast their projects in a more real-world focus. They should seek intern or part-time opportunities in an architect's office. Just being around an architect's office would be beneficial. Ultimately, if you're going to be an architect, you're going to have projects built. Therefore, you have to recognize the constructability of—and a certain *reality* to—projects. And this is not to imply that they're uncreative. Some of us practicing primitives may have a useful perspective and would be delighted to serve as resources.

Case Study | ABC/Prieto Haskell*

Rick Prieto and Larry Haskell settled comfortably in the overstuffed chairs on the porch of the cabin overlooking Lake Tahoe. The two had driven up to the lake to spend some time together reflecting on their future prospects as the partners-in-charge of the San Francisco office of the Los Angeles based architectural firm, Alvarez, Beckhard, and Crane. The San Francisco office had been run as a separate profit center from Los Angeles for fourteen months, as ABC/Prieto Haskell (ABC/P-H). It

was the first step in what Rick and Larry hoped would be an eventual buyout of the San Francisco practice from the founders in Los Angeles. Rick and Larry each owned a nominal 1 percent of the business. They had been unable to reach an agreement about a buyout with the majority shareholder and firm founder, Ed Alvarez.

As Rick gazed across the calm, blue expanse of the lake he mused, "I wonder how ready we really are to break away from L.A.?"

History of Alvarez, Beckhard, and Crane

The Early Years

Alvarez, Beckhard, and Crane (ABC) was founded in 1962 in Los Angeles by Ed Alvarez and two partners. Ed owned over half the firm. Although his

*This case was written by Martha A. O'Mara, PhD candidate in Organizational Behavior, Harvard University, under the direction of Adjunct Professor John Seiler, Harvard Graduate School of Design. It was written as a basis for class discussion and does not illustrate either an effective or ineffective handling of an administrative situation. © 1992 Harvard University Graduate School of Design.

partners brought in some developer-built housing, Ed obtained most of the firm's work. He was well connected with many minority group organizations in Los Angeles that were involved in the development of public housing projects.

A major source of work for the firm resulted from subcontracting from larger engineering or architectural firms that were required to include a minority-owned firm on their team of consultants to be awarded a government-funded project. These projects typically included large-scale renovations or construction of military bases, transportation support facilities, and other public infrastructure. ABC also obtained work on "set-aside" projects where it was mandated that the design firm be minority owned. These projects included housing, building renovation, and small jobs on military bases or for public transportation agencies.

While these projects occasionally contained some opportunity for creative design, much of it was routine production work. As Rick Prieto described it: "These contracts just require a basic drafting service. Ed has a lot of folks in the back room cranking this stuff out. He will take on whatever work that brings in income. To Ed, a fee is a fee is a fee. Within these limits, however, he has been very successful. He is a very dynamic person, and he knows how to make and use contacts."

Larry explained some of the disadvantages in this type of work: "Engineers who are the prime consultant on a big job will only think of you as fitting in a particular slot where they need you to qualify for the project. They rarely give you more than the mandated minimum amount of work and you never get direct control over your work or any visible credit for it."

Most public agencies had a policy of limiting the amount of work they could award to any one firm within a particular period of time. Ed Alvarez felt that the firm had reached a ceiling in the Los Angeles area, so he and his partners began to look for work in northern California to expand their client base.

The San Francisco Office

The San Francisco office started in 1976 as a branch for ABC's participation in the design of a Bay Area Rapid Transit (BART) station. That agency, as was frequently the case, required firms to have an office in the local area. ABC initially moved into the offices of the large civil engineering firm that was the prime contractor on the project. A separate location was later leased to be supported by local fee income.

Ricardo Prieto, a talented young designer, was hired to head the office and was joined two years later by Larry Haskell, an architect with a great deal of building renovation experience. Both had master's degrees in architecture and were members of the AIA.

Rick Prieto described the arrival of ABC in San Francisco: "The engineering firms in the area were glad to see ABC come into town because it was a credible, minority-owned firm with a good track record and reputation. And the partners in Los Angeles were glad to get the type of repetitive production work the engineers offered."

Coordinating the practice between the two locations was often difficult, especially on projects that shared production tasks. A management consultant hired to help with this problem suggested that the entire firm organize its operations in the form of a "matrix." With this arrangement, the senior people would be responsible for a functional job, such as design or production, for both offices, but have a specific home office location and responsibility for local projects. This meant that Rick, who was the most design-oriented of the partners, was now not only in charge, with Larry, of the San Francisco office but also directed design for the entire firm. As a result, he spent a great deal of time commuting between the two office locations. Rick and Larry became dissatisfied with this arrangement. Travel was wearing on Rick, and both Rick and Larry felt that the San Francisco practice suffered because the Los Angeles projects were always given priority over those in San Francisco. They were also annoyed by Alvarez agreeing to take on work for the San Francisco office before he discussed it with them.

In the early years of the San Francisco practice, Ed Alvarez took an active role in developing business with public agencies in northern California. He had gradually stopped doing so in recent years, and now Rick and Larry took full responsibility for it.

As the San Francisco office grew and became more independent, Rick and Larry wanted more control over how it was run and a share in the profits of the firm. They approached the three partners about the possibility of obtaining a greater share in the partnership that more closely fit with the contributions of the San Francisco office. When the partners declined to share their interest in the total company and instead offered Rick and Larry a small share of the San Francisco office alone, Rick and Larry proposed buying out the entire San Francisco practice. Ed Alvarez was strongly opposed to the idea. Rick attributed this to Ed's desire for future financial security. "I think Ed sees this office as his retirement nest egg, a source of continuing income. Anyone who might have taken over the leadership of the L.A. office has left the firm. We're the only 'second generation' he has left."

As a compromise, so that the contribution of the San Francisco office to the total company's profits could be more clearly assessed, the San Francisco office became a separate profit center and separately incorporated. The name of the office was changed from Alvarez, Beckhard, and Crane to ABC/Prieto Haskell. As part of this transition, the Los Angeles office "loaned" the San Francisco office $250,000 as working capital to cover administrative start-up costs and to carry accounts receivable. At the same time, Rick and Larry moved the office into new and more desirable quarters south of Market Street. Now, after a year and two months of this arrangement, Rick and Larry wanted to assess their position.

Current Operations of the San Francisco Office

Rick got up from his chair and went into the cottage, returning with two cold beers. "First of all," he said to Larry, "We need to look at our current operations and see what sort of raw material we have to work with." Larry nodded as he reached for the beer his partner had brought him. "I agree. Let's start with a look at our people."

Staffing. The San Francisco office had a staff of twelve. In addition to Rick and Larry, there were three experienced architects. Rob Schwartz, who Rick and Larry considered a potential future partner in the practice, was informally responsible for managing the drafting room, as well as several major projects. According to Larry, "Rob knows how to give the right answers to clients. He is politically sensitive. He knows he has a lot at stake with us, and he is willing to work hard."

David Richey, sixty-one years old, had worked for many years at one of the nation's largest firms. He had strong technical competence but shied away from project management. Explained Larry, "He knows what he is good at and what he likes to do. He lives close by and partly for that reason, came to us for a job about a year ago. He really knows how to put a building together. But he marches to a different drummer. For example, he wears an earring."

The third of the senior staff members, Alfredo Castrita, was trained in urban planning and worked on his master's degree in design part-time. He planned to go back to Argentina in a few years to run an architectural practice owned by his father.

Two other employees, Wanda Winston and Diana Rossi, had been with the office for several years. Larry saw them as "thorough, hard working, but not fully experienced. Both Wanda and Diana have a lot of confidence—maybe it's more accurate to say ego—and they say they feel held back by the type of work we usually do in the office. I could see Wanda being made a partner some day. Diana is defensive about having an architectural degree from another country and can be rather abrasive." The women were encouraged to take on some project management responsibilities when the work was similar to projects they had worked on before.

The office also had four drafters, although the number fluctuated. One was a student intern, two were students working on their master's degrees who were only there for the summer and part-time during school, and one was a full-time employee with an architectural degree from Turkey. There was considerable turnover among this group of people. The office also employed a full-time secretary and shared a receptionist with another design firm. Rick and Larry had also employed a marketing coordinator, but that person left, and they felt they could not afford to replace her.

Project Management. Rick and Larry were actively involved with every project in the office. Rick was usually responsible for design, while Larry tended to coordinate engineering tasks. The project managers—Rob and Alfredo, and, to a lesser extent, Wanda and Diana—monitored the overall production of a job and visited the field. David Richey preferred not to have client contact.

People tended to work on most of the projects in the office at one time or another. Since project schedules changed frequently, job assignments were made on a weekly or biweekly basis. Rick described the method for doing this: "We look at what is a priority in the next two to three weeks, then schedule the work. This requires flexible project teams. People here have to view projects not as 'their' jobs but as the 'office's' jobs. Assignments at any given time depend on three factors: who is working in the office at that particular time, what projects are currently underway, and the timing of the project's schedule."

Rick reflected on the current organization. "At this scale it works. If things continue to grow as we expect they will, we will soon get to the size where Larry and I can't be so heavily involved in every project. I'm worried about losing the collaborative feel we have tried to maintain in the office. And, I wonder if our project managers are ready to take on more responsibility."

Larry shared his concern: "Right now most of our work is similar to previous projects—a lot of repetition. But we are starting to expand the sort of work we do, and I wonder if we have the kind of staff capable of switching to unfamiliar types of assignments."

Rick and Larry felt they needed to hire more people to cover the heavy workload in the office. Everyone in the office was working on a heavy overtime basis, for which there was no premium paid. According to their accountant, they could not afford to hire anyone else at the present time. However, they had decided to replace a senior project manager who had left the office two months earlier.

There was no established way of recruiting new employees. Larry stated: "We really didn't deliberately plan to have a staff structured the way it is. Usually, people come to us for work by word of mouth." Newly hired employees started out on a three-month "probationary" period, at the end of which their initial salary was reviewed. Reviews were then conducted yearly.

Compensation. Salaries in the San Francisco office were competitive with other local firms. "We're not some superstar design office that can pay people peanuts and still attract good ones," said Larry. The office did not have a bonus system, and since it lost money the previous fiscal year, the issue had not been addressed. Larry and Rick expressed the hope that they would some day be able to give out some form of bonus based upon performance, responsibility, and tenure.

Management Control Systems. The accounting system that the San Francisco office had been using was contracted to a data processing firm. It received its information from staff in the Los Angeles office. Larry felt the accounting system used was very sensitive to human error in data entry and was slow to report project-billing expenses. "There were always a lot of mistakes in the numbers. We weren't getting the kind of timely information we needed to make sure our projects were within budget. So, we had to do all the numbers over again by hand in San Francisco."

Rick and Larry thought the Los Angeles office was slow to collect receivables. The firm had over 1.5 million dollars in uncollected accounts in comparison to last year's income of 4.5 million dollars for the two offices. Even after the San Francisco office became a separate profit center, the Los Angeles office still received payment checks for San Francisco's work. "When they run short of cash, they use our money," growled Rick. "Ed Alvarez apparently feels justified in doing that since we owe him the $250 grand."

After its first twelve months as a separate profit center, the office was losing money. (Exhibits 3–1 and 3–2, pages 113–114, contain financial performance information for the second

Exhibit 3–1
ABC/Prieto Haskell
Harvard Graduate School of Design

Balance Sheet
April 30, 1986

ASSETS

CURRENT ASSETS

Cash	$ 35,966	
Accounts Receivable—Retainage	24,143	
Accounts Receivable	127,260	
Loans Receivable—Officers	3,000	
Joint Ventures—Capital	46,061	
Total Current Assets		$236,430

FIXED ASSETS

Furniture and Fixtures	$ 6,344	
Less: Accumulated Depreciation	1,959	
Total Fixed Assets		4,385

OTHER ASSETS

Deposits		5,958
Total Assets		**$246,773**

LIABILITIES AND STOCKHOLDERS' EQUITY

CURRENT LIABILITIES

Accounts Payable	$ 47,933	
Due to Engineers	28,464	
Loan Payable—ABC	238,704	
Payroll Taxes Payable	7,311	
Loan Payable	4,197	
Excise Tax Payable	228	
Total Current Liabilities		$326,837

LONG-TERM LIABILITY

Deferred Corporate Income Taxes		2,072
Total Liabilities		**$328,909**

STOCKHOLDERS' EQUITY

Capital Stock	$ 3,000	
Retained Earning (see Exhibit 2, page XX)	(85,136)	
Total Stockholders' Equity		**(82,136)**
TOTAL LIABILITIES AND STOCKHOLDERS' EQUITY		**$246,773**

six months of operation.) Although Rick and Larry thought that the next six months performance would make up for the current deficit, they were very concerned about controlling current expenses.

"We have a difficult time monitoring profitability," Rick elaborated. "One of the reasons we are losing money right now is because a lot of our government work is based upon a fee structure and overhead rate that was negotiated

Exhibit 3–2

ABC/Prieto Haskell
Harvard Graduate School of Design

Combined Statement of Income and Retained Earnings
For the Six Months Ended April 30, 1986

EARNED INCOME

Fees	$318,576	
Less: Engineering Cost	<u>66,964</u>	
Net Fees		$251,612

COST OF OPERATIONS

Direct Labor—Staff	$ 73,631	
Direct Labor—Officers	25,104	
Direct Labor—Office	<u>3,225</u>	
Total Job Costs	<u>$101,960</u>	

Direct Job Costs:

Blue Prints	$ 2,483	
Other Costs	<u>21,487</u>	
Total Job Costs	<u>$ 23,970</u>	
Total Direct Costs		<u>$125,930</u>
CONTRIBUTION TO OVERHEAD AND PROFIT		$125,682

OTHER EXPENSES

Overhead Expenses (Schedule 1)		<u>$225,394</u>
INCOME (LOSS) FROM OPERATIONS		($99,712)

OTHER INCOME

Rental Income	$ 7,600	
Interest Income	<u>137</u>	
Total Other Income		<u>$ 7,737</u>
INCOME (LOSS) FROM OPERATIONS		($91,975)

INCOME TAXES

Excise Tax		<u>228</u>
NET INCOME (LOSS)		($92,203)
RETAINED EARNINGS—BEGINNING		7,665
Less: Prior Period Adjustment		<u>598</u>
RETAINED EARNINGS—ENDING		<u>($85,136)</u>

SCHEDULE 1: Combined Statement of Income and Retained Earnings
For the Six Months Ended April 30, 1986

INDIRECT SALARIES	$67,536
FRINGE BENEFITS	45,495
BASIC OVERHEAD EXPENSE	
Office Expense	$63,105
Other Financial Charges	22,770
Insurance	7,955
Promotion	5,431
Auto Expense	4,723
Petty Cash	3,737
Dues and Subscriptions	2,066
Professional Fees	1,784
Blue Print and Photo	361
Employment Fees	263
Seminars	114
Contribution	54
Total Basic Overhead Expenses	$112,363
TOTAL OVERHEAD EXPENSES	**$225,394**

a long time ago. But now our overhead is a lot higher because of the new office and other start-up costs related to being a separate profit center. It takes a long time to renegotiate a higher rate with public sector clients. You have to open all your books. As we finish up these projects and get new contracts at better rates, we should be able to start making some money. However, the amount of profit that can be made on a publicly funded project is limited by law."

Rick and Larry had recently selected a different accounting software package that would allow them to customize the project reports. They arrived at the number of available hours for a given job by first subtracting the estimated profit and overhead costs, and then divided the remainder by the average hourly salary cost of the people that would work on the project. That constituted the maximum number of hours for each phase of work.

The office used a personal computer with a word-processing software package for most correspondence, proposals, and reports, and some software for cost estimating. They hoped to purchase a CAD system within a year, and Larry had been spending some time reviewing available systems. CAD was not used in the Los Angeles office.

Clients. A major portion of the work completed by ABC and the San Francisco office was in either transportation or housing. The transportation projects were for the local rapid transit system or Contrail. On half of these projects, an engineering firm served as the lead designer and the primary client contact. Larry noted: "Over time, we've gained a lot of respect from the local engineering firms, and now they are inviting us on projects that aren't connected with minority participation requirements."

Most of the housing projects in the office were for public agencies, including housing for a military base, rehabilitation plans for a number of public housing projects, and new housing units.

While the minority ownership of the firm was a factor in a majority of the office's projects, Rick and Larry hoped to reduce the incidence of obtaining new business that way. Rick expressed his mixed feelings about their "minority-owned" status: "We don't want to be a minority-owned firm by law, although we qualify. It may at first open doors for you, but then it stereotypes you. We do want to be a minority firm in that we want to work with minority groups in the community. I feel we can bring a special sense of understanding, which has been very effective in our housing work. Yet I recognize that minority set-aside work has been helpful in establishing the practice and is a good source of income. We feel responsible for keeping the office busy, and our employees employed, so we have continued to accept this type of work if there is a substantial role for us in it. Our goal is to have no more than 30 percent of our work on this basis."

Ed Alvarez continued to rely on minority-firm contracts for most of the new business in the Los Angeles office. "Ed only seems to feel comfortable pursuing that kind of work. It's where all his contacts are. I don't see him deliberately going after the type of private sector development work we want to obtain," said Rick.

Both Rick and Larry felt that the San Francisco office was capable of doing more sophisticated design work than Ed Alvarez aspired to. "We want to better utilize our experience, particularly in rehabilitation and community projects, and there is a good market for that type of work in San Francisco right now. The local economy is very healthy here," said Larry. Rick elaborated: "We want to get more work in the private sector, with developers, and more creative design work on public projects. I think we have both the talent and experience to do so, but we certainly have to become better known in the community."

Recently, the San Francisco office received a large commission to rehabilitate public housing at various sites throughout the city. The agency in charge had deliberately approached ABC/Prieto Haskell because of their reputation in housing. In addition, a private developer had asked them to design a condominium project. To Rick and Larry, both these jobs represented an increased recognition of the firm's abilities beyond its "minority-owned" status and signs of a payoff from a year-long marketing and promotional effort.

Business Development. The pursuit of new business consumed over one-third of Rick and Larry's time. Publicly funded projects typically required extensive written proposals detailing the firm's experience and the background of project team members. Until recently, the San Francisco office had employed a full-time marketing coordinator who was responsible for responding to requests for proposals, preparing brochures, press releases, and other promotional materials, and monitoring contacts and leads on potential new business. When she had the time, she would also make "cold calls." This entailed finding a developer or public agency that might have work coming up and sending them a brochure and a letter asking the company to consider using ABC/P-H on their next project. Then, about a week later, she or Rick or Larry would make a telephone call to the targeted company or agency and try to speak with the person in charge of selecting architects. If there was potential for new business, they would try to make a personal appointment to present the firm's qualifications. A "cold call" campaign in recent months to local public housing agencies had resulted in several potential design opportunities.

When the marketing coordinator moved east to attend graduate school, Rick and Larry decided to wait until the office became more profitable before replacing her.

Shortly after moving the office, Larry retained a graphic designer to develop a new letterhead and other visual materials. He contrasted this approach with that of the Los Angeles office: "They do their paste-ups in-house. Nothing matches and they use cheap paper and ink. They don't seem to care about the image they project. It's the same with project photography. We hired a professional to go out and shoot our best work and tried to get the L.A. office to share the cost. But their idea of photography was sending someone out with a Brownie."

The Desire to Own the Practice

The sun was setting over the lake as Rick and Larry finished their review of the San Francisco office. Larry stood up and stretched. He looked over to Rick and said: "I have a sense that things are moving in the right direction. But we haven't made much progress in our negotiations with Ed Alvarez. How hard and how fast should we push the buyout issue?"

Negotiations with the Los Angeles Partners

When the San Francisco office became a separate profit center, an outside consultant hired by Alvarez had put a purchase price on it of $300,000 that would be paid to the three Los Angeles–based partners in proportion to their share of the ownership. Neither Larry nor Rick had the money available to make such a payment, and they were advised by both their lawyer and their accountant that the price was too high. Since that time they had been unable to reach an agreement with Ed Alvarez on an alternate amount. Negotiations came to a complete standstill a few months ago when Beckhard decided to leave the company and demanded a financial settlement that was currently under litigation.

Not owning the San Francisco practice worried Rick and Larry because it meant that, legally, the Los Angeles partners could fire them at will. Larry noted with irony: "Right now the office isn't making any money so you really can't value it according to its income stream. But the harder Rick and I work to make the office successful and profitable, the higher its value will be and, consequently, the more we would have to pay to purchase it."

Larry and Rick had considered leaving and setting up a practice on their own, but because most of the work in the office was for governmental agencies, with binding contracts with ABC, they would not be able to take any of those projects with them. Rick estimated it would take at least six months to generate any fee income if he and Larry went out on their own.

Rick summed up the mixed feelings he and Larry shared: "We still feel a lot of loyalty to Ed Alvarez. He gave us a real break early in our careers and has been a mentor to us in many ways. But we have a fundamental difference of opinion as to the future direction of the firm and our share of that future. I can't see any way to resolve those differences."

Case Study Analysis | A Firm in Search of a New Identity

JOHN SEILER was an Adjunct Professor of Architecture and Urban Design at the Harvard University Graduate School of Design where he taught professional practice classes. He is an architect who consults with design firms on management issues and with schools on campus planning. Professor Seiler's publications include contributions to *The Instructor's Guide for the Architect's Handbook of Professional Practice* (Washington, D.C.: AIA Press, 1988), "Architecture at Work" in the *Harvard Business Review,* (vol. 62, No. 5 (September–October 1984), and *Systems Analysis in Organizational Behavior* (Homewood, Ill.: Irwin, 1967).

Introduction

What follows is not intended to be a model analysis. Probably no two people will choose to attack a case study in just the same way. The author of this analysis approached the case the same way he does when he is preparing to teach it to his students in the architecture program at the Harvard Graduate School of Design.

First, he proceeds as though he had never seen the case before. His reason for that is to try to experience the case the way his students will, so he has a reasonable chance of understanding what students are talking about in class. Normally, however, he does not let himself reach a value position on the case. In fact, he wants to avoid thinking about what the actors in the case should do so that he can more accurately hear what students think should be done. That habit of recommendation prohibition has been lifted for the purposes of the analysis here.

The author starts his analysis by reading the case attentively once; then, with greater care, he starts digging into those aspects of the material that make him most curious. There is no particular pattern to this initial probing. He expects that the pieces of information he is finding will eventually suggest their relationship. What follows is a rough reflection of this gradual process of finding meaning from undigested facts.

What Do the Pieces of This Case Mean?

Rick Prieto and Larry Haskell have ambitions that break through the practice boundaries of their mentor and boss, Ed Alvarez. They have taken some steps at their branch office to start to realize those ambitions. At the same time, they necessarily continue to ply the old trade as Ed Alvarez envisioned it. Being partly in a new kind of practice, but mostly in an older one, creates some conflicts from which we may learn something about the organizational behavior of an architectural practice.

Differences Between the Two Types of Practice

ABC was a "production shop." Ed's clients wanted him to produce construction documents for routine projects such as repairing roofs of buildings used by government agencies. The tasks to be undertaken were well understood, technically and in terms of the standards that the agencies expected firms like Ed's to follow. Ed was good at this kind of work.

Because very little creativity was required, relatively lowly skilled drafters could perform to specification with a minimum of instruction and supervision. Consequently, Ed's organization looked like a flat pyramid, with Ed at the top spending most of his time getting new projects, two partners below him seeing that the work got done, and a great many drafters actually producing drawings. Wages for this type of work

were modest, and overhead costs—those expenses like rent that do not vary by the volume of work—were low. Ed cared very little about his firm's image from an aesthetic point of view. We may assume that the economics of this type of work had been efficiently applied, since Ed had spare capital to lend to the San Francisco office.

In contrast, Rick and Larry sought to attract developer clients in the private sector for projects that would require a considerably higher level of design skill, for which Rick had a reputation. Although they had only recently secured their first contract of this type, they apparently had been hiring staff and leasing office space with this possibility in mind.

How Does the San Francisco Office Operate?

The organization at Prieto Haskell (P-H) was oddly shaped:

Rick and Larry

Senior Project Manager	Senior Project Manager	Senior Project Manager
	Technical Specialist	
Junior Project Manager		Junior Project Manager
Drafter	Drafter	Part-Time Drafter	Part-Time Drafter

The organization has a relatively small top, a small bottom, and a bulge in the middle. This sort of organization structure seems overqualified for the routine work being done in conjunction with the Los Angeles office and better suited to the more creatively demanding kinds of projects that Rick and Larry were trying to attract to P-H. David Maister, in an article titled, "Balancing the Professional Service Firm" (*Sloan Management Review,* Fall 1982), calls Ed Alvarez' kind of organization a "Procedures" firm, whose main attraction is low-cost efficiency. The P-H firm would probably fall into his "Gray Hair" category, in which experience is the prime value being offered. Where a more advanced form of creativity is sought by clients, Maister would call that form of practice "Brains." Of significance is the coexistence in the P-H firm of a Gray Hair organization and a predominately Procedures practice. That is a piece of information whose implications we need to examine. (See Peter Piven's discussion of firm classifications in this chapter, pages 72–76.)

The work scheduling system in the San Francisco office was on a weekly assignment basis, with everyone working on every project at one time or another. This method of manning projects was flexible, probably a reflection of the heavy work load in the office and the reluctance of the partners to increase expenses by hiring more staff. This scheduling system would place higher priority on getting the work done than on assigning the most appropriate person to do the work. It is likely that some of P-H's drafting work was being done by staff above the drafting level.

Why Is the San Francisco Office So Unprofitable?

[Refer to James Cantillon's Financial Management Primer in Chapter 5, pages 171–198, for background in understanding financial statements and for help in interpreting the numbers.] To answer this question, we can look at the relationship between what ABC/Prieto Haskell got paid and what it cost to provide the direct labor for the fees received. Exhibit 3–2, page 114, of the case study provides these figures for a six-month period. Net fees were about $252,000. Direct labor was about $102,000. Dividing the former by the latter:

Fees: $252,000 / Direct Labor: $102,000 = 2.47

For every dollar of direct labor spent, ABC/Prieto Haskell received $2.47 from its clients. So, after paying for each direct labor dollar, P-H would have left over $1.47 to pay for its other direct job costs and its indirect or non-project-related expenses. At first glance, that sounds like a reasonable ratio.

Unfortunately, the method of reporting direct labor cost at ABC/P-H does not include the cost of the fringe benefits that were paid to those who provided that direct labor. The firm's fringe benefits, listed in Schedule 1 of Exhibit 3–2, page 115, amount to about 26 percent of all labor costs (about $45,000 in relation to a total labor cost of about $170,000). Adding 26 percent for fringe benefits to the previously cited direct la-

bor cost brings total direct labor cost to $128,000, and the ratio of direct labor including fringe benefits to fees is now 1.96. Many firms would find it difficult to pay for their other job costs and overhead expenses with less than a dollar for every direct labor dollar. And that would be the case even for firms whose overhead-cost level was consistent with the kind of practice they were conducting. We may suspect that P-H did not enjoy that consistency.

Our assumption that some drafting was being done by staff paid above drafter rates would probably be one element in the explanation of ABC/P-H's unprofitability. The San Francisco partners say their losses are due to the fact that their allowable fee base had not been renegotiated with government agencies since their move to new, more expensive quarters.

We can believe that explanation. Office Expense in Schedule 1 is 25 percent of fees received. That high a percentage reflects the partners' desire to move up on the design ladder. The clients they seek to serve will expect their architects to be successful enough to afford, if not an impressive office, at least a respectable one. However, how likely is it that the government agencies that currently provide most of ABC/P-H's work will be sympathetic to arguments that their design contractor needs a more impressive office?

There were other overhead reasons for ABC/P-H's lack of profitability. Indirect salaries, about $68,000, were 27 percent of the fees collected, or about two-thirds of what it cost to do the work itself. Remembering that, after paying for each direct labor dollar, P-H only has 96 cents left to pay for everything else, that seems like a high proportion.

What is included in indirect costs? Rick and Larry each spent a third of their time getting new work, so that would be part of the $68,000. So would time spent by secretarial, accounting, and other staff doing work not directly related to projects themselves. We may also suspect that some of that large indirect expense was created by hours put into work on client projects that could not, by the limitations of the contract, be billed. That could be either actual hours worked beyond the number of hours budgeted for the work, or it could represent the unbillable premium that a project manager was paid when he or she was doing drafting, as we have previously surmised.

The other noticeable overhead cost is the finance charge. ABC/P-H's total loans outstanding from Exhibit 3–1, page 113, are about $243,000. Its finance charge of about $23,000, a little over 9 percent of the loan amount, seems reasonable until we remember that Exhibit 3–2 is only for a six-month period. We might presume that the interest rate for the whole year will, therefore, be double that for six months, or in the 18 percent range. That is a very high financing rate, though not entirely surprising for a start-up firm suffering from lack of profitability and an uncertain future. What is somewhat surprising, however, is that most of the loan comes from P-H's parent firm, ABC. A suspicious observer might assume that such a high rate is Ed Alvarez' way of getting a return on his money without having to share it, through distribution of P-H profits, with his San Francisco partners.

What About Getting New Business?

The only other overhead expense that is worthy of mention is for promotion. We know that the San Francisco partners, in an effort to reduce indirect salaries, have decided not to replace their marketing coordinator, who left a month ago. That is regrettable if the firm is to establish itself in a market more directly related to its existing organization and economic structure.

The last six-months' promotion expense was only 2 percent of fees received, which would be considered low even for a more established firm. Of course, we have already noted that Rick and Larry spend a third of their own time on project promotion work, and that represents a significant amount of money. However, to be most effective, especially when entering a new market, and when the partners are engrossed in current projects, the firm needs staff assistance to research prospects, set up appointments, provide promotion materials, and to follow up on established contacts. The current 2 percent of fees being spent on such work is inadequate. The partners are caught in a squeeze between their marketing ambitions and their out-of-balance financial condition.

Why Do They Need That Big Loan?

Another feature of P-H finances has to do with the supply of cash needed to run a business like Rick's and Larry's. Most of the reason why P-H needs a loan, adding up to almost six-month's worth of its fee income, is so that it can pay its employees and its suppliers without having to wait to do so until it can collect on its billings to clients. Except in those rare cases where a contract has a provision for advance payments, the timing between cash spent to do contracted work and the receipt of funds for that work is a critical factor in a firm's economic profile.

ABC/P-H's balance sheet, Exhibit 3–1, page 113, shows total accounts receivable of about $150,000. We want to find out if that amount of uncollected billings is appropriate for the amount of work the firm has been doing. We can answer that question by finding out how long after sending out its bills P-H had to wait to get paid. We can calculate that by dividing the total billings for the six-month period by the accounts receivable that were outstanding during that period. We can think of this calculation as telling us how many times our receivables "turned over," or were paid off in the six-month period.

Net Fees: $250,000 / Total Accounts
    Receivable: $150,000 = 1.67 pay-off cycles

P-H got paid by its clients at a rate of 1.67 times over the last six-months. What does that mean in terms of how many months, on the average, P-H has to wait to get its money from the time it sends out its bills?

6 months / 1.67 payment cycles
        = 3.6 months per payment cycle

We are told that the firm's typical clients, government agencies, are notoriously late payers. If other commercial credit relations between architectural firms and their clients were payment in 30 days, the San Francisco firm would be carrying an excess of receivables worth 2.6 months' of loan financing. P-H is currently producing about $42,000 of billings a month.

$42,000 × 2.6 months = $109,000

If we assume that the cost of carrying these receivables is 18 percent a year, as previously calculated, then:

$$\$109,000 \times .18 = \$21,000$$

P-H is spending about \$21,000 a year more for its receivables than it would with 30-day paying commercial clients. (That amount represents about 23 percent of the last six months' losses.)

Another way to picture the receivables situation is to ask what would happen if ABC/P-H were able to get its clients to speed payment by 30 days. That is easy to answer, since we calculated that a month's billings were about \$42,000.

$$\$42,000 \times .18 \text{ interest} = \$7,600$$

That reduction represents about 12 percent of the last six months' loss.

What Do the Partners Seek as a Client Market?

Of course, there are many other, nonfinancial factors that Rick and Larry have to analyze as they seek to develop a growth and, assumedly, an independence strategy for their young firm.

The partners want to reduce their dependence on minority set-aside work to about 30 percent, from its present level of almost 100 percent. However, they also want to work with clients in the minority community, because they believe they have an advantage in understanding that community's needs since Rick is of minority origin and others in the firm also have a personal understanding of minority issues. So this is one market target in which they may have a competitive advantage.

They have also recently been chosen to work on a public housing rehabilitation project, not because of their minority eligibility but because their past work of this kind has been highly praised. This reputation has also led to a private condominium commission. Since Rick is a talented designer, the more the firm's projects require design input, the more his value to projects will increase. And, of course, the more the firm is able to use its talents effectively, the greater its ability to increase its fee level and the efficiency by which it uses the talents of its staff.

What About Technology?

Larry is determined to depart from ABC/Los Angeles' traditions in other ways than just in the markets the firm targets. He wants to put a CAD system in place in the office in the next year. The case does not dwell on this subject, but it may portend a way to free itself from its financial dependence on ABC. It has already been remarked that P-H has an oddly shaped organization, one not well suited to its parent's business. We know that Rick and Larry did not choose this kind of organization; it just happened. Can they proceed effectively to make a market transition with this organization?

We have speculated that part of the firm's lack of profits may be caused by some of its staff performing work beneath their skill and salary levels. If Larry is successful in bringing high-end computing technology to P-H, he may be able to design work assignments so that staff members can become more self-sufficient, both in project management and in design and drafting. We could imagine an eventual practice profile that omitted the drafting level almost entirely, with each staff member doing schematic, design development, and construction documentation on his or her projects, creating a project integration that had inherent communication efficiency and delegation of responsibility. If so, even the more routine projects could possibly be carried out by upper level staff with an efficiency matching the fee structure for such jobs.

The Partners' Strategy Challenge

Rick and Larry seem to be caught between two priority positions. One is to contain costs to achieve profitability. The other is to obtain new forms of business that are better suited to the firm's existing cost structure. Unfortunately, the cost reduction path, in its job development curtailment, prevents or seriously delays the firm's ability to approach more design-oriented clients. On the other hand, devotion of funds to replacing the marketing coordinator will tend to prolong a period of unprofitability.

The San Francisco partners have defined their long-term market goals. Their "mission" in service to clients has received appropriate attention. "Mission," as defined by John Pearce in his article, "The Company Mission as a Strategic Tool" (*Sloan Management Review,* Spring 1982), "describes the firm's product, market, and technology in a way that reflects the values and priorities of the strategic decision makers . . . basic goals, characteristics, and philosophies . . . a basis for a culture that will guide future executive action . . . statement of purpose that distinguishes a business from other firms of its type."

However, Rick's and Larry's operating and financial mechanisms have not been analyzed sufficiently. If the partners are going to adopt a cost-reduction plan to put themselves in a position to buy their office from Ed Alvarez, they need to reduce their overhead—their office cost and their financing cost—and their ratio of direct labor to fees. That probably means moving to cheaper quarters, renegotiating the finance charges with Alvarez, finding ways to encourage public clients to pay their bills faster, and reducing the impact of less cost-effective staff, either by replacing them or rapidly finding a way to make them more efficient, such as through adoption of high-end computing technology.

If they are going to attack the profitability problem by obtaining more design-oriented commissions, they need to find a source of financing that will allow them to replace the marketing coordinator, increase the budget for promotion, and support an organization and office that is better suited to the design-oriented than the minority set-aside client.

It is doubtful that a disinterested source of funds, such as a bank or a small business investor, will want to run the risk of carrying P-H into its hoped-for profitable new design-oriented form of practice. The risks are too great and the expected rewards are too small. There is, however, an interested potential investor, and that is Ed Alvarez. Rick and Larry are his only "next generation." He is thought to look to them to take care of him financially in his retirement.

Ed may be smart enough to know that the San Francisco partners will never be satisfied with the kind of practice that he has been so good at. If he wants a stream of income over the long run, he may have a better chance of receiving that stream if he does so as an investor

in the kind of practice Larry and Rick want to establish. The latter will have to do a good job of constructing the financial and marketing analyses that demonstrate that P-H can earn at least as much money as a firm with a major share of its market outside the set-aside relationship as it can within it.

Even if the partners can demonstrate this vision of the future, they will also have to show Ed how he can protect his investment while, at the same time, giving over control of the firm to his young colleagues. It will probably be necessary for Larry and Rick to be creative in establishing baseline financial operating minimums below which Ed will be allowed to regain some amount of decision authority until the minimums are exceeded.

(Hopefully, some of the students who are exposed to the ABC/Prieto Haskell case will find themselves in positions similar to Rick's and Larry's when they get out in practice. To help them think about ownership transitions in broader terms than have been discussed here, students are encouraged to read two brief articles that appeared in *Architecture's* March 1992 issue, titled "Branching Out to New Generations," by Andrea Dean, and "Basics of Ownership Transition," by Peter Piven.)

What Happened?

The author generally tries to resist responding to this question at the end of a case discussion because, if he really knew the answer, his response would simply start off a new round of case discussion, but with insufficient information to conduct a decent analysis. However, this case prompted the writer to break with this tradition because the answer surprised him when he learned about it.

He would have predicted that Rick and Larry, as wonderfully creative as they are in real life, would never manage to gain financial control of their P-H office. He could not see how they were going to make the office sufficiently profitable to produce the kind of excess capital that would satisfy Ed Alvarez. Especially, he could not see how they could achieve economic independence while striving to enter an entirely new market. He does not know just how they succeeded in doing both of those things, but succeed they did.

The office took on a new partner with skills complementary to Rick's and Larry's, and that obviously helped in operational ways. Larry succeeded in computerizing the office, and it became a model of how to revolutionize a working organization through the effective use of technology. Project managers were not only enjoying delegation of design responsibility, but they also took on project management tasks usually performed by staff, such as client billing and payment follow-up activity. Larry reported that these innovations gave middle-level firm members a motivation to make a project work in every sense of the term because they felt as though they were running their own, small design firm.

This success story makes the author want to go back to this firm and collect data for a new case, one with enough information in it so this analysis could start all over again.

Case Study | Rose/Knox Townhouses, or Architects Build Cheap Houses for Themselves

This is a compelling case study about how three young architects acted as their own developer to create live and work spaces for themselves. Cost and design were paramount! This case reveals multiple dimensions of professional practice in action. In a single project, the architects learned about real estate development, finances, and how great design can support marketing and garner awards and publications.

DONNA KACMAR, AIA, is a Principal in the firm Architect Works, Inc., and an Assistant Professor at the Gerald D. Hines College of Architecture at the University of Houston. She received a National AIA Young Architects Award in 2004. © Donna Kacmar, AIA.

Three former architecture school classmates, now professionals, joined forces to enter first-time home ownership. The investigation focused on how three individual units might be developed within an inner-city neighborhood in Houston, Texas, using an efficient configuration of 1,600 square feet of living space per townhouse. Low-cost and low-maintenance materials prevalent in the warehouses and bungalows of the diverse neighborhood were explored.

The final solution incorporates a Galvalume-clad "living" box and a cementitious fiberboard-clad "utility" box sitting on a load-bearing concrete masonry unit (CMU) first floor. Prefabricated floor trusses, concrete-masonry firewalls, and plywood decking were left exposed to maintain a construction cost of $50.00 per square foot in 1997.

Project Process

In early Spring 1996, my apartment porch started falling apart, and I began considering other housing options. My good friend and former classmate Mary Ann was starting to look at older houses she might buy and renovate. I asked her and our mutual friend Chris if they would be interested in considering building three separate houses next to each other. After dinner in a neighborhood Cuban restaurant we agreed to proceed.

We began looking at available sites.

On weekends we would drive around and make lists of available properties, look through real-estate listings, and coordinate this search with a map of the city. We looked in close-in neighborhoods near where we all three were currently living.

As we looked at sites we drew up potential layouts on the configuration of the site bound-

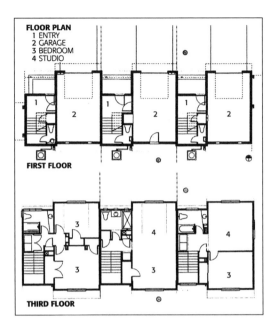

FLOOR PLAN
1 ENTRY
2 GARAGE
3 BEDROOM
4 STUDIO

FIRST FLOOR

THIRD FLOOR

Figure 3-12 Floor plans showing floors one and three, with studios, of Rose/Knox Townhouses. Courtesy of Donna Kacmar, AIA.

aries to see if that particular site configuration would work for us. We looked at square lots, double lots, lots that backed up to each other. We soon discovered that we would only be able to afford one lot and would have to build connected house units in lieu of the three freestanding houses we had originally envisioned. We looked at townhouses currently in the market and projects published in architectural publications.

As we continued our search for an appropriate site, we also began to meet with construction-loan officers and bankers. We wondered if there was a standard percentage of improvements to land costs. Since we were going to look for an institution to finance this project, we needed to make sure we were within standard ratios.

We began to narrow our search for land. We drove by sites at night, noted the location of street lights, traffic signs, access, bus routes, street activity, schools, and nearby commercial property. We went to the homeowner's association meetings in areas we were interested in and let them know we were looking for land on which to build three houses but that we were not developers.

We investigated if there were any deed restrictions or if city wastewater, water, and storm water drainage-capacity units were available. We investigated city setback requirements. We started drawing up potential building masses that accounted for any city right-of-way easement requirements.

As we refined our project budgets, we investigated city replatting requirements and talked with a civil engineer.

We finally felt comfortable enough about a site. It measured 50 × 115 feet on a corner. We then made an offer on the site and had thirty days to conduct design investigations to determine if what we wanted programmatically was feasible.

Once we closed on the site, we each felt committed to the project. We started to wonder about our relationship to each other. We investigated forming a limited partnership or other legal entity to develop this project. We understood that the project depended on all three units getting completed. What might happen if one of us could not get financing, if one of us backed out, or if one of us died during construction? While that would certainly be difficult for us to handle emotionally (and perhaps ruin our afternoon) it would also put us in a difficult place financially. Would that hold up the construction process?

We decided to each take out a life insurance policy that named the other two as beneficiaries with the amount of the construction loan determining the amount of the policy so the project could be completed.

Was this the only way to handle the situation? If something had happened to one of us would this really have provided adequate protection?

We began our design work in earnest. We met each evening after work and presented design options to each other. We discussed alternatives. It actually helped that we had very little money: Sometimes design disputes were settled by asking, "What is the cheapest way to do that?" During the design process we had a dispute about the type of masonry to use. We investigated different concrete masonry units and colored block and got prices on each type of unit. When we found out that the limestone colored, split-face block was out of our budget it settled what may have become an aesthetic argument.

We continued to work with a civil engineer and started working with a structural engineer. We wanted the structural materials to be exposed, so we were even concerned with what the wood floor trusses looked like so they could be exposed. One oversight in the review of the shop drawings led to one of the living room ceilings receiving an unplanned layer of gypsum board.

We met with potential contractors and selected one to work with so we could get pricing

feedback along the way. Often our clients requested competitive bidding for their projects in the hope that they would get the lowest price. We felt that we needed to get a good handle on the budget from the get-go, so we needed to work closely with one builder.

We worked in the evenings and on weekends trying to equally share the research, design, and drawing time.

By working with a contractor from the project's inception, we ended up with a negotiated contract for construction instead of the traditional design-bid-build mode of project delivery. What are the advantages and disadvantages of this arrangement? Under what conditions would you feel comfortable with this arrangement?

One of the three of us was a registered architect at the time. The other two were architectural interns. Who is the responsible party for the drawings? Did our individual responsibility and professional risk differ?

Once we received a preliminary design from the structural engineering consultant, made some material selections, and completed a pricing set we asked for a construction-cost estimate from our contractor. As often happens with my clients, the price came back over budget, and we had to look for ways to cut the costs. I remember from my professional practice course that the budget is a result of scope and quality and time. We needed to reduce two of those items, but we had plenty of time! We looked at all of

Figure 3-13 Preliminary exterior elevation sketch of Rose/Knox Townhouses. Courtesy of Donna Kacmar, AIA.

our material selections. In lieu of stucco, we decided to use Hardi panel. In lieu of a recessed flashing joint between the panels, we developed a batten system. Our builder told us that "you cannot afford the guy who can hang the panels straight," so the batten gave the installer some wiggle room.

We investigated other unusual materials and applications of standard materials. Doing a house for ourselves gave us the opportunity to try things out that we would not try out on our clients. Using the $1^1/_8$-inch Sturdifloor for the final finish floor was an idea we wanted to explore though we had never done it on a project. Now I can recommend it to a client with an awareness of the advantages and disadvantages of the selection.

We soon revised the drawings and material selections, signed a contract with the builder, got a building permit, and started construction.

We had weekly site meetings with all three of us and the builder. Things went smoothly, but it was a construction project after all. When the sewer connection was found to be much lower we understood another quote from pro practice class—"the owner pays." Because we had a construction loan that rolled into a permanent mortgage, any change orders would be paid by us in cash (or check). Each detail was decided by us. Where would the telephone come in to the building. I had never put that on a drawing for a client's house. When it rained for two months I understood why there are structural materials and finish materials. We wanted our plywood sub floor to be the finish floor, and therefore we could not drill a hole in it to allow the rain water to drain off the floors. Instead, we would go up there after each rain (and there were several rain storms that spring) to squeegee the water off the plywood.

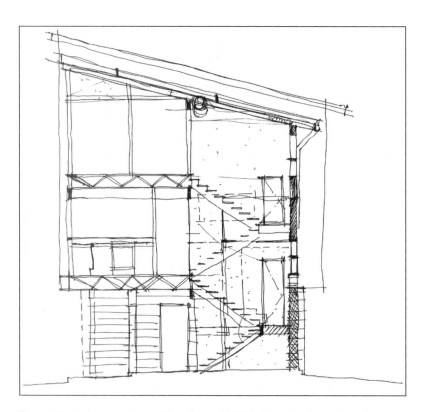

Figure 3-14 Cross-section with stairs and HVAC ducts for Rose/Knox Townhouses. Courtesy of Donna Kacmar, AIA.

The construction process also gave us more design opportunities within our prescribed allowances. For example, we designed a mailbox to fit in a CMU opening (see Figure 3-15, below). We reviewed each window order, door order, and exterior floodlight. We did all of the things that we would like to do for our clients but that the project fees usually do not allow us time to do. In this case we had no project fee, so our time was only limited by our other commitments (namely our full-time jobs). Typically in an architecture firm we do not review door orders. We want the contractor to be responsible for all ordering. Architects do not want to be liable for paying for an ordering mistake. In our case we just wanted things to move smoothly. And we were interested in each detail.

Did we take on any added risk as we reviewed the window orders? Did we assume that risk as an architect or as an owner? What type of contract should we have signed with the contractor? Can you describe an ideal contractual relationship between each of the owners?

Construction was completed almost within the six months allowed by the bank. After securing a friendly extension, we all moved in during July. Mary Ann's move-in was almost delayed due to a careless plumber leaving her shower supply open. When a worker opened up the water service, water came flowing out of her shower head. Unfortunately the drain was not plumbed in yet, so the water overflowed the tub and came down to the second and then the first

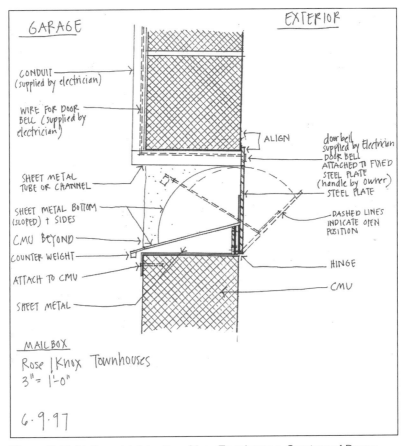

Figure 3-15 Mailbox detail for Rose/Knox Townhouses. Courtesy of Donna Kacmar, AIA.

floor. I stopped by the job site at about 7:00 P.M. and heard some noise, and when I unlocked the door, I saw water coming down her stairs. Soon we had the builder out with his towels and his shop vac. Luckily most things dried quickly and did not need to be replaced.

The project provided us with more than a place to live. We understood all of the pieces of a residential project.

We understood the difference between project cost and construction cost. Each of those soft costs has a name and is reflected in the register in my checkbook.

We developed a respect for a builder's hesitancy to use a new material or an old material in a new way. It is hard to invent.

We also had quite a bit of luck. Because we were working for architectural firms, we had vast resources and knowledge pools from which to seek advice. We knew consultants and contractors we could trust. We had friends ask us to submit our project for publications, and when we submitted our project for a design award we won. The area where we purchased our lot has changed dramatically in the last eight years. The property values have doubled. Not only did we have a great professional experience but we will also benefit financially when we sell. One of the biggest lessons has been the reminder that rewards come from informed risk-taking.

Project Information

Project Name: Rose/Knox Townhouses, Houston, Texas

Completion Date: August 1997

Architects: Donna Kacmar, AIA, 5811 Rose Street, Houston, TX 77007; Chris Craig, 5813 Rose Street, Houston, TX 77007; Mary Ann Young, 5815 Rose Street, Houston TX 77007

Project Team: Donna Kacmar, AIA Chris Craig, Mary Ann Young

Owners: Donna Kacmar, Chris Craig, Mary Ann Young

Contractor: S. Paul Rife Construction, Inc., Paul Rife, Superintendent

Structural Engineer: Matrix Structural Engineers, Peter J. Hurley, Principal

Civil Engineer: Karen Rose Engineering and Surveying, Karen Rose, Principal

Construction Budget: $90,000.00 per unit

Size: 1,600 square foot air-conditioned space per unit

Materials: Hardi-panel siding, Galvalume C-Panel siding, standard gray concrete block with "Dry Block" additive, Alenco aluminum windows, Carrier HVAC equipment

Chapter 4

Project Management

The thing that is so intriguing about project management is the variety of *people* (clients, consultants, suppliers, constructors, and staff), along with their particular agendas, that must be coordinated during the complex process of transforming a program into a building. The project manager is essentially the quarterback who, on a daily basis, organizes, directs, coordinates, monitors, and takes responsibility for the myriad tasks required to move the job toward completion in accordance with the firm's contractual obligations. Some of the general tasks of a project manager include the following (as defined by National Council of Architectural Registration Boards, the NCARB):

- Negotiate contracts with clients
- Consult with clients on project development
- Prepare and monitor project schedule
- Prepare and monitor project budget
- Review project accounting
- Document project construction time and progress
- Monitor the processing and quality of schematic, design development, and construction documents and drawings
- Administer construction contracts
- Participate in project construction progress meetings
- Prepare progress reports
- Assign and monitor project staff
- Direct and/or coordinate the work of consultants

So the project manager performs well-defined tasks while endeavoring to optimize the balance between *budget, schedule,* and *quality* requirements through all phases of a job. In sum, project management is a creative process that supports the pursuit of design excellence and the implementation of the project as intended by the architect and owner.

There are a number of popular software packages that help to generate status reports linking budget, schedule, and personnel, among other things. For example, Microsoft Project and Primavera Expedition are common tools used by architects to plan the milestones and delivery dates for a project.

A basic, commonsense, and elegant formula for project management, which incidentally is not specific to architecture, has been set forth by Alan Rudolph and Barry Posner.[1] They suggest: first plan, then manage the plan,

---

[1]"What Every Project Manager Need to Know About Project Management," *Sloan Management Review* 29, Summer (1988): 65–73.

and then continue to plan and manage, plan and manage until done. They outline four key principles for planning projects, then six principles for managing them:

Planning Projects
1. Set a clear project goal.
2. Determine the project objectives (for team members).
3. Establish checkpoints, activities, relationships, and time estimates.
4. Draw a picture of the project schedule.

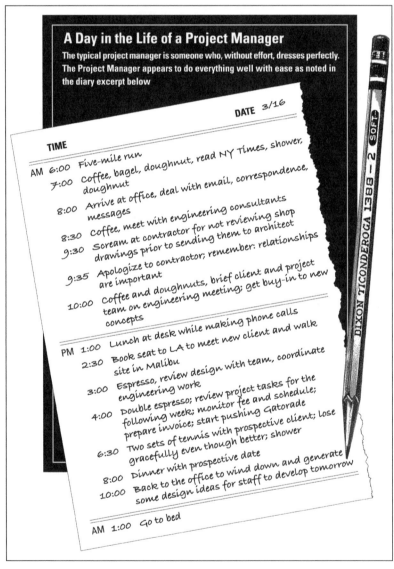

Figure 4-1 The author's take on a day in the life of a project manager.

Managing Projects

1. Direct people individually and as a project team.
2. Reinforce the commitment and excitement of the project team.
3. Keep everyone connected with the project informed.
4. Build agreements that vitalize team members.
5. Empower yourself and others on the project team.
6. Encourage risk taking and creativity.

The material in this chapter is intended to present an overview of the roles and specific strategies available to a project manager; this information can be generalized to many job situations. Martha A. O'Mara suggests, later in this chapter, that as team leader, the project manager must be able to work effectively with, and direct the efforts of, participants. O'Mara offers explicit guidance on how to work effectively in groups and touches on issues of leadership and delegation. Jeremiah Eck then talks about some seemingly common sense, "street-smart" strategies project managers should be aware of as they communicate with clients. You can't be an android and *just* perform well—there is a human component that must be considered. Eck completes his remarks with a frank discussion about cost issues. The chapter includes a special treat—a description of David Wisdom's place in Louis Kahn's office—Wisdom is perhaps one of the great role models for aspiring project managers.

Managing the Process Versus Producing the Product

An effective project manager does not need to know all the answers. A project manager focuses on managing the process and does not necessarily produce the product. That means, as a project manager, you find the right resources and people to whom you refer and delegate in order to successfully accomplish the work. Being a project manager is analogous to being a film director or orchestra conductor: you assemble and manage disparate talents to produce the vision.

Charles B. Thomsen is one of the pioneers in developing innovative methods for service and project delivery in architecture and construction, so who better to ask about the essence of project management? Predictably, Chuck very succinctly and efficiently answered my questions for the interview transcribed below, which is intended to get you thinking about *process*. Appreciating the creative potentials in the process will help the profession of architecture not just survive but flourish well into the twenty-first century. (Please see Thomsen's essay on project delivery strategy in Chapter 9, pages 289–304; it includes information on fast-track, design-build, bridging, construction management, and other contracting methods for design and construction.)

Chuck B. Thomsen is Chairman and CEO of 3D/International of Houston, Texas, and formerly President and CEO of the CRS Group, Inc. He has worked on projects in most states and in twenty-two countries, directed over thirty branch offices and more than a dozen subsidiary companies, and participated in numerous acquisitions. He is also the author of *CM: Developing, Marketing and Delivering Construction Management Services* (New York: McGraw-Hill, 1982), and *Managing Brainpower: Organizing, Measuring Performance, and Selling in Architecture, Engineering, and Construction Management Companies* (Washington, D.C.: AIA Press, 1989).

AP: What are the important elements of doing architectural project management in an artful manner?

CBT: Project managers, in architecture or any other discipline, must realize that their job is to *manage the process,* not to produce the product. They have to be process oriented. Most discussions between architects and engineers immediately turn to, "What's the building going to be made of, and how is it going to be configured?" People do not talk enough about how decisions are made, the sequence of those decisions, and what kind of information people require before they make decisions. I suppose the artful quality lies in how you actually accomplish the acts and weave together the players to produce the results. The project manager is managing a process, managing work. This is distinctly different than focusing on the product itself.

There are four big things that must be controlled: cost, schedule, quality, and contracts. Control systems have to be created for each of those four activities. And you have to control them during project definition, design, construction documents, and construction.

AP: In terms of controlling them, to what degree should a project manager rely on office conventions for running a project (the monitoring forms, time management, communications protocol, and so on) versus tailoring the approach for an individual project?

CBT: You've got to do both, don't you? I never saw a project that would fit a standard management template. But I never saw one that wouldn't benefit from the templates that have been developed in the past.

You can be as creative about the process as the product. You need to analyze the process and study it as much as the product.

AP: So you are viewing the process as a design problem in itself?

CBT: Exactly! Take the logic this way: If all work is a process, the quality of the product is going to be influenced by the quality of the process.

Faculty tell us a great deal in architecture school like, "You have an individual project; you need to think about the program, the proper expression for the purpose of the building, the context, the environment, the orientation, circulation, the scale, material, and so on"—all the factors that must be considered when you design a building. There are unique requirements to which you must respond in the course of design.

Unique requirements also exist in the process! You're not going to produce a lot of uniqueness with the same process time after time. If you have a knowledgeable client, you may have a different process than if you have a naive client. If you have a client with lots of pressures on time and money, that presents a challenge different than somebody who's got plenty of both.

I remember that soon after I got out of school, I was working for a firm that got a job to do a spec office building. The senior partner came to me and said, "Just put your dream down—design something that is your imagination of what a great looking office building would look like." I failed miserably; I couldn't begin to sit down and design an office building. The boss thought I wasn't any good. Looking back on it, I realized that putting down your dream is not how you design a building. I remember doing research on office buildings, developing a computer program that would analyze the best floor plate geometry, the optimum number of floors for the land value and configuration, and so on. Some very good office buildings came out of that, and there was some quite interesting architectural expression in those schemes that reflected responses to the issues of cost and income from income-making buildings. These designs were driven by the economics of the geometry, structure, and how you house people in a knowledge-worker environment. All this falls into place when you study the problem!

We don't do enough of this in school. Students are generally taught that the look of the thing is the principal issue, and too often the look of the thing is not derived from much genuine intellectual rigor. But you might get better results if you asked students, "What's the process you're going to use to produce this design? How are you going to research the issues? How are you going to define the form givers?"

AP: What can a student or young intern do to become a happy and effective member of a project team upon entering the workforce?

CBT: Work hard! Be a great team player. Everyone's got good ideas, but not very many people know how to work collectively to execute them. When we are able to find the people who are great workers and appreciate that architecture is a team sport, they're soon vice presidents.

If an individual focuses and works hard on trying to do an extraordinarily good job or a task that is performed better, faster, in more innovative fashion—they put their effort toward creating that unique thing—that would be more desirable than working hard to produce large quantities of average work. This is the value of quality over quantity.

AP: When you have real rapport with a client and there is a very positive emotional tone, are there times when a handshake is sufficient to make a deal and written legal specifics can dilute the feelings of mutual trust?

CBT: There are certainly times when a handshake is just fine. We often start work for clients whom we trust based on verbal agreements. But I do think that it's helpful to write down an understanding of the relationship, particularly if it's a beginning relationship. I remember many years ago putting together a joint venture with Nick Petry in Denver. We wrote a one-page agreement on how we were going to work together. Then we got another job and I wrote him a letter and said, "Let's do this one like the other one." I saw him a few days later, and he said it was fine. We wound up doing sixty projects together. Finally he sold his company to another large construction company, and there was no written agreement between us on how we would joint venture these sixty projects. My lawyer told me that if we had a written agreement that was different than the way we were working together, it would be overridden by our consistent pattern of working with each other on past projects—it would take precedence over any written agreement anyway.

However, I would never encourage anybody not to have a contract. And I would always encourage people to have a contract with a client when it's a first relationship.

AP: What practice issues should students be aware of as they engage projects in the design studio?

CBT: The big difference between school and practice is the diversity of unusual real-world issues you confront. A student is easily trained to work well within a limited amount of time, but it is far more difficult to simulate restrictions on cost, the realities of construction, the conflict of personalities in teamwork, changing technology, and how it is that the client actually acquires the product.

The great challenge is to develop project definition and translate it into a design compatible with the constraints of the real world. We architects (compared to the medical, legal, and accounting fields) learn in an isolated environment and really have a hard time with that. I think that most architecture schools are fundamentally art schools, and those issues are not really understood and therefore not taught.

Many knowledgeable architects and clients, particularly large corporations or government clients, such as the Army Corps of Engineers or the General Services Administration, would love to be invited to the schools and participate in design reviews. We're all extremely flattered when we're asked to help in this fashion. This is a large, untapped resource for both students and faculty and a great opportunity to help bridge the gap between academic and professional communities.

Making Group Projects in Studio Work for You

Thomas Fisher has said that today's building climate is not one in which "the misunderstood romantic genius is going to thrive. The task that lies ahead for the schools is how to construct curricula that go beyond romantic individualism. And the task that lies ahead for the profession is how to work in an increasingly participatory environment without simply giving in to whatever the majority wants." There is simply no doubt that architecture is, in fact, a team sport, and project managers are central to ensuring collaborative success. Moreover, there is an organizational trend toward flatter office structures—less hierarchical—as a result of computerization facilitating information sharing.

Everyone on a team has an obligation to strive for the group's success. Martha A. O'Mara elaborates below the challenges of the group process and how individuals can best contribute. William Caudill was prophetic in his book, *Architecture by Team* (New York: Van Nostrand Reinhold, 1971), where he stated, "The team is a genius."

MARTHA A. O'MARA is the author of *Strategy and Place: Managing Corporate Real Estate and Facilities for Competitive Advantage* (New York: The Free Press, 1999). She lectures in executive education at the Harvard Design School, where she taught real estate and urban design for eight years. She received a PhD in organizational behavior from Harvard University.

The lone student hunched over a drawing table in glorious solitude is frequently used as the defining image in design-school catalogs. The one-on-one interaction between student and studio critic is often considered the most essential element of a design education. However, once in practice, much of a designer's work is collaborative. Today, many architects spend as much or more time working in project teams as they do working alone at the drawing board or CAD station. All but the simplest projects typically involve several designers collaborating together in concert with the client, the developer or user, the builder, and the applicable public agencies. Business organizations are also more frequently using teams to solve complex problems because teams can perform better and faster than the traditional divisions of labor through a hierarchy or in specialist departments.[2] The ability to work effectively in a team is now critical to career success. It makes sense that students graduate from design school with the ability to work well in teams.

The Challenge of Group Projects

The challenge facing educators in the design professions is how to best prepare students for professional practice by replicating the collaborative conditions of practice within the artificial confines of a semester-long studio. This essay discusses the use of group projects in design school and offers some tips, based upon my experience in working with student teams, for getting the most out of your projects. The purpose is to help you not only survive your next group project but to help you identify ways to make the most of it and to become better prepared for professional practice.

Many instructors use groups in their studios without having the development of practice skills as a deliberate goal. Groups may be required because many of the most realistic design problems are complex and beyond the ability of a single student to tackle in a few short months. Some sort of division of labor in the studio or classroom is essential. In a group format, the challenges facing the student are to hone professional practice skills while further developing his or her individual analytic and design

---

[2]The effectiveness of teams is well documented by Jon R. Katzenbach and Douglas K. Smith in *The Wisdom of Teams.* (Boston, Mass.: Harvard Business School Press, 1993).

skills. The students endeavor to maximize their learning from the studio while minimizing the pain and suffering frequently attributed to group projects. It is important to note that, while the terms "group" and "team" are often used interchangeably, the word "team" implies a higher degree of collaboration and interdependence that is often achieved only after experience and effort. All teams are groups, but not all groups are teams.

Group Process Issues for Both Students and Instructors: The Harvard GSD Experience

As a studio instructor teaching complex urban development studios at Harvard's Graduate School of Design (GSD), I found myself wondering if there were better ways to prepare our students for collaborative work. Is there a place and a purpose for group work in the design studio? I decided to use our own students' experiences working on group studio projects to provide some insight into these questions. Since 1971, GSD students have worked in studio teams examining the development potential of actual urban and green-field sites, often with graduate students from Harvard's schools of business, law, and government. Both the urban design and landscape architecture departments have presented such studios. In an effort to closely emulate professional practice, students work with a developable site and a real client, often a public agency or land owner, who underwrites the studio's expenses. The complexity and scale of development-studio problems necessitate a collaborative effort; so students work in teams of three to five people, mixing degree programs, backgrounds, and experience. Their final product is similar to a formal development proposal and includes: a site plan; schematic design drawings; models and renderings; market research and marketing plans; pro-forma spreadsheets, showing costs, income, and overall return on investment projections; and a financing proposal. Sponsors assume a "client" role and brief the students and comment on their proposals.

When I began coteaching the development studio, the conventional wisdom I heard around the school was that students viewed the development studio teams as a necessary evil—a nuisance to be endured in an otherwise interesting studio. Drawing upon my background in management and organizational behavior, I wondered if this attitude were endemic or if the students were simply realizing what the people working in organizations already knew—group work can be difficult. Instead, my coinstructors and I decided to present the group work experience in a different light;[3] it is not an inevitable unpleasantness but rather a critical element of the development studio pedagogy. After all, part of learning about development *is* learning about interdisciplinary teamwork.

In past development studios, students were put into teams in a variety of ways and then the "group process" issues were largely ignored for the rest of the semester. Past instructors usually felt it was up to the teams to

---

[3]Over the years I have had the privilege to work with Studio Critics Richard Graf, Miltos Catomeris, and Leland Cott, all of whom actively supported this research.

work out their own problems and were uncomfortable getting directly involved in group process issues. We started by making learning about teamwork an important objective of the studio and directly addressed the peculiarities of group dynamics through discussions and exercises.

I also wanted to get a better picture of what students were actually experiencing, so in two recent studios that I did not teach I distributed anonymous questionnaires covering three points in the semester: at the beginning, to understand initial expectations; at the midterm review point, to see how the teams were progressing; and at the end of the semester, to assess their satisfaction. The comments from these students greatly influenced the "Lessons Learned" discussion below.

Deliberating the Embracing of "Group Work"

Our approach to the studio's format drew upon a model of successful group process based on the research of Harvard professor Richard Hackman.[4] Rather than a "touchy-feely" approach, focusing on the internal dynamics of a group's interaction, Hackman highlights the importance of external factors influencing group performance; these include the reward system, the skill and knowledge of the team members, and the resources available to the team. This meant that, as instructors, we needed to make the studio's performance criteria clear and achievable, to compose the groups with the right mix of skills and experience, and to provide the students with the necessary instruction and information.

Getting to Know Each Other

We also realized that we could more fully exploit the different modes of learning present in the development studio format. The concept of "learning styles" recognizes that people have different preferences for how they learn and approach solving problems. Individuals vary according to their emphases on either abstract conceptualization or concrete experience with the real world and on their preferences for reflective observation versus active experimentation. These orientations form four different learning types: *convergers* prefer technical tasks that apply theory; *divergers* prefer to observe action and reflect on a range of points of view; *assimilators* are most attracted to abstract ideas and concepts; and *accommodators* learn from hands-on experiences with people. These learning types, defined over the years by McBer and Company, a Boston-based organizational consulting firm, can be diagnosed through a simple questionnaire. The students discussed their learning types with each other in studio and used this information as a way to begin sharing their expectations and goals. By becoming more aware of the different ways people prefer to learn and, therefore, the types of tasks they gravitate toward or avoid, we helped open up communication within the teams so they could anticipate potential areas of conflict early on. Rather than resist each other's differences, we encouraged the

---

[4]See Richard J. Hackman, ed., *Groups That Work (and Those That Don't)* (San Francisco, Calif.: Jossey-Bass, 1990).

students to use those differences to approach more creatively both their work process and the studio problem.

Other steps were taken to build awareness and communication skills in the studio. Since it is a natural tendency for all groups to pay far more attention to the product of their work—"the what"—than to the process by which they work together—"the how"—we made process an explicit activity. Early in the semester we held a discussion on group process and suggested tactics for increasing communication. We encouraged students to talk about process throughout the course of the studio. In the first weeks, students got to know each other better. Dinner at an instructor's home, field trips, and experiential learning exercises promoting group interaction all helped the students to become more cohesive. We did not form teams until a few weeks into the semester. Although the instructors put the teams together, students could confidentially request not to work with a particular individual. In actuality, students rarely make such a request.

Of course, any sorts of different team-building activities, whether formal or informal, can be used. The critical element is that improving the group process is a clearly recognized task in the studio. It should be given both time and attention regularly throughout the semester.

Performance Evaluation

Part of Hackman's perspective on groups is that a satisfactory product outcome is only one indicator of a group's success. A successful group experience also builds technical skills, enables members to work better together in the future, and contributes to individual personal growth. We evaluated a student's performance in the studio, not only on the quality of the team's development proposal but on the level of cross-disciplinary collaboration evident within their team. Although the tendency is for students to gravitate toward those tasks where they feel most competent, we encourage designers to "run the numbers" and nondesigners to lend a hand building models and producing site documents. We try to recognize and reward that behavior.

Lessons Learned

Based upon five years of either teaching or observing group projects in the studio, as well as reviewing the management literature on group process, I've compiled some basic guidelines for deriving the most from the group project experience in design school. They include comments made by students on the questionnaires.

- *Know yourself.* What are your personal learning priorities and expectations? How can these be made to best fit with the group's task and the other members' goals? Establish clear goals together.

It is difficult to establish what you expect of others unless you are in touch with your own expectations. What do you personally want to get out of this particular project? If you want to learn new skills, you will want to work on parts of the problem that are new to you. If putting your existing skills to the test is a greater priority, you will want to emphasize your special interests. Are you looking to build your portfolio? If so, you will be especially concerned about the appearance of the final presentation. By being in better touch with your own priorities, you may be more willing to take on a larger share of the load at times without feeling resentful or pulling back when others need more time.

Listen to what others want. Where is there common ground? Make sure that learning, rather than merely doing, is the objective. Students with positive group experiences noted:

> "What contributes most to success is the willingness of people to support, stand in for, and encourage other members—to have a common respect and an ability to listen."

> "Everyone understands their responsibilities and is willing to commit."

> "Our group worked well because we had a clear goal."

> Respect your differences:

> "The team members with less professional experience wanted to spend more time exploring alternatives."

> It's also important to remember that: "Different perspectives increase the learning."

- *Communicate your expectations of each other clearly.* Realize that different people will make differing levels of commitment. Get this issue out in the open early.

The most common complaint about group projects is that people do not equally share the burden of work. In reality, it is inevitable that members of your group will have different levels of commitment to the project. For some, this may be their dream project, and they may want to devote most of their time to it. For others, it may be just another course requirement to get out of the way. Some people have greater personal pressures on their time. One person may be working part-time to pay for school, and another may have young children and not be able to work in the evenings. A great deal of resentment can build if one or two people feel they are unfairly carrying the workload of others. However, if people make their levels of commitment explicit at the beginning of the project, the group can take steps to make the most of each person's available time and talents. The critical point here is to be open about your expectations of each other and flexible about how you work together.

- *Process counts—make it a priority.* Have strategies in place for dividing up work, for bringing ideas together, and for making decisions.

Set time aside at the beginning and periodically throughout the studio to discuss how the process is working. How are you doing as a team? Get help on setting up corrective procedures if the process breaks down.

Although it is a natural tendency to divide up the work according to what people do best, this may not contribute to the most learning in the studio so be open to other approaches. If you have well-established goals and expectations, it will be easier to assign tasks. One team I observed made each person responsible for a certain part of the analysis and then also assigned each person the task of serving as a "critic" for another part of the work. This increased the flow of ideas in the studio, reduced the amount of time needed to review ideas with the entire group at once, and let members experience more than just one part of the project. This tactic can be a good way to work with differing levels of experience in the team—the less experienced person can take the first crack at the problem and the more experienced one can then help critique and refine the approach. Other groups shifted responsibilities throughout the semester so that everyone got some experience with different parts of the problem.

The biggest stumbling block in the studio is one that differs greatly from practice. As one student explained: "In practice there is someone being paid to make the final decision. There is no final authority in a student-run group." Therefore, an agreed-upon process for making key decisions is needed. The ability to make a decision, any decision, will often result in a better outcome than in trying to keep everyone happy through an incomplete resolution. Remember that reaching consensus does not require total agreement. Consensus means that everyone agrees to support the decision, even if they would personally choose a different solution.

The issue of group "leadership" is often sticky. On the one hand, the studio needs a central point of coordination. On the other hand, since all are supposed to be peers, it can be difficult or uncomfortable to acknowledge someone as being the leader of the group. As one student noted, "We're of the same age group with similar training. No one had the obvious experience to lead the group." Some groups find it helpful to assign certain leadership responsibilities to particular members. For example, one person might be in charge of the final "look" of the presentation and another for coordinating report preparation. Remember that there are several ways to lead. The person at the front of the room writing ideas on the board may be less of a leader than someone who thoughtfully reflects upon the comments others are making and helps find synthesis. It is only natural for the most experienced or talented students to informally lead at times and many students enjoy learning from their peers. Try to "check your ego at the door," and be open to the talent of others.

- *Realize it takes time to build a team.*

You won't get it all working well right from the start. Someone noted, "It takes time for a team partnership to form. You get thrown in with people you don't know and it takes a while for you to learn what they can do." Another said, "It took time to understand different group members' methods of working."

It is helpful to review how well you are working together at the end of every major group meeting. This doesn't have to be arduous. Such simple questions as "What is working well about our process together?" or "What do we need to do a better job?" can open up communication. Search for solutions, not scapegoats.

- *Generate documentation early and often.* Leave a "paper trail."

As a project moves along, it can be difficult to remember why a particular decision was made. Keeping good records of what work has been completed and what decisions have been made aids communication and helps avoid revisiting old issues. This documentation will also make pulling together your final presentation a lot easier at a time when people are exhausted and nerves are frayed.

Work schedules are especially helpful. It is okay to change the schedule as your understanding of the project changes, but make sure you understand why you are changing it. If you think someone is not carrying through on his or her commitment, catch it early. You'll help avoid resentment and not get stuck at the last minute with a critical piece of work incomplete. One group mentioned that, "We coordinated schedules, having some people carry more of the load at certain times."

- *Be open about your differences.* Remember, you are not "friends," you are "colleagues" in this project. Don't avoid confrontation in order to "keep the peace"—it won't.

For many team members, their personal relationships with each other will live on long after the project is over. This can make conflict even more uncomfortable. In one case, "problems arose because we all knew each other and wanted to be friends." Again, communication is the key. One student attributed his successful group experience to open communication: "We were forthright in expressing individual opinions and ideas while respecting those of others. We resolved problems at one sitting, not letting problems linger."

Ideological differences were often cited as barriers to effective teamwork in the studio. Design school is a time when aesthetic values are most passionately felt and some matters of style and form are difficult to compromise. This is a time when your studio instructor can help, not as a referee between warring factions but as a source of insight. Rarely in the "real world" does a designer's vision get realized in its purest form—now is the time to learn the fine arts of collaboration and compromise.

- *Remind yourselves of the larger goals you have established.* From my perspective, learning is as important as doing.

You will never have it all your own way in a group project. We learn more about our own beliefs when they are challenged. When others question our assumptions, it makes us think through the problem harder. Group projects help us realize that we can also learn not just by doing new things but by teaching others about what we already know. A student with more work experience than others on her team understood the need to pull back at times: "I decided school should be a learning experience for the team members, not a situation of having the most qualified person do a job. You have to take assigned team members as they are and work from there. Letting the team members learn in a loose environment created inefficiencies in producing the end product. However the studio product is transitory, and hopefully the learning experience will be lasting."

In the end, keeping in mind your overall learning objectives will make those momentary frustrations easier to manage and will better prepare you to become an effective, articulate practitioner.

Client Relations: Of Timing and Schmoozing

Developing and maintaining good relationships are crucial to mastery of project management. A fundamental truth about success in project management has to do with the quality of personal relationships among the client, stakeholders, consultants, design team members, and constructors—everyone with whom you come into contact on the project. This may sound self-evident and common sense, but establishing rapport, developing trust, and maintaining respect and integrity are characteristic of the best project managers. High-quality relationships along with high-quality work will yield enormous benefits perhaps not even imagined: a great project, repeat work, referrals, and the ability to resolve disputes expeditiously.

Good timing combined with the ability to schmooze with clients and other industry players is all part of being a successful architect—and an excellent project manager. You must exercise common sense in your relationships with people! I know this sounds obvious and simplistic, but read Jeremiah Eck's experiences carefully—they will help to illuminate this underrated and surprisingly ignored aspect of professional practice.

JEREMIAH ECK, FAIA, is a principal of Jeremiah Eck Architects, Inc. in Boston, Massachusetts. He is a former lecturer in architecture at the Harvard Design School, a landscape painter, and author of The Distinctive Home (Newtown, Conn.: The Taunton Press, 2003).

A lot of what we do in life is, as the saying goes, about timing. Over many years of practice in a small architectural firm, I've found timing to be a particularly important part of how I conduct my practice. I might even go so far as to say that it is even more important in a small practice than it is in a larger one, because timing issues are more critical to a fewer number of people who are accountable to the design and building process. As a result, a sense of timing should be very finely tuned.

For a student of design, time is usually well defined. You're given a defined project within a defined period. For the most part, you are solely responsible for the execution of the design, production, and presentation of the drawings. How you time the process is, with the exception of the start and finish point, yours to determine. But in a small practice, the number of variables that may influence a project can vary both in number and occurrence, and how you handle their timing can often determine whether a project will succeed or fail.

I should say that I'm using a rather broad definition of timing. What I mean is adjusting any action or reaction that is part of keeping a project going—from getting the job through construction. In another sense, it means having good street smarts—being wily and aware all the time. You can make the right call to the right client on a particularly overcast and gloomy day, and I would define that as bad timing. You can show your knowledge of a few technical details during an otherwise philosophical design discussion with a client, and I would call that good timing. Basically my definition means *saying or doing the best thing at the best time.* I would even go farther and say it's creating the right thing to say or do at the right time. Good timing means you have a good imagination; it doesn't mean you just know the right thing to say or do. Many people know what that's all about, but they don't know how to get a job or keep it going once they've gotten it.

I have fond memories of a particular incident that illustrates what I mean. I was once asked by a couple to do a renovation of their top floor apartment in Cambridge, Massachusetts. After looking at the job, I realized it was too small and recommended a former employee of mine to do the job. She did the project for them and they were quite pleased. So pleased in fact that they asked me back for some design consulting on a completely different job. This time I took the job, thinking I could get in and out completely without the normal hassles that often make small jobs unprofitable. What I didn't know at the time was that they were about to get a divorce, and as a result of their disengagement, I never got paid for my work. I sent a couple of friendly, professional sounding letters over the next few months, but to no avail. Finally I wrote it off to experience; it wasn't enough money to really get excited about anyway. I figured they were having problems enough of their own, and I would probably get paid someday. Almost a year went by and no word. Then one day I got a call from the ex-wife. I was at first tempted not to take the call or to say something nasty when I picked up the phone, but I decided not to. She was quite civil on the phone, recognizing that she/they was/were long past due and would do what she could to make good the debt. And oh, by the way, she enjoyed working with me, appreciated my professional patience, was on the board of trustees at a local small college and had recommended me to the president to design their new fine arts center. Within two weeks, I had gotten that job, and it turned out to be one of the best jobs—and fees—I had ever gotten. Incidentally, she/they never did pay me, but who cares?

I consider that story to be one of timing. The absolutely right thing to do would have been to keep demanding the money owed, even to take the clients to small claims court. Or the right thing to say, when she called, would have been, "I've waited long enough; where is my money, you irresponsible client!" But I didn't do either. Instead, I first used my good common sense, trying to recognize their situation by not constantly demanding payment. Second, when the ex-wife called, I decided to let her talk for a while. Both of those actions fall under my definition of timing, or put another way, having street smarts.

Good timing means you know how to adjust to the ever-changing circumstances that surround a practice. In any one day, I can be told I've won a great job or lost another one, be praised by a happy client or yelled at by an unhappy contractor. I can be on a job site with mud on my shoes early in the morning and in a downtown conference room in the afternoon, talking flashing details on the site and philosophy in the conference room or,

Figure 4-2 The Fine Arts Center. Photo courtesy of Jeremiah Eck Architects Inc.

for that matter, vice versa. The point is that to have a successful practice you need to be able to adjust, to gauge your timing in a creative fashion.

Timing is not always reactive. In fact, in some ways the most creative timing is proactive—knowing when to act. I often call many of my clients on high-pressure weather days. Normally everyone feels better when the weather is great. So I take advantage of that fact by associating with my clients on such days. If it's the weekend and I'm driving by a site, I may drop by to say hello, or if it is after hours I may call a client at home, letting them know subtly that I am in the office. I may not be working on their job, but they often think I am.

One of the most important project issues regarding timing is momentum. Project momentum often involves proactive timing. In my experience, no project just goes along by itself with you and the other participants in the project conferring or acting at just the right time. A project takes constant attention, or good timing, to help move it along. I'm convinced that the major reason most of our designed projects get built is that we know how to keep the project momentum going, how to satisfy the various needs of all the parties each step of the way. Examples abound: Knowing when to insist on a design point of view to a client is one of the most obvious. But not so obvious is knowing when to give out good or bad news to either client or contractor, knowing when to insist that the contractor change something to comply fully with the drawings, or even knowing when to send out invoices as they relate to the client's perception of what has been done.

Cost Issues for Small Projects

Very much related to project momentum, and probably the most troublesome project issue of all for any office, and one that requires impeccable timing, is cost control. Cost estimating, especially for small jobs, is difficult at best. There isn't enough money in any fee on small jobs to afford a professional estimator, and my experience has shown that relying on contractors' preliminary estimates can often be misleading. As the saying goes, I'd be a rich man if I had a quarter for every time a contractor told me, looking over my preliminary drawings, that there wasn't enough detail to give an accurate price, only to insist after construction documents were complete that the reason their final price was so much higher than their preliminary price was because my drawings had so much detail in them!

The point is that estimating for small jobs is not really a science and relaying project cost information to an owner is an art requiring good timing. Obviously, you want the owner's imagination to flow freely in the early stages of the design project, and you don't want to inhibit the client's excitement with constant reminders of what the likely cost might be. We handle the problem through a cost-averaging process that includes a number of likely cost inputs, including various contractor estimates and our own past experience estimating. There are a number of advantages to this approach. Most important, it doesn't cut the owner's imagination off at the knees early on in the design process. But it does help all involved to be more realistic in the preliminary design phase rather than waiting until final bidding at the conclusion of construction documents to see if design expectations match price expectations. This approach also engages the owner in the estimating process, making him or her aware early on that price is a big part of design. I feel our pricing process is about timing. If you get one high preliminary bid in, do you call the client right away without knowing what the other estimates are? No, that's bad timing. But do you call the client right away if you get a low bid in? The answer is probably yes. After all, when design and price expectation match, you have a happy client. But my point about timing is that, if they don't match, reflect a bit first and determine when it might be best to give out the information. I'm not suggesting that you ever withhold pricing information, but that you use the information at the right time in an effort to keep project momentum on track.

As I mentioned earlier, I think such timing is particularly important in a small practice. Usually, all the people involved in small projects do, or will, get to know each other quite well. It's not a cliché to say that the architect is a conductor of sorts, choosing when to up the tempo or soften the sound. *If you see yourself merely as an expert on design or construction, you'll never have a fully successful practice.* You have to see yourself as a facilitator—a facilitator with impeccable timing.

Designing Your Time

Typically in architecture school, bad work habits become ingrained. The macho stay-up-all-night mentality is valued by students and actually viewed as a badge of honor. This habit may lead to terrible time-management practices in the real world.

There is no question that it takes a long time to design a building thoughtfully. For many of us, the creative process is stimulating, boring, engaging, tortured, filled with self-doubt, and satisfying in varying degrees and sequences, depending on the particular project and frame of mind. Because creativity is so idiosyncratic and often quirky, it may be very difficult to manipulate all the variables and forces toward planned inspiration. But plan you must to promote, to the extent possible, balanced, healthy, stress-free, and productive professional and personal experiences.

Consider time management as a design problem, as management expert Nancy Greiff explains in the next essay. Baby steps! If at first things seem overwhelming, just chip away one small step at a time. (And don't forget to take a running jump at that first step.)

NANCY GREIFF, PhD, owns Positive Resolutions, an Albuquerque, New Mexico–based training and consulting business specializing in people skills for the workplace. She enjoys helping client organizations with negotiation, win-win conflict resolution, customer service, and time management. Formerly a professor at Cornell University, Dr. Greiff now leads events and training programs nationwide. © Nancy Greiff.

One of the greatest ironies of professional training is that we are taught a vast array of complex skills but not how to manage our time so that we can use these skills effectively! This short essay provides tips for some of the most common time challenges at work and at home.

The Difference Between Efficiency and Effectiveness

You can be very efficient at completing tasks before you, but if these tasks do not contribute to the career and the life you want, then you are not using your time *effectively*. It is possible to be very good at doing the wrong things! Here is a wonderful story that highlights the difference between efficiency and effectiveness.

> A team of managers was supervising a crew building a road through a jungle. The crew was working steadily, clearing trees and brush, grading the road, installing drainage—doing all the tasks necessary to build a good road. The road looked to be a great success.
>
> Then the project leader arrived and climbed up a tree to get an overview. After surveying the activity below, he called down to the managers, "Wrong jungle!"
>
> The managers, undaunted, called back to the leader, "Shut up; we're making progress!" (Adapted from *First Things First*, Stephen R. Covey, A. Roger Merrill, and Rebecca R. Merrill [New York: Simon & Schuster, 1994.])

Sometimes we are so caught up in the heady feeling of getting things done efficiently that we do not ask ourselves if these things are leading us in the right direction. *Efficiency* is about building a road with a minimum of wasted resources, such as time, effort, and materials. *Effectiveness* is about building a road through the right jungle!

To be effective, figure out—and write down—your long-term goals. This may require some careful soul-searching, as well as discussion with partners in your plans (your spouse or significant other, your boss). Then make sure that each day includes actions directly relevant to these goals. Study that state-of-the-art building material you would like to be using in your designs. Play with your kids. "Now" is the only time you have. "Later" never comes.

A good way to head in the right direction is to ask yourself: "What are three things I could do today (or this week, month, or year) that would most benefit my organization (or career, work group, or project)?" This will help you set priorities and act on them.

Ask yourself frequently, "What is the best use of my time right now?" If the answer is something other than what you find yourself doing, consider switching to the more important task.

Create Goals That Are Specific and Meaningful

To use time more effectively, set specific, measurable goals and create an action plan to achieve those goals. Vague and ill-defined New Year's resolutions, for example, tend to fade away into the haze of good intentions. "Get in shape this year" is not specific and measurable. Even, "Go to the gym three times a week" is too vague. Go to the gym and do what? "Swim a half-mile three times a week" is an example of a specific and measurable goal.

Once you have set specific and measurable goals, you can identify the tasks necessary to accomplish them. Then decide the order in which these tasks should be done and what resources are needed. Set reasonable deadlines. For example, if you want to build your family vacation home in the mountains, first set a time frame; otherwise, dreams remain in the future and fail to become present realities. Then determine how much money you must save, where you want to build, and so on.

Keep your action plan in a visible place, not tucked away. Believe it or not, in the daily crush of small tasks, you can forget to move toward your most important goals.

At the end of each day, take a few minutes to organize your desk and lay out your top-priority task for the next day. This will give you a "jump start" in the morning and will encourage you to do important things first. Starting the day with the most important task will give you a feeling of success and progress and eliminate that feeling of something unfinished hanging over your head.

Resist the Path of Least Resistance

Sometimes the really important things seem too overwhelming, so we take the path of least resistance. We spend time doing things we know are not very important but that give us the illusion that we are in control.

It *is* satisfying to cross items off the list. The trick is to divide important tasks into small blocks and use those as the easy-to-handle items. That way you make progress on the big tasks. It is so much easier to get started if the task before you does not seem huge and daunting.

Interrupt the Vicious Cycle of Interruptions

When asked to name their most frustrating time-management problems at work, most people mention interruptions. Even coworkers who make their desk their "second home" probably feel that interruptions are a big problem for them too.

People are right in feeling that interruptions often waste time. On average, you can finish three times as much work in a stretch of uninterrupted time as you can in the same period of time with interruptions. In other words, a half-hour of uninterrupted time is equivalent to an hour and a half of stop-and-start work.

The trick to controlling interruptions is to understand that everyone at work feels that the day gets too chopped up to make a concentrated effort. Enlist your coworkers' help, even your boss's help, in implementing the following suggestions:

- Schedule "closed-door" time, where you can only be disturbed for genuine emergencies. If you have a door, close it and put a sign on the door with some message such as, "Back at 10 AM." Even if your workspace does not literally have a door, you can do this simply by letting others know that this is your uninterrupted time, and you will be available both before and after this time.
- Determine what your peak energy time is, and make this your closed-door time. Do high-priority work during your most alert times.
- During closed-door time, let voice mail pick up the telephone. If your job depends heavily on telephone contact, it will help if you change your voice mail message during closed-door time to let people know when you will be returning calls. "Hello, this is John Smith. I will be in a meeting between 9 and 10 AM today and will be returning voice messages from 10:15 to 11:30 AM. I would like to speak with you, so please leave a message." Most people care more about knowing when they will speak with you than they care about doing so now.
- Encourage others to treat themselves to closed-door time as well, and respect their time. This gives them a great incentive to leave you alone during *your* no-interruptions time. With bosses, it helps to cite the "3-to-1" rule—"I know it is difficult not to have access to me for that hour in the morning, but it means I can finish the project you gave me three times faster!"
- Understand that you may be the chief interrupter of your own work. Perhaps you are scheduling your most important projects in "residual time" when you do not have a meeting or some other activity scheduled. Instead, make appointments with yourself to work on big projects. Write these in your calendar, and treat them as you would

treat an appointment with an important client or with your boss. Schedule other things that come up around them, just as you would with any other important commitment.

- Set time limits on less important work that interrupts progress toward your major goals. Defer or shorten low-priority or low-value tasks. For example, do not read your junk mail.
- Minimize self-interrupting by scheduling similar tasks at the same time. Switching mental gears takes time. Return telephone calls all at once, write memos in a chunk of time devoted to that, and so on.

"Tickle" Your Papers

"If we're moving toward the paperless office, how come I still cannot see the top of my desk?"

Along with interruptions, most people name organizing paperwork as a large time robber. Many people create piles of paper, little by little. You might think, "If I don't leave this memo about submitting my budget request where I can see it, I'll forget to do it before the deadline." The trouble with this approach is that each reminder is soon covered by the next must-see item, again and again, until you find yourself in a maze of paper.

The solution is a tickler file. A tickler file is a series of 43 folders, the first 31 of which are labeled 1 through 31, and the last twelve of which are labeled with the names of the months. Paper that needs to be saved because some action will be required on your part goes into the tickler file. So, if you receive an item on April 10 that you will not use until April 20 (directions to an April 20th meeting, for example), put it in the folder labeled "20." If you receive an item on April 10 that only becomes important in June, place it in the June folder. At the end of May, take out the June folder and arrange the accumulated items into the appropriate "1" through "30" folders.

If today is April 10, then at the end of the day take the "11" folder out of the filing cabinet and place it front and center on your pile-free desk. All the pieces of mail and other papers you'll need for the next day will then be waiting when you arrive at work the next morning.

Here are a few other simple tips:

- Always refile what you take out, and create new files for new items.
- Process mail on a daily basis. Incoming paper goes into one of three places:
  1. Your filing cabinet, if it is important enough to keep but does not require action.
  2. Your tickler file, if it is an action item.
  3. The trash. The trash is a great place to put paper. Be honest with yourself about all those things you save because you'll get to them "someday."
- Clean out files as you use them. Cull outdated items while you're using the file. Then you won't have to clean your files because they no longer fit in your cabinet! And your mind will be working much more

effectively and efficiently than it would if you have to do many files at once.

- To vanquish existing piles of paper, just process five to ten pieces a day. Before long, your backlog will be gone.

Defeat Defeatism

If you use even a few of these tips, life really will become easier. But we all fight against years of habit, and we fear that we will not have the energy or discipline to change. A natural tendency is to conjure up all the reasons why a new strategy will not work (others will not cooperate, and so on). Remember that even if a new strategy does not solve the problem completely, any improvement *is* improvement. You may reduce unwanted interruptions by only one-third at first, but even one-third means that life is better. You now have one-third more time to concentrate on major projects—or even play with the kids.

Finally, be sure to congratulate yourself for changing your use of time! And enjoy the results!

Experimental Drawing—Drawing to Steal

"Good artists borrow, great artists steal." — T. S. Eliot

JEAN PIKE is an architect and artist who teaches drawing and architectural design at the Pratt Institute and the New Jersey Institute of Technology. She received a master of architecture degree from Yale University.

In the professional world, where creativity and innovation are valued commodities, it is important to stay fresh and keep looking. Keeping up with what is currently being done in one's field, visiting and inhabiting great buildings, asking questions about how their designs are relevant to contemporary architecture—or not—and looking at the past through new eyes can provide fertile territory for invention in architecture. Drawing is a vehicle for seeing, committing to memory what one sees, and finding possibilities for transformation that can eventually make a work observed become a vision that anticipates.

The drawing shown in Figure 4-3 is a fantasy of what might happen if the inscribed imagined space of a wall-painting at the House of Venus Marina at Pompeii became three-dimensional space and collided with the actual architecture. It is a study of idealized architecture in counterpoint with what literally exists. The question then hangs as to how the design of different dimensional planes might affect one another, creating a new experiential whole, and how this might occur in contemporary practice.

In drawing there are rules, but there also exists the terrain for experimentation that could lead to new insights and possibilities in creative work. What is important is to make one's drawing, one's way of seeing, and the thing that is drawn, one's own.

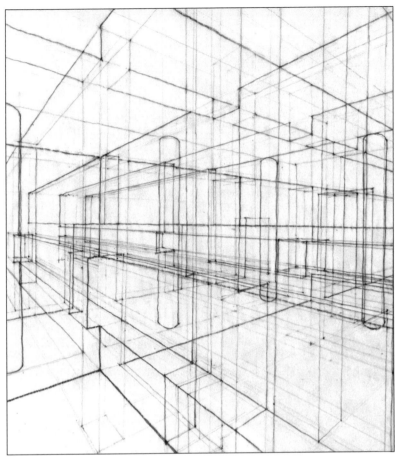

Figure 4-3 Courtyard at the House of Venus Marina, Pompeii, pencil on tracing paper, 2004, Jean Pike. Courtesy of Jean Pike.

The Ultimate Manager: The Role of Wisdom in Louis Kahn's Office

The process of design continues until the building is occupied by the users. Of course, the focus of design changes scale—detailing and coordination become more relevant as construction documents are developed. Unfortunately, as has been alluded to, and noted previously, this production end of practice has an unfounded reputation (as Michael Borowski indicates so well, below) of being subservient to conceptual design. It must not be regarded as any less creative or artful; it just has a very different focus. David Wisdom was one of those people dedicated to the production phase; his role was clearly critical in the successful completion of projects in Louis Kahn's office, and his work underscores the importance of complementary (and overlapping) strengths on the execution of complex building projects.

MICHAEL BOROWSKI is a practicing architect in Albuquerque, New Mexico. He received a Master of Architecture from the Harvard University Graduate School of Design in 1982 and has taught at Arizona State University and the University of New Mexico. Mr. Borowski would like to thank Henry Wilcots and Anant Raje for sharing with him their experiences working with David Wisdom in Louis Kahn's office. Their insights into the work produced there helped him prepare this profile. © Michael Borowski.

Louis Kahn was a man of tremendous vision. However, the process of transforming that vision into architecture was a complicated one, and he needed the help of others for its realization. Although much has been written about Kahn's work, little has been said about the role that David Wisdom played in the production of that body of work. How does Wisdom figure in that achievement and what was his contribution?

David Wisdom passed away in January 1996 as a storm moved into Philadelphia, blanketing the city with a heavy layer of snow. When news of his death reached those who had worked with him in Kahn's office, they expressed their grief at such a significant loss. The word that came to many lips, the word that perhaps best described David Wisdom, was "mentor." It seems that this shy, quiet, unassuming gentleman, who was not one to pat his own back, had been a mentor to many. Anant Raje wrote from India saying, "It is sad news that Dave Wisdom passed away. I was extremely grieved. I had learned a lot from him. He was sympathetic, friendly, and undoubtedly a strong prop in Kahn's office! It wasn't an easy job to put Kahn's ideas and concepts into working drawings."

Born April 8, 1906 in Media, Pennsylvania, David Wisdom became associated with buildings through his father, who managed commercial real estate. While in his teens, he worked after school as an office boy for Stewardson & Page in Philadelphia. Word has it that the architects there saw potential in young David, and they encouraged him to go to college and become an architect. Following their advice, Wisdom went to the University of Pennsylvania, where he received a Bachelor of Architecture in 1931. After graduation, he worked for a number of architectural firms in both Pennsylvania and New Jersey. Then in 1943 he took a job with Oscar Stonorov and Louis Kahn. After Stonorov and Kahn ended their partnership in 1947, he continued to work with Kahn and was associated with him until Kahn died in March 1974.

Although there were no titles in Kahn's office, Wisdom was the old-time classic "chief draftsman," and no doubt at all, he was a major force and presence there. If Kahn was the soul of the office, then Wisdom was its heart. He made it tick. He kept it running. With Kahn's busy teaching and lecture schedule, the office needed a steady cornerstone, and the literal fact of Wisdom being there provided it. He began to play this role in 1950, when Kahn was at the American Academy in Rome for three months and Wisdom was left to help run the office. According to Henry Wilcots, a long-time colleague of both Kahn and Wisdom,

> Dave *was* the office. Of course everyone knew that there was only one architect in the office, and that was Lou. Yet, Lou was in and out. Dave held

things together. He was the day-to-day person. He was there every day. He was involved in every project that came through that office. Oftentimes when a new job came in, the first person Lou talked to was Dave. He was involved in every job at the very beginning. It may not be much, but Lou would talk to him about it. When it came to the production of working drawings, Dave was basically it. During the working drawing stage, he was consulted by everybody who was in charge of a job. They would go to Dave about things: "How should this work?" He would sit down and work out the detail. When you had a problem, you went to Dave. Sometimes, Lou would come in and say to Dave, "What do you want me to do? You tell me." And Dave would say, "Do such and such."

In Kahn's office, the production of working drawings was not subservient to design. In fact, they were typically mixed together with little separation. Wilcots described the process of Kahn and Wisdom working together in this way:

> Lou was part of the production. He did not design something and then go away. A building was designed until the last stone was laid. For example, the hallway and the door had to be a certain dimension. It didn't have anything to do with code. It had to do with the design of the building and what he felt needed to happen as you walked through that space. Lou would say, "Oh, no! We can't have a three-foot hallway. We need five feet!" Lou always talked about two people walking side by side and somebody passing and they're greeting somebody, so it needs to be such and such a dimension. Of course, Dave was right there by his side saying, "Well, how are we going to do this?" Dave's details were all very practical. Dave would say, "I don't know, Lou. What's this for? What's it going to do? It's meaningless!" He was just very practical, and Lou didn't always agree with him. Sometimes Lou would get angry with Dave and would go storming out, because it wasn't what he was looking for or the excitement wasn't there. Maybe he wouldn't like the result because it was so practical, but it worked. However, he would go back to him the next day. Lou has said that Dave was his best critic.

Both men shared a profound respect for the nature of materials and the act of construction. Despite his sometimes extravagant ideas, Kahn was really very utilitarian. According to Wilcots, "Dave learned from Lou about the respect for materials, but one could say he helped reinforce it because he could carry it through." While Kahn had the inspiration, Wisdom could sit down and think a thing through. He could go step by step by step. Wisdom's approach was one of attempting a truthful and pragmatic search for simplicity in the making of a building. It was the impulse that drove the character of all his details, which were practical to the extreme. Through logical reasoning combined with a respect for the nature of materials, he was able to produce details that were pure, pragmatic, and precise.

The art of detailing was an important element that Wisdom contributed to Kahn's work. Kahn would draw a sketch of something, and Wisdom would transform those lines into a workable, buildable solution that had economy and simplicity. Wisdom's detailing is characterized by its clarity and directness of approach. There was nothing showy about him. If Kahn gave him something that was overdone, he knew how to simplify it and express the essence of the detail. This was useful to Kahn.

There is a story told of Kahn coming back to the office after being away for a while. Wisdom was looking for answers when he came in, and he started asking him questions, one right after another. Evidently, Kahn did not have such a good time on the recent trip, and he snapped, "What is this, the Spanish Inquisition?" It didn't phase Wisdom one bit. He just asked another question. Because to get things going, for the office to move, to produce those drawings, he had to have answers. It was all part of the search for the right solution, which Kahn sought in a work of architecture.

Wisdom is described by various people who worked with him as always devoted, always inquisitive, and always inventive. There was in his nature a profound desire to learn. This was the virtue of Wisdom. Henry Wilcots recalled that,

> Throughout his life I've heard him say, "What did I learn?" He'd come out of a meeting, and he'd say, "What did I learn?" He was constantly trying to learn. You could sit down and have a conversation or work on a detail with him. Afterwards, he'd get on the train to go home and he'd say, "What did I learn?"

David Wisdom has left this earth, but thankfully the evidence of what he learned and the effort that he selflessly put into Kahn's vision remains to be experienced in the built work. In it we are witness to the loyalty, devotion, and intelligence he gave to Kahn's architecture. It was David Wisdom's quiet gift to us. It is simple, clean, and rock solid.

Case Study | Anne Cahill (A) and (B)*

One of the inevitable and key roles of a manager is to work toward resolution of conflict among people who must work together. When these people are talented, headstrong, complex, and male and female (as they often are in the architect's office), life can become quite challenging. The roles of manager as participant in conflict and as mediator of conflict are addressed in the Anne Cahill case study. Following the case, this author proposes an analysis. See if you agree.

Anne Cahill (A)

Anne Cahill, 28, was in her second year as a consultant at McCormick and Swell, a small, professionally respected consulting firm based in New York. She had recently been assigned to a multiphase project for the Continental Manufacturing Company, a large industrial manufacturing company that had been a client of McCormick's for several years.

Anne had passed her first-year performance reviews at McCormick with glowing commen-

*Copyright © 1981 by the President and Fellows of Harvard College. Harvard Business School Cases 482-023 and 482-024. These cases were prepared by E. Mary Lou Balbaky and Michael B. McCaskey as the basis for class discussion rather than to illustrate either effective or ineffective handling of an administrative situation. Names have been disguised. (All events are reported from the point of view of Anne Cahill.) Reprinted by permission of Harvard Business School.

dations and was beginning to take on project management responsibilities. Larry Strodbeck selected her for the project team because of her analytic skills, her experience in developing management training courses, and her interest in international marketing.

Strodbeck was the senior partner at McCormick who negotiated the current contract with Continental, and he had been studying the politics of strategic decision-making within Continental for several months. He believed that the company was now ready for a more comprehensive planning effort that would involve an international market analysis in collaboration with some of Continental's competitors. A related project was developing a program of managerial effectiveness for 150 of Continental's top-level managers, roughly 150 men whose skills lay more in engineering and technical work than in the management of people.

Anne was assigned to work closely with Peter Grant, the project manager, who was to oversee the day-to-day schedules and budgets for the various phases of the project and keep it on course. John Sarducci and Martha Weber, both in their first year at McCormick, were to work on the project full-time. Other McCormick people with special expertise, such as Judy Samuelson, a research associate, and Earl Sanchez, a top training specialist, would be assigned to the project when, and to whatever extent, their services were needed.

From the very beginning, the team members seemed to click together and enjoyed each others' ideas, abilities, and company. At McCormick, consultants generally valued being egalitarian and supportive rather than hierarchical and competitive, and the team operated according to these values.

The management of Continental Manufacturing Company had a reputation for being very tough, no-nonsense people in engineering, manufacturing, and other technical fields. From the start, the project team members realized that it would be a challenge to gain the cooperation and acceptance of Continental's executives and managers. Many Continental executives harbored an unspoken distrust of young professional consultants handing them expensive, impractical advice about how better to run their business. They wanted to see performance, guaranteed methods, straight answers, and organizational directives that looked like wiring diagrams.

Because of this reputation, Anne felt a certain nervousness before the first meeting with the president of the company, several executive vice presidents, and a director. Early one morning, Strodbeck, Grant, Cahill, and Sarducci flew to Continental's headquarters in Pittsburgh for a full day of meetings and presentations. When they were ushered into the executive suite, Larry introduced the team members but did not specify their exact roles. Anne settled herself into one of the large leather chairs around the highly polished conference table. She listened and watched intently as she tended to do in new situations. At present, there was a lot of new information to take in.

Larry and Peter presented the various phases of the project and their rationale for them. Although he had carefully introduced the financial analysis and conclusions to the president over the last few months, Larry formally reiterated the analysis and conclusions to the executives. At one point Anne added to what Larry had been saying. She spoke clearly and at length. The Continental executives seemed surprised, almost cold in responding to her comments, and she was slightly unnerved. Why did they act so surprised?

During the lunch break, one of the vice presidents gave Anne and John a tour of the Continental headquarters while Larry and Peter had lunch with the president of the company. Just before the afternoon meeting reconvened Anne cornered Peter, whom she trusted and liked, and asked him directly about the "incident" in the morning: "Did you notice anything strange in the reaction to my comments this morning? Or am I being overly sensitive?"

Peter was somewhat embarrassed but also a little amused.

I hate to tell you this. But they didn't know who you are—what your role on the project team is. You know there are very few women managers at Continental and so they are not used to seeing women in responsible positions. They thought you were a secretary—maybe a research assistant. But in either case, they resented your speaking. They finally asked Larry. But, when they learned that you are a consultant they reflected that what you had to say was rather intelligent, they became intrigued to know more about you.

In the afternoon meeting the group discussed the next two phases in the overall strategic planning effort. The second phase involved individual interviews with all the divisional vice presidents at Continental and with the top executives of their major American competitors. The companies were involved in a collaborative study on breaking into the international market.

The third phase of the current work was to be a joint project between McCormick and a group from Continental's Human Resources Department. McCormick was to design and test a program for developing managerial flexibility and effectiveness. The upper-level management training program would stress training for flexible, creative thinking, long-range planning, as well as standard communication and change-management skills. The goal was to develop within this technically oriented company an upper-management cadre to deal with organizational complexity and rapid, strategically motivated changes.

Near the close of the meeting, Anne was introduced as the team member with primary responsibility for the interviews with the divisional vice presidents and the chairmen of Continental's collaborating competitors. There was an awkward pause at the table and the executive vice president who was to arrange the interviews said: "Ahh . . . I don't know . . . whether that is such a good idea. Women on the work floor or in the plants are considered to be bad luck in our industry."

The executive reddened. The meeting turned silent and those eyes not looking downward looked at Anne. After a moment she responded, "Well, if that is the case, then, you must definitely make sure that I visit every one of your competitors." The room erupted in laughter. Although the matter was not discussed

further, the unspoken sense seemed to be that Anne could go ahead with the interviews even though not everyone was comfortable with the idea.

On the flight home from Pittsburgh, Anne wondered if she should stay on the project or not. If she accepted the commitment, would these men take her seriously? Could she get the information she needed from the divisional vice presidents and the chairmen? And most important, would the executives at Continental trust her to plan and navigate what was to be a crucial new thrust in their organization—the training program for upper management?

With mixed feelings, Anne decided to continue with the assignment, and she began to interview the divisional vice presidents of the Continental Company. Despite the misgivings expressed at the introductory meeting, she was welcomed and treated with courtesy and interest.

The weeks passed and the project team began to work closely together. The four of them—Peter, Anne, John, and Martha—analyzed the interviews Anne had conducted with the chairmen and the divisional vice presidents. They also developed a series of programs for use with different levels of top management. Anne greatly enjoyed the give and take of working in the group and trying to mesh different perspectives into a coherent whole.

In the course of the work, Anne saw how each member's particular abilities surfaced and how they assumed or were pressed into the roles they did best. As the team leader, Peter kept close track of scheduling and organizing, and he worked to keep the team within their time and financial budgets. Anne and John had the best conceptual and writing skills and so, although they would meet with the group to discuss general concepts, they would then go off on their own to do the actual course design and writing. Anne sensed that Martha wanted to do more course design work, but Peter, Anne, and John felt her conceptualizations were fuzzy. They, therefore, channeled her into liaison tasks where she could use her substantial interpersonal skills. She was a great facilitator and problem solver and very supportive of others. People came to rely on her increasingly as the liaison with Continental's personnel staff, who were to be the eventual in-house instructors of the training programs.

Peter decided that Anne and Earl Sanchez, the training specialist, should test the prepared programs with the prospective instructors at Continental. They were to spend three weeks at the company headquarters in Pittsburgh teaching the materials to the Human Resources Department personnel. Then Anne would spend another three weeks supervising several of the instructors as they ran pilot courses for some of Continental's own managers. The course would then be revised. Sanchez would also be involved in the supervision of the instructors but more in the capacity of a part-time advisor. He would be the on-site project manager for this six-week period in Pittsburgh.

The weeks chosen for the pilot field training were difficult for Anne. She was in the midst of a serious fight with her fiancé precisely over the demands that her job placed on her, especially the time she was required to spend traveling. When she arrived in Pittsburgh, her phone calls home to Jay, her fiancé, were doubly strained by his unfavorable reaction to her working in an all-male environment. She received very little support from him, and worse, she began immediately to have conflicts with Sanchez.

At McCormick where there was such a strong emphasis on team cooperation and equality, Anne had found Sanchez easy going and charming. He had a reputation for being a charismatic trainer—spontaneous, intuitive, with lots of flair. At McCormick, his contribution to the group was occasional and basically suggestive. In the field, however, he clearly expected to be the leader and when there was a disagreement, he reverted to an older, more ingrained style of male authority. In the masculine environment at Continental, Sanchez used a male style of camaraderie—sexist jokes and a deliberately male vocabulary—to establish himself with the managers and trainees.

Anne felt deserted. She was scared to be teaching an exclusively male group, most of whom were older than she was. "*You* are going to teach me about leadership and management?" one manager demanded incredulously. "I was

doing groups when you were in diapers!" Despite the comment, most of the men were more sympathetic to her situation than she had expected.

Anne had written most of the programs and was personally invested in seeing them tested as written. On the other hand, Sanchez was used to changing formats spontaneously, depending upon his mood and the feel of a group. Sometimes only hours before a group session was to begin, he would point out changes he wanted to make. Anne resented his style and his presumptuousness, and she became very adamant about teaching the sessions the way she had designed them. If these methods were going to be used generally throughout the company, she argued, they had to be tested in a specific form. Furthermore, the new instructors did not have Sanchez's "feel" for group process nor his confidence. Anne also felt uncomfortable with too little structure, and she knew that the training staff would have even more need for routine and formula. They had to be introduced slowly to the ideas of freedom and ambiguity.

Every afternoon, Anne and Sanchez had incredible fights when they went over the next day's sessions. Anne found herself resisting his ideas on points where she knew he was right and had something to add. She tried to confront him directly on what was happening, but he responded that she was a raving feminist and overly sensitive. One time, trying to be conciliatory, he added:

> I admit you do irritate me for other reasons, too. You're too attractive to be so smart. If you were ugly, I could accept your smartness and if you were dumb I could see you being so attractive. Having it all gives you too much power. You should back down once in a while.

His style and behavior continued to infuriate Anne. When she didn't go along with him on course changes, during that class he would sit in the back of the group, cover his eyes, shake his head, and look disgusted.

The afternoon before the last session on goal setting, Sanchez told her that the way she had designed the session would flop. He proposed changes that would require the preparation of a whole new set of forms. Anne told him he was out of his mind. Twenty minutes before the morning session began, he came up to her and said:

> Are you still determined to do it your way? Look, I worked all night figuring a way that you could change the format and still use the forms that you have. See, I compromise.

Anne refused and was very gratified when the session seemed to go extremely well. Several instructors told her that the programs were excellent. Even so, Sanchez tried to discount what she had done. Anne could hardly speak to him after that.

Upon cooling down, Anne saw the irony of the situation. One of the skills they were trying to teach was how to cope with resistance to change. Another was how to communicate. She and Sanchez would be in Pittsburgh for another three weeks, and she wondered what, if anything, she should do?

Anne Cahill (B)

After some thought, Anne decided to approach Sanchez about a problem she faced. One of the instructors she was supervising turned out to be an alcoholic. He did well in the morning sessions but drank heavily at lunch and was embarrassingly ineffective in the afternoon sessions. During personal feedback sessions, the instructor denied that his drinking affected his teaching and refused to discuss the matter.

Anne asked Sanchez for his advice about the alcoholic instructor, but their communication was still extremely strained. He first suggested that she coerce the instructor into drinking less at lunch by threatening a low rating or dismissal from the program, but Anne thought this was totally unrealistic. Sanchez then said that he would have a "man-to-man" talk with the instructor and took him out for drinks.

Anne was skeptical but in fact the instructor was sober for the next two days. When he appeared drunk on the third day, she considered

going over Sanchez's head and calling Peter at the home office, but she decided not to. Instead she struggled on with the often incoherent instructor, putting great effort into guiding his every step. In her report to Peter on this phase of the project, she recommended that this man be dropped from the program, but still she felt a sense of failure at not finding a better way to assert herself. She also regretted her inability to compromise with Earl Sanchez.

When Anne returned to New York, the team threw itself into the task of analyzing the results of the pilot study and revising the programs. Sanchez was not involved in this part of the work, and Anne avoided him around the company. She told Peter Grant what happened in Pittsburgh and said that she'd be happy if she never had to speak to Sanchez again. Peter advised her to find some way to mend the relationship. After all, they were communication experts.

"I've had that kind of antipathy toward someone here at McCormick for five years—arguments, fights, the whole thing—and it's *not* a pleasant experience when you're in the same company and at times are required to work on the same project."

"So, why don't you repair *your* relationship?" Anne suggested.

"I can't *stand* the guy," said Peter.

Peter had several other projects urgently demanding his time, so the brunt of the work of revising the courses was left to Anne and John. Christine Riviere, a hard-working editorial assistant, was brought in to help them, and the three worked efficiently together. Martha Weber continued to act as a liaison person and had weekly meetings in Pittsburgh with the personnel people at Continental. She introduced the revised programs to the company instructors and tried to deal with questions and problems. Although Martha seemed to be doing very well, she quietly complained to Peter that the Continental people regarded her as the "nonthinking" member of the team and went around her to Anne, to John, or to him whenever there was a serious conceptual question. Peter subsequently mentioned this to Anne and asked that she include Martha more in the conceptual work.

However, a week later, he added Judy Samuelson, a research associate, to the team because of her training and conceptual skills in adult development.

At first Judy was not welcomed onto the team. Anne, John, Martha, and Christine thought they had evolved rather smooth and effective patterns for doing the work, and a new entrant would force some realignment. They also though the team was developing very high quality and innovative training materials, and they wondered if the new person could maintain the same high standards. In addition, it quickly became apparent that Judy liked to work by herself and then bring completed work back to the group, but other team members typically preferred to conceptualize as a group so that everyone understood how the parts fit together. For her part, Judy seemed to resent Anne. She wondered how Anne could call herself a feminist and dress as femininely as she did. Anne's guess was that Judy, who was married, resented the attention that Anne received from some of the men at McCormick.

There was some tension. Judy was not often invited to lunch by other team members. In group meetings, less attention was directed toward her. Her ideas were not solicited, and she didn't receive much support for her ideas when she volunteered them. She was given parts of the course to work on that Anne and John viewed as less critical. "Once she 'proved' herself on the less important material and after she recognized the value of *our* approach, and the two seemed related," Anne later recalled, "she received more important work." In time, Judy became a full member of the team.

Despite Martha's reassurances that things were going well at Continental, Anne's investment in the program was so great that she continued to worry about how the instructors were receiving the revised programs. She knew that there had been some resistance among the instructors to accepting a "package" prepared wholly by McCormick. Anne had wanted to set up a collaborative effort, but early on it was clear that the McCormick people were the experts on training and the theory behind the training, and should be the lead people in designing the course. However, the course did need to be closely tailored to Continental's needs and peculiarities.

Both Peter Grant and Earl Sanchez felt that the course should be constructed and tested without encouraging any substantial revisions or additions from the client group. Guidelines had been set up jointly; now the ball was in McCormick's hands. Peter and Earl knew from experience, they said, that no matter how much input the client had early in the design process, they would want to change things again in the revision stage just to affirm their ownership of the course. They'd want to reinstate exercises that they had rejected earlier when they hadn't understood them. In their eyes, the policy showed foresight, and time and budget constraints reinforced its reasonableness.

Another problem arose because the person at Continental who had worked most closely with the team in planning the course became very ill and was replaced by a new man, Gary Greer. Greer was an innovative thinker and excited about the project, but his ideas about the thrust of the program were quite different from his predecessor's ideas.

Now that the final materials were being prepared, Anne thought it would be a good idea if she and John went to Pittsburgh in person and briefed the group of instructors on the finished version of the course. The first-hand encounter would allow the instructors to bring up any problems, questions, or troubles they were having with the course and to hash them out with the course designers from McCormick. Martha had indicated that the group of instructors, as a whole, had difficulty with ambiguity and many of the latest versions of the exercises deliberately evoked ambiguous situations.

Anne called Greer to set up a meeting with him and the twelve staff members who were to be the instructors, but he was unenthusiastic. She gave him a few days to mull it over, then called him again. This time she was adamant. It was absolutely necessary to have a joint planning and review session before she and John could go ahead with the final six weeks of writing.

Greer acceded and meetings were set up for the following Monday and Tuesday. When

Martha returned to the office that Friday she said that everything had been arranged and that all the instructors would attend. Anne and John had also been scheduled for a brief meeting with the head of the Human Resources Department on Monday morning.

On the early Monday morning flight to Pittsburgh, John napped and Anne studied a twenty-page outline she had written on the conceptualization and theoretical underpinnings of the course design. Most likely this wouldn't be necessary, since the Continental group would probably have lots of specific questions and the two days would be full of give and take, demonstrations, role plays—very interactive. But she didn't know what the head of Human Resources wanted, and she felt it never hurt to be over prepared.

Greer met Anne and John before the meeting and was friendly but restrained. When they went into the meeting with the instructors, they were met with silence, then stiff formality—quite unlike the cordiality of previous visits. Something serious was brewing. Gary started the meeting by suggesting a contracting period: What were McCormick's expectations and goals? Anne said that she had expected to participate in open question and answer sessions around specific lessons. She thought the instructors would want to discuss any troubles they were having with the course and to clarify conceptual questions they might have. One of the instructors spoke out tersely:

> I will tell you what we want. McCormick talks. *We* listen. We want a complete overview of the program—how and where and why the course fits our company!

Several other instructors commented in this vein. Anne tried to get them to talk directly about why they were angry. One instructor responded:

> We don't want you to give us any touchy-feely stuff on how you want us to look at the course and to tell you what we think it says. We want *you* to tell us what *you* meant to write.

At this point the group broke for coffee while Anne and John left for their meeting with the head of Human Resources. As soon as they left the room, Anne asked Gary: "What's the matter with this group? I've never seen them so uncooperative and hostile. We had no idea there were any serious problems here. Why didn't you warn us?"

"I guess we are very angry," Gary replied. "There's a lot of feeling that you haven't been consulting with us and that you haven't used our input in designing the course. I tried to dissuade you from coming here when everyone's temper is so riled up but you insisted—and maybe you're right. This could get some communication going but you're not going to find it easy. Some of the men are also angry at having been pressured into a meeting before *they* felt ready for it."

The meeting with the department head was perfunctory and ceremonial. As they returned to the group of instructors, Anne realized how scared she was. She had never been confronted with a group as angry as this before. She was also livid that Martha had given them no warning of the anger and impending trouble. In the minutes before the meeting reconvened, Anne and John tried to decide on a strategy for the coming confrontation. John himself admitted that he was terrified.

"*Another* fine mess you've gotten us into, Ollie!" he muttered. "*What* are we going to do?"

Anne looked at the group of angry instructors who were waiting for her to speak. She felt that the best thing to do at this point was not to open any sores or address the anger directly but instead, to try to go ahead with the task. She knew that her work and thinking were good. She knew that she, John, and Peter had put together some very good ideas about how to restructure the course. It *could* be a very exciting program if she could convey this to the men convincingly with the kind of enthusiasm she sometimes felt toward it all—on good days. She also knew that the only way to get through to this group of hard-nosed men was to be competent beyond all ordinary standards. She just had to go straight at them with no evasiveness. She had to talk intelligently and concisely about what McCormick was proposing and why. It was the only way she could have any credibility at all.

Inwardly Anne was shaking like a leaf as she started to lay out her conceptual overview of the project and how it fit into, but extended, the human relations work with which the group was familiar. For an hour and a half she mainly lectured about the course design, mentally hugging herself for having been so overprepared. John broke in occasionally to add a point or to clarify something that Anne couldn't immediately find the words to explain. When an instructor raised a particularly difficult question, Anne and John would look at each other to see who they felt could answer it best. John also rephrased hostile questions to make them more constructive. About halfway through, she *knew* they were making sense to these people and that the anger was beginning to dissipate. She felt she and John were giving the tightrope walk performance of the century. To be able to do this sort of thing was one of the pleasures of her job!

By the end of the session, the group was starting to come around and ask interested questions. Some of the hostility was still there, but Anne was feeling a huge glow of success at having tamed these angry lions.

By 4 or 5 o'clock in the afternoon, the group was able to talk peripherally about the anger of the morning and to joke about it. But it was not until the next day that Anne and John tried to confront directly the leftover hostility. "It will be a good learning experience for everyone," John suggested, "If we look at what happened in detail and talked about how you felt and why. There may be lessons for how important participation is for teaching and learning about change management, flexibility, and effective planning." The Continental people said no. They wanted to go on with the work of the previous day instead. Anne was disappointed, for the incident was a great demonstration of the perils of poor communication. But she knew that the McCormick group had to back off. The meetings ended cordially and Anne and John resolved to find ways to make the communication and feedback process more efficient and tangible.

The first step in improving communications was dealing with Martha Weber's almost disastrous oversight—if it was an oversight. How could she not have known that the Continental people were angry? What was the best way of handling this one?

Author's Case Study Analysis | Portrait of a Project Manager

Based on Anne Cahill's actions described in the (A) case, this author believes she has enormous potential as a project manager. She may require a few more years of experience in order to consistently appreciate and effectively control the myriad of challenges presented both by her own firm and by clients, in the context of a male-dominated power structure.

With only a year at her present job, Cahill demonstrated moments of brilliance under extreme pressure. She handled a belligerent comment from a Continental executive with perfect and lightning wit. Her message of excellence and confidence in proceeding with interviewing was a marvelous initial move. Moreover, Cahill demonstrates potential as a fine team player. She relishes and her work benefits from group interaction (as described in the interview analysis/program development phase). She has superb communication abilities ("best conceptual writing skills," and "she spoke clearly and at length" at the initial meeting).

Cahill has an intuitive sense regarding the utilization and evaluation of other team members. However, she was unable to positively redirect her feelings of anger toward Sanchez during the field work phase. She was placed in a very difficult circumstance but did not yet have the skills to engage Sanchez as a collaborator or ally on any level. The tension with her fiancé is an elegant metaphor for the gender politics aspect here: How does a capable, attractive woman assert her talent and ambition without threatening men who may be uncomfortable and frankly insecure in the presence of such women? At the end of (A), Cahill reflects on what she should do to improve the situation. This is impressive: She is self-aware and has identified the problems, but needs more tools/experience to fully rise above and achieve excellence. My guess is that she has the intelligence and motivation to overcome the obstacles; she cares about the needs of the people she works with (and for) and has sensitivity for the bottom line.

If I were Cahill's project manager (Peter Grant), I would ask her to design and implement a strategy to break the pathological pattern of interaction with Sanchez. If I were not in a position to be a direct role model (to demonstrate such a strategy), I would relate similar situations that I had encountered personally and managed with varying degrees of success or failure. I would certainly acknowledge the difficulties (and inevitabilities) of conflict among distinctive and talented personalities, but I would also offer concrete examples of approaches to managing clashes. I would quickly point out that everything in this realm is magnified when one of the principal actors is female. The message, first and foremost, is that the problem is normal, and second, that it is survivable, negotiable, and may even constitute an opportunity. Relationships that endure tough start-up may turn out to be the most gratifying and meaningful.

One approach that has stood the test of time and transcended gender differences is to effect a more self-effacing posture, and ask for help, suggestions, or guidance based on the other person's legitimate experience and achievement. In other words, diffuse the chip-on-the-shoulder by making it into a helper and mentor. Incorporating suggestions, even at the expense of some of your own ideas, is likely to serve you well—and you may learn something too. Development of more genuine personal bonds is then facilitated, and with the passage of time, it will be easier to disagree without emotional or professional cost.

The tension Anne and John discovered on their arrival at Continental could have been avoided if Continental had a significant level of participation in the "diagnosing process" (see Schein's Process Consultation Model from "A General Philosophy of Helping: Process Consultation," *Sloan Management Review,* Spring 1990). The McCormick team allowed Continental to essentially "distance themselves" and therefore create a situation in which nothing short of a stellar performance was required of Anne and John. Moreover, Anne appears a little unimaginative and perhaps rigid in her shock at the resistance demonstrated by Gary and company. Certainly Martha's liaison failure was the immediate cause of the tension, but we know from the beginning that Martha deferred to Peter, Anne, or John each time there were questions of any weight. Martha's work was further undermined by Peter's decision to add Judy to the team, a move that seriously diminished Martha's opportunity to grow in her job. It is appealing to speculate about the effect of Judy's addition upon Martha's morale and investment in the entire project.

Anne and John were able to transcend the accumulated tension by directly addressing the task. Communicating the rationale behind and excellence of the program with focus, pace, and enthusiasm was the only way to penetrate the group's collective hostility. Reinterpreting antagonistic questions to promote the analysis and strengths of the program was a graceful tactic.

Cahill continues to demonstrate how capable and articulate she can be under pressure. That she derives tremendous satisfaction from educating and influencing clients is very evident, and her teamwork with John is impressive. These are all traits that will contribute to her success as a future project manager. Cahill's "need for achievement," however, has to be moderated. Her insensitivity to the group dynamics following Judy's addition to the team, in conjunction with her failure to register the cues from Gary and the Continental crowd, represent a problem area. Anne is similar to the star player on a basketball or football team; she brings fabulous talent, but "hot-dogging" won't do it— Anne has to be "coached" to be aware that winning is achieved by learning to adapt to, and work with, all elements of the team. When this occurs, Anne will become a star project manager while she is now only a star performer.

Case Study | Drawing as a Means to Practice

PAUL STEVENSON OLES, FAIA, is a practicing architect, experienced teacher, and highly-regarded perspectivist. As an architect, his work in housing and energy-efficient design has received wide recognition. He has taught at RISD (Rhode Island School of Design), Yale, MIT (Massachusetts Institute of Technology), and Harvard, where he was also a Visiting Scholar and Loeb Fellow in Advanced Environmental Studies. He is a cofounder of the American Society of Architectural Perspectivists (ASAP, later ASAI), the author of numerous articles and two major books on architectural illustration, and has lectured and exhibited worldwide.

Beginning with the terms of this book's title, "professional" and "practice," it may be useful to separate the two and provide some context, however subjective, for their accepted meanings. Architectural *practice* has been succinctly defined by Richard Eribes as *design translated into service*. Since architecture is an allographic art (one in which instructions by the artist guide others in the realization of art), it could be argued that design *is* the service provided by architects. We don't, for the most part, appear on the building site with hammer and saw but rather with a roll of contract documents, that is, instructions.

The word "professional," as a noun or adjective, is usually connoted in a very positive way, suggesting expertise, integrity, and concern for the client (as distinct from "customer"). There is, however, a dark side to the term—that of exclusivity, turf-guarding, and sometimes even deliberate mystification to enhance the perceived indispensability of services. For our purposes here, I refer only to the former admirable and edifying aspects of the term.

In that vein, the conscientious professional seeks to serve the interests of the client, rather than using opportunities presented by practicing primarily for his own pleasure, amusement, or enrichment. It has become increasingly clear

as the practice of architecture becomes ever more complex that the *sharing* of the many facets of practice usually provides a superior service to relying merely on the contributions of a single individual, however talented or energetic. This is a manifestation of the larger, indeed ubiquitous, phenomenon of specialization, which itself leads to the eventual "professionalization" of every field of endeavor.

This specialization phenomenon is largely responsible for the trajectory of my own career, but more importantly can be shown to have influenced the design of one specific piece of consequential architecture—the East Building of the National Gallery of Art in Washington, D.C. Establishing context for this case study requires some detail about my own history and the chain of events leading to the design of the building.

I received my undergraduate education in architecture at a technological college in the southwest (Texas Tech University) in the late fifties, where the Bauhaus revolution in design that was ushered into this country twenty years earlier by Walter Gropius had not quite arrived. Accordingly, the early part of my training was along Beaux-Arts lines, with its attendant emphasis on drawing. In those days, verbal presentation of projects was not even allowed, and therefore academic survival required the development of adequate skills of graphic communication. Although there were no courses offered in "rendering," per se, everyone learned to present effectively by observing the work of more senior students.

Armed with this unintentionally acquired skill of drawing, I continued my graduate education at Yale University and took my first job after graduation at The Architects Collaborative in Cambridge, Massachusetts. I later learned that the reason I had been hired was because of that skill, which was in short supply on the East Coast due to the dominance of the very revolution that had not reached the plains of Texas during my early training. To

Figure 4-4 Wax-based pencil drawing of the East Building, National Gallery, Washington, D.C. made prior to construction in 1971. The challenge—for the renderer as artist—was to visualize before construction the building in normal light and use. All drawings by Paul Stevenson Oles, FAIA. Courtesy of Paul Stevenson Oles, FAIA.

Figure 4-5 Photograph of the completed East Building, 1978. The correlation with the drawing (Figure 4-4) in geometry and lighting is quite precise, although there are a few discrepancies: the bollards in the foreground and the lintel over the major opening reflect design decisions taken after the drawing was made. Courtesy of Paul Stevenson Oles, FAIA.

Figure 4-6 This 1969 drawing of the main interior space of the East building, taken from the vertex of the acute angle formed by the triangular plan, shows most of the design elements under study at the time. The space had not been previously rendered with such accuracy and was seen by Mr. Pei as too dark, "heavy," and "barnlike," which led to the subsequent series of studies and the glazing of the entire central roof. Courtesy of Paul Stevenson Oles, FAIA.

Figure 4-7 This four-hour sketch from almost a year later represented an attempt to reduce the oppressiveness of the central roof by introducing the triangular opening at the right. The intention was to admit additional light and to give a sense of the public space continuing above the coffered ceiling. The scheme seemed awkward and needed further work. Courtesy of Paul Stevenson Oles, FAIA.

compound the irony, my first direct superior at TAC was the person who was, indirectly, the cause of my local usefulness—Walter Gropius himself!

After some time in the role of "the Gropius pencil," I became known locally as a guy who could draw and began to receive offers for moonlight work in presentation. Resisting the siren call of money (consistently twice the rates commanded by drafting services), I continued for years to seek the holy grail of generalized practice that is the ideal of most architects. It became clear eventually that it was an uphill battle, however, so I decided that if I were to work as an artist for other architects, it should be only for the very best in the nation. Accordingly, I

sent a letter with examples of my drawing work to the five architects for whom I had the greatest respect, and I received a response from only one—and that one happened to be my first choice.

The fateful phone call came one evening as I was working late in the small home/office of my then-employer in Cambridge. Stepping through the dining room, over the kitty litter box and past the uncleared dinner dishes to take a call in the kitchen, I put the phone to my ear to hear an energetic, slightly accented voice intone "I. M. Pei here." I nearly dropped the telephone! To condense the story only slightly, Mr. Pei soon made it known to me that he had recently received the "commission of a lifetime"

Figure 4-8 This subsequent five-hour study shows the earlier ceiling opening as substantially expanded, admitting more light into the space, although the scheme introduced circulation problems with the long bridge on the left. Mr. Pei and the design team were encouraged by the increase in openness and light, which set the stage for glazing the entire roof as shown in the remaining drawings. Courtesy of Paul Stevenson Oles, FAIA.

and that he wanted the graphic representation of that project to be in one hand, and that hand should be mine. So much for my resistance to drawing!

That remarkable project was, of course, the East Building, and the year was 1968—the beginning of a design process that was to continue into 1971. During the latter part of those years, I often spent three or four days a week in Pei's New York office as a consulting member of the project design team. At the time my work began, the shape of the exterior envelope of the building had been almost completely determined by the architect, generated largely by the National Capitol Planning Commission's site setback requirements and height constraints set by the U.S. Commission of Fine Arts. The major design issues then remaining were those of the scale, circulation, and character of the resulting central interior space.

Pei's wisdom was in having someone on the working team who could provide real-time representational visualization of ongoing design decisions made among a talented and strongly opinionated group of designers—headed, of course, by the architect himself. The nature of the main space—basically a nineteen-degree isosceles triangle in plan, determined by the famous L'Enfant street plan of Washington—was so deceptive that simple elevations would not suffice as design feedback. Even perspective drawings could not eliminate the spatial ambiguity inherent in the unconventional geometry, but they were the most useful tools at hand. The effectiveness of interior study models was limited by the fact that they had to be of a fairly

Figure 4-9 Several intervening studies confirmed to the architect that the space should be opened entirely to the sky to show more of the "houses," the small hexagonal galleries located in the corner towers. The scale and repetitiveness of the conventional space-frame module became an issue of concern at this time. Courtesy of Paul Stevenson Oles, FAIA.

Figure 4-10 This concern led to the idea of exploring a hybrid combination—a large-module structural-space frame located at a lower spring point supporting a folded plate frame above, which held the glazing. Courtesy of Paul Stevenson Oles, FAIA.

Figure 4-11 The resolution of the roof enclosure issue came finally with the adoption of a single space frame of a very large module that combined both the functions of structure and glazing, as shown in this sketch. Courtesy of Paul Stevenson Oles, FAIA.

substantial size and required a great deal of time, expense, and design commitment to construct.

My main task, therefore, was to produce very rapid sketches of tentative design changes that were deemed worthy of further study. These drawings, some of which are included here, provided a basis for discussion and revision by the design team, along with the brilliant client, the late J. Carter Brown, then Director of the National Gallery, who was frequently present at the working sessions. Those design sessions in the office, centered on an elegant lunch often graced by a fine wine from Pei's own cellar, were usually attended by most of the core design team, which included the seven members of the firm. In addition to Pei himself, the team included Jim Freed, Leonard Jacobson, Bill Pedersen, Shelton Peed, Didi Pei, Tom Schmitt, and Yann Weymouth. The ideas proposed and tentatively ac-

cepted would result in quick drawings, which in turn would stimulate subsequent (passionate but always civil) argument, new ideas, and more drawings. Thus the work progressed throughout most of 1969 and all of 1970.

It was evident to everyone on the team during those years that this was not just another project. Given the profound cultural responsibility, the open-ended schedule, the elastic budget (the Mellon fortune), and eventually the unprecedented national visibility, we realized that this was almost certainly a defining project in each of our careers. Because of this, and the intense professional dedication of all the participants, no effort was spared to make this the best work possible within each of our capacities.

The elapsed time between the original commission for the design and the official

Figure 4-12 This 1971 wax-base pencil drawing represents the final scheme as built. The drawing illustrates the large (35- by 45-foot) module of the compound space frame with semitransparent exterior lattice screens to modulate the amount and quality of direct sunlight. The irony inherent in the large module is that it is seen to make the space less overpowering and more humanely scaled than the smaller, more repetitive modules of the earlier schemes. Courtesy of Paul Stevenson Oles, FAIA.

opening in June 1978 was almost exactly a decade. The initial critical reviews before and after the opening were virtually all raves, and reports from attendees, exhibitors, and users in the ensuing years have been predominantly positive. The building seems to have been embraced by the people of this nation beyond the most extravagant hopes of all of us who labored on it.

It was seen as a popular and critical success, but how did fellow architects—the profession—view the work? The agency charged with the maintenance, monitoring, and advancement of professional standards in our field is, of course, the American Institute of Architects. Positive professional behavior is encouraged by an extensive program of commendations and prizes, which includes their annual "25-year award." This is perhaps the most meaningful

recognition of all because of its removal from the prevailing design "climate" of the moment. To be selected for this award, a building must have stood those most stringent tests of continued use and the passage of time.

The granting of the AIA 25-year award in 2004 to the East Building was more than merely a celebration of the genius of its architect. The award occasioned more than the pleasure of everyone associated with the project (including the remarkable corps of dedicated construction workers who actually built it): it effectively verified the process by which the building was designed and brought to realization. That process was characterized by inclusiveness, civility, and genuine collaboration—reflections and extensions of the values of a paradigm of professionalism, I. M. Pei himself.

Chapter 5

Making a (Financial) Statement

Did you hear the one about the architect who inherited one million dollars and continued to practice until he went broke?[1] Or the one about the lawyer who complained about a plumber's bill. "I never earned $200 an hour!" exclaims the lawyer. "I never did either," replies the plumber, "when I was a lawyer."[2] Is the often repeated refrain that architects don't make any money a self-fulfilling prophecy?

This chapter, on financial management of architectural firms, introduces students to some of the fundamentals: planning for profit (i.e., so you design-oriented folks know that it is possible to balance making money with achieving design excellence), understanding financial statements, cash-flow projection, accounting systems, project budgeting, and so on.

(1) You have trouble balancing your checkbook, and (2) you have less money coming in than going out every month. If either of the above is true, study this chapter and also consider seeking help (i.e., an accountant). This material can inform your search for other references or for assistance that can provide more details when needed. It is essential that you have sufficient background to communicate meaningfully with a number-crunching specialist, and this chapter can help. Architects must be able to understand and interpret financial reports (and their implications for all phases of design), and they must know how to perform simple record-keeping tasks to monitor the economic health of individual projects and of the firm in general.

The following two selections—a brief primer on financial management (including the fundamentals previously noted) and a more applications-oriented review of fees, compensation, and project monitoring—set forth basic definitions and principles from which you can pursue further study. The message is to understand that you must plan—or design—the financial aspects of practice so you can maximize both design and play time and ensure a profit. Design skills and business acumen should not be mutually exclusive traits for the practitioner.

---

[1]Oliver Witte. "The Compensation Crisis," *Architectural Technology* Winter (1985): 42.

[2]Roger Yee. "Who Needs Designers?" *Contract Design* December (1995): 8.

Figure 5-1 Financial management does not have to be puzzling if you take the time to do a little planning. Graphic by Iris Slikerman.

Financial Management Primer

Financial data, statements, and their analysis underlie important management decisions. This information reveals the firm's existing financial state, outstanding or unresolved problems, and potential for the future. If you ever doubt the gravity of financial management, remember that without money there is no practice, no architecture, no design.

In the essay below, Jim Cantillon pulls off a most difficult job. In a light-hearted manner, he comprehensively but succinctly highlights the basics—it is a great place to start to learn about these issues.

JAMES J. CANTILLON, principal of Boston-based Cantillon & Associates, was formerly Chief Financial Officer for the architectural firm Finegold Alexander & Associates. He currently provides financial and business management services to design firms. Jim holds an MBA from the Simon School at the University of Rochester, Rochester, New York, and conducts frequent presentations to industry groups, including the Boston Society of Architects and the Society of Design Administrators.

A common goal of many architectural students is to "make a statement" in their profession. And like all matters, some will accomplish that objective—others may fall short. *Any* architect who decides to run or manage a business will indeed have no choice but to make a statement; in fact, it may be several. And I am talking about the dreaded *financial statements*, the "score-keeping" devices that you and others will want *and* need.

So there goes all the fun; suddenly architecture is becoming too much like work. Well hopefully that is not so—the business management aspects of the design profession can be kept simple and manageable and, in fact, be a terrific tool to support good design. So let's take a look at these financial statements—what are they and how do they help?

Financial Statements

There are two fundamental accounting reports, or financial statements, that describe the financial status of a firm. They are the *income statement* and the *balance sheet*. The income statement reflects just that—the income, or profit, of the firm. It covers a discrete current period of time, customarily a month, as well as the year to date. The year is defined as the accounting year, referred to as the *fiscal* year, which may or may not be the same as the calendar year. The income statement reflects revenue, expenses, and the difference between the two—profit or loss. (*Loss*, being a four-letter word, is clearly the label to avoid.) We discuss later how the income statement can be interpreted and serve as a foundation for appropriate action.

The balance sheet reflects the financial condition of the firm at a *point in time.* While the income statement reflects profitability, the balance sheet shows what the firm owns (assets) and what it owes (liabilities); the difference is the net worth of the firm, essentially the *cumulative* profits of the firm since its inception. The income statement and the balance sheet are directly related. And while profitability (as shown on each year's income statements) should mean a strong balance sheet, that is not necessarily so—but it is a good start.

Just why do you need to distract yourself with these dastardly financial statements? First, they can help *you* understand the financial strengths and weaknesses of the firm, and they allow you to make well-informed business decisions. Additionally, any bank or lending institution will require such reports as a condition of providing financing to a firm; such credit from banks is typically in the form of equipment loans or a revolving line of credit, the latter allowing you to bridge those inevitable valleys (thank goodness for the peaks). Further interest in your financial statements may come from your clients, especially if they are in the public sector. Financial statements are, I'm afraid, here to stay, so try to make them as simple and effective as you can.

The Balance Sheet

A simple balance sheet and its components is reflected in Exhibit 5–1, page 174. The format lists all assets of the firm on the left-hand side; liabilities and the net worth of the firm are on the right. And notice that the sum of the assets is the same as the total of liabilities + net worth, reflecting that *exciting* concept known as the "debits equaling the credits." A review of key balance-sheet accounts follows.

Cash

The first asset listed under "assets" is cash, the essential ingredient to a business, not unlike its importance in one's personal life. It allows you (or prevents you) from doing what you want to do. Where does this *cash* come

Exhibit 5–1
Balance Sheet $(000s)

Assets:		Liabilities:	
Cash	20	Accounts payable	110
Accounts receivable	185	Car loan payable	15
Equipment	15		
Equipment depreciation	−5		
Total current assets	215	Total current liabilities	125
Buildings	0	Long-term debt	0
Total assets	215	Total liabilities	125
		Retained Earnings:	
		Current year	23
		Prior periods	67
		Total net worth	90
Total assets	215	Total liabilities and net worth	215

from? Essentially three sources—the owner's personal investment, outside funding such as banks, and lastly your clients, through *timely* paying of your invoices. Cash planning is very important, both on a short- and long-term basis. A simplified cash-flow projection is shown as Exhibit 5–2, page 175, reflecting cash requirements and expected cash receipts, in this case over a three-month period. All planning requires a solid starting point— an understanding of where you are and where you've been. Accordingly, an effective cash forecast will be built on a solid working knowledge of the firm's financial condition as found in the income statement and the balance sheet, as well as in related management reports. Managing the cash "additions" (i.e., collecting receivables and maintaining bank sources) will allow you to handle those "expenditures"—and maintain positive relationships with those who support your firm (employees, vendors, and so on).

The cash needed to support the operating costs of any firm will flow primarily from client payments, the foundation of long-term positive cash flow. Those unpaid invoices are *accounts receivable*, as they appear on the balance sheet. The speed with which you turn over (i.e., convert your receivables to cash) is critical to your cash balances. Low turnover is only good with respect to your employees, not with your receivables! If your payment terms are thirty days, which is fairly standard, depending on your client base, you can probably expect payment no sooner than forty-five days from the time your invoice is sent. It is important to avoid any further delays. So here are a few practices that will assist you in the prompt payment of invoices:

Exhibit 5–2
Cash Flow Projection $(000s)

	Month 1	Month 2	Month 3
Cash balance—Beginning of month	20	10	10
Additions:			
Client payments	90	70	120
Bank loan	0	35	0
Cash available	110	115	130
Cash expenditures:			
Payroll	45	45	45
Nonpayroll	25	25	25
Subconsultants	30	30	30
Equipment purchase	0	5	0
Bank loan payback	0	0	20
Total expenditures	100	105	120
Cash balance—End of month	10	10	10

- Ensure that payment terms are included in your contracts and that they are clearly understood *as the project begins.*
- Invoice promptly; the clock will not start with your clients until they receive your invoice.
- Call the client after your initial invoice on a new project to ensure that the invoice was received and by the right person. Also ask if everything is clear; then inquire about the likely turnaround time for payment. This discussion resolves any administrative issues immediately (not after the invoice is past due) and also establishes both the client contact and payment expectations—*for the duration of the project.*
- Following up immediately if payment is *not* received; banks are in the business of providing money to others, not architects (just think how you'd feel if banks started doing design work).
- And let's not forget those *retainers*—deposits made by clients as projects are initiated; ask . . . you may be pleasantly surprised.

Other Assets

An additional type of asset is "fixed assets" or equipment, including such items as office furniture, the cost of leasehold improvements at your office, computer equipment, and so on. These are recorded on your balance sheet at their cost and then depreciated (written off) over time, say three to five years. The balance sheet reflects the initial value of these assets, as well as the depreciation write-down; such depreciation is shown as an operating expense on the income statement.

Liabilities

So much for what the firm *owns*—the assets shown on the balance sheet. The other side of the balance sheet (both literally and figuratively) is what the firm *owes*—its *liabilities*. The primary liabilities will be *accounts payable*, your unpaid bills to vendors and consulting engineers and subcontractors. Another typical liability is loans, for equipment or automobile purchases, as well as any unpaid balance on your line of credit. As mentioned previously, the difference between the assets and the liabilities is the firm's net worth. And note that the net worth includes both current profitability (shown as year-to-date profit on the income statement), as well as any profit or loss from prior periods. Current year profit contributes to the net worth; but any "sins of the past" (prior losses) are not forgiven.

Balance-Sheet Analysis

So now we have the numbers—they are all in orderly columns and rows, and they even add up! And just what does it all mean? Other than the fact that you want the *net worth* to be as high as possible, the *relationships* tell the story. And this will be equally true in our discussion of the income statement. So what are those relationships, or ratios, found on the balance sheet?

The "current ratio" is a fundamental measure of the *liquidity* of the firm—it is the current assets divided by the current liabilities. A standard target ratio is 2:1 (i.e., $2 of current assets for every $1 of current liabilities). The *working capital* of the firm is directly related, consisting of the dollar difference between current assets and current liabilities. The following example shows the dynamics of the current ratio and working capital, as impacted by a single event, described below.

In this example, life is simple—we have only cash and accounts receivables as assets, and only payables and a loan as liabilities. The baseline condition of the firm includes a past-due client bill, whose delinquency has caused the firm to borrow money from the bank. The "revised" condition assumes client payment of this receivable and the related loan payoff. Notice how this activity does not impact the working capital dollars but significantly improves the current ratio:

	Baseline	Revised
Cash	20	20
Receivables	260	185
TOTAL ASSETS	280	205
Payables	110	110
Loan (credit line)	75	0
TOTAL LIABILITIES	185	110
Working capital ($)	95	95
Current ratio	1.51	1.86

Another ratio is the relationship between receivables and sales, a ratio called "days sales outstanding" (DSO). This ratio measures how quickly you are collecting your receivables. The industry average is about 65 days, as measured from the end of the billing or accounting month. This ratio can therefore be strongly influenced by the speed with which you send invoices to your clients.

While DSO can be derived in several ways, a simple method is to divide accounts receivable at month end by recent average daily billings (say, the past three months). An example follows, again reflecting conditions before (baseline) and after (revised) the client payment of your past due invoice:

	Baseline	Revised
Receivables	260	185
Three months sales	270	270
Daily sales rate	3.0	3.0
Days sales outstanding (DSO)	87	62

Notice that the firm's ratios improved dramatically by that one event, the large client payment. The firm improved its financial strength, although nothing impacted the income statement; only balance sheet changes occurred. So the income statement does not tell the whole story. In this case, even though the firm was making a profit, its assets (accounts receivables) were at risk, and the firm was using its available cash to pay off a needless loan, with interest. Believe me, a strong balance sheet with positive ratios will definitely help your banker sleep well, and sometimes there's nothing better than a well-rested and content banker! Then *you* can focus more fully on design. Life *is* good . . .

The Income Statement

The basics of the income statement (P and L, as in Profit and Loss Statement) are revenue (what you bill or earn) and expenses (your costs). A standard income statement, showing current month and year-to-date results, is included as Exhibit 5–3, page 178. Normally you will have much more control over your expenses, such as payroll and office-related costs, than over revenue, simply because the *prospective* clients have significant "input" on any new projects and contracts you attain, and *current* clients have a direct influence on the timeline with which you complete the contracted work (i.e., earn the fee). A review of the methods to influence revenue follows in the Project Finances section, page 180. For now, let's look at the ways you can manage the expenses of the firm.

Expense Control (and Technical Staffing)

The elements of your expenses can be separated into payroll and nonpayroll, as they are managed in entirely different methods. Payroll costs are a significant cost to any architectural firm, representing as much as two-thirds of a firm's overall expenses. The size of a firm's technical staff should, of course, be directly related to the project work under contract, a "moving target" as projects start and end. Regular tracking of your backlog (the unbilled bal-

Exhibit 5–3
Standard Income Statement $(000s)

	Current Month	Year to Date (Six Months)
Revenue	105	550
Expenses:		
Salaries	45	245
Payroll costs	4	21
Benefits	3	17
Subcontractor costs	35	175
Rent	3	18
Insurance	2	12
Depreciation	0	3
Office supplies	2	10
Marketing	4	10
Accounting	1	4
Utilities	2	12
Total expenses	101	527
Profit/(Loss)	4	23

ance of contracts) facilitates technical staffing decisions; that backlog information is found in management reports, *not* the financial statements.

The key is to maintain a meaningful relationship between technical staff and project revenue; an error in *either direction* is a problem. Having too few people may cause you to miss project deadlines or to deliver a substandard product. Too many people are, of course, a cost to the firm with no offsetting revenue (definitely not good for the long haul). Technical staffing is not a simple matter, and its implications are significant, both short- and long-term. Make sure that the responsibility for technical staffing is defined and that staffing decisions clearly reflect the workload, as measured by the backlog of unearned fees. When the workload is unclear, consider part-time, short-term, or temporary staffing. *Keep those options open.* And remember, people are your largest cost; they are also your greatest asset—do not take the matter lightly.

Managing the Labor Force

MICHELLE NEWSOM writes this brief sidebar on how firms typically lose (and gain) staff.

Firms can "manage technical staff"—to help balance staff with project needs and company profitability—via these common occurrences:

1. *Attrition*—The company does not fill vacancies created when underutilized employees seek employment elsewhere.
2. *Retirement*—The company does not fill the vacancy created by an employee who permanently leaves the workforce.
3. *Reduction In Force (RIF)*—The firm must "let-go" the employees for whom no project needs exist.
4. *Outsourcing*—The company can enlist the efforts of an underutilized employee from another firm, particularly during peak project pushes or for "quick-burn" projects.
5. *Employee Contract*—The company provides a contract to the prospective employee that stipulates that the term of employment will coincide with the term of the project.

Support Staff

While there are general guidelines regarding the number of *support staff* to technical staff (say, 1 per 5 technical), the "correct" number of support staff should reflect the workload (as with technical staff). This "workload," however, is not as clearly defined for support staff as with the backlog's relationship to technical staffing. You will need to define the "job descriptions" of support staff (i.e., what are the duties and responsibilities of each person or position?).

Support activities include reception and secretarial, marketing, and accounting. Such staffing decisions should be considered investments; there should be a definite payback on the benefits to be obtained. For instance, if an architect is answering the phone or making prints when he or she could be doing project work on a billable basis, the payback for an office person is the additional revenue generated by the architect. If an owner is assembling the marketing presentation, again in lieu of his or her billable time on projects, that too is justification for investing in marketing support. And if you are not capturing all your costs for billing to your clients or you are writing off client invoices because no one is following up on your accounts receivables, the benefit of accounting support becomes clear. So spend that money on overhead positions prudently, but don't fail to invest in the support you *really* need. It can and should be a good investment.

Nonpayroll Expenses

The other broad category of costs to a firm are nonpayroll costs, such as benefits, office-related expenditures (rent, phone, utilities, supplies, and so on), marketing costs (other than payroll), computer and systems expenses, and insurance (liability, workers compensation, and business insurance). The fundamental methods of controlling such nonpayroll areas include:

- Having someone in charge of each element, with a budget or target.
- Doing comparison shopping *regularly*, on your insurance, benefits package, supplies, and so on.

- Asking for better prices, especially if you can anticipate increasing volume and have a reputation for prompt payment.

Remember, just as you need to invest in support staff, investing in marketing can also be money very well spent—*control* that spending, don't *stop* it!

Project Finances

Other than overhead expenses, all financial activity of the firm is project related, including revenue, subcontractor/engineering costs, and direct labor. Project tracking is therefore a key managerial need at the project and firm level. Systems that integrate project management and accounting represent an inexpensive and effective addition to a firm. A basic system for a smaller firm (say, less than ten employees) can be purchased for under $1,000. Just as you should supply your technical staff with the tools to do their jobs, you should likewise support effective financial management of projects (and the firm) with effective systems. You will find it an invaluable investment that simplifies the process, captures your project costs and revenues in a meaningful and usable fashion, and provides the basis for controlled growth in the future.

Exhibit 5–4, page 181, presents an income statement suitably formatted for architectural firms to better understand their business. Revenue, subcontractor costs, and direct labor are project related; the non-project portion is the overhead spending. So, as you will note, there are really only three elements a project manager must address to control and monitor his or her projects. *Only three*—pretty simple so far, eh? Ways to control those elements follow. *Revenue* can be impacted by several actions, such as:

- *Negotiating an appropriate fee;* your contracts should be clear and mutually beneficial, allowing the client to satisfy his or her goals within an acceptable timetable and *permitting the architect to be fairly compensated.*
- *Ensuring that your billing rates are in line with your actual payroll costs by person or category;* keep these billing rates up to date by reviewing and revising them at least once per year.
- *Pursuing extra compensation* immediately, *as soon as services exceed the contracted scope of work;* delays will seriously jeopardize your position.
- *Maximizing the types of project expenses that are reimbursable and with a reasonable markup (say 15 percent);* do not underestimate the potential profit opportunity on project expenses.

Project costs for engineers/subcontractors are, as with your fee, initially influenced by the negotiated contract. Be sure to obtain good engineering support at a cost level that is backed up by your fee. You can't give others dollars you don't have. Also, make sure that the terms of the con-

Exhibit 5–4
Architectural Firm Income Statement $(000s)

	Current Month	Year to Date (Six Months)
Gross revenue	105	550
Subcontractor costs	35	175
Net fee income	70	375
Direct labor	27	143
Overhead:		
Indirect labor	18	102
All other overhead*	21	107
Total overhead	39	209
Profit/(Loss)**	4	23
*Same as details on Exhibit 5–3		
**Net fee income less Direct labor		
and Overhead		
Ratios:		
Billing multiple	2.59	2.62
Overhead rate	1.44	1.46

tracts with your client are mirrored in your contracts with engineers (i.e., contracts should generally be similar in terms of fixed fee or cost plus invoicing, proportion of fees by phase, inclusion [or exclusion] of reimbursables, and so on).

Each project should have a labor budget for *direct labor*, which is the payroll cost of the time charged to the project. This "budget" does not have to be complex—keep it simple, but do it! This direct labor can be best managed by taking the budgeted labor hours and differentiating them into two discrete elements—timeline (weeks and months) and the size of the project team during each phase or task. That can generate worker hours or worker weeks and provide two identifiable and measurable elements—the number of people working on the project and the length of time involved. And be sure that anyone and everyone working on the project fully understands the time allotted (budgeted) to each phase or task. *Use that system you bought* to track project activity. Respond immediately if and when the project gets off track.

If the tasks are then accomplished with fewer people, or in less time, or with individuals at a lower pay rate than assumed (a plus not only in economic terms but also with respect to personnel development), you will have succeeded in underspending your budget. *Yes!*

These three financial elements of a project converge into a single statistic or ratio, the "billing multiple." It is defined as the gross revenue less project expenses ("net fee income"), divided by direct labor dollars. It is the firm's return on its investment on any project(s), and this return is discussed below as part of the income-statement ratios.

Income-Statement Ratios

As with the balance sheet, there are certain ratios or relationships that will allow you to focus on the financial issues. The primary financial ratios are the billing multiple and the overhead rate, both of which are shown at the bottom of the Architectural Firm Income Statement (Exhibit 5–4, page 181). And here's the simple litmus test: If the billing multiple is higher than the overhead rate (plus 1.00), the firm will be profitable. (The break-even multiple *is* the overhead rate plus 1.) And what do you know, the income statement does reflect a condition where the billing multiple (2.62) *is* higher than the break-even multiple (1.46 + 1, or 2.46). And, voilà, the firm shows a profit—would I fool you? (Overhead rate is defined as "total overhead" divided by direct labor dollars.)

How do you accomplish the goals of keeping your billing multiple up and your overhead rate down? Project managers must take responsibility for their own projects and manage them effectively, using some of the techniques described in the Project Finances section (page 180). And remember, all projects are not created equal; some projects will be more profitable than others. Some may even be undertaken with below break-even targets and budgets, as a means of attracting a new client or entering a new market. This is not an unacceptable proposition, as long as *most* projects are profitable, with higher than break-even multiples. And no, despite what you may have heard, you can't make up losses on every project with *volume.*

Overhead expense includes two major components: the nonpayroll categories, whose control was discussed in the Cost Control section (page 177), and indirect salaries, representing any time not charged to projects. Indirect labor consists of those "investments" in support staff, whose time is generally 100 percent indirect or overhead, as well as the "indirect time" (i.e., time not charged to projects) of technical personnel. These project versus nonproject activities can be effectively monitored by "time analysis" reports, which track direct and indirect time both by person and for the firm. Such time reporting is an integral part of any project-oriented accounting system. Industry statistics for technical staff *utilization* (hours charged to projects as a percentage of all hours) is about 82 percent; for the firm as a whole, it averages about 62 percent.

The caution here is that if you have a decline in workload but no corresponding change in technical staff levels, your breakeven will rise. While you should not see a decline in your billing multiple, your overhead rate (and breakeven) will increase as you have both higher indirect (nonproject) time and therefore higher overhead costs. Observe the dynamics that follow, with a shift of 10 percent in the proportion of time (and dollars) charged to projects, as direct labor:

	Baseline	Change	Revised
Net fee income	375	−37	338
Direct labor*	143	−25	118
Overhead:			
Indirect labor*	102	25	127
Other overhead	107		107
Total overhead	209		234
Profit/(Loss)	23	−37	−14
*Memo: Total Payroll	245		245
Ratios:			
Billing multiple	2.62		2.62
Overhead rate	1.46		1.98

Same billing multiple (but on less volume)—higher overhead rate—and a profit position for the firm has turned into a loss. Or viewed differently, you have less revenue dollars but the same costs. This underscores the need to be proactive in your staffing and to maintain as much flexibility as possible with your technical staffing needs.

Summing It All Up

The practice of architecture can be fun; it should be fun. You can make statements with your work. You can even make greater contributions, and for a longer time, if you have a profitable, healthy practice that allows you to invest in the best people, the best technology, and the best marketing and promotional efforts. Making a profit while you practice good design is not an either/or proposition. You can do both, and it doesn't have to be burdensome to stay focused on the business aspects. The basic rules are:

- Negotiate contracts for *mutual* benefit with the client (be paid fairly).
- Manage projects by focusing on the three key elements.
- Maintain flexibility with your staffing (it's a volatile world).
- *Invest* in support staff and activities, based on tangible paybacks.
- Designate specific people to manage the overhead components.
- Don't be a banker—bill promptly and expect clients to pay *on time*.
- Get a system that will work *for you.*
- Establish a banking relationship—before you even *need* it.
- Understand where you are *(check those ratios)*—respond as needed.

Whatever you do, don't become an accountant; the world needs your design contribution. But also don't ignore the numbers; they are important. But keep it simple—it really can be.

The Real Meaning of Green Design: Fees and Schedules

Norman Rosenfeld, FAIA, is a prominent New York City practitioner. Here he shares his candid views of how he arrives at setting fees and implications of this for design time. If he is unable to negotiate a contract with what he feels is adequate compensation to produce high quality architecture, he says, "No." Even in this enormously competitive environment, he will not compromise the project or his reputation for another commission. So the cliché, "Get the job, get the job, get the job," should not be an absolute until appropriate terms are discussed. You don't want to be in the position described by William Fanning: "Architects end up paying tuition for a design education, and then paying for a business education through poor compensation."[3]

Because projects are circumstance specific (they're all different) and because the nature of architects and clients is so variable, it is impossible to prescribe any one specific method for establishing a fee for services. In general, the more defined the project, the more precise a fee estimate can be. Mr. Rosenfeld's approach below is quite common and combines a number of methods related to specific phases—to both determine and cross-check the numbers. For example, if project scope is ill-defined, at the start of a project, an hourly rate is fair; a stipulated (lump) sum can then be used on subsequent phases, once scope is pinned down. In some cases, time is difficult to predict in the construction contract administration phase; therefore, an hourly rate may be a viable option here too. Notwithstanding how fee is determined, budgeting for profit is essential, and should be a management priority.

NORMAN ROSENFELD, FAIA, is the founding principal of Norman Rosenfeld Architects, a New York City–based architectural firm, since 1969 specializing in the programming, planning, and design for health-care, education, and commercial projects.

Fees

To keep projects on-time and on-budget, our firm develops a project schedule (see Figure 5-2). We compare the documentation time-period (whether it's schematic, design development, or construction documents) with the fee. We perform various iterations of fees and projections of time.

Figures 5-3 and 5-4 show all the tasks in the project to which we attribute time (or staff hours; the initials represent the individuals involved). Multiplying the total hours by an assumed average rate per hour results in the gross cost. This particular example was a simultaneous equation. The client finally gave us the go-ahead in January; we knew the project had to begin construction in June, so we used the time frames from the schedule and then assigned hours to the various tasks that needed to be accomplished.

---

[3]Thomas Fisher "Who Makes What," *Progressive Architecture,* December (1995): 95.

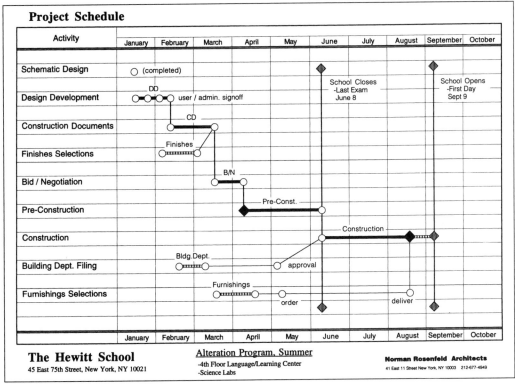

Figure 5-2 Project schedule. Courtesy of Norman Rosenfeld Architects.

Our fee is always based on time. That is what all professionals are selling—their time. Sometimes it's sold at a higher rate or a lower rate. It's time, but it's also related to the market and the ultimate fee a client expects to pay for a particular project (clients have conventionally thought of fee as a percentage of construction cost). We have a long history of doing certain projects and know the total effort that they will require, so while we will not necessarily relate it to a percentage of construction cost, it is a valid second check. For example, a 10,000 square foot renovation for a high-tech environment will require x number of hours in programming, y number of hours in schematic design, z number of hours in construction documents, and so on. We then project that to arrive at a number at the end. Then we cross-check it against the anticipated construction cost of the project to determine the percentage fee. It's not a science; it's an art with a little bit of science mixed into it.

The fee for our example project is likely to be about 15 percent; since much hand-holding to develop the project was required, it is speculative as to whether this fee level will generate a profit. When the project is complete and we know that we're in a slight loss position, that may be as a result of the factor of overhead—the cost of running the office. The number of people and projects in the office and the amount of total fees affect the proportion of fee that may be attributable to overhead. The office expenses are fixed, and if there is more work and more projects, then the overhead

THE HEWITT SCHOOL							ALTERATION PROGRAM	
45 East 75 Street, New York, NY							4TH FLOOR & SCIENCE LABS	

TASK BUDGET

TASK NO.	TASK DESCRIPTION	STAFF HOURS					TOTAL HOURS	GROSS COST
		NR	LM	JH	SR	EI		
PRE-DESIGN								
	FIELD SURVEY		4		4		8	$760
	PREPARE BASE DRAWINGS		4			8	12	$1,140
	USER PROGRAM MEETING		4	4			8	$760
	SUB-TOTAL - PRE-DESIGN	0	12	4	0	12	28	$2,660
SCHEMATIC DESIGN								
	DEV./CONFIRM PLAN & ELEVATIONS	1	6	20		6	33	$3,135
	USER REVIEW MEETING		6	4			10	$950
	RESEARCH LAB EQUIP.		4	2			6	$570
	FINISHES SELECTIONS	2		8		12	22	$2,090
	PRESENTATION	2		12		12	26	$2,470
	MTG. MINUTES / ADMIN		14	8			22	$2,090
	SUB-TOTAL - SCHEMATIC DESIGN	5	30	54	0	30	119	$11,305
DESIGN DEVELOPMENT								
	OUTLINE SPECIFICATIONS	1	6	2			9	$855
	BACKGROUNDS TO ENGINEERS					6	6	$570
	ENGINEERING MTG. / WALKTHRU		6				6	$570
	DEVELOP SPECIAL DETAILS		24	12	6		42	$3,990
	LAB LIGHTING DESIGN / CEILINGS	1	6			6	13	$1,235
	RESEARCH CODE ISSUES		8				8	$760
	MTG. MINUTES / ADMIN	1	16	4			21	$1,995
	SUB-TOTAL - DESIGN DEVELOPMENT	3	66	18	6	12	105	$9,975
	SUB-TOTAL THRU D.D	8	108	76	6	54	252	$23,940
	ASSUMED AVG. RATE/HR							$95

Figure 5-3 Task budget for predesign, schematic design, and design development phases. Courtesy of Norman Rosenfeld Architects.

decreases and it costs less to do a job. Things are slower now than we'd like them to be, so this job is bearing a high burden of overhead. That can't be billed or reflected in a fee to a client, since they are not responsible for the high overhead at that particular point. We analyze fees and profitability at the end of a year on an annual basis to see how many projects we had and how the overhead is allocated. It is possible to take a capsule view of a particular project, but its real profitability will shake itself out at the end of the year.

One of the things we try to avoid is committing to lump-sum fees for things over which we have no control. For example, for some projects we will not establish a fee until we've done a study, which then provides us with an understanding of the scope and complexities of the project, its budget, and how it is to work with that client. All clients have their own vagaries, and certain clients are more costly for the architect to work with: They're indecisive, they can never arrange or attend meetings on time, they will hold decisions for weeks and not respond because they can't get consensus from their organization, and they will frequently change their minds—you learn that very quickly when you do a preliminary study for them.

The other end of the project is during construction, where we will establish a lump sum to do construction observation. If the contractor turns

TASK BUDGET

TASK NO.	TASK DESCRIPTION	STAFF HOURS NR	LM	JH	SR	EI	TOTAL HOURS	GROSS COST
CONSTRUCTION DOCUMENTS								
	(2)-CONST. FLOOR & CEILING PLANS		16			16	32	$3,040
	(1-1/2)-ELEVATION DRAWINGS		6			8	14	$1,330
	(2)-DETAIL SHEETS							
	-TYP.		8	2		16	26	$2,470
	-SKYLIGHT/ROOF		12	2	2		16	$1,520
	FINISHES COORDINATION		6	2		16	24	$2,280
	(1)-SYMBOLS/SCHEDULES/NOTES		8	4		8	20	$1,900
	LANDMARKS SUBMISSION		4				4	$380
	BLDG. DEPT. SUBMISSION		8			12	20	$1,900
	SPECIFICATIONS		30	6	2	8	46	$4,370
	COORDINATION/CONSULTANTS		8	1		4	13	$1,235
	MTGS./MINUTES	1	8	1			10	$950
	SUB-TOTAL - CONST. DOCS.	1	114	18	4	88	225	$21,375
BID PHASE								
	PRINTING OF DOCS./NOTICES		3		2	3	8	$760
	ATTEND PRE-BID MTG.		4		2		6	$570
	CLARIFICATIONS/ADDENDA		8		2	12	22	$2,090
	REVIEW BIDS/RECOMMEND.	3	12		3		18	$1,710
	SUB-TOTAL - BID PHASE	3	27	0	9	15	54	$5,130
PRE-CONSTRUCTION ADMINISTRATION								
	SITE VISITS/MEETINGS/MINUTES		12				12	$1,140
	SHOP DRAWING REVIEW		50	4	2		56	$5,320
	SUB-TOTAL PRE-CONSTRUCTION	0	62	4	2	0	68	$6,460
CONSTRUCTION ADMINISTRATION								
	SITE VISITS/MEETINGS/MINUTES		34				34	$3,230
	SHOP DRAWING REVIEW		20	2	2		24	$2,280
	PUNCH LIST		10				10	$950
	SUB-TOTAL -CONST. ADMIN	0	64	2	2	0	68	$6,460
	SUB-TOTAL THRU D.D.	8	108	76	6	54	252	$23,940
	(FROM PAGE 1)							
	GRAND TOTAL	12	375	100	23	157	667	$63,365
				ASSUMED AVG. RATE/HR.				$95

Figure 5-4 Task budget for construction documents, bid and negotiation, pre-construction administration, and construction administration phases. Courtesy of Norman Rosenfeld Architects.

out to be a poor performer, however, who slows it all down and costs the architect more field visits, we may seek an increase in our fee for these additional services.

A time budget must be established to monitor how you're spending time and fee. This helps to ensure that you don't fall into a hole too fast, and it lets you discover problems earlier rather than later. Some problems can't be corrected (i.e., some projects have certain built-in problems that could not have been anticipated); such a project becomes a sinkhole. Sometimes you have a client who is very difficult and indecisive, and you have to suffer. But on balance, we have run a profitable practice; some projects have been very profitable, some less so. Profit is very important so that you can be in practice (business) to do the next project and can invest some of that profit in new computers and software, for example, to stay current with technology. Some of the profit goes to marketing—developing printed ma-

THE HEWITT SCHOOL 45 East 75 Street, New York, NY						ALTERATION PROGRAM - 4TH FLOOR AND SCIENCE LABS		

TASK BUDGET

TASK NO.	TASK DESCRIPTION	STAFF HOURS					TOTAL HOURS	GROSS COST	% OF TOTAL
		NR	LM	JH	SR	EI			
SUMMARY									
	PRE-DESIGN	0	12	4	0	12	28	$2,660	4.2%
	SCHEMATIC DESIGN	5	30	54	0	30	119	$11,305	17.8%
	DESIGN DEVELOPMENT	3	66	18	6	12	105	$9,975	15.7%
	CONSTRUCTION DOCUMENTS	1	114	18	4	88	225	$21,375	33.7%
	BID PHASE	3	27	0	9	15	54	$5,130	8.1%
	PRE-CONSTRUCTION	0	62	4	2	0	68	$6,460	10.2%
	CONSTRUCTION ADMINISTRATION	0	64	2	2	0	68	$6,460	10.2%
	TOTAL LABOR	12	375	100	23	157	667	$63,365	100%
	ASSUMED AVG. RATE/HR.							$95	
	TOTAL LABOR							$63,365	76.5%
	MEP							$7,000	8.4%
	STRUCTURAL							$1,500	1.8%
	EXPEDITER							$1,000	1.2%
	(EST.) CONSULTANTS							$9,500	11.5%
	(EST.) DIRECT EXPENSES							$500	0.6%
	TOTAL EXPENSES							$82,865	100%
	(EST.) CONST. COST							$756,600	
	FEE %							11.0%	
	FURNISHINGS?								

Figure 5-5 Task budget summary. Courtesy of Norman Rosenfeld Architects.

terials, photography, and so on. How to spend your profits is a necessary business judgment. A lot of those profits go to bonuses to staff at the end of the year; good staff is the most important resource of any office. We think it is an important responsibility to recognize our staff's contributions with bonuses and salary increases.

Staff Compensation

The economics of how staff are compensated is another issue. Some offices don't pay for health insurance, but we do: We think that's very important. Some offices don't give bonuses and don't recognize employees' contributions to the firm in a financial way. There are other firms that extract enormous overtime without paying for it. While we do not pay directly for overtime, we do recognize extra effort in both base compensation and in bonuses. Sometimes bonuses are given semiannually. We employ highly competent people and they should be recognized financially—New York is an expensive town to live in. Our staff should be paid at least as well as the

THE HEWITT SCHOOL		ALTERATION PROGRAM	
45 East 75 Street, New York, NY			- 4TH FLOOR AND SCIENCE LABS
		PROJECT BUDGET	
PROJECT AREA	1. SCIENCE LABS	2. LEARNING CENTER	3. LANGUAGE CLASSROOMS
Construction Budget**	$160,000	$190,000	$115,000
Construction Contingency- 10%	$16,000	$19,000	$11,500
Equipment***	$40,000	$20,000	$20,000
Furniture and Furnishings****	$10,000	$4,500	$20,000
Furniture and Furnishings Fees	$1,500	$500	$2,500
Architectural and Engineering Fees			
Through Const. Documents(80%)	$32,000	$24,000	$16,000
Bid Neg. & Const. Observ.(20%)	$8,000	$6,000	$4,000
Total(100%)	$40,000	$30,000	$20,000
SUB-TOTAL	$267,500	$264,000	$189,000
Project Contingency- 5%	$13,400	$13,200	$9,500
PROJECT COST	$280,900	$277,200	$198,500
		*TOTAL PROJECT COST	$756,600
		*FEE SUMMARY	
		Architectural and Engineering	
		Through CD's(80%)	$72,000
		Bid / Const. Obs.(20%)	$18,000
		Total(100%)	$90,000
		Furniture and Furnishings	$4,500
		TOTAL ARCHITECTURAL FEES	$94,500
		(separate projects)	
		Through CD's(80%)	$66,000
		Bid / Const. Obs.(20%)	$16,500
		TOTAL ARCHITECTURAL FEE	$82,500
		(Combined Projects)	
Notes:			
* Does not include Expediting and other reimbursable expenses.			
** Per adjusted Cost Estimate by Riskin Contracting			
*** Science Lab and other equipment costs to be verified by Hewitt.			
**** Furniture budget estimate to be verified by Hewitt.			

Figure 5-6 Project budget. Courtesy of Norman Rosenfeld Architects.

clients with whom we are working. They certainly should be paid as well as some of the craftspeople working on the jobs, but many architects are not paid as much as plumbers or electricians, and I find that to be totally skewed. Contributions of architects are very poorly valued by society. Architects have chosen to sell themselves short. Architects compete on fees with a very damaging result. Lawyers or physicians don't do that (although with health-care reform physicians' fees are being brought into line).

Monitoring Projects

People fill out time cards on a daily basis. [The time card, for all firm members including principals, is perhaps the most significant tool for establishing and tracking the cost to produce projects.] The time cards are recorded by our bookkeeper biweekly (corresponding to our pay periods). That time goes into a computer, and job cost reports are developed that indicate how much time has been spent (and by whom) on the project. If you see that you are exceeding the budget, you will do one of three things: You will nod your head and keep going; you will determine what you should be doing in the next period to correct the overexpenditure of the previous period (and see where you went wrong); or you may attribute some particular project- or client-specific reason to it—and perhaps seek an additional fee from the client. You may determine that the additional fee might be appropriate but that it is politically not correct to ask for it at that juncture. After the architect's economics at the end of the project are known, you may then seek a fee adjustment, since you can demonstrate to the client the real costs incurred for the work done on the client's behalf. Often you will do nothing but run scared to the next phases of the project and let people know that they should try to be more efficient and effective in coming out at the end.

The project architect (or manager) monitors what people are doing—monitors the progress being made against the budget that has been created. I'd like to add that, in our office, design quality is never compromised. That is a problem because we provide our services, and so represent to our clients, that we can only turn the faucet on full. Because of our reputation (the client's selection of us has usually been based on the quality of our past work or on what others have said about us), there's no way that we can't do what we had represented or what the client expected from us. It is an enormously competitive environment, and there are other firms that are getting projects because they are quoting lower fees than we are. We are letting these projects go because we simply can't perform at that lower fee level without compromising quality along with our reputation. This is a very big dilemma these days.

Streamlining Production

One of the things we can do in this very competitive environment is to carefully analyze how we produce work and identify where we can seek effective shortcuts in documentation—not in design or quality but in being smart about recording information from which the contractors can build. We take a very active role during the construction phase, including analysis of contractor claims for changes. Doing a lot of up-front work (particularly in the area of renovations) by gathering good information so the documentation closely reflects the existing conditions allows thoughtful construction detailing that minimizes change orders at the end. Similarly, intensive programming with the client up-front is more likely to satisfy that client's complicated needs.

We are able to validate higher fees in part because of our very active role during construction. If there are contractor changes, we negotiate with the contractors on behalf of the client—and this is significant. We have found that on occasion we have saved our total construction administration fee due to our ability to negotiate change orders with the contractor. Once the contractor knows that's who you are, he backs away, and doesn't pursue unreasonable and inflated costs for changes. So we don't compromise service. But we do have *complete* drawings so that all the necessary information is documented, which leaves little opportunity for ambiguity and little basis for the contractor to claim misunderstandings.

We try to improve our delivery—the documentation component—by being lean and tight in both drawings and notes, while hopefully taking less time. It does take time, however, to learn how to edit.

We are experiencing a trend toward smaller projects. In an office this size, smaller projects are very expensive to produce. We can do a three-million-dollar project for almost the same amount of effort it takes to do a one-million dollar project. But we can get almost three times the fee for the three-million-dollar project! There are smaller projects around, and we are trying now very seriously to (1) submit competitive fees and (2) develop tight office budgets against those fees, then seek the ability to execute them efficiently and economically, maintaining the standards of design, planning, and quality of product. We will take on only quality projects (which does not necessarily mean high cost)—that's a given. Our clients want that, and understand it requires some greater effort, and recognize it in a higher fee. Some of our up-front planning efforts have saved staffing costs—if we save one full-time employee to operate a facility, that can equate to $50,000 a year or $1 million over a twenty-year life—a significant value added service to our clients. This planning effort requires a large amount of professional time to understand our client's operations and then to devise a workable plan to effect this operational savings. That effort can certainly command a premium fee. Some client projects simply don't warrant that level of quality, and we would not likely be doing work for those clients. We seek clients who appreciate the work that we do, will pay for it fairly, and be happy with the results. This is the secret to repeat client projects.

Conventional Versus Progressive Real Estate Development

CHRISTOPHER B. LEINBERGER is a real estate developer, author, consultant, and teacher. He is Chief Executive Officer of the Historic District Improvement Company and a partner in Arcadia Land Co., a New Urbanism development company. He is also a consultant with Robert Charles Lesser & Co., the largest independent real estate consulting firm in the United States. He has written for numerous national publications, including the *Atlantic Monthly, Nation, Urban Land,* and various Brookings Institution publications. Mr. Leinberger is a graduate of Swarthmore College and the Harvard Business School.

American real estate development, how we build our metropolitan areas and invest over a third of the country's capital, has become commoditized and formularized over the past few generations. This has happened due to the need to more rationally regulate the flow of capital into this huge asset class, an asset class equal in importance to the other three major asset classes: stocks, bonds, and cash. The form and substance of these commoditized formulas have been based upon the experience of the past sixty years, since the end of the Second World War. The driving force of these formulas has been to accommodate the prevailing transportation system of our era, just as transportation has always driven the form of our cities throughout recorded history. In the modern era, that transportation system is based almost entirely upon the automobile and truck.

The formulas by which America develops its built environment are collectively known as "conventional development." The elements of conventional development include:

- *Single Product Type*—Every development can only employ one product type, e.g., neighborhood retail, walk-up rental apartment, entry-level single-family housing, etc. A single product type keeps the development simple and does not complicate it with complex financing, marketing, and construction.
- *Modular*—Every development must stand on its own for parking, access, signage, marketing, management, etc. The only thing a development project uses in common with other developments is the roadway in front of the property.
- *Segregated*—Real estate development is generally aimed at defined income classes, which usually translates into racial segregation as well. Mixing income classes in a single development is not generally done, particularly with housing, since it is felt that significantly lower income households in the same neighborhood would threaten housing values. And since a household's home is usually the largest part of their net worth, any threat to the value is resisted.
- *Car and Truck Access and Visibility*—Conventional development is defined by its access by automobile (residential, commercial, and industrial) and truck (commercial and industrial). The visibility from the street is also a defining factor that, added to access, determines how the buildings address the street and the large setback so as to provide lots of visible surface parking.
- *Parking*—The parking available on the site determines the amount of buildable floor area. Since most parking is at-grade due to the economics of surface lots, it usually occupies the majority of the site and, as mentioned above, is almost always in the front of the site.
- *Short-Term Financial Return*—Due to how conventional development is underwritten (the financial analysis and financing process), the financial returns must be short-term. This means that construction costs must be minimized, both to insure a project's ability to quickly cash flow and not to tie up capital in a location that might become obsolete since sprawl will eventually take the demand further to the fringe.
- *Disposable Product*—The result of the above practices is that conventional development results in buildings and developments that have a short-term life, generally in the seven-to-ten year time frame—before there is a decision made whether to completely renovate or to assume a lower-level clientele and therefore a lower-level valuation—generally as a result of sprawl.
- *Suburban or Semirural Character*—Conventional development will almost always result in very low-density product. Conventional development has been suburban in character (0.2–0.4 floor area ratio) for

nearly all development between 1950 and 1990 and has been becoming increasingly semirural (floor area ratio of under 0.2) after 1990.

Conventional development is the type of development that is legal (zoning assumes it), financeable (banks and investors understand it), and architects and construction firms have significant experience designing and building it. Conventional development is encompassed by the nineteen standard product types (see Exhibit 5–5), which are the types of develop-

---

Exhibit 5–5
The Nineteen Standard Real Estate Product Types

Third Quarter, 2004

These real estate products are the easiest and most acceptable to the conventional investment community. They are generally single product type, stand-alone developments with self-contained parking, though some mixed-use developments are now possible.

Income Products

Office
Build to Suit Office
Mixed Use Urban Office/
    Retail/Restaurant
Medical Office
Multi-Tenant Office

Rental Apartments
Garden Apartments
Urban Apartments

Industrial
Multi-Tenant Bulk Warehouse
Build to Suit

Miscellaneous
Self Storage
Mobile Home Park

Retail
Grocery Anchored Retail
Big Box Anchored Retail
Lifestyle Center
Outlet Mall

Hotel
Not Possible Without Subsidy

For-Sale Products

Housing
Entry Level
Move-up Housing
Luxury Housing
Retirement/Assisted
Resort/Second Home

Source: Arcadia Land Company and Robert Charles Lesser & Co.

ment projects that can be easily built and financed and are legal. Virtually every one of the nineteen standard product types must be built in a suburban or semirural character and is generally described as sprawl.

In contrast, progressive development has completely different characteristics and resulting character. Progressive development is comprised of a long list of relatively new alternatives, such as New Urbanism, conservation development, downtown revitalization, corridor redevelopment, among others. The public policy side of progressive development tends to be promoted by various smart growth initiatives, generally at the state and regional levels. In fact, much of what is referred to as progressive development is actually "old urbanism," having been common throughout the history of city-building for the past 5,000 years, probably reaching a pinnacle between 1893 (the Chicago World's Fair, which led to the City Beautiful Movement), and the Depression of the 1930s, which virtually stopped construction in this country. The forty years between 1893 and the early 1930s saw the flowering of some of the finest modern urbanism, which combined the growing requirements of moving and parking the car without sacrificing what was special about "old urbanism." After the Depression and the Second World War ended in1945, the development industry in the United States seemed to get collective amnesia, gobsmacking old urbanism, and introducing what has come to be known as conventional development in its place.

The elements of progressive development include:

- *Complex Mix of Product Types*—There is a need to build a much more complex set of products within close proximity of one another to encourage a walkable environment. This can include multiple types of products (residential, retail, office, hotel, etc.) next to one another or even in the same vertical configuration as a mixed-use project, e.g., housing over retail at the ground level. These types of projects may not be legal, based upon current zoning. In addition, investors do not understand this kind of development, and architects and contractors have little or no experience with this type of development.
- *Integrated*—The concept is to build seamless communities that integrate uses and income classes, bringing all elements of the region together, whether to visit, work, or live in the development.
- *Multiple Transportation Options*—Getting to and from progressive developments is critical and plans need to include as many transportation options as is feasible. This includes cars and trucks but also walking, transit, and bicycles.
- *Parking*—While the car needs to be accommodated, once their car is parked, occupants should be able to get around the progressive development on foot or by transit for the rest of their visit. The initial phases of a progressive development will require conventional parking ratios—e.g., four spaces, 1,000 square feet of retail—but over time, those ratios will drop as more people get to the development using alternatives such as transit, walking, and bicycle. There is a probable eventual need for structured parking to make most progressive developments work if there is a major commercial component in the development to maintain walkability.

- *Mid-to Long-Term Financial Returns*—For 5,000 years, real estate has been a long-term investment class. The IRS allows fixed commercial real estate assets to be depreciated over thirty-nine years, a very long period of time for a conventional financial investment. By approaching real estate with a mid- to long-term financial perspective (six to twelve years for midterm and over thirteen years for long-term), the progressive development can be much better built, using materials that will not only last longer but will actually improve with age. Conventional development tends to use sidings and windows made of vinyl, for example, which have a sixteen- to eighteen-year life, and roofs made of asphalt, which has a twenty-year life. This is opposed to more expensive but longer lasting materials such as steel-frame and brick siding, which has a hundred year life, and tile or slate roofing, which has a forty-five-year life. However, this quality level costs much more and means lower short-term returns. As a result, progressive development financing requires significant "patient" equity, combined with conventional equity and debt, to achieve the quality level that results in buildings that will last for decades to come. The financial results can be among the best in the real estate business since an "upward spiral of value creation" kicks in once critical mass is achieved in progressive development. This will result in value ratios that are as high, if not higher, than any other location in the respective metropolitan area, but only in the mid- to long-term.
- *Built for the Ages*—Progressive development gets better with age due to the construction quality and the importance of design. These are buildings that evoke an emotional response, so much so that when the buildings need to be rehabilitated, generally in forty to sixty years, the then owner will spend more money modernizing the building and probably making it even better than when it was originally built rather than the probable cheaper alternative, which is to tear down and build a new structure. This cannot be said for conventional development, say, a big box retail store in the middle of a twenty-acre surface lot, which has questionable long-term rehabilitation value.
- *Walkable Urban Character*—The center of any progressive development will have an urban character (floor area ratio over 1.0), creating a special walkable place. Since walkability has always been a radius of about 1,500 feet, until people look for an alternative mode of transportation, this translates into a place that is about 80 to 120 acres. Densities can step down outside of the urban core to suburban and even semirural development, but there needs to be a center for a progressive development to have a focus, ideally with a sufficient critical mass of mixed-use commercial and residential buildings. The walkable urban place is not only one of the major competitive advantages of progressive development but it puts a governor in fear of real estate developers and owners—overbuilding—since there is a natural limit on competition in a confined urban area defined by its walkability.

Today, there are significant barriers to progressive development. These barriers are legal, financial, and design-, and construction-oriented, which makes it much more difficult, time consuming, and risky to do. Eventually with more experience and case studies of financially successful projects, these barriers should begin to be lowered, though it will probably take at least a decade for progressive development to be considered an acceptable alternative to conventional development for local government, investors, and banks. However, it is apparent that a significant underserved market exists for special places where one can live, work, and play within walking distance. What the market wants, the market generally gets.

Case Study | Downtown Albuquerque Theater Block

CHRIS LEINBERGER demonstrates the application of his progressive real estate development ideas in the following case study of an astonishing downtown revival.

On May 4, 2000, the management team of the Historic District Improvement Company (HDIC) was meeting to discuss two significant decisions they had to make about the first major project kicking off the redevelopment of downtown Albuquerque, New Mexico. The project was a highly unusual mixed-use development comprised of a fourteen-screen, 50,000-square-foot movie theater, immediately surrounded by seven individually designed buildings with restaurants and retail on the ground floor and possibly office space on the second and third floors. There were commitments from a national movie theater to be the anchor tenant and from a regional restaurant for the 7,000-square-foot anchor space next to the entrance to the movie. However, the rest of the space (53,000 square feet, or 48 percent of the project) was not yet leased. It was the most complex project ever built in the Southwest, totaling 110,000 square feet, and supported by a 180,000-square-foot, 630-space parking deck on the next block. The $14 million Theater Block was going into a downtown that had not seen a private sector building permit in fifteen years and was generally considered to be clinically dead.

The strategic plan for the redevelopment of downtown had been established in October 1998, and HDIC was formed late that year to be the "catalytic developer," the firm responsible for taking above-market risks to "kick start" the redevelopment process. HDIC's job was to demonstrate to the rest of the Albuquerque development and investment community that taking a risk to learn a more complex method of building and financing projects was worth it. The downtown strategy had met with early success, such as the establishment of a privately funded business improvement district with an annual budget of $800,000 on enhanced safety, cleanliness, and promotion. The downtown strategy included throwing out the existing zoning and replacing it with: a "form-based," New Urbanist code; a way-finding system of signs; the conversion of one-way streets to two-way; festivals; special events at night; and attracting the back office headquarters of the GAP downtown (from San Francisco), among many other things. Yet the retail real estate market was very weak, rents averaging between $8 and $10 per square foot annually (triple net). The office market was even weaker, having an 18 percent vacancy rate and rents between $12 and $18 per square foot annually (gross, which translates into $6 to $12 per square foot, triple net).

There were two major decisions HDIC management faced on that warm May day. The first was whether to build the office space on the second and third floors of the building, which represented 25 percent of the project square footage. It was considered suicidal to put more office space into the very weak downtown market. Who would be the tenants? Would these tenants pay what it cost, even at a break-even rent level ($21 per square foot), which was far above the market rent? Yet this was the gateway into downtown. One story of retail space immediately in front of a sixty-five-foot high movie theater, exposing forty-five feet of cinder block wall above the twenty-foot restaurant on the ground floor, was felt to be a terrible first impression of downtown. And if the downtown revitalization was successful, not building the second and third floors would be considered a wasted opportunity five to ten years down the line (adding the second and third floor later was not considered feasible since it would mean closing the first floor retail and restaurant space, something the lease with the restaurant would not allow).

The second major decision was whether to continue the joint venture with the "building development" partner, which was one of the world's largest and best capitalized development firms. HDIC's strategy was to be the "land developer," providing the land, parking, tax abatement, the lead tenants (movie theater and restaurant), and other incentives. The building developer was to arrange for financing (splitting the equity investment between the two firms), bank loans, construction management, and property management. However, the building developer had only built conventional, suburban projects. They had never built such a high density, complex, mixed-use project, though it was considered a small project in size to them. As such, they wanted to build it to a quality level that was comparable to their suburban experience, estimating the construction costs for the shell at $35 per square foot and the contribution to tenant improvements (furniture, furnishings, and equipment, or FF&E) at $25 per square foot. HDIC management had concerns that replicating a suburban quality project would not attract people back to downtown.

HDIC management had to make up their minds within days as to whether they were going to build the office space and whether their partners were right in building a suburban qual-ity project in downtown Albuquerque. The financial projections showed that the project worked, but only at the conventional construction- and tenant-improvement budget HDIC's building development partner assumed. If this project failed financially, the downtown revitalization that was just beginning would probably die. If the project was viewed as a little piece of suburbia placed downtown, what would be the competitive advantage of downtown? Downtown was considered scary to most suburbanites, so there had to be real walkable "urbanity" for the project and downtown to succeed.

The Decisions and Results of the Decisions

HDIC's management decided to build-out the office space, which would have doomed the project from a financial perspective if it did not lease up at the top of the rent range (or higher) in downtown. HDIC also insisted that the overall budget of the project be increased to achieve the high-quality urban construction that people walking in a downtown, rather than driving by at 45 miles an hour in the suburbs, would expect. This increased the construction budget to $80 per square foot and the tenant improvement budget to $50 per square foot, a total of 117 percent over the original budget. The HDIC building development partner felt the project could not be financed, and the risk of building the office space was far too high. As a result, HDIC decided to assume the role of building developer, having a friendly parting of the ways with their partner. HDIC had never been a building developer, increasing their risk even higher.

The financing of the project meant increased "patient" equity to make it happen, which HDIC provided, even though it meant they had to postpone other projects they were hoping to begin by diverting their limited equity to this project. The management of HDIC had to aggressively market the project themselves, since the conventional leasing companies in Albuquerque did not believe downtown revitalization would happen, so they did not offer their services.

Figure 5-7 The theater block project, highlighting the Century Theater. This mixed-use project has become the new gateway to downtown Albuquerque, New Mexico. Courtesy of Christopher B. Leinberger.

The results were that the movie theater opened in November 2001, and it achieved patronage 40 percent over national averages. Nearly all of the retail and restaurant space was leased within a year of completion, achieving rents between $20 and $27 per square foot (triple net), which was two to three times the downtown rates and just below suburban regional mall rents. The office space was almost completely leased within a year of the completion of the project at $18 per square foot (gross). While these rents were less than breakeven, the superior retail and restaurant rents made up for it financially. The project began to have a positive cash flow within a year of completion, about two years before it was expected, and at nearly twice the levels projected.

Two years after the project was completed, a senior executive from the national building developer who was the initial partner came to town and toured the project. His reaction was that their firm could not have financed the project and therefore could not have built it. Their experience with conventional suburban development did not give them the financial capacity or development experience to do a progressive, urban project of this kind. The risk of building a suitable gateway project to downtown, which included adding the two stories of office space and dramatically increasing the construction budget, was successfully met, though not without many sleepless nights on the part of HDIC's management.

Chapter 6

To Market, to Market

" . . . to buy a fat pig. Home again, home again, market is done." What might be wrong with this last line of the classic Mother Goose nursery rhyme? Right, "market" is *never* done! Marketing should be an ongoing and enjoyable part of doing architecture, not a necessary evil to be done only when we are desperate for a job. Be happy, relaxed, and confident; do good work; demonstrate design and project management expertise; and, most important, research prospective clients thoroughly (i.e., really be *responsive* to and *understand* the client and the project's operational needs), and you will improve your chances for success. This is not to suggest that it is easy. Witness architect Carol Ross Barney's marketing experiences from internship to ownership:

> When I was a young architect working at Holabird and Root, I was sent out on many interviews with their old, corporate clients. I thought it was a lot of fun; I had a great time. I very much enjoyed talking about the work that needed to be done. I thought that was marketing. That's all I ever had to do—I never had to make the sale.
>
> At another firm, my marketing experience was quite different. We had a hands-on seminar that started off with one of those self-analysis tests. The founding principal called me in to his office and told me that the tests had been graded, and I was the only person in his firm that had any aptitude for marketing. I was appalled. It did, however, give me a little bit more confidence about doing marketing. But it is still hard—there are times when I just sit and grind my teeth. I must keep remembering that the rejections aren't directed at me personally; it's all about business. Whenever I get turned down too many times, I think about all the hard-working copier salesmen who call, and somehow I feel better about what we are doing.
>
> Now, as principal of my own firm, I do the marketing and the sales, and most of our people miss the majority of the rejections. The marketing process is lengthy—there are usually no quick fixes. It is a *process of building relationships,* which take time to mature, and (like anything worthwhile) it's a full-time challenge to keep those relationships going.

Perhaps the single most important strategy in marketing is providing excellent service to *existing* clients (i.e., maintaining good relationships and doing good design, with all that this phrase implies). *Repeat clients and referrals from existing clients amount to a huge chunk of new business for architectural firms.*

Briefly, other effective strategies fall under the category of public relations and publicity: giving talks, writing articles, publishing projects, and winning awards. The audience for all these efforts, however, must be carefully considered. Other design professionals are a group not likely to produce project leads, but reprints of articles in architectural, engineering, or construction journals can help establish credibility. Exposure to potential *client* groups will likely yield more contacts. Exposure and initial leads, by themselves, are not enough! Follow-ups with appropriate supporting material are essential to begin a dialogue and nurture a *personal relationship*.

The client (or prospective client) relationship is as basic to getting jobs as it is to shaping the architecture. Always remember this crucial point in conducting professional practice in any capacity. It seems to be the one element common to all successful firms, large or small.

Marketing is a complicated art and science, so, for this chapter, I enlisted one of the world's best at doing it—Gene Kohn—to introduce some general concepts along with stories illustrating how they are applied. Topics include proactive and reactive marketing, diversification of project types and geographic markets, promoting specialized knowledge (i.e., what makes you distinctive), anticipating opportunities, brochures and promotional material, interviews, proposals, and competitions.

The chapter opens with a top-ten list: David Koren, a Senior Associate and Marketing Director at Gensler, shares his rules of marketing. They are indeed words to practice by. The chapter also includes tips on presentation skills, key elements for creating an architecture firm Web site, and concludes with a powerful case study by two noted Fellows of the Society for Marketing Professional Services, Jean R. and Philip F. Valence.

Top 10 Rules of Marketing

DAVID KOREN is Marketing Director for Gensler's 250-person New York office where he is responsible for marketing strategy, strategic alliances, market research, and public relations. He is cochair of the marketing committee of the AIA New York chapter and is an active member of the Society for Marketing Professional Services. David is the author of *Architect's Essentials of Marketing* (New York: John Wiley & Sons, 2004), which is endorsed by the American Institute of Architects. © 2004 David Koren.

Marketing isn't just about networking, submitting proposals, and making presentations. It's about communicating your message to your intended audience—your prospective clients—using a wide variety of methods, including everything from your Web site to the way you answer the phone. What does your Web site say about you? What does the way you answer the phone say about you? Marketing is central to your business and touches everything you do. It doesn't start when you need work, and stop when you get it. It is a continual ongoing process of using communication to develop your business.

To be a successful marketer, you need to develop habits that encourage clear and immediate communication with your clients and prospective clients. In your firm, you need to strive to develop a culture of marketing, so that in effect everyone in the firm, from the person who answers the phone to the person who signs the checks, is promoting the same message with regard to who you are as a company.

Here are top ten basic rules that underlie a successful marketing practice:

1. Never Wait

Work is not going to come to you, at least not usually. Don't just sit there: do something! Pick up the phone, write a letter, think about your strategy. Don't be passive, allowing your success to be in somebody else's hands. Take action. Now!

2. The Client is the Center of Everything You Do

Whatever your message, your client or prospective client is your intended audience. Your work, the level of service you provide, and your communications should all focus on the client and their needs and issues. In everything you do, strive to get your message to your client. It's not about you; it's about the client.

3. Relationships Are Vital

Build relationships with everyone you know. People don't hire you because you're the best for the job or because you proposed the right fee. People hire people they like and trust. Trust is strongly reinforced by third-party endorsements, when somebody other than your client or you tells them that you're great. The endorsement can come from anywhere, at any time.

4. Do Great Work

No matter how good a marketer you are, you have to have something to sell. Since you're selling design services, it's crucial that you have a good portfolio. But more than this, you need to do your best work on every project, whether it's a "portfolio builder" or not. Your work says who you are as a person and a professional. If you aren't doing great work, your clients and others will notice, and will probably tell others.

5. Get the Word Out

When you do your best work, make sure everybody knows about it. Utilize the media intelligently to spread the word about your projects to the right audience. Think about whom you're trying to reach and what is the best way to reach them. What magazines do your clients read? How can you get your projects into those magazines?

6. Always Have a Plan

So you've got it rolling: You're working on projects, you're getting new work. Now what? Where do you want to go? What do you really want to be working on? How do you get there from here? If you don't know where you're going, you'll probably have a hard time getting there. So make a plan of where you want your business to go, and figure out how you get there from here. What's the next step?

7. Be a Professional

There's no excuse for bad behavior. Behave like a professional and people will take you seriously. Act with integrity at all times, and people will want to work with you. Be honest, be forthright, be ethical, and, most importantly, be who you are.

8. Remember Your Friends

Marketing really is a lot like life. Cultivate business relationships with people you like, and do what you can to help them. They'll remember you, and they'll return the favor. Build up a collection of good will in those around you, and your business will benefit.

9. Be Passionate

What do you care about? Don't be afraid to tell people about it. Why do you want this particular project? Figure out a good reason, connect the project to your passion, and let your passion propel you forward. If you're passionate and energetic about a project, if you seem like you really care, how can anyone doubt your commitment to do your best work?

10. Dream Big

Don't be afraid to dream big. Where do you really want to go? Who do you really want to be? What do you really want to do with your practice and your life? Don't be satisfied with humble ambitions. Allow yourself to reach for the stars. You don't get to be a leader in your field by accident.

Marketing for Success

In the extremely competitive environment in which architectural commissions are secured, successful marketing strategies are more important than ever. Good strategies have driven the rapid growth of the architectural firm Kohn Pedersen Fox and made them a legend in their own time. Gene Kohn is largely responsible and generously shares his wisdom for getting clients and landing big projects. *Architecture* has reported that Gene researches the business background of every prospective client so fastidiously that he is often praised for knowing more about their hometowns and company histories than they do. In Gene's words: "Developing anecdotal common ground with clients is essential to understanding the goals and aspirations for a project."

A. EUGENE KOHN, FAIA, RIBA, JIA, is President of the internationally renowned architectural firm, Kohn Pedersen Fox Associates, PC (KPF). Gene was assisted in writing this piece by Elizabeth C. Pratt.[1]

Why Market?

Philip Johnson, one of America's most well-known architects, has stated on a number of occasions, "The first principle about architecture is, 'Get the job.'"

This may or may not come as a surprise, but most architects, even those with international reputations, often fight tooth and nail for a project. The number of good architectural firms is constantly growing, and consequently the competition for projects is becoming increasingly stiff. While having a good reputation for excellence in design and project management is certainly essential to a firm's marketability, these qualities are not always enough to win a project. Architects are beginning to realize that if they do not invest more time and money into their marketing efforts now, they will lose in the long run.

One of KPF's most frequently asked questions is how the firm was able to grow so rapidly. When the firm was founded in 1976, there were a total of four architects on staff; now the firm has close to 250 members. I strongly believe that much of KPF's success is due to the emphasis we have placed on strategic marketing and, most importantly, our willingness to take risks. As an example of the kind of time, money commitment, patience, and determination often necessary to bring in work is the following true story of how Kohn Pedersen Fox won the commission for the Bond Building/ Chifley Square in Sydney, Australia.

A Success Story

In 1987, Richard Travis, an architect from Sydney, visited me at my New York office. The purpose of his visit was to form a professional relationship to pursue projects together in Australia. Earlier in 1987, I had attended a conference that was comprised of developers, builders, investors, financiers, and related real estate persons, as well as architects and planners. One of the keynote speakers at the conference had been an economist who pointed to the audience and said, "If you are not international by 1990, half of you will not be in business by the mid-1990s." With the words of this economist echoing in my mind, I realized that working with Richard and his firm, Travis Partners Pty. Ltd., might open the doors for us, not only in Australia but in Asia as well.

Soon after that meeting, Richard called to tell me that Alan Bond, unquestionably one of the most powerful and successful businessmen in Australia, was planning to build the best new major office and retail tower in Sydney and was bidding for a prime site at Chifley Square. As the result of a contract within the Bond Organization, Richard's firm, along with KPF, was asked to evaluate the site and create a conceptual study to be used in the bidding process. We were led to believe that if Alan Bond was awarded

---

[1]Courtesy of A. Eugene Kohn, Kohn Pederson Fox Associates, 111 West 57th Street, New York, NY 10010.

the site, our team would be named the architects. Thus when Alan Bond did obtain the site, Norman Kurtz (of the mechanical, electrical, and plumbing engineering firm Flack + Kurtz Engineers) and I headed to Sydney to discuss the project and negotiate the fee. However, upon our arrival we learned that, rather than awarding our team the commission, Alan Bond was planning to hold a design competition among some of the best architects in the world, and we were to be included.

Needless to say, the idea that we had traveled all the way to Sydney to be included in a design competition left us frustrated and extremely disappointed. We decided to give ourselves a deadline of one week to turn Alan's thinking around and win the project without a competition. Achieving this goal would require a flawless strategy and unyielding determination.

The first goal was to meet with Mr. Bond himself, which would not be easy because he was traveling in Australia all week and would be nearly impossible to contact. Also, we were told, even if we were fortunate enough to see him, it would only be for twenty minutes because Mr. Bond was a very busy man. Nonetheless, Phillip Isaacs, an Australian associate of Norman Kurtz, focused on trying to locate Alan while I worked with Richard and Norman to schedule time with Steve Goslin, the head of Alan Bond's Sydney office, who would be the project director. Luckily, we were able to meet with Steve the next day, but while he seemed very impressed with our work, he still felt that a design competition was the way to proceed.

This was not good enough for us. In a second attempt to impress Steve, we invited him and his wife, along with Alan's son John and his wife, to lunch at Phil Isaacs' local yacht club. Lunch, though formal enough to warrant place cards, was most relaxing and enjoyable and afforded us an opportunity to meet with John Bond and set the stage for a more formal meeting with him in his office later that afternoon. By that time we had formulated a convincing argument as to why a competition would not be in their best interest. First of all, it would be costly for both the Bond Organization and the participating architects; second, valuable time would be wasted—at least two or three months; and finally, competition designs are often completed without the client's participation and may not take cost and other local factors into consideration.

We had certainly made progress with John, but the key was to meet with Alan. Fortunately, we had developed a strong telephone relationship with his secretaries in Sydney and Perth and discovered that Alan would be in Sydney on that Friday. One of Alan's financial advisors, located in Scarsdale, New York, was a neighbor of Norman's; at Norman's suggestion, the neighbor phoned Alan. That call, coupled with our persistence, persuaded Alan to meet with us at 9:00 AM on Friday.

We worked very hard that Thursday evening, defining our strategy and putting together a slide show and accompanying dialogue. When we finally met Alan, he seemed impatient, opinionated, and gruff, but as soon as we began our presentation, he became more friendly and engaging, although interrupting our presentation by asking us excellent questions. At the end of an hour, we were preparing to leave when in walked a very beautiful woman. We were not introduced to her, but after she and Alan talked privately for a few minutes, he told her that he wanted to show her something interesting. He asked me to put the slide show back to the beginning and to go through it again, but instead of letting me do the talking, he presented the projects one by one himself, with the same enthusiasm and detail I had shown in presenting them to him.

I knew at that moment we were going to be the architect and sure enough we were selected that day. As a side note, Norman and I, along with our wives, celebrated that night at a wonderful intimate restaurant called the Kiosk at Manly beach and took a romantic ride on the ferry back to Sydney. Chifley Tower, now owned by MID of Osaka, Japan, led by Mr. Sekine, is over 1.2 million square feet and is regarded as one of the most outstanding buildings of Australia.

I have not been as excited about winning a project since that day, mostly because we created a strategy, followed it, and succeeded. We had tremendous enthusiasm, energy, and focus, as well as a client who responded positively. These were the components that helped to win this project. *However, while the ingredients in the recipe for success generally remain constant, their proportions often vary.*

Marketing Strategies

The most effective marketing techniques vary from firm to firm and from project to project. While specific marketing strategies depend greatly on the age and size of a firm, as well as its experience, there are generally two approaches to marketing: proactive and reactive.

Proactive Marketing

Proactive marketing is the best way to create new opportunities where none exist. It is an aggressive approach that involves making new contacts, exploring new markets, and coming up with new ideas that will interest a potential client.

Proactive marketing naturally played a much larger role in our promotional strategy when we were a younger and smaller firm. I remember contacting a potential client by telephone in hopes that he would consider KPF for a project he was planning. Apparently, he had already short-listed a group of architects and was about to make a selection. Before he could hang up on me, I blurted out that KPF was going to be the best architectural firm in the country and that he would be making a big mistake if he did not consider us. As soon as I said it, I wanted to take back this comment (I am not usually this boastful, although I do think very highly of our firm), but somehow this approach got us an interview and ultimately the commission. This former client and I are now good friends.

Characteristic of this bold marketing approach in our early days, we also approached the American Broadcasting Company (ABC) for a project. We had read about ABC's purchase of the Armory on 66th Street in New York City in the *New York Times Real Estate Section* and decided to contact the broadcasting giant for an interview. This project involved the conversion of the Armory into daytime soap studios. KPF's enthusiasm for taking on the modest 60,000-square-foot renovation project, which most larger firms may have considered too small, combined with personal contacts that Shelly Fox and I had at ABC, won us the project. This project was the start of a fifteen-year-plus relationship with ABC, throughout which we have completed a total of fifteen projects.

Marketing for Diversification

KPF's growth is partly the result of having diversified its base of projects from high-rise corporate office buildings, which made up the core of our portfolio in the 1980s, to include university work, convention centers, hotels, and cultural, retail, and entertainment facilities. Diversification, or not putting your eggs in one basket, is a type of company insurance for longevity; it also keeps the practice challenging and ultimately fulfilling.

Domestically, KPF has recently had success pursuing our first project in the health-care industry. When we first received the Request for Information for an 850,000-square-foot medical and research facility for the National Institutes of Health in Bethesda, Maryland, we were wary that our limited experience would work against us for such a high profile project. As part of a creative strategy to compensate for this inexperience, we joined an architectural firm in Washington, D.C., whose knowledge of this industry would complement our design reputation. Our joint qualifications submission was a gallant, customized effort to emphasize our sincere enthusiasm for the project as well as our capacity to complete it. To our delight we were asked, along with five of the most experienced firms, to join the design competition, for which we were ultimately awarded third place. While we did not win this commission, we view this experience as an extremely positive one. It has increased our knowledge of this project type and better positioned us to win this type of project in the future. In fact, just before this essay went to press, we were selected to be part of a three-firm team to master plan a new medical center at UCLA (University of California, Los Angeles).

Marketing for Globalization

Foreign commissions have provided tremendous design opportunities for architects in the United States in the last five years as the economic conditions here have become so unpredictable. As a rule, we try to avoid being heavily committed to any market. One of the advantages of working globally is that it allows us to ride out the down cycles in certain markets through the up cycles in others.

Marketing for commissions overseas is a task in itself. There are three approaches that professional firms can take in pursuing clients and projects overseas. The first is to maintain a home office and send partners and professional staff abroad on a project by project basis. The second is to open satellite offices in the markets that are most active. The third is to form affiliations with local firms overseas and work collectively on projects.

Anticipating Opportunities

It is most important to anticipate which countries will be in the market for foreign talent. If a foreign client would like to augment its local architects, the reason for doing so is most likely one or more of the following: the project requires technical skills unavailable in the host country; the client is interested in the design expertise of a particular architect abroad; or the client simply wants an internationally known architect whose involvement with the project might ultimately enhance the leasing value of a building.

Opening Satellite Offices

KPF has established a full-service office in London that serves and evolves within the European community. The opening of this office followed a five-year period in which we were involved with numerous projects in Europe. More importantly, we are now able to obtain commissions in Europe and Asia that we would have been unable to pursue from our New York office.

While we are particularly pleased with the results from our London firm, KPF has always been especially cautious of establishing satellite offices. For one, local offices are often regarded with hostility by the local firms of a country—instead of being a potential collaborator, you become the competition. Also, there is concern that the quality of work generated through satellite offices may not be as high and, consequently, the end product would suffer.

Promoting Specialized Knowledge

A specialized knowledge or expertise in a particular building type is a potential source of projects. For example, through our ongoing work with some of the major communication and media companies, we are one of the most experienced architects in this quintessential information-age building type. Recognized for this specialization, we were awarded the design of a TV studio complex for the government of Singapore's broadcasting service (although the project did not proceed).

The greatest architectural achievement, and consequently one of the most desirable exports of the United States, is arguably the skyscraper. While Asian cities may be more populated, many American cities, similar to Tokyo and Hong Kong, are generally concentrated, with downtowns of unprecedented densities. Asian urban communities are growing and with the cost of land increasing, skyscrapers are recognized as good investments. Hence developers in Asia are looking toward the United States for assistance. New York has set the example for architectural development in Asia, not only because it is the only American city approaching the population of Asian cities but also because it is home to some of the most famous skyscrapers in the world. KPF has had great success designing high-rise buildings in New York and in many other cities in the United States, and our success domestically with this building type has assisted us in winning commissions abroad.

Cultural Assimilation

Working in different countries with different cultures, languages, history, and traditions, certainly presents new challenges. However, there are inevitable risks involved in working in foreign countries. Outside of the difficulty of assimilating culturally with the host country, there are more pressing concerns, such as the political climate and its effect on the country's economic stability and tax considerations. Also, it is essential for the foreign client and the American architect to foster a strong working relationship. This is simply to understand each other's policies and working standards and to reduce miscommunication when the job is underway. We have a responsibility to respect the traditions of our host country while introducing them to our own. As architects working abroad, we act as ambassadors of America. The weight of that obligation must be recognized.

Repeat Clients

In the United States, we have had the privilege of completing numerous projects for certain clients because they were impressed with our previous work for them, our approach to design, and service. Though we have only been in Asia a short while, we have already been commissioned for several projects by repeat clients.

A good reputation is also beneficial when it comes to collaborating with Asian firms. While some local firms may be hesitant to work with foreigners, the hesitant firms feel it is to their advantage to work with internationally recognized architecture firms and value them much like brand names. Often, it is the local architect who is responsible for identifying us as a potential candidate for a project. This has been particularly true in Korea, Singapore, Indonesia, and Taiwan.

Reactive Marketing

Reactive marketing, as the name implies, involves responding to calls, letters, requests for proposals, and invitations for interviews and competitions from potential clients. While proactive marketing is necessary in order to diversify and to respond to the needs of a changing economy, reactive marketing results in opportunities for which we are generally very well qualified. Although we do not pursue every opportunity that is presented to us, long-range thinking requires that we follow up on a wider range of project types rather than only those that match our past experience. After twenty years, KPF is fortunate to receive requests for information and proposals very frequently. Also, we have enjoyed many positive relationships in association with other architects and consultants, who assist us in identifying potential projects. However, as I emphasized in the beginning of this discussion, while we may be qualified to do a project, we have to work very hard to beat our equally qualified competitors. We find that all marketing efforts require an intensive, focused effort from firm brochures and project qualification packages to formal proposals, interviews, and presentations.

Marketing Brochures and Promotional Material

As a rule, all marketing material, including text and graphics, must be high quality. Producing high quality standard firm brochures is particularly critical because they introduce a potential client to the firm and play a large role in defining the firm's identity to the public. Therefore, text, including firm descriptions, design philosophies, and project descriptions, should be well-written, concise, and informative, emphasizing the strengths of the firm without being overly complimentary or boastful.

Graphics should reflect the design sensibility of the firm. Also, logos, text fonts, and page formats should be consistent from one promotional piece to the next. To ensure high graphic quality, the first step is to hire a talented graphic artist and skilled photographer who can help the firm build a library of project images.

Proposals

Proposals provide a great opportunity to customize marketing material to address the needs of a particular client. KPF might mail several brochures to prospective clients per day; however, we try to limit our proposal efforts to one or two per week. Proposals generally respond to formal RFPs (Request for Proposals), which are normally issued several weeks before the proposal due date. The size and complexity of a proposal depends on the requirements outlined in the specific request and the nature of the specific client. Clients in the public sector, such as the General Services Administration, require firms to present their credentials through standard forms, which somewhat limits creative freedom. Private sector clients may ask for specific information, but they do not require the use of a particular format. Herein lies a window of opportunity.

Interviews

Almost every selection process involves at least one interview. The interview is often the first time that the client and the architect are meeting face to face, and because the success or failure of this meeting has a profound impact on the chances of winning the project, architects are under great pressure to make a good impression.

Aside from improving your presentation and public speaking skills, the best advice I can offer to assist you in making a good impression is, "Know the project." While part of the interview may involve showing the client all the beautiful projects you have completed, your main purpose is to demonstrate your familiarity with and interest in the project at hand. It is important to research the project and recognize the forces influencing the design such as the site, program, budget, schedule, and regulations. *Understand the client's goals and objectives for the project and emphasize your commitment to addressing all the issues.*

Perhaps the most complicated and time-consuming selection processes that KPF has ever undergone was the one for the Procter & Gamble General Offices Complex in Cincinnati, Ohio. In addition to a qualifications package and formal proposal, the client scheduled several interviews requiring, in some cases, slide-show presentations and very preliminary design concepts. Like a playoff in sports, each interview, like each game, was crucial. If the interview went badly, you were out. KPF was fortunate to have made it through the preliminary interviews to the final, but we were competing against Skidmore, Owings & Merrill (SOM) and I. M. Pei. SOM, an excellent firm, had designed the existing buildings, and the Pei firm was already recognized internationally for their outstanding achievements.

I feel certain that our success during these interviews was due to our enthusiasm, desire, and determination to be selected against great odds. *We spent extra time preparing in an effort to completely understand the issues.* Bill

Pedersen and I were nervous as we went into our last meeting after being selected by the Interviewing Committee. This last interview was just with the Chief Executive Officer, John Smale, and the Chairman, Brad Butler. We needed their blessing for the final selection. After this last interview, we left the executive floor for the lobby to catch a cab to the airport, without knowing if we had the job. Just before we left the building, however, the Chairman ran up to us and said, "We want you to have a good trip home; you have been chosen for the project." Bill and I could hardly believe the outcome of this long, in-depth process, considering the young age of our firm. We were on such a high, we barely needed a plane to fly home!

Competitions

While KPF has received some of its most valuable projects through competitions, we participate in them only when they make sense to us. Our London office enters many competitions because in Europe they tend to be short in duration and inexpensive, plus they are frequently part of the selection process for a project. In the States, however, competitions are costly and frustrating; they often require an intense effort and an enormous number of resources, frequently for no gain. KPF usually will not do a competition without getting paid; however, if we will gain valuable experience learning about a new building type or if the client or location of the project is special, we will make an exception. It is unfortunate how many architects are eager to do competitions without a fee; this is harmful to the profession as well as to the architects themselves. These architects are giving away their most valuable assets, creative ideas, and no other professional does that as frequently as an architect.

The Marketing Team

In addition to the Design and Administrative Partners, who have prime responsibility for business development, the official marketing team at KPF includes the architects who will be involved in the project as it goes forward, a marketing staff composed of architects skilled in writing and communication, and a full-time graphic designer, who is responsible for integrating graphics and visual materials. It is also important to realize that everyone in the firm plays a role in marketing from the person who answers the telephone and directs calls, to the receptionist, the support and technical staff, and the partners. Performance at all levels creates an impression of a firm. Treating all clients, construction people, suppliers, city officials, employees of these entities, in fact treating all people, with respect is very important to building a successful firm and to creating a proper perception of a firm.

Community Involvement

To be successful as an architect, it is a good idea to gain exposure outside of the building industry. Publishing articles in mainstream magazines, newspapers, and books is one way to introduce yourself to the general public. Another way is to participate in various associations and organizations beyond architectural or real estate related fields.

Being creative by developing bookmarks, Christmas cards, announcements, internal and external newsletters, and by sponsoring art shows and other events can also be very helpful to building rapport with community and clients.

Accepting Losses

Finally, accepting losses and learning to gain from those losses is critical. The odds are in your favor if one out of every ten proposals is a winner. This means that no matter how many awards you have won, or how much experience you have with a particular project type, or how fervently you pursue a project, another architectural firm will, nine times out of ten, be chosen over your own.

The reasons for this unfortunate statistic vary and are sometimes never identified. In my experience, politics or "who you know" often plays a large role in the selection of an architect. As I have mentioned, name recognition helps bring in work, but your good name cannot compete with an architect who may be close friends with the client or even a friend of a friend of the client. Another unfortunate reality is the extent to which fee drives the selection process. As the competition for projects increases, many architects have succumbed to submitting unreasonably low compensation requirements just to win a project. We cannot compete with this strategy, nor do we want to. Architects provide a valuable service and should receive appropriate compensation for their work. Upholding this principle is one of an architect's primary responsibilities.

Selling Architectural Services

The following list of basic principles of selling architectural services that may seem elementary are, in actual practice, very important and unfortunately quite often overlooked. They are reprinted from David Dibner's book, *Dreams and Schemes: Stories of People and Architecture.** It is simply not possible to underscore enough the significance of *common sense* and street smarts.

- When you are selling your company, you are, more importantly, selling yourself, since architecture is such a personal service.
- The client is not just a company, but a group of individuals who must be approached as individuals. Your challenge is to convince each of them (or at least a majority) that you are the person, and your firm is the service provider, that can be trusted with the project.
- While past experience in similar projects is important to display, since each project is different, the seller must always keep in mind the phrase, "and here is what this (previous project) means to your project." In other words, the examples shown must always not only be relevant to the project at

*David R. Dibner, *Dreams and Schemes: Stories of People and Architecture* (Philadelphia, PA: XLibris Corporation, 2001), pp. 134–135.

hand, but the seller must also identify what the direct relevance is. This is based upon the understanding that everyone's experience and perception differs.

- The seller must always keep attuned to the buyer's reactions. Learn to be an active listener. Ask them questions to demonstrate your interest in them. (The seller often becomes so entranced with his or her own voice and firm's activities that they seem not to care about listening to the buyer's requirements and specific concerns.)
- Don't waste the buyer's time with materials unrelated to the client or the project. This might indicate to the client that, should you get the job, you will continue the same practice of overlooking their needs.
- Don't assume that the client has seen, read, or understood anything that you have previously sent them. Start from the beginning.

There is nothing that substitutes for doing research in order to understand your potential client's history, preferences, etc., and the potential project's requirements. This includes visiting the site in advance of the interview and understanding its challenges.

Top 10 Presentation Skills

DAVID GREUSEL, AIA, is a principal of HOK Sport + Venue + Event in Kansas City, Missouri, and is author of *Architect's Essentials of Presentation Skills* (New York: Wiley, 2002). He has more than twenty years' experience in every major role in architectural practice, including management, marketing, design, and technical aspects of projects. He draws hundreds of attendees to his featured lectures at AIA National Conventions, where he is consistently rated one of their best speakers.

1. Show Up

"Showing up" means preparing physically, and it also means being able to move comfortably and confidently during your presentation. Most architects are altogether too good at standing still—move around! Get out from behind the podium. If you grow rooted to one spot, your audience will find your presentation—and you—less interesting.

Another aspect of showing up is stage presence. Stage presence is the degree to which you comfortably inhabit your body and thus take command of the space around you (the stage). So stage presence can be thought of as the quest to be *visible rather than invisible*.

2. What's My Motivation?

Ask yourself, "What *specific action* do I want my audience to take as a result of this presentation?" The answer to this question is your motivation for making the presentation, and that motivation should animate every word you say. Once you have defined the goal of your presentation, you can tailor the presentation format to serve your objective. The worst presentations are a laundry list of unrelated facts. Better presentations have a narrative flow, or at least a coherent outline. But the best presentations are built around a central theme, story, idea, or metaphor. Never tell your audience more than they want to know—about you, about your firm's history, about the design, about other projects that your firm has done. The secret of being interesting is to ask the simple question, "Is this point of more interest to me than it is to my audience?" If the answer is "yes," drop it.

Your motivation (what you want to accomplish) not only drives the selection of format but also influences how you present material. Options include memorization, use of an outline or notes, or extemporaneous. Extemporaneous speaking means improvised, spontaneous, unrehearsed, spur of the moment, impromptu, offhand, or unpremeditated. This is the best way to talk. Speaking from an outline is next best, and memorized or scripted speeches are typically the worst way to present ideas orally.

3. Know Your Lines

If you don't give a speech so often that you know the subject backwards and forwards, at least know your key points well enough that you don't have to read them from the three-by-five index cards clutched in your sweaty little palm. *The key to public speaking is mastery of the topic.* Another term for mastery of the topic is *preparation*. Nine of the ten biggest flops I have ever seen in public speakers were not that the speaker couldn't speak—they are that the speaker was unprepared. So where does a speaker's confidence come from? From the usual places: experience and preparation. One reason architects can be weak presenters is that we tend not to think of presenting as part of our normal work—we see it as something we only do occasionally. For many architects, this picture is simply not accurate.

It is difficult to practice a speech. The *practice paradox* is this: you can practice speaking, but you can't practice a speech. A professional actor can memorize a speech and make it sound spontaneous. You can only practice speaking, not a particular speech. Architects should take any and every opportunity to make public presentations, because it is only through the collective experience of dozens of humbling and embarrassing moments that you become a truly polished speaker.

4. Find Your Light

Finding your light simply means moving to where the light is. Finding your light is important because if the audience can't see you, they also can't hear you. One aspect of finding your light is the need for you to understand the physical setting of your presentation. Public speaking is like construction projects in this regard: it is not enough to say that things *may* go wrong. Things *will* go wrong, and a good presenter is prepared to deal with contingencies as they occur. The key is to acknowledge up front that some factors are beyond your control. Therefore, it is essential for you to have a backup plan.

5. Face Out

No one is sure why turning your back on the audience is a bad thing, but it is universally agreed that it is. Along with the simple command to face out come a host of other implied values: keep smiling and the five Es (energy, empathy, enthusiasm, engagement, and entertainment).

Energy equals pitch plus pace. Architects often speak very deliberately, then wonder why their presentation seemed to lack energy. People are able to listen much faster than you are able to talk!

Empathy is the establishment of common ground with your audience. Strategies for developing empathy include self-deprecating humor, dressing appropriately (i.e., like your audience), and showing basic courtesy.

Enthusiasm is literally the spirit within you. If you are not happy to be there, your spirit will show it and your audience will know it instantly.

Engagement is the difference between speaking with a group and speaking at them. The key to engagement is *interaction*: your ability to establish a dialog. Engagement is the most important of the five Es because it is the most often overlooked.

Entertainment content has a physically relaxing effect on both the teller and the audience, and it helps to build empathy and rapport. No presentation should be completely devoid of entertainment.

6. Keep Going

Unless there is a genuine emergency, it is best to keep your presentation moving ahead in the face of difficulties. Clients and others don't appreciate a presenter who quits when things start to go wrong.

One disaster that can befall a presentation, particularly one to a hostile group, is inappropriate audience feedback. How to handle inappropriate feedback? Acknowledge that you heard the point, affirm what the speaker said (not the same as agreeing with it), record the point somehow, and continue. You handle appropriate feedback exactly the same way.

A good way to overcome *stage fright* (which is very common) is to have every person on your team say a few words early in the presentation. This helps prevent an unmanageable build-up of nervous tension.

7. Project

To *project* simply means to speak in such a way that the most distant person in the space can hear you. This skill was more important in the days before the invention of microphones, but it still works when it has to. Projection is not yelling. It requires support from the diaphragm and open breathing.

Projecting also requires that you control your breathing. For better projection, you should breathe low, from the diaphragm, not high, from the chest. Generally, we all tend to breathe low when we are relaxed (i.e., asleep) and high when we are tense (i.e., when we are giving a speech).

8. Be in the Moment

Being *in the moment* means being able to react to the things that are happening around you as they are happening. Not being in the moment is when you are thinking ahead, to what you are going to say next when someone else is talking, or worse, thinking behind, to something you should have said or not said a minute ago. Delivering a canned speech that you have given dozens of times before is the opposite of being in the moment. When you are "in the moment," you will turn on the projector at the right time, react promptly to interaction from your audience, and be aware of changes in the environment—and take appropriate remedial action.

9. Remember Your Props

All architects use props—otherwise known as visual aids. Choose a presentation technology that supports your objective for the talk, not the one that everyone else is doing. Here are some common presentation props:

35mm Slides: Long the gold standard for photography, slides are an inflexible medium that require darkened rooms and loud projectors.

Traditional Overheads: Perhaps the most reliable and effective presentation technology known to man and virtually unknown to architects. Poor image quality makes overheads less desirable for design presentations.

Computer Overhead Projection: Dynamic multimedia presentations allow you to face the audience and your notes (on a laptop). Varied lamp colors and resolutions make photo reproduction iffy at times, but this technology is constantly improving.

Presentation Boards: High-touch medium allows you to mark on the drawings in real time. Cumbersome and expensive, boards fail as a presentation medium when you have more than a dozen images.

Video: Though entertaining and at times awe-inspiring, computer animations and videos are expensive and time-consuming to produce, and they sometimes result in audience disengagement because of the passive nature of viewing.

Go Live: The best visual aids are the ones you make in the presentation room. Take advantage of the architect's natural sketching and lettering skills to make your own presentation graphics in real time.

The most important thing about your props is that you are comfortable and confident with the presentation technology that you use. No one wants to see you stumble through a technology you are not capable of handling.

10. Know When to Get Off

Time moves at different rates for a speaker and his or her audience. What seems a mere moment to a speaker can seem hours to an audience. A timed speech will *always* take longer in reality than in rehearsal. If you have a rigid time limit, cut your remarks to leave yourself a comfortable cushion.

Variety in pace is also important. You can emphasize the importance of a point by slowing down or by pausing to let the point sink in. But, in general, most architects should talk faster. And louder. Above all, recognize that presenting is a dance not a download of intellectual content. Learn to dance.

Top 10 Principles for Design on the Web

TIMOTHY DOWNING, Design Principal, and **JUSTIN STONE,** Managing Director, lead Design & Co., an award-winning firm providing design and technical expertise to individuals, institutions, and corporations for the production of digital and printed media, including Web sites, CD-ROMs, printed identities, brochures, books, and other promotional materials. Design & Co. has been awarded first place for Web site design by the Society of Marketing Professional Services/Boston in the 2002, 2003, and 2004 Marketing Communications Awards Programs. Tim Downing received a Master of Architecture from Yale University and a Bachelor of Architecture from Cornell University. Justin Stone received a Bachelor of Arts from Bennington College.

Key Elements for Creating an Architecture Firm Web Site

Having worked with architecture firms and been intimately involved in the marketing of design services, we believe that the Web site is the single most important tool for any marketing effort. It can provide a comprehensive overview of your firm to any potential client, any time, any place—quickly. As you already know, more and more people—prospective employees, architect search committees, and individuals at both home and work—utilize the Web as an information resource to make decisions about consumer products and services. Different from a firm brochure, access to information on the Web is omnipresent and relatively easy to update. A brochure is also limited by its linear hierarchy and by the amount of control you have to "feed" the viewer content. On the Web, you can access information in a linear fashion, but you can also quickly move horizontally across links.

How does one approach the design of a Web site for a *designer*? More specifically, what are the particular demands placed on a designer's Web site that are different from most other Web sites? It may seem obvious, but a designer's Web site, above all other considerations, must first provide a strong framework for the work.

Further, we believe that Web sites today must create a presentation that penetrates beyond being simply a resource for "boilerplate" information that characterizes many Web sites within the architecture and engineering industries. We believe that the more a Web site communicates the specific skills and assets of the firm, the more appealing the company will be to prospective clients and employees. Here is the Top 10 List, Key Elements of Architecture Firm Web-site Design:

1. Design as a Designer

We find that most Web sites are grossly inadequate in their capacity to provide a strong framework for the presentation of artwork. On the other hand, the few Web sites with some design facility and formal "muscle" place a premium on sophisticated graphic identity and animation techniques at the expense of content.

Your training in architecture provides the foundation for a unique approach to design for the Web. As designers working in the built environment, you know that a set of complex factors exert pressure throughout the design process. The practice of architecture has developed a rigorous and deliberate design process to resolve these complex issues. Use this same process to design for the "virtual" environment. Here, factors include technical constraints, content requirements, budgetary constraints, marketing opportunities, and needs of the site visitor. This means that it is of foremost importance to use design to communicate precisely how you approach your work and the variety of services you offer, while serving the needs, interests, and limitations of site visitors. In this way, you can create a meaningful design solution that speaks directly to the needs of your firm and prospective clients.

Not unlike architecture, we recommend organizing the design process into a design phase and an implementation or construction phase. It is very easy to become lost in a maze of disjointed content when you try to design as you build!

2. Know Your Competitors and Make Your Advantages Obvious

While the field may be saturated with architects competing for the same kinds of projects you are, no two firms are alike. Every architect brings a unique perspective, design sensibility, and personality to their work. Your Web site should clearly represent your unique advantages from the first moment a visitor arrives at your home page (perhaps earlier, if you are promoting the Web site online or through conventional media).

We recommend researching firms that can reasonably be considered competitors. If nothing else, this competitive analysis can be a useful exercise in determining what not to do. Most importantly, it will help you refine your Web site's aesthetic to more thoroughly distinguish your practice from your competitors.

3. Know Your Target Audience

It may seem obvious, but knowing your audience is often overlooked when architects are either consumed by the nuances of their own work or enticed by a particular Web technology. While presenting the work and character of your firm in a sophisticated manner, the Web site *must* serve your audience in every way possible.

Don't try to be everything to everyone. It is vital to understand the markets in which you engage, and evaluate priorities accordingly. More often than not, architecture and engineering services are considered luxury service items. This typically means that you are appealing to a fairly sophisticated user in a very competitive design landscape. There are, however, exceptions, making this a critical question to answer early in the design process. And don't forget prospective employees!

Ask yourself: Who am I designing for? Once you have identified your target audience, constantly test your site design against two questions: What do visitors want to get out of visiting my site? What do I need them to come away with?

4. Allow Clear Access to Content

Before the sophisticated graphics and cool animations are developed, make sure you haven't subverted content. For many visitors, this will be the first glimpse of your firm. What information you show, and how you present it, will say a lot about the priorities of your office.

Creating a Web site requires the development of a structure for information. Although intuitive, the design process for a Web site requires the scheming of a structure that provides a clear hierarchy among information elements and a series of primary, secondary, and tertiary pathways to access that information. Avoid site pages that leave a visitor "trapped," with no obvious pathway to other areas of the site. To this end, it is almost always best to keep your primary links in the same location and order on all site pages.

In particular, you will need to consider the way in which your projects are organized (by building type, region, scale, etc.), and how to show a lot of work without making the site cumbersome. A typical site visitor will spend a limited amount of time at your site. The Web site should be designed so that the visitor is exposed to as much site content as possible within that window of opportunity. It is always preferable to keep a visitor moving forward through the site, rather than forcing them to return to a page they have already seen.

5. Form Realistic Assumptions about Technology

In the last four years, we have seen a marked improvement in the carrying capacity of new broadband services, as well as a significant jump in their popularity. Few businesses are still on dial-up, while some thirty-percent of home users are now on broadband in some form. This, combined with the development of other software and language programming facilities to support and often replace straight "html" programming, have increased the range of possibilities for designers to promote their work by lending a much greater degree of control over the manner in which their work is experienced online.

Evaluate the technology of your site visitors, and set boundaries for your presentation technology accordingly. If you are designing for a fairly sophisticated clientele, you can assume a higher degree of technical capability for end-user systems. If, however, you are designing for a nonprofit organization of low income families, you will not want to build a Web site requiring a recent version of Macromedia Flash Player, a fast computer processor, or high bandwidth for animations and large, high resolution images.

In general, design for your higher-end clientele, but allow easy access and compatibility for your more "technically challenged" users. Do your research. There are many resources online where you can learn about the market penetration of computer operating systems, Web browsers, and specific presentation technologies. It is critical to remember that a Web site that looks good on your computer may be completely incompatible with different or older systems. Remember to consider the age of your clientele as a factor in forming assumptions about technical constraints.

6. Decide How Detailed or Dense Your Site Will Be

An information-rich Web site is not a problem as long as you are very careful about how you provide hierarchy to site elements. But consider carefully your audience and your goals for the site. Is this effectively an online brochure? Is it a portfolio? A gallery? Is it a mechanism for communicating with, or presenting documents to, clients and contractors? Will the site help change the focus of your firm's work in some way?

A Web site is not necessarily an encyclopedic reference for your body of work. There is no right or wrong answer to the question of how much to show. Your solution will depend in part on the diversity of your portfolio, the quality of your photographs and renderings, budgetary constraints, and your goals for the Web site.

If you have completed ten residential projects and two institutional projects but want to shift your firm's focus toward institutional work, you will probably want to show only two representative projects of each type. Limiting the number of projects shown online is a simple but effective way to level the playing field in terms of your firm's focus and strengths.

7. Define Your Budget

For most firms, the commitment to build a high-quality Web site will be a substantial investment. This investment includes the in-house work of assembling information—including scanning and formatting images, creating and editing copy, and seeking approval from all principals. A Web site is no different from your physical office, graphic identity, signage, etc., in terms of the quality and attention that is required. In the online marketplace, it is your store front, demonstrating your sensibility and sophistication in a competitive environment. When considered in context of the greater Internet, and in particular your competitors, all of the decisions that go into your Web site will say much about your firm.

Begin by defining what you need: what the site should be to best serve the needs of your firm and clientele. Using this defined need as your benchmark, buy as much Web site as you can afford! Work backwards, editing and reducing content and scope to fit your budget. The quality and sophistication of your Web site is a direct indication of the character and success of your firm. Remember also to account for the cost of Web site updates.

The only "external" factor that should influence the budgetary constraint you set for your Web project is the shelf life of the Web site. How often will the site need to be replaced or completely redesigned to accurately present the character of your firm online? When will it be outdated technologically? Three to four years is probably a reasonable assumption, although this will depend on the incremental modifications you make over the course of time. Certainly, some firms opt to keep their sites longer. Other firms evolve rapidly enough that two years is a more appropriate shelf life. Every case is different, but this must be a factor in your budgeting considerations.

8. Get Noticed: Search Engine Penetration

The ability of search engines to find your Web site is more important to some firms than others. Certainly, not accounting for this in your development process guarantees that your site will be difficult or impossible to find. Many people believe that if they put a Web site on the Internet, prospective clients will find it easily, ensuring a steady stream of inquiries, clients, and revenue. This is a terrible misconception. Individual Web sites, particularly those in saturated markets such as architecture, are actually very difficult to find through search engines. Even if the user enters the firm name precisely, it is not likely to appear in search results if the site has not been built to certain specifications.

Be realistic about the amount of time you are willing to devote to this aspect of your project. Search Engine Optimization and Marketing are specializations best left to the professionals. Unless you are one of the fortunate few firms operating within a niche with little competition, making your Web site prominent within relevant search engines will be a full-time effort for at least several weeks, requiring specialized knowledge and experience and a significant ongoing commitment.

There are several things you can do to at least make your Web site accessible to search engines. First, you need to come up with several combinations of relevant terms (including variations of your firm's name) your clientele are likely to enter as search terms. Use these term combinations strategically when developing the site content. Search engines will exhibit a preference for content-rich (aka text-rich) Web sites that feature relevant key term combinations early and often on multiple pages and in page names. Be careful! Search engines are also increasingly successful in identifying gimmicks that might artificially boost a site's relevance. The penalty for these kinds of tricks is often removal from the search engine database altogether.

Beyond building a site well, techniques proven successful in improving the ranking of a Web site include formally registering with as many search engines and Web directories as possible, updating your Web site frequently (particularly the home page and other areas saturated with relevant terms, such as principal and staff bios and press releases), pay-per-click advertising programs with prominent resources (such as top search engines), and positioning links to your Web site with prominent industry resources online.

An old-fashioned mailer is often the best and fastest way to begin driving traffic to your new Web site.

9. Create a Realistic Schedule

We find the time and resources required for information gathering to be consistently underestimated by firms. We recommend there be one person in the office—preferably with good editing skills—whose responsibility is acquisition and preparation of all images and texts for the Web site.

If you are producing your Web site in-house, be realistic about timing. We have found that many in-house sites sit for years in various states of completion. You must approach this process with as much rigor and discipline as you bring to your client's projects. It needs a dedicated team, formal schedule, and clear milestones.

10. Have a Plan for Ongoing Site Maintenance

Maintenance is vital and should be considered during the development process. In addition to the obvious content-related changes you will want to make over the life of the Web site, the evolution of technology may necessitate other changes and adjustments. Just because all browsers read your design structure accurately today does not mean that the next versions will. We recommend technical evaluations of a Web site at intervals of three months to one year, depending on the complexity of your Web site. You don't want to learn from a client that all of your project pages have been "broken" for months.

If you will be updating the site in-house, make sure that the site will be built in such a way that content will be accessible to those who will be doing the work. You must also be realistic in expecting that you will always have somebody in-house with the knowledge and time necessary to manage this effort, somebody who will not allow the site to remain unattended, or become sloppy, or dated.

If you have hired a development firm, make sure that they account for ongoing maintenance as part of their development process and are able to estimate costs based on assumptions you provide about the frequency and volume of changes.

Case Study | Richards Roth Caruso, Inc.*

JEAN R. VALENCE, FSMPS, is a Principal and Director of Strategic Development at Symmes Maini & McKee Associates, Inc., in Cambridge, Massachusetts, where she leads both marketing and staff development. A Fellow of the Society for Marketing Professional Services, she is a recipient of SMPS' highest honor, the Marketing Achievement Award. Jean is also the author of *Architect's Essentials of Professional Development* (Hoboken, N.J.: Wiley, 2003).

PHILIP F. VALENCE, FSMPS, is founder of Blackridge, Ltd., management and marketing consultants. With more than thirty years experience in the design and construction professions, Phil assists firm leaders in the creation of strategic plans that are anchored by a set of driving values and marketing plans that reflect client concerns and issues. Phil is a Fellow of the Society for Marketing Professional Services and a frequent speaker and writer on matters related to professional practice and client satisfaction.

*This case was developed for use in class discussion and is not intended to reflect either effective or ineffective conduct regarding administrative matters. © 2004 Jean R. and Philip F. Valence

Part 1

On a bright September afternoon, staff members of Richards Roth & Caruso, Inc. (RRC) have just returned from The Soup Cellar, a favorite gathering place for the firm to celebrate the acquisition of milestone projects, the conclusion of demanding design and document phases, the occasional win in the Boston-area architects' softball league, and, as was the case today, the departure of a valued employee. In their converted 1891 fire station in Wellesley, Massachusetts, an historic New England town twelve miles southwest of Boston, Marc Caruso sits across from William Richards, at the latter's desk. The two of them gaze at the red and yellow foliage and iron gates that mark the main pedestrian entrance to Wellesley College, the alma mater of the marketing coordinator, Rena, whose farewell party they had just hosted.

Rena Francis had joined RRC as a part-time administrative assistant three years earlier, during her senior year at the Ivy League women's college. Having married an MBA candidate at nearby Babson College, Rena was happy to accept a full-time job at the firm, where her writing and graphic skills quickly signaled a better application to proposals, interview preparation, and the coordination of publicity. Now Rena's husband has finished his degree, and he has accepted a position in Phoenix.

William, who had earned his MArch in Cambridge, Massachusetts, had started the firm twenty-two years ago when he returned to the area after a brief postgraduation stint at a New York City firm. Having begun by designing home additions and community buildings, William quickly added small library additions, town halls, and school renovations to his project list. He was as effective at handing multi-constituency clients as he was at design, and he was increasingly sought out to lead complicated projects. After twelve years, William added two partners within six months of each other. Marc stepped into a design leadership role, applying his experience in education facilities and his expertise in historic preservation to the firm's growing K–12 portfolio. Jessica Roth, a registered structural engineer with business savvy and strong management skills, took charge of the finance, operations, and administrative matters.

Today, RRC is fifty-one people practicing architecture and planning. Seventy-five percent of its revenues is generated by public K–12 school work, much of it renovations and additions. William is the primary marketer, and all three serve as Principals-in-Charge on projects.

The Hiring Question

Rena's departure has spurred a reassessment of marketing in the firm, which in turn has led to a decision to replace her with someone with more marketing experience who can help RRC capture commissions with greater design potential, preferably in the private sector. William and Marc are taking the lead in finding a Marketing Manager and have placed ads in the AIA chapter newsletter, the job bank of a marketing association, and the help-wanted section of the region's major newspaper. They were thrilled to receive more than fifty responses, which they culled to six people for interviews.

The interviews have, however, given them pause. Their first surprise was the subjects that candidates raised once the firm's history and marketing process were explained. Although all five women and one man praised RRC's offices—which had been featured in national as well as local architectural press—and seemed impressed with the firm's portfolio, most of the candidates' questions had less to do with the firm's work and more to do with business matters. All six had asked whether the marketing role would be focused on communications or on business development, and they also quizzed them on their marketing databases. Three were interested in the firm's target markets, beyond K–12. Two asked about RRC's approach to networking with consultants and general contractors, and one, startlingly, was interested in meeting a few of RRC's "next generation of leaders."

The second surprise was candidates' compensation expectations, which would place at least one of them at a project manager level.

In William's office that fall day, William and Marc shared their thoughts:

WILLIAM: This is the time to channel our resources into a new market, like colleges and universities. How many times have we heard school superintendents talk about declining preschool enrollments and changing demographics? It's worth investing in someone who can get out, meet people, and network. We must take marketing more seriously, and more people than I have to be willing to get out of the office and generate business.

MARC: We do excellent work for our clients and manage to get so much repeat work from them that our competitors just want to throw in the towel when they see us win our first project in a community. We "get out" and generate repeat work every day. The best way for us to market ourselves is to pay more attention to design and to get more publicity, enter more awards programs. If local demographics are an issue, then let's take K–12 farther and form alliances with design firms out of state. One thing we can certainly do is make more of our historic renovation expertise. We have a better portfolio in adapting aged buildings to effective and, by the way, stunning reuse than any other school architect I can think of around here.

WILLIAM: "Around here" is the problem. Trying to do public schools out of state is like pushing Jello uphill. How many firms can you think of that have done that successfully? If we want awards and want to make sure the firm stays healthy in the future, we need to move into the private sector. Private schools and higher education have more need of our skills, more money to spend on good design, and a much greater need to invest in physical facilities for the long-term.

MARC: We have a real niche in K–12. Our schools get some coverage in local media, and our network with superintendents is great. Whatever we do we can't give that up. Maybe we should look for a senior architect who has some experience in schools and colleges.

WILLIAM: Way back when I brought in Jess, she relieved me of inside tasks so I was able to get out, bring in business. Maybe we need another good inside marketing person who can pay more attention to the media, get us organized so we can chase independent schools and some universities. You could take over my networking activities with school administrators, and I could shift all of my marketing time to the new mar-

kets. Some of our engineering consultants and general contractors have ties with independent schools and the higher education market, and they could give me some ideas and introductions.

MARC: I barely have time to attend to my projects and to the design side of things. Maybe I can help with the media, but I don't see myself golfing with your school administrator pals any time soon.

After this exchange, through a friend, William was introduced to a marketing consultant, Joe Guarino. Three weeks later, William, Marc, and Jess meet with Joe at The Soup Cellar to discuss their quandary. After listening to William and Marc describe the process they had been through and their indecision, Joe asked them three questions: "What is your long-term plan for the business? Do you need a good inside person to manage the marketing effort, or an outside person? If you need an outside person, do you want a seller-doer or someone who just develops business?"

WILLIAM: We have a good tracking system for identifying potential projects, our promotional materials are up-to-date, and everyone pitches in when we have proposals or presentations to prepare. We could probably do better at client follow-up, but that's primarily my responsibility and I can ramp up that effort. Maybe a senior-level insider person isn't so important.

MARC: I agree. We have good processes, so a marketing manager isn't critical. I can spend some more time at client follow-up. And we can find an architect with education experience to develop alliances, speak, and go to other parts of the country to expand our practice.

JESS: I can certainly take a more direct role in watching over marketing here in the office to be sure nothing falls through a crack. My concern is that William and Marc, despite good intentions, will not be able to do as much client follow-up as we need. William is already over-committed and Marc is too involved in projects, and that is never going to change. What we really need is more help.

After a moment of silence, William and Marc nod in agreement.

JOE: Okay. An outside person it is. What about the other two questions? Let's discuss the last question first: a business developer or a sales person? Business development (BD) means that you actively establish and maintain contact with a predefined group of organizations and individuals—a target list, basically. Your goal is to win project work at some time in the future. BD is people and relationship focused, and generally you have a long time to fruition, perhaps as long as two to three years. Sales is another active process, but in this case you are pursuing a specific project with the objective of closing on it. Sales is project-focused, rather than relationship-focused, and it has a short time frame to fruition. BD and sales are different, and for most design firms they require people with different approaches and skills."

Marc points out that approximately eighty percent of their work is through public agencies, which means that they just have to watch for project announcements in the press. Therefore, they should hire someone to spread the net wider and bird-dog those announced projects. William warns them of their extreme dependence on the public K–12 market.

Joe observes: "A classic dilemma. You are having trouble with answering the 'Whom do we hire?' question because you are unclear about what you want to be doing in the next three to five years. Which gets to my first question: What is your long-term plan for the firm?"

Joe suggests the partners think about creating a business and marketing plan that reflects their long-term goals for the practice. The plan will provide a solid basis for making critical decisions in the future about staffing, services, markets, fees, and project pursuits.

Marc responds that they know what their plans are because they talk about it all the time. Jess agrees, but points out that they have never actually agreed on specific goals in terms of markets, client types, revenues, staff size, and the like. And, more importantly, they've never talked about what they would have to do to

achieve them. The partners agree to continue the conversation tomorrow back at the office.

The next morning Jess and Marc stare glumly at their coffee, as William acknowledges that he had not thought about marketing the firm in the context described by Joe. Sales and business development have always meant the same thing to him, and he's always had the future outlined in his head and simply acted on that basis. He expressed regret that through the years of growth he hasn't encouraged them to set goals and talk substantively about where they are going with the practice. William suggests that they take the time now to establish plans so that they have a clear direction for marketing.

Marc agrees that they all should have been more insistent about doing the planning part, but states clearly, "For now, I am not interested in taking the time or spending money we can't spare to hire Joe or some other consultant to help us do a plan. Maybe in a year or so. Rena has been gone for over a month, and we need someone to replace her right now. We have enough information to decide what kind of person we need and to make the hire." Jess agrees.

Marc and William return to themes of their conversation several weeks ago on Rena's last day, and Jess, who hadn't understood their concerns and hopes about continuing in the public K–12 market (and about pursuing private schools and higher education), speaks up.

JESS: You both make valid points about what we need. Marc, I agree we have an excellent reputation and solid experience base in the public K–12 market, which we should exploit by forming alliances to work regionally. We agreed yesterday that we do a good job at tracking leads and project opportunities, and everyone pitches in when we have proposals or presentations to prepare. However, I am concerned, like William, about the low profit margins in public work and about our dependence on a single market. So I wonder if we can even maintain our K–12 practice at current levels if we continue to do what we are doing now.

And, William, I am persuaded that we should diversify our market and client mix to reduce our exposure and that the higher ed market is a reasonable step based on our historic renovation expertise and their needs. But we are an unknown entity to these clients, and we had better understand what that means. I know this will require a significant investment of time, perhaps two years, as Joe said—and money, say, $200,000 just for hard costs—before we see a good return on investment. I like your suggestion of an architect with knowledge of the market who could be both a business developer and a project manager. Are we willing and able to support such a person for the duration? As well as replace Rena?

DISCUSSION POINTS

1. What would be your position on hiring a "seller and doer" for the college and university market? What opportunities would it afford? What are the risks of such a hire? What kinds of information would help you make this decision? What could you do to mitigate the risks and maximize the potential?
2. Should William, Jess, and Marc rethink the idea of hiring an experienced Marketing Manager? If so, based on the kind of questions the candidates were asking, should RRC aim for a marketing professional with more communications expertise or one with more experience in business development?
3. Are there other options the firm should consider to solve their marketing concerns?

Part 2

A year later, Joe Guarino, the marketing consultant they had lunched with last fall, is sitting in RRC's main conference room. He has been retained to facilitate a weekend retreat.

The firm's new college specialist architect, Gerry O'Sullivan, does not seem to be working out as the principals had hoped. RRC has not won a single higher education project and appears to be no closer now than they were nine months ago when they hired Gerry. Three qualifications packages have been submitted to the state for different community college projects, all of them renovations, but the firm didn't make the short list for any of them.

Wrapping up a day of private interviews with the principals and Gerry, Joe is reviewing his notes:

William's Concerns

- I've been reading about changing demographics in our region; I'm concerned that the need for new schools is leveling off. When I'm golfing with some of my general contractor pals, they tell me that the college and university market is exploding and that we had better hurry if we want to participate in it.
- Gerry has some great ideas about this, but it is so embedded in projects that he hasn't time to do anything with it.
- Gerry has raised concerns about whether or not the firm is ready to do things differently if and when we actually get college work. I've pointed out that we have already done that once. We dramatically altered our approach to projects for the independent-school market to reflect their particular expectations and needs, and we are still refining our design and delivery processes accordingly.
- Regardless of what we do, our marketing effort is disorganized. This is my fault; with all the proposals we are doing, I haven't spent enough time with the new coordinator to plan publicity or to talk to her about other things we should be doing.
- I haven't gotten other people—especially Marc and other senior staff members—involved in marketing.
- Maybe we need to bite the bullet and adjust our staff mix, so that Gerry isn't the only person with recent experience in the university market.

Marc's Concerns

- We are doing really well right now, getting new and renovation K–12 projects and more school feasibility studies that will turn into school projects in the future.
- We've fallen off in getting PR (public relations) help. No one has time to spend talking to editors with all the work, and we aren't entering our projects for awards as we used to.
- Gerry is really good; a very effective presenter, as well as a project leader. We have to figure out how to keep him.

- We should either partner with an out of state firm that wants to do college and university work here, or we should hire a senior project manager to support Gerry and give him more time to market. In either case, Gerry has to understand that we want him to do the kind of institutional work that he really loves.

Jessica's Concerns

- We're really busy right now, but we keep talking about new marketing ideas that we simply can't afford. We are lucky if our projects earn us four-percent profits, and the studies we are doing barely break even. We always seem to do whatever it takes to solve clients' problems, which means they love us. But they can't pay for services beyond their funding. Fee negotiations are getting tougher, and study clients are asking about design-build options on future projects.
- We need to expand our markets. But the K–12 market is what we know, and the learning curve to enter a new market will bounce our overhead.

Gerry's Concerns

- Our percentage of public K–12 work is way too high, even higher than it was when I joined the firm. We go after everything, and then, when we get it, we complain that the fee is too low and that we don't have time to market universities.
- Most of the people here don't realize that the approach to marketing and serving a private college is completely different from getting and doing work in the pub-

lic sector. Marc and Jessica assume that all we have to do is scan the public announcements for higher education facilities; respond to an ad, preferably from a community college in a town where we have done a successful school; highlight my résumé and the firm's budget versus actual track record on schools; and then be handed a project.

- People here think that all of our current services—from programming through construction administration—would be provided to a university the same way as to a public school system.
- William is savvier. He wants to be clear about what we can bring to these clients. He and I have talked about marketing our expertise in renovating and adapting late nineteenth-century and early twentieth-century masonry buildings.
- RRC's talent at converting old buildings to new uses is absolutely transferable to the college market, but are William, Marc, and Jess serious about this? We need a target list and a mailing campaign, different visuals, a client-centered approach to proposals and interviews, basically a whole new approach to marketing and to project delivery. If I'm supposed to be leading this effort, then tell me and give me the time to do it all.

DISCUSSION QUESTIONS

1. What three or four critical issues need to be discussed at the marketing retreat? Should Gerry be invited to participate?
2. What kinds of information and background data will participants need to help them address issues and make decisions?

Chapter 7

Laws and Order

This chapter focuses on the formal (legal) relationships and specific obligations between (1) architect and client and (2) architect, client, and contractor. It includes general discussions about the applicable AIA documents, considered to be the industry standard. These discussions, written by Robert Greenstreet, Dean of the School of Architecture and Urban Planning at the University of Wisconsin–Milwaukee, and attorneys Timothy Sheehan and David Gorman, communicate pragmatic material and associated theoretical underpinning that is essential background for students and emerging architects.

The intent of this material is to provide an overview of the roles and responsibilities of the primary players, not to offer legal advice. (Legal assistance, if and when needed, should always be sought from an attorney experienced in construction law.) Refer to numerous other texts on legal aspects of architectural practice by J. Sweet, R. Greenstreet, N. Walker, and the AIA's *The Architect's Handbook of Professional Practice* (Hoboken, N.J.: John Wiley & Sons) for wider and more detailed coverage of legal cases and issues such as the Architectural Works Copyright Protection Act, plan stamping, legal ramifications of transmitting electronically formatted construction documents to clients and others, and so on. The AIA's *Handbook* includes the full range of sample AIA documents (available at most local AIA chapters) with accompanying commentary (for the most popular documents) that explains or clarifies many of the clauses contained therein.

The chapter includes two fascinating case studies on the impact of numerous codes and regulations on both the context and design of architectural projects.

Res ipsa loquitur.

Thinking Ahead in the Architect-Client Relationship

There is no question that the quality of the architect-client relationship is the driving force behind successful projects. Bob Greenstreet describes, in the following, how formalizing this relationship *presents an opportunity* to educate the client about the process of doing architecture, to develop realistic expectations, and to remove any ambiguities about the nature of the

THE FAR SIDE® By GARY LARSON

© 1990 FarWorks, Inc. All Rights Reserved/Dist. by Creators Syndicate

The Far Side® by Gary Larson © 1990 FarWorks, Inc. All Rights Reserved. Used with permission.

Suddenly, a heated exchange took place between the king and the moat contractor.

Figure 7-1 Typical of contractor-owner interaction.

project, its design, and construction administration. For example, the architect should inform unsophisticated clients about the professionals' standard of reasonable care and competence. The law doesn't require the architect to perform perfectly, rather, the "architect is required to do what a reasonably prudent architect would do in the same community and in the same time frame, given the same or similar facts and circumstances." The landmark case, *City of Mounds View v. Walijarvi*, defines the current negligence standard (which comprises 1.1 in the *NCARB Rules of Conduct*): "The architect need be careful but need not always be right." Moreover, architects provide a service, not a product—which requires exercising professional judgment. No amount of care can fully anticipate the nature of the unique built result of the architect's design; the similar caution in medicine is that doctors can't guarantee that a patient will get better despite the best care.

ROBERT C. GREENSTREET, RIBA, PhD, is
Dean of the School of Architecture and Urban
Planning at the University of Wisconsin–
Milwaukee. He is an architect specializing in legal
aspects of professional practice, and he has also
written extensively on presentation techniques and
graphics. He has authored and coauthored the
following books: *Legal and Contractual
Procedures for Architects* (Boston: Architectural
Press, 2004), *Architectural Representation* (New
York: Prentice-Hall, 1991), *The Architect's Guide
to Law and Practice* (New York: Van Nostrand
Reinhold, 1984) and *Law and Practice for
Architects* (Oxford, UK: Architectural Press, 2005).

Think about the design process that students invariably go through in their studio experience. Each project may differ in scale and building type, and the focus can change depending on the level of the studio and the interest of the instructor, but the notion of the client remains pretty much the same—a static source of funding with a fixed definition (private householder, school board, and so on) and therefore finite program requirements. Of course, some schools go out of their way to introduce "real" clients who outline their needs at the beginning of the project and comment on the work at its presentation, but the full interaction between architect and client is usually something that can only be guessed at in school.

While an understandable omission in design studio, given the plethora of competing educational requirements jostling to be part of the curriculum, the critical importance of developing a sound working relationship between architect and client should not be underestimated. It is, after all, the cornerstone of the practice of architecture where architects, working in a commercial profession, need to attract and retain a fee-paying clientele in order to survive. Client-handling skills are particularly important when one surveys the structure of the architectural profession in the United States. An AIA survey found that of the over 13,000 architectural firms owned by AIA members, less than 5 percent of them employed more than ten architects, and a huge 62 percent were one-person practices, a group that was estimated to be growing by 1 percent each year. Given the growing number of small firms, it is reasonable to infer that there is likely to be greater contact between each architect and his or her clients and that the importance of the relationship will be fundamental to professional success.

That success, it would seem, is not necessarily a prerequisite of contemporary practice, as a survey of recent court cases involving architects demonstrates. While it is the spectacular collapse or splashy bankruptcy that captures headlines, studies indicate that a surprisingly large number of cases originate, not from failure in the construction process, but from problems erupting in the design phase, where the architect and client are the major players. Many of the issues derived from errors in construction documentation, but a significant number involved breakdowns in the architect-client relationship and were not necessarily connected to design errors.

The American Institute of Architects (AIA) recognizes the importance of establishing a strong architect-client bond. In addition to the stipulations laid down in Canon III of the Code of Ethics and Professional Conduct, entitled "Obligations to the Client," they publish a booklet entitled *You and Your Architect* on their Web site (www.aia.org); it is an especially useful guide (that is periodically updated) for clients or potential clients who have limited experience in dealing with architects. However, the onus of ensuring a continuous, harmonious relationship really lies more with the architect, the professional whom the courts will inevitably hold to a higher standard of performance than the client should problems arise. A study of major pitfalls, areas where architects and clients have legally clashed, may therefore be useful for highlighting the sensitive zones within the architect-client relationship and give some indication of better practice procedure, which can reduce problems and lead to a more productive outcome.

The Legal Landscape

Much has already been written of the grim threat that has faced the architectural profession since the 1960s, the threat of extinction by legal liability. There have been major improvements since 1985, when a breathtaking 43 percent of insured architects reported a claim against them, although the current statistic is still uncomfortably high. Many of the cases that are reported involve architects and their clients and often result not from design failure (a relatively unusual source of conflict), but from a breakdown in the contractual relationship due to misunderstandings, miscommunications, or a general lack of comprehension of the relative responsibilities of both parties. The essence of a good working relationship lies in a successful "meeting of the minds," where each side shares exactly the same understanding, not only of their own rights, responsibilities, and duties, but also of those of the other contracting party.

While it is possible to achieve this mind-meeting through extensive discussions, letters, and recorded minutes of meetings, the use of a contract provides the obvious vehicle to establish the ground rules, and the more standardized the contract, the better. Some architects and, increasingly, clients try to produce their own contracts in an attempt to create a more tailored set of conditions, and certainly there is no need to have a contract at all—work can be carried out by a simple oral agreement or briefly worded letter. Unfortunately, less thorough forms of contract, while perhaps creating a more informal or tailored relationship, tend to omit important issues, such as arbitration and mediation clauses or ownership of documents, in their quest for brevity. More importantly, they do not necessarily set out the parameters of the relationship, the details that constitute the structure of the interaction. Without these, the potential for misunderstanding or omission is much higher and increases the chances for disagreement and, ultimately, conflict.

The "meeting of the minds" objective needs two essential elements to be successful. First, the exact details of the relationship need to be spelled out so that both sides fully understand them, and second, the establishment of the mind-meeting needs to be achieved *before* the contractual relationship is formalized. In both cases, standardized forms of contract are very useful. They establish the ground rules in a way that is fair to both parties—the AIA Standard Forms have been developed over many years, through as many as fifteen editions, by representatives of all parties involved in the building industry, and because of their extensive usage have developed a nationwide consistency of understanding as to the meaning and interpretation of the various articles. The latest edition of B141 (1997) represents a departure from previous versions. It is intended as "a flexible contracting package that allows Architects to offer a broad range of services to Owners spanning the life of a project, from conception to completion and beyond."

Critics of standardized forms include attorneys who like to draft their own contracts on behalf of their clients and architects who feel they are too restrictive or impersonal. In fact, however, the range of standard architect-owner contracts is broad enough to cover a wide range of contingencies:

B Series/Owner-Architect Documents

B141	Standard Form of Agreement Between Owner and Architect
B141/CMa	Owner-Architect Agreement, Construction Manager-Adviser Edition
B151-1997	Abbreviated Owner-Architect Agreement for Projects of Limited Scope
B163	Owner-Architect Agreement for Designated Services
B171	Interior Design Services Agreement
B177	Abbreviated Interior Design Services Agreement
B181	Owner-Architect Agreement for Housing Services
B188	Owner-Architect Agreement for Limited Architectural Services for Housing Projects
B727	Owner-Architect Agreement for Special Services
B801/CMa	Owner-Construction Manager-Adviser Agreement
B901	Design/Builder-Architect Agreement

While the contract itself is invaluable in establishing the ground rules between the parties, it also has a useful secondary function as a tool of enlightenment, and it can be used by the architect to "educate" the client-to-be (particularly the individual[s] who has [have] little previous experience in the process) into the roles and responsibilities each side is expected to take. This is a particularly useful exercise during contract negotiations, where the architect can lead the client through the process, pointing out the range of architectural services as well as the client's responsibilities. This last activity is wise, not only to help the client, but also to provide some protection to the architect in the event of legal action. Pointing out that, say, the improper securing of a necessary easement or an up-to-date site survey was not the architect's fault, as both are clearly stated as client's responsibilities, may not be an adequate defense in court. In some instances, juries have found against the architect for not clearly pointing out to the client their responsibilities and subsequently checking to make sure they have been carried out. This is part of the architect's obligation to "consult" with the client (AIA Document B141.2.1.1.), which creates a broad spectrum of obligation for the expert in the relationship to make sure that all duties are carried out regardless of the party to whom they are assigned. A walk through the contract articles prior to contract formation both alerts the client to intricacies of his or her role and provides something of a defense for the architect that the consultation, and therefore architectural duty, was carried out. Of course, a detailed analysis of the complexities of the process during contract formation is considered by some to be less compelling or interesting than the discussion of design ideas, and too much reference to the difficulties and intricacies of the construction process may, it could be argued, frighten off a potential client. This is possible, although it is probably better to lose an uncertain client before work begins than during the process, and a forewarned party is less likely to be suddenly surprised by subsequent events and blame the architect at a later stage.

Undoubtedly, even using the most trusted standard contract and diligently wading through its contents with the client cannot completely ensure a problem-free association. Misunderstandings, misinterpretations, and unexpected occurrences will always happen and can lead to problems that disrupt and even rupture the working relationship. Here, then, are the author's *Top Ten Areas* to look out for, based upon research into the problems that have arisen in the past between architects and their clients:

1. When Should the Contract Be Signed?

It is not unusual for architects to provide a few sketch designs at preliminary meetings with clients prior to any contract being signed. This is not necessarily a bad practice, and it is seen by many as a kind of "fishing" period, often necessary to secure clientele. However, the production of an excessive amount of free work is economically questionable and should be kept to a minimum. The discussion of the project at the outset should go beyond basic design requirements to include matters of construction procedure and project administration, stressing the importance of a contract between all relevant parties at the earliest possible time. Should the client appear hesitant to enter an agreement with the architect within a reasonable time (and after a limited amount of work), the future of the relationship should be carefully evaluated. It may be better to lose a potentially troublesome client than to risk problems in the future (although the prevailing state of the economy may make this strategy seem impractical). Of course, some architects charge a consulting fee for all preliminary, precontract meetings, either at an hourly or fixed rate, although this may be an approach limited to those in heavy demand or with a substantial workload already in hand.

2. What Does the Client Really Want?

At some point, it may become clear to the architect, hopefully before the contract has been signed, that the client has not developed an entirely clear idea of the program to be followed. While AIA Document B141 clearly states that this is the client's responsibility (Article 2.2.11), the architect is charged with reviewing the program to "ascertain that it is consistent with the requirements of the project."

Should work continue too long without clarifying the client's needs, the architect may spend fruitless hours producing schemes that are not satisfactory to the client, leading to further repeated, abortive, and expensive attempts to provide a satisfactory result. In the worst possible case, a misunderstanding of the clients needs could result in major problems. In one recorded case, a firm of English architects designed a printing works and were subsequently sued by the owners, who claimed negligent design. Apparently, the second floor of the building was failing due to heavy rolls of paper being stored and moved by forklift trucks across them. The architects' defense—that the client had not told them that the second floor would be used in this way—was considered inadequate. The court held that the architect had the responsibility to find out what the client wanted and design accordingly.

Obviously, architects need to carefully probe the client's program so that the ultimate design can successfully meet the stated requirements. However, it must be made clear at the outset that the architect is only paid to review and clarify the client's program. In the event that it is apparent that the client does not have a sound idea of his or her needs, the architect can offer to provide assistance in determining the necessary information. It should be pointed out that such services fall under Programming (Article 2.8.3.1) and therefore require additional payment. This will prevent any misunderstandings later in the project, should the client assume that all such work is part and parcel of the overall fee.

3. When Do I Stop Designing?

Article 2.4 of the Owner-Architect Agreement (AIA Document B141) describes the Design Services, which include the production of preliminary designs for the client's information and approval. Although no warranty is given guaranteeing satisfaction, it would nevertheless seem incumbent upon the architect to provide a scheme that fulfills the client's expectations. If the client proves to be difficult to please, the architect may be faced with the prospect of producing a seemingly endless supply of sketch designs not previously budgeted for in the percentage-fee or fixed-fee methods of payment. Disputes may then erupt should the architect request extra payment that the client refuses, claiming that the work is still part of Schematic Design Documents (Article 2.2.2).

In the event that this situation can be predicted in advance (as, for example, with a particularly demanding client body or a complex, confusing, or incomplete program), it may be possible to limit the number of sketch designs produced at the contract formation stage, providing a formula for additional payment if this number is exceeded. This, of course, would require client agreement, which may not be readily forthcoming, and contract amendment and should be handled with great care.

Alternatively, a payment structure could be agreed upon to provide an equitable formula for payment for the actual work undertaken, as in the Multiple of Direct Personnel Expense or Multiple of Direct Salary Expense methods (Article 1.5.). Again, this will require client acquiescence at the time of contract formulation. In the event that a standard percentage fee has already been agreed upon, it is unlikely that renegotiation of the architect's fee will find favor with many clients, and it may be expedient to continue to produce designs until the client's approval is obtained, rather than force the issue and risk dispute. Obviously, the ability to foresee and therefore plan for contingencies such as these, although difficult, may help to prevent conflicts or the inconvenience of undertaking excess work without suitable compensation.

4. How Accurate Should My Estimates Be?

When the project requirements have been adequately identified, the architect prepares an estimate of the cost of the work (Article 2.1.7.1). This will be updated and refined as the design process progresses through the completion of the construction documents. However, a preliminary estimate of construction cost is all that is required, and accurate cost prediction is not considered to be necessary beyond the judgment normally expected of design professionals. Should detailed estimates be required by the owner, they should be provided by appropriate consultants or by the architect as part of Detailed Cost Estimating (Article 2.8.3.16)

Where only the preliminary estimate is required, the degree of accuracy of the architect's predictions has been brought into question, and legal action has stemmed from cases where final project costs have substantially differed from those originally projected. In the cases that have been recorded concerning this issue, it would appear that less than a 10 percent deviation between estimated and actual costs may be acceptable, although differences in excess of this may render the architect vulnerable to liability claims. However, such factors as size of the project and differing decisions made in courts throughout the country make any generally applicable formulas impossible to recommend. When dealing with questions of cost, the architect should be careful not to raise the client's expectations of low budget without careful consideration. Should these expectations be later disappointed, a greater chance of conflict between client and architect is likely.

5. What If There Are Delays Outside My Control?

Where delay occurs in securing necessary approvals, the architect has no obligation to expedite the process. Rather, it should be explained to the client at the beginning of the project the possibilities of delay in certain circumstances that should be taken into consideration. If proposed designs are rejected by zoning or building code officials and the client wishes to appeal or seek a variance, the architect's additional fees should be clarified. In all cases concerning outside forces affecting the project, the client should not be shielded or misled as to the realities of the procedures involved and should be made fully aware of any likely delays or limitations as soon as possible in the process.

6. What Is the Extent of My Services?

There can be a tendency, especially when working without a standard form of contract, to assume that the architect's services are all-encompassing and that the roles of advisor and consultant cover pretty much everything in the design realm. Both clients and architects may fall into this trap, which does not serve the interests of the latter well at all. Either the architect is doing too many tasks for a limited fee—not a financially advisable situation in a profession where fees are at best minimal to start with—or the client potentially becomes annoyed or surprised when bills for additional services are later presented. Neither scenario is particularly agreeable.

To avoid the expansion of architectural services beyond normally accepted parameters, the architect needs to have a clear understanding of all 68 Categories of Services and to communicate this understanding adequately to the client. AIA Document B141, Owner-Architect Agreement, an excellent document to "walk through" with the client before any contractual agreement is signed, is a useful guide to defining each stage that the client can anticipate and the extent of the duties of the architect in each. By reviewing each phase of service—project administration, planning and evaluation, design, construction procurement, construction administration, and facility operation—and articulating the architect's responsibilities in each, the owner's requirements will hopefully become much clearer. Where additional work is warranted, the architect can refer back to the Categories of Services, so that the client can choose whether or not the extra expense is warranted. In this way, when the contract is signed, both parties should have a clear expectation of the services the architect will provide.

7. What Do I Do on Site Anyway?

The short answer is, of course, relatively little, although there are numerous instances of architects acting, often in good faith, beyond the limitations of their contractual obligations and getting into all sorts of trouble. The General Conditions of the Contract of Construction (AIA Document A201) are an excellent model for determining the extent of the architect's role. The document clearly outlines what the architect can do (Article 4.1) and therefore, by omission, what he or she should definitely *not* do. The latter category includes some fairly important, and occasionally surprising, items such as stopping the work, instructing the contractor on how to build from the construction drawings, changing the work (except for minor changes specified in Article 7.4), commenting on safety and procedures on site, or terminating the contractor. While maintaining an important role as the client's advisor and consultant in all these matters, architects have gotten into trouble by exceeding their authority.

In the first place, acting beyond the contract—for example, giving the contractor instructions or advice on how to build in conformance with the contract documents—is essentially providing free work, which, while very charitable, does nothing for the financial well-being of the practice. Secondly, should that advice turn out to be faulty and lead to damage, delay, and so on, the architect can be held liable for the consequences. A careful reading of AIA Document A201 and the relative responsibilities of the architect, client, and contractor can help to prevent unnecessary work during the Construction Phase (a phase for which the architect, after all, only receives approximately 20 percent of the overall fee) and to assist clients by reminding them of *their* duties.

8. How Many Site Visits Should I Make?

The architect working under AIA contract conditions agrees to visit the site "at intervals appropriate to the stage of the Contractor's operations" (AIA A201., 4.2.2). Many factors may influence the frequency and duration of these visits, including the nature of the project, the stage of worked reached, or a special event (i.e., testing or covering over of work), although in total they must be sufficient in number to ensure that the architect has checked that all work conforms to the contract documents.

In cases where subsequent failure of a building has brought the adequacy of inspection into question, the extent to which the architect should have been present on the site has been a key factor in determining liability. Briefly, it would appear from decided cases that, unless otherwise specified, the architect should not be expected to provide continuous inspection duties. If adequacy of site visits can be proven on the basis of reasonable professional behavior, which will involve frequency and relevance of visits, thoroughness of inspection and record keeping (notes, logs, photographs, videos, and so on), a claim may be successfully defended despite actual building failure. There is by no means a reliable measure of such professional behavior, however, and where construction appears to be of a nature that may require close inspection, the client should be advised of the merits of employing either construction management services or providing a greater architectural presence on site (AIA B141 2.8.3.17—On-site Project Representation).

9. When Should I Get Paid?

It has been said that, regardless of the architect-client contract type, three elements are essential—an accurate description of the work, the architect's fee, and when the fee is paid. While seemingly least important, the last category can cause some problems, and sometimes needs some skillful handling. AIA Document B141, Owner-Architect Agreement, clearly lays out the basis for compensation (Article 1.5), including the type (Percentage, Multiple of Direct Personnel Expense, Fixed Fee, and so on), reimbursable expenses (Article 1.3.9.2), and a compensation worksheet used for estimating costs and appropriate compensation. An initial payment to the architect is required on execution of the agreement, and subsequent payments should be made monthly, usually in proportion to the services performed within each phase.

Problems can arise if the architect has difficulty in receiving payment—not a particularly unusual condition in a profession where as much as $70 million a year in architectural fees remain uncollected in the United States. While no amount of care can prevent a recalcitrant client from not paying, the architect can at least make it easy to pay by explaining payment procedures in the precontract negotiations and billing regularly, sending polite reminders where necessary.

When all else fails, the architect may have to consider legal action to recover fees. While studies indicate that over 75 percent of architects win such cases, careful consideration is necessary before going to law because of the cost, time, and potential public relations damage involved. Other alternatives—arbitration, mediation, mechanic's liens, or even collection agencies—may also be considered.

While there are no guarantees with any method of fee collection, standardized procedures for billing clients and collecting unpaid accounts are a sensible practice. Early client education regarding methods and amounts of payments, followed by prompt invoicing and excellent record keeping, are essential, and a consistent office policy of dealing with unpaid bills—the content, timing, and means of delivery (by hand, registered, and so on)—will provide an overall strategy that means less time and anxiety spent dwelling upon or dealing with fee collection and more time spent concentrating on increasing practice productivity.

10. When Does the Relationship End?

The architect is required to hold two meetings with the owner at the conclusion of the project, one after substantial completion and the second before the expiration of one year from the date of substantial completion to review the building's performance. However, it is not uncommon for the architect to revisit each project after completion to check out any complaints or questions from the owners. This constitutes something of a free service in most cases, although is often undertaken out of professional care or as a public relations function. The number of these visits may vary, and at some point give rise to some reflection on the part of the architect as to the advisability of providing continued free services.

The number of post-completion visits that an architect may willingly undertake beyond those contractually required will depend entirely on the nature of the project and the client; although at some stage it may be necessary to require payment for further services or point out the contractor's responsibilities under warranty. Explanation and discussion of such details at the beginning of the project may help to avoid embarrassing refusals by the architect to undertake more work without payment and prevent bad feelings after the project has ended.

The Relationship of the Architect and Contractor

Here, attorneys Tim Sheehan and David Gorman provide valuable insight on the most significant AIA Document: A201, *General Conditions of the Contract for Construction.* It is considered *the* "Keystone" document by the AIA, since its "central role as a reference document for the major contracts makes it the glue that binds these contractual relationships." In other words, it's rather important and is linked to other AIA documents. Sheehan and Gorman also provide valuable insight on another AIA document mainstay: A101, *Standard Form of Agreement Between Owner and Contractor.*

As with the AIA Agreements for professional services previously discussed, these standard form documents (A101 and A201) are often supplemented or amended (with the advice of an attorney who specializes in construction law) as a function of specific project circumstances and location.

TIMOTHY M. SHEEHAN has practiced law in Albuquerque, New Mexico, with the firm of Sheehan, Sheehan & Stelzner, PA, since 1974, primarily in the field of construction law. His clients include sureties, public and private institutional owners, general contractors, subcontractors, suppliers, and design professionals. Mr. Sheehan is a member of the American Arbitration Association and the Association of Attorney-Mediators. He is an adjunct professor of law at the University of New Mexico Law School and is the author of the revised and expanded text, *Construction Law in New Mexico* (Albuquerque: New Mexico Law Institute, 1996).

    DAVID P. GORMAN practices law in Albuquerque with the firm of Sheehan, Sheehan & Stelzner, PA, primarily in the fields of construction and public procurement law. His clients include general contractors, public owners, architects, and sureties, and he has represented clients before the state and federal courts. Mr. Gorman is a member of the American Arbitration Association and frequently writes on topics in the field of construction law.

The most common contractual relationship in the construction industry remains the triad of owner, architect, and contractor, where the owner is in direct contract with the architect and independently in direct contract with the contractor, but there is no direct contractual relationship between the architect and the contractor. The most commonly used owner-contractor agreements for fixed price construction are the AIA Document A101-1997, *Standard Form of Agreement Between Owner and Contractor* (Stipulated Sum), and the AIA Document A201-1997, *General Conditions of the Contract for Construction.* These documents not only give the architect certain rights associated with its contractual duties to the owner but also impose responsibilities on the architect that run to both the owner and the contractor. The AIA family of documents binds the architect to these responsibilities by the incorporation of the A201 by reference into AIA Document B141-1997, *Standard Form of Agreement Between Owner and Architect with Standard Form of Architect's Services.* For the architect, the potential for conflicts and liability exposure arises both from the architect's role in advising the owner regarding the use of the appropriate owner-contractor agreement and in connection with attempting to balance the architect's duties to the two parties to the A101 and A201 in these critical areas: accuracy of contract documents, certification of payment requests, review and acceptance of work, substantial completion of the work, and claims.

    An example of how document selection can create a serious financial impact on the parties is the provision in the A201 General Conditions (Article 4.3.10), which provides that the owner and contractor waive claims against each other for consequential damages. For the owner, this includes rental expenses, loss of use, lost profits, lost income, extended financing costs, and loss of management and employee productivity. This is one of the few areas where AIA contract documents deprive an owner of a remedy that it would otherwise have against a contractor. In commercial, retail, and entertainment projects such damages to an owner can run into hundreds of thousands or even millions of dollars. The fact that this provision appears in the A201 General Conditions rather than in the A101 Agreement may make it an unwelcome surprise for owners who are unfamiliar with the documents. If the architect is taking the lead in providing or recommending contract documents to the owner, the architect may want to highlight such a provision during the document selection process.

The A101 Agreement and the A201 General Conditions are intentionally complementary documents. The A101 Agreement is a relatively brief and simple document given the complexity of the construction process. It does little more than provide a framework for the relationship between owner and contractor by establishing the scope, price, and time period for the work to be performed, enumerating the documents that comprise the contract and providing basic payment terms. For example, Article 5 of the A101 Agreement provides the timing and other basic terms for submitting and processing the contractor's payment applications, but the actual details of the process are covered in much greater detail in Article 9 of the A201 General Conditions. The A101 Agreement gives no detail of the key role played by the Architect in the administration of the contract between the owner and the contractor.

The A201 General Conditions provides the details of the relationships between owner, contractor, and architect during the construction of the project. The general duties of the architect in administration of the contract are addressed in Article 4 of the General Conditions, but the Architect's role is also woven throughout the other Articles of the A201. The duties of the architect in Article 4 include being the owner's representative during construction, facilitating communication between the owner and contractor, reviewing and certifying of contractor's applications for payment, rejecting of nonconforming work, preparing change orders, establishing substantial completion of the work, interpreting the contract documents, and deciding claims and disputes between the owner and contractor. Because it is vested with the right to make and receive communications on behalf of the owner, the architect's actions and inactions have the power to bind the owner. These actions and inactions may create liability to the contractor, and the owner may look to the architect to recoup the financial impacts of the architect's actions and inaction. Conversely, the owner normally has an expectation that the architect will be diligent in protecting the owner against poor workmanship and excess costs while the contractor has a strong interest in expeditious decisions and maximizing its recovery for errors in the plans and specifications. Recognizing the tension between the duties to owner and contractor created by Article 4 and the other provisions of the A201, AIA has artfully drafted the A201 to minimize the architect's potential liability in areas of the greatest potential conflict.

Plans and Specifications

One of the key points of contact between the architect and the contractor is the plans and specifications. Typically, these documents originate with the architect or the architect's subcontractors. And, in most cases, the owner is relying on the architect's expertise in designing and specifying a constructable project. Under Article 3.2 of the A201, the contractor is responsible for a careful review of the plans and specifications and is required to report to the architect when the contractor discovers errors, omissions, or inconsistencies. The contractor's duties under this provision do not extend to ascertaining whether the plans and specifications are in accordance with applicable laws or building codes but only to report variances that it discovers (Article 3.2.2). The contractor is only responsible for damages resulting from errors, omissions, and inconsistencies if it discovers them and knowingly fails to report them to the architect (Article 3.2.3). These provisions reflect the common judgment that the owner, through the architect, is responsible for the accuracy of plans and specifications. The A201, while recognizing this common judgment, also makes the architect the initial judge of contractor allegations of errors and omissions in the plans and specifications. This quasi-judicial role demands an objectivity that may be difficult for the architect to muster. Denial of meritorious contractor claims can lead to acrimony and disputes. The cost of contractor claims allowed on the basis of errors and omissions must be borne, in the first instance, by the owner. But the owner may be inclined to seek damages for such errors and omissions from the architect and the architect's professional liability carrier.

Construction Observation

The architect may also feel torn between the interests of the owner and the contractor in the area of observation of construction. The A201 requires the architect to make observations of the progress of the contractor's work (Article 4.2.2). The A201 is very protective of the architect in the role of observer of the work. Article 4.2.2 states that the architect is not responsible for exhaustive or continuous inspection of the correctness of the work. Nor does the architect have control over the means, methods, techniques, or scheduling of the work by the contractor or responsibility to the owner for the contractor's failure to carry out the work in accordance with the contract documents (Article 4.2.3). These provisions insulate the architect from responsibility to the owner for the contractor's poor workmanship. Other provisions related to shop drawings and submittals absolve the architect from responsibility for their accuracy or completeness (Article 4.2.7). Yet, the A201 does give the architect significant power over the contractor's work. It provides that the architect can reject work that does not conform to the contract documents and can require additional inspection or testing of the work, regardless of whether the work in question has been completed (Article 4.2.6). If it turns out that the questioned work conforms to the contract documents, it is the owner who will bear the cost of the additional testing or rework. If the rejected or retested work does not conform to the contract, the contractor bears the cost of correction (Article 12.1.2). Since it is the architect who, in the first instance, decides whether the work meets the contract requirements (Article 4.2.11), the architect may be subjected to pressure by the owner to find deficiencies in the retested work, and the architect's objectivity may be questioned by the contractor.

Changes to the Construction Contract

Few projects proceed without difficulties. These difficulties can take the form of problems with the plans and specifications, the site, weather, or acts of

God. The A201 provides a change-order process to allow adjustments in the contract to take these difficulties into account. The architect plays a key role in the change-order process. Sometimes changes are obvious (as where the owner orders extra work), but more often they are initiated by a contractor or owner claim. The architect generally has the responsibility for determining whether there has been a change. If there is agreement between the architect, owner, and contractor on the change and the amount of time and money by which the contract should be adjusted, the architect prepares a Change Order (Article 7.2.1). If the contractor disagrees, the architect prepares a construction change directive, which directs the contractor to perform the changed work and establishes a method for determining the impact of the change (Article 7.3.3). The contractor is free to disagree with the price and/or time adjustment for the change but is obligated to perform the change whether agreement has been reached or not (Article 7.3.4).

Because the contractor is obligated to complete the work, even while disagreeing with the architect's determination of whether a change exists or what the appropriate adjustment to the contract is, the change-order process is a fertile area for inception and growth of disputes. Contractors are particularly sensitive to change directives or denials of change requests that burden the contractor with unanticipated costs or eliminate particularly profitable work. Owners, too, are sensitive to changes, since they can materially increase the cost or time of the project. Some owners also use changes, particularly those deleting work, to control the overall cost of the project. Either party, or both, may attack the architect's determination of the existence or magnitude of a contract change.

Disputes

The A201 gives the architect the power to decide claims and disputes between the owner and the contractor. All claims (including those for the architect's errors and omissions) are referred, in the first instance, to the architect for decision (Article 4.4.1). The A201 provides a framework, both in terms of time and appropriate actions, for the architect's decisional process (Article 4.4.1–.7). While the A201 does not offer any specific protection for the architect for assuming this decisional role, case law is quite uniform that the architect will not be liable for the decision so long as the architect's consideration and decision on the claim have been made in good faith. Unfortunately, some contractors tend to discount the architect's ability to be fair in determining disputes between the owner (who has hired the architect and is far more likely to be a source of repeat business) and the contractor. These contractors may make their presentation of claims to the architect rather perfunctory, preferring to rely on the right to have the dispute mediated or arbitrated by a neutral or panel of neutrals (Articles 4.5 and 4.6).

Payments to the Contractor

The architect is also intimately involved in the processing of the contractor's progress payment and final payment requests. This is a sensitive area for both the contractor and the owner. The owner does not want to overpay the contractor for work or pay in advance for work not actually completed. And the owner has a strong financial incentive to expend funds as slowly as possible. Conversely, contractors generally have no desire to finance the work for the owner. They must pay their own employees and suppliers independent of the time of receipt of payment from the owner, and it is in their interest to obtain payment as work progresses. As with so many of the sensitive areas where the architect must balance the interests of owner and contractor, the A201 provides a mechanism that deflects as much liability as possible away from the architect. Before making the first application for payment, the contractor submits a schedule of values to the architect (Article 9.2.1). The schedule of values assigns a value to each component of the work, and this schedule becomes the basis for measuring the degree of progress on the project. The schedule of values determines the proper amount due on the contractor's periodic requests for payment (Article 9.3.1). The architect needs a certain degree of sophistication about construction costs to evaluate the schedule of values, as it is common for the contractor to weight values toward tasks that take place early in the project. The architect may well object to a schedule of values that is "front-end loaded," as it may decrease the contractor's incentive to complete the undervalued tasks at the end of the project. If the schedule of values is acceptable, the architect's periodic visits to the construction site (Article 4.2.5) will confirm the degree of progress on scheduled items for the purpose of evaluating the contractor's pay request.

The contractor's payment application is submitted directly to the architect, and the architect has seven days to either certify to the owner the proper amount payable or to inform the owner and contractor why payment is being withheld (Article 9.4.1). If the architect certifies the contractor's application for payment, the A201 provides that the architect only represents that to the best of his or her knowledge and belief the work has progressed to the point indicated (Article 9.4.2). Even this representation is qualified and limited by a number of caveats (*Id.*). The purpose of the limited and qualified nature of the architect's representation is to provide the architect with the maximum possible protection from liability to the owner for overpayments to the contractor. The A201 also offers the architect a degree of protection when the architect decides not to certify the contractor's pay request in whole or in part, by enumerating several reasons for the architect to withhold certification for payment, including: defective work or persistent failure to carry out the work in conformity with the plans and specifications, the filing or probable filing of third-party claims, the contractor's failure to pay subcontractors and suppliers, or reasonable evidence that the contract cannot be completed within the remaining contract time or for the remaining contract balance (Article 9.5.1).

Occasionally, unscrupulous or financially strapped owners will pressure the architect to find one of the enumerated grounds for withholding payment. Withholding certification for payment can be financially devastating to the contractor, and the A201 provides that once the noted grounds are corrected, certification will be made for amounts previously withheld (Article 9.5.2). Once certification for payment occurs, the owner is obliged to pay the amount certified within seven days, or the contractor may, with seven days additional notice, stop the work until payment is received (Article 9.7.1). The contractor has the same right if the architect (through no fault of the contractor) fails to issue a certificate for payment within the architect's seven day deadline (*Id.*).

Project Completion

The architect's role in establishing substantial completion and final completion of the project also has important financial ramifications. Generally, the amounts retained by the owner during the project as security for the completion of the project ("retainage") are payable in full, or in large part, upon substantial completion. Under A201, the architect determines when the contractor's work has advanced to the degree that the project is substantially complete (Article 9.8.4). The A201 requires the architect to determine substantial completion through inspection but makes it the contractor's responsibility to provide a list of items ("punch list") that remain to be completed (Article 9.8.2). Similarly, the architect conducts an inspection when notified by the contractor that the work is ready for final inspection and acceptance. Acceptance by the architect is the trigger for final payment to the contractor (Article 9.10.1).

The punchlist can be the source of considerable friction. The architect is not bound by the contractor's punch list and has a right and duty to insist that the project conform to the plans and specifications before final acceptance. Opinions may differ on whether particular items on the punch list affect whether the project is substantially complete. Also, contractors are usually anxious to demobilize their forces from a job site and move them to other jobs and may attempt to rush the evaluation of final completion.

The three-party relationship on the typical construction project places the architect in the position of mediating between the very different interests of the owner and contractor. To carry out this role, the architect must strive for the respect rather than the friendship of either of the other parties. The A101 and A201 documents are carefully designed to insulate the architect from the dangers of charges of favoritism in carrying out its functions, but they alone cannot win the trust and respect of the other project participants. Ultimately, only the architect's own demonstrated integrity and candor in the face of competing interests will earn the respect of the construction industry.

Scenario for Discussion

The owner of a hospital wants to add new space to and renovate a portion of its existing facility. The owner asks its architect to design systems and specify materials for the new and renovated portions consistent with, as much as possible, the portions of the hospital that will not be changed.

The architect reviews plans and specifications for the existing hospital and specifies wall coverings to match the existing portions of the hospital. Unknown to the owner, architect, and contractor, the wall covering that is specified meets prevailing building codes but is no longer permitted for hospital use by an independent hospital accrediting organization. The specifications contain a general provision requiring the contractor to provide materials that conform to all applicable codes.

The contractor, who has been selected in part because of its experience with similar hospital projects, checks the plans before construction but does not detect the issue. The contractor submits information on the wall covering that, unlike the submissions on a number of other materials, does not contain any indication that it is approved by the accrediting organization. The submittal is approved by the architect and the material is installed in the new portion of the hospital.

The owner occupies the new portion and begins moving its employees and equipment into the new space. The contractor moves on to renovation of the portion of the existing facility previously occupied by the equipment and staff that is now in the new portion. The contractor submits a request for information to the architect concerning how to install the wall covering where the renovated space and the new space meet. Not finding an answer in its library, the architect contacts the accrediting organization for guidance and is informed that the material is unsuitable for use and that the organization will not accredit the hospital with the material in the new and renovated spaces. The contractor already has the material for the renovated space and is ready to proceed with installation. Removal of the material in the new space will require the owner to shut down the space and create substantial expense for decontamination of the installed equipment.

DISCUSS THE FOLLOWING OPTIONS FOR THE ARCHITECT

1. Should the architect notify the contractor and owner at once, or should the architect first attempt to determine an appropriate solution to present to the owner and contractor?
2. While the architect is pondering the appropriate solution, the contractor notifies the architect that progress on the renovation portion of the work will be delayed if it does not receive a response to its request for information within forty-eight hours. Is the architect obligated to inform the owner of the problem now?
3. Should the architect order the contractor to suspend work while the issue is under consideration?
4. Can the architect insist that the contractor remove and replace the wall covering at the contractor's expense because the contractor should have known the accrediting organization's standards?

Top 10 Legal Implications of Electronic Documents

STAN MARTIN is a partner and member of the construction industry practice group in the Boston law firm, Holland & Knight LLP. He concentrates his practice in construction law, with an emphasis on contract negotiations, procurement, performance and claims, arbitration, and litigation.
© 2005, Stanley A. Martin.

Data-file transfer via the internet has become commonplace, and architects' and engineers' drawings and specifications are no exception. But what is your response when the HVAC (heating, ventilating, and air-conditioning) subcontractor, who has the same software as your firm, asks you to send the drawings via email? Should you be concerned? Do you have an obligation to share this information? How do you deal with this situation? A number of issues arise in this context, some of them practical, some of them contractual, but all with potential legal ramifications. What follows are legal implications that arise from the use and distribution of electronic documents.

1. Set Up a Company Protocol

Have procedures in place on how to deal with exchange and transfer of files electronically. Topics include: under what circumstances will files be shared and with whom; who is authorized to send files; what cover e-mail or letter must accompany the files; and what written records (read: hard copies or a log) must be maintained.

2. Provide by Contract What You Must Share, When, and How

Specify in the appropriate contract (e.g., with the project owner, if you are the prime designer) what information is to be shared electronically, when during the project, and the format. Any qualifications or caveats to accompany shared electronic data should be set forth. This is the best opportunity to shape the nature and extent of file sharing; don't wait until someone is ready to hit the "Send" key.

3. Designate a Person Within the Company Who Must Approve Dissemination

Someone has to monitor the file sharing and make the call—yes, no, or otherwise—when the request for files arrives in the e-mail inbox. Don't let each employee make his or her own decision, as you will quickly lose track of what has been sent out. This should not be a low-level employee but someone with authority in the organization.

4. Don't Just Give the Documents to Anyone Who Asks

This is the toughest one. Who is entitled to electronic files? Establish this by contract, so you know what to do when an electrical contractor bidding the work asks for a set in order to forward, in turn, to a supply house. If not in the contract, then follow your company protocol—do you send files only to those who are actually working on the project or only to designated parties? Otherwise, you will be assailed from all sides for your "refusal" to cooperate.

5. Follow the Company Procedures, Protocols, and Your Contract

A company procedure left to gather dust on a shelf is worthless. Implement the procedures, and follow the guidelines. If something turns out to be impractical, modify the company procedure, after considering all the issues. Be wary of making exceptions in the heat of the moment.

6. Transmit Documents with Appropriate Qualifications or Disclaimers

Certain things must be clear in the transmittal:

- The purpose for transmitting the file (e.g., only for use in preparing as-builts).
- State that you are NOT conveying any copyright interest or license, or right to prepare derivative works, other than as specifically identified in the transmittal.
- Disclaim responsibility and liability for: file corruption or viruses; the obligation to furnish updates; any discrepancy between electronic and paper versions; third-party claims arising from improper use or dissemination.
- Demand that the recipient indemnify and defend you against third-party claims arising from the recipient's failure to abide by the terms of the exchange.
- Demand that the recipient obtain your permission in writing before sending any of the files to another party.

7. Keep a Record of What Was Sent, by Date and Version, When, and to Whom

Even if not by hard copy, you must be able to re-create, one year from now, what was sent yesterday. Track the version of each document or set of documents transmitted, and keep a record or log of the transmittal and any stated restrictions or qualifications. Keeping paper copies of each transmittal will be cumbersome—that's why you're sending them electronically in the first place—so look for another means of documentation.

8. Get Agreement or Confirmation from Noncontracting Parties as to Their Intended Usage

Before you send the files out the virtual door, get the intended recipient to state in writing the purpose of seeking electronic files. Reiterate this purpose with your transmission.

9. Protect Your Own Copyright Interests

Make sure each document is identified with a copyright notice, year, and name of person or company owning the copyright. If the project is significant enough, register your copyright with the U.S. Copyright office (www.copyright.gov). Although copyright interests are only transferred in writing, be wary of taking any action that could be construed as conveying a license to use your work.

10. Pursue Violators Who Come to Your Attention

If someone improperly uses your files, and it comes to your attention, don't just sit there. Take action, or else you could be deemed to have waived your rights. At a minimum, notify the scoundrel in writing of the violation and of your intent to hold that person responsible for any liability or damages as a result, and demand that the violation cease. You will have to use your judgment, and should seek counsel, on what might be appropriate follow-up, but at least go on record with your objections.

Case Study | Minor Setbacks

Codes and regulations are promulgated for the public good. However, they may overlap, conflict, or even be inappropriate for some projects and communities, as Steve Schreiber elaborates below. And they certainly can have a big impact on shaping designs. When codes and regulations present a special hardship, fail to accomplish their original intent, are outdated, or do not promote excellence in the environment, it behooves the architect to challenge the status quo. Whether that means applying for a variance on behalf of a client, or participating in a planning meeting with building officials at city hall and lobbying for change, change for the better is indeed possible. And depending on the circumstances, nothing less than some change should be accepted without a fight.

STEPHEN SCHREIBER, FAIA, teaches and practices architecture in Tampa, Florida. He is a professor and former dean of the University of South Florida School of Architecture and Community Design, where he teaches architectural and urban design and introductory drawing courses. His design work has been published in *Architecture, Designer/Builder, Cracking the Codes,* and other journals. Schreiber is currently serving as President of the Association of Collegiate Schools of Architecture. Courtesy of Stephen Schreiber, FAIA.

The Context

A substantial part of an architect's work involves understanding and addressing the multiple codes and regulations that affect building proj-

ects. These laws include zoning regulations, environmental protection rules, building, mechanical, electrical codes, fire safety laws, federal mandates (such as the Americans with Disabilities Act), design covenants, and transportation rules. Any architect can attest to the lack of coordination among the various codes and the hours spent reconciling conflicting laws. This lack of coordination has a serious impact on the development of the built environment.

For example, the comprehensive master plan for Albuquerque, New Mexico, emphasizes the need to "infill" vacant lots in the city's older neighborhoods. Albuquerque, like many North American cities, is sprawling at its edges but stagnant in its core. This policy is intended to encourage the development of underused or vacant property with the existing urban grid. Through creative infill, the city could substantially grow without further increasing the need for more utilities, streets, sidewalks, or bus lines. In short, the city can become more efficient and environmentally sustainable.

Albuquerque's building, zoning, and public works departments require that all new buildings satisfy a demanding set of requirements that are difficult to meet on sites that were planned under old guidelines. Many property owners find it impossible to develop older parcels of land in older neighborhoods such as Old Town, downtown, and the university areas. Codes, which are often contradictory, govern issues such as handicap accessibility, landscaping, off-street parking, and traffic movement. The numerous constraints, designed for suburban areas, are a major reason why so much land in older neighborhoods (such as the center city) is left vacant.

The Project

In 2000, my firm was asked to design a new retail commercial building for East Central Avenue in the "University Area" of Albuquerque, near the University of New Mexico. This project would occupy an underused property in this bustling pedestrian district. The University Area supports active business and neighborhood associations, which developed (with the city planning department) a sensitive set of design guidelines. The "sector plan" favors infill construction, urban "street walls," and active storefronts. It aggressively attempts to deemphasize automobiles. Since the commercial building would be one of the first completely new buildings to be constructed on Central under these guidelines, it also became a major test of the conflicts between a well-intentioned sector plan and relentless city, state, and national building requirements.

The site, on the southwest corner of Princeton and Central, is located on the edge of the university area's robust commercial district. The relatively flat 150 foot by 150 foot parcel houses an historic tile-faced laundromat (built in the early twentieth century). This 2,500-square-foot structure sits on the property line at the corner

of Princeton and Central. A poorly maintained 3,700-square-foot warehouse sits on the southeast corner of the site. The property is served by a midblock alley that runs north-south (Figure 7-2, below). My client, the operator of the laundromat and warehouse, felt that his property could be more fully developed as a small shopping center, with retail spaces ranging from 1,500 to 3,000 square feet in size. Initial programming demonstrated that the site could support about 8,500 square feet of retail space, including the laundromat, on one level. (That is about the same amount of conditioned space in the existing laundromat and warehouse.)

The design guidelines for the area require that buildings be constructed to the edges of the property line. The sector plan prefers that parking be accessed only at the alleys (not Central Avenue) and that parking lots be hidden from the main street. The document also suggests that façades be broken into 50-foot bays (maximum) where possible (Figure 7-3). A reduction in off-street parking is allowed if adjacent property owners, the neighborhood associations, and the "zoning hearing examiner" all agree.

Modern Albuquerque zoning codes normally require one parking space for every 300 square feet of retail space. Therefore, every square foot added inside means that one square foot of asphalt must be added outside (for park-

Figure 7-2 Existing conditions. Courtesy of Stephen Schreiber, FAIA.

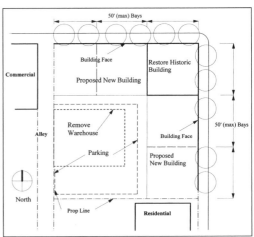

Figure 7-3 Design guidelines. Courtesy of Stephen Schreiber, FAIA.

ing and drive lane). The zoning code has a more intense parking requirement for some commercial uses, such as restaurants.

After exploring several options, the client agreed on an L-shaped scheme, with the laundromat situated at the intersection of two retail wings. One wing would face north toward Central and another wing would face east toward Princeton. The parking in the rear would be entered and exited at the existing alley, which feeds a number of other lots. The retail wings could be entered from either the parking area or the public sidewalks. All entrances were designed to be wheelchair accessible (Figure 7-4). So far, so good.

The Problems

Just before the working drawings were to be submitted for the building permit, the owner's surveyor found out that the eastern edge of the property was located in a flood plain. This discovery meant that the interior floor slab would have to be raised almost 3 feet above the level of the existing slab for the laundromat (and the existing city sidewalk). It also meant that it would be difficult to allow wheelchair access from Central or Princeton. (The south side of the property, on the other hand, could be easily regraded.)

The New Mexico building code requires all entrances that face public ways (such as Central

or Princeton) to be accessible with ramps. Building officials said that we had three choices:

1. Find a place for a ramp.
2. Do not allow anyone access from Central or Princeton (make everyone enter from the rear).
3. Move the building back from the street and it would no longer be "facing a public way."

All options violated the admirable intentions of the university area design guidelines. Eventually a solution was reached where public ramps penetrated the building at two locations. The ramps would lead from the city sidewalks to the rear of the new retail wings. The laundromat, which was grandfathered into the old code, could be entered from the existing sidewalk. The new retail wings would have to be entered from the parking-lot side.

The last group to review commercial working drawings in Albuquerque is the Transportation Development department. We had reviewed the schematic design with this department because of the difficulties of fitting new buildings into old street and alley layouts. After initially approving the site plan, the department later demanded that the owner widen the city alley from 16 feet to 24 feet (with the extra 8 feet taken on his property)

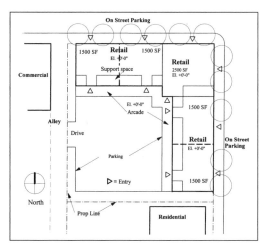

Figure 7-4 Proposed design. Courtesy of Stephen Schreiber, FAIA.

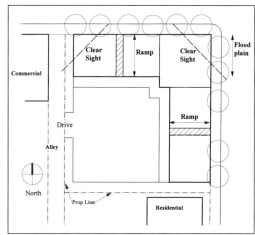

Figure 7-5 Ramps, flood plain, and triangles. Courtesy of Stephen Schreiber, FAIA.

and that he provide 25 foot by 25 foot "clear sight triangles" at the corner of Princeton and Central and the alley and Central (Figure 7-5).

The only way to meet these requirements would be to put the building in the middle of the property. But the design guidelines (and common sense) rendered that solution unacceptable to the planning department (Figure 7-6). Again, the project seemed to be undevelopable. The department eventually found an exception in the traffic codes that, in fact, do not require clear sight triangles on certain corners. The officials also slightly relaxed the 24-foot alley width requirement when it discovered that a row of existing power poles and a brand new dumpster enclosure (required by another department) would sit in the middle of a newly widened alley.

The Solution

The final design is slightly smaller than the owner anticipated (7,900 square feet versus 8,500 square feet originally planned). Because of this, the client's efforts to finance the project have been delayed several years. The raised floor levels will prevent store entrances from facing major streets, but generous shop windows will help activate street life (Figure 7-7).

The difficulties encountered in this modest-size project are poignant reminders of why Albuquerque remains a suburb "in search of a city." Only the most optimistic and persistent property owners and architects can maneuver the multiple contradicting codes for even seemingly simple jobs. It is easier to develop a completely new parcel of land on the edge of the city, regrade where necessary, plunk the building in the middle of the property, and surround it with parking. If cities such as Albuquerque truly want to become denser and more urban by a process of infilling, they must start by setting new priorities for their code processes.

DISCUSSION QUESTIONS

1. What are the major trade-offs on a project such as this?
2. Should the architect have known about the conflicting code requirements before completing schematic designs? Before completing working drawings?
3. Should the authors of the sector plan have known about the conflicting code requirements before drafting the design guidelines?
4. One of the major design conflicts had to do with the city's requirement for clear sight triangles, which forces many buildings back from street edges. When should the rights of pedestrians outweigh those of drivers?
5. Another conflict arose because of the requirement for wheelchair access to a site that had to be raised above a flood plain. What are different ways this conflict could have been handled?

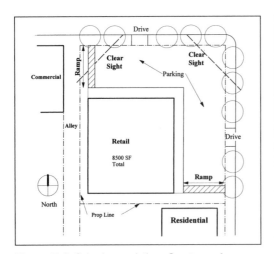

Figure 7-6 Suburban solution. Courtesy of Stephen Schreiber, FAIA.

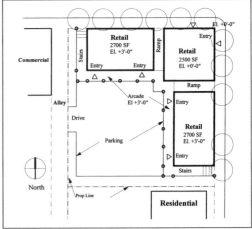

Figure 7-7 Final floor plan. Courtesy of Stephen Schreiber, FAIA.

Case Study | Accounting for Terraces—Dealing with Unclear Regulations

BARRY D. YATT, FAIA, NCARB, CSI, CDT, is a tenured associate professor of construction technology and practice at The Catholic University of America and an architect with almost three decades of experience. He provides peer review and expert witnessing services and is a nationally recognized producer of professional educational programs and texts. These include the AIA's *Promises, Promises: Forging Healthy Project Relationships* (Washington, D.C.: American Institute of Architects, 1996) and the John Wiley & Sons/NCARB monograph, "Cracking the Codes: An Architect's Guide to Building Regulations." © Barry D. Yatt.

Prologue

Regulations are written to give members of the public, through the government, some degree of control over actions taken by individuals and businesses that might affect them. One kind of regulation, the zoning ordinance, gives them some control over the way individuals and businesses develop and use land, or "real property." But control can be tricky. The issues that both individuals and communities face can have many shades of gray, and regulations can too easily be simplified abstractions that see things as black or white. In an effort to moderate regulations to better fit the realities of life, to address unusual or atypical situations that simple rules can't handle, regulations are often written with built-in exceptions. But with exceptions come questions. Under what conditions can an exception be claimed? How much of a condition must exist to trigger the exception? And when is an exception not an exception but a credit?

These questions arose in the case of rules for maximum building height found in the zoning ordinance of Montgomery County, Maryland. In section 59-C-1.327(a), the county code sets a maximum building height of 35 feet. This dimension is meaningless, however, without agreement on the location of the top and bottom points for measuring height. For the case we are about to examine, the critical issue was agreeing on a definition for the bottom point.

According to the "Height of Building" definition in code section 59-A-2.1, there are three ways to measure building height: one for buildings located within 35 feet of the street, another for buildings located more than 35 feet from the street, and an "exception" for buildings that sit on a "terrace." This range of approaches suggests that the bottom point for measuring height is complex or, at least, recognizes that not all site conditions are equal. It says:

> *Height of Building:* The vertical distance measured from the level of the approved street grade opposite the middle of the front of the building [to the top of the building] . . . except that if a building is located on a terrace, the height above the street grade may be increased by the height of the terrace. In the case of a building set back from the street line 35 feet or more, the building height is measured from the average elevation of finished ground surface along the front of the building. . . .

The ordinance, in other words, establishes that the bottom point for measuring the height of a building is the height of the street where it passes by the center of the front façade in cases where the street's elevation is close enough, either horizontally (within 35 feet) or vertically (not on a terrace), to be relevant.

It appears that, like the formula used for buildings located more than a minimum horizontal distance from the street, the terrace exception to the maximum height rule is intended to provide an alternative formula for buildings that are located at some vertical distance from the street.

One might interpret these horizontal and vertical distance formulas as allowing buildings to be higher up if appropriate as a result of site-specific topographical differences without allowing for maximum heights that exceed the allowed 35 feet. Alternatively, one might interpret the terrace exception to allow a building to be taller, lest it exceed the usual maximum height when a terrace is present. This latter interpretation is potentially far more generous. It could easily be argued that, under this interpretation, the terrace exception to maximum height doesn't just change the bottom measurement point but actually increases the allowed maximum height.

So this ordinance has created some confusion. Are building height and "height above street grade" the same thing, or are they not? One interpretation suggests that the entire building height can be increased when a building is on a terrace; the other suggests only that the bottom point used for measuring the height of a building can be lifted so that soil is not included when calculating the height of a façade. Worse, the ordinance includes no definition of the word terrace, nor does it include any clarification of whether the terrace must remain in place in order for its height to be added to a project built where the terrace once existed.

The clause could have been drafted to say "if a building is located on a terrace, the height of the terrace will not be counted toward the maximum allowable height of the building." It also could have included a definition of the word "terrace." Either might have helped reduce the ambiguity of the formulas.

The consequences of this terrace exception clause for a specific project are the subject of this case study.

The Situation

On the north side of Exfair Road in Bethesda, Maryland, a developer applied for a building permit for a single-family residence. Since Exfair Road runs across the face of a hill, the north side of the street is higher and the south side is lower. The developer claimed that the rise along the entire north side was a terrace, including the property on which he wanted to build. He applied for a building permit for a house that, without the exception, would have exceeded the allowed 35 foot maximum height restriction. He claimed that his project should be granted a permit on the merit of the terrace exception. The developer's position was that any increase in grade from the street amounted to a terrace and that

Figure 7-8 The terrace on Exfair Road, Bethesda, Maryland. Courtesy of Barry Yatt. © Barry D. Yatt.

the grade increase entitled him to build a building that exceeded the maximum height restriction whether he kept the terrace in place or not.

The county's Department of Permitting Services (DPS) granted the permit, with an exception of 7 feet, allowing a building whose upper measurement point could be a maximum of 42 feet above street grade. But since the design included a garage on the front façade, a garage whose floor was approximately at street grade, DPS' approval permitted the developer to remove the terrace from in front of the house and build the house at street level while benefiting from a formula intended for projects whose ability to reach the maximum allowed height was limited by the presence of a terrace.

All was set for construction. But an architect neighbor, who obtained a copy of the developer's permit set from DPS, became concerned about the intended height of the building. The architect filed an appeal with the county challenging the DPS decision to grant the permit as allowing a building that was too tall and, therefore, illegal.

The Appeal

Each party involved in this appeal had a different role. The neighbors were in the role of "appellants," since they were appealing the ruling of the county. The county was the party whose acts were being challenged by the appellants. The developer's role was only as an "intervenor" since although it had a financial stake in the outcome of the case, its actions were not being challenged. It was not considered a party to the appeal since the legal issue was the propriety of the government-issued permit.

The appellant filed her appeal within thirty days of the issuance of the building permit. That complied with a rule in Montgomery County that requires appeals of any agency's actions to be initiated within thirty days of the action, which in this case was DPS' decision to grant a building permit. While this rule lets construction proceed with minimal risk of delay, it does limit the time available for the public to appeal. People must act quickly to figure out what is being proposed, figure out what implications it has

for them, obtain related documents including copies of permits, secure technical advice if needed, and file their appeals. In the case of a building permit, understanding technical issues related to construction or law requires special training, expertise in reading construction drawings, and an understanding of codes.

A lawyer, who lived next to another nearby property that was granted a permit under the same clause, also filed an appeal with the county. The two cases were granted a joint hearing.

The Facts of the Case

The two neighbors looked for something in the ordinance that might help them argue their point and force the county to rescind the permit, thereby forcing the developer to reduce the height of the house. Part of the problem in arguing the issue was that all of the existing houses were small—none was near the maximum allowed building height—so even a fully compliant building would have seemed tall if it used all of the height allowed. And a building that is out of scale with its neighbors is not illegal so long as it meets the required limits.

But when the appellants saw that the new building was more than 35 feet high relative to the elevation at the street, they wondered how it had been granted a permit. Then they noticed the reference to terraces and realized that it was the basis for the added height. It seemed reasonable, but then why did the new house seem so tall?

The front façade, they realized, *was* tall. The developer had removed the soil in front of the house all the way down to street grade. They cried foul, noting that while all the other buildings were sitting atop the existing topographic ridge, this property had undergone a "terrace-ectomy" to allow a street-level garage. How could a terrace exception be granted for a property whose terrace had been removed?

The Arguments

DPS defended their decision to grant the permit, claiming that the terrace wording applied. The developer testified that since the ordinance didn't define "terrace," the remaining soil constituted a terrace.

For their part, the appellants claimed that allowing use of the terrace exception was inconsistent with the purpose, limitations, and plain language of the ordinance. They noted that the purpose of zoning ordinances is to maintain property values and community ambiance. They said that the new project would reduce the value and livability of their properties by blocking light and air. They further argued that the look and feel of their community would be changed for the worse by the presence of this new, too-tall building.

The issue returned to establishing what Montgomery County meant when it adopted the terrace wording and the reasonableness of applying the terrace exception to the project. They called for testimony from three county employees and a civil engineer. Each used a different definition of terrace.

The first was the plan reviewer who had initially reviewed and granted the permit. He identified a planter box located in front of the building as a terrace, saying that he had been instructed to consider any raised land feature at least 6 feet wide to be a terrace.

The second, a senior member of DPS staff, said that the house, as built, was "in a little valley" but that there was a terrace nonetheless because of the remaining grade change from the front to the rear of the property.

The third to testify, the zoning supervisor, said that every DPS employee had the same understanding of what a terrace was. He said that the testimony given by the first two employees reflected long-term practices at DPS.

The civil engineer said that a small peninsula of land remaining from a larger original terrace could also be defined as a terrace. He identified a strip of land in front of the building as a qualifying terrace, since it extended from the building more than 6 feet and was more than 6 feet wide. He cited a DPS memo as his source for this definition.

The memo to which he referred was an internal County memorandum of a meeting held several years earlier when DPS staff attempted to define the term "terrace." The memo included the following item under "a summary of issues covered during the last meeting":

> The definition of the term "terrace" was discussed, since there is no definition in the zoning ordinance. It was decided that whether a terrace exists would be determined on a case-by-case basis. The following criteria provide some guidelines:
>
> • Flat surface
> • Slope not to exceed 1:12
> • Is the terrace a natural element in comparison with adjacent lots
> • Terrace must be no smaller than x feet wide

Regarding this last criterion, no elaboration was included as to how many feet would constitute "x." Neither was there any indication as to whether the term "wide" refers to measurements made perpendicular to the street or parallel to it.

The memo makes it clear that those present recognized the need for further definition of the term "terrace." No date is listed for the meeting, and there is no listing of participants, although it is on DPS stationery and is addressed to "staff." There is no indication that any members of the public were present at the meeting or notified of it or its conclusions. In fact, the memo was never finalized and never officially approved by DPS or issued in draft to the public for public comment.

The appellants argued that this memo should not be allowed to influence the case, since it had never been made public.

Unpublished rules based on internal discussions to which the public was not invited are, in fact, quite common, and plan reviewers are often given wide latitude in deciding whether a given project should be granted a permit. Of course, this makes the job of the person applying for a permit difficult, since it's hard to design a building to meet rules that aren't published. It also makes it difficult for the public, on whose behalf a code is supposedly written, to confirm or deny the appropriateness of the new rule. Following procedure for notification, comment, and publication is all the more important for deliberations like this, where the issue involved was general and could have affected future projects, rather than specific to a particular project.

DPS argued that, although the memo was clarifying long-term practice, it served only as a "guideline" and was "not necessarily applied in all cases." Nevertheless, it maintained that all plan reviewers followed the same rules and that the point of the memo was to make sure that all plan reviewers were "on the same page."

The Board of Appeals also commented, noting that "the guidelines were not incorporated into the Ordinance. DPS has not used any formal procedure to adopt the guidelines, including issuance in accordance with the Montgomery County Administrative Procedures Act."

On a different issue, the appellants argued that the wording of the building height definition implied that terraces were meant to be seen as exceptions. Legally speaking, exceptions have clear implications and are meant to be applied rarely. The appellants pointed out that while a terrace did exist prior to construction, the design of the house included removal of the terrace. They argued that the conditions required for the exception were no longer met and that consequently there was no justification for applying the exception, especially since the terrace no longer existed along the street, the place where height is measured.

DPS countered by labeling the exception a "credit," despite the use of the word "except" in the height definition. Because the intent of credits is that they be routinely applied, DPS maintained that the "terrace credit" was intended to be generally available.

Finally, DPS, with support from the developer, claimed that the building was designed in the only way possible to fit a garage on the site. The appellants argued that regulations are not written for the convenience of those regulated but to fulfill their greater purpose and that in any case a garage could have been included in a number of other ways if the house had been designed differently. The Board of Appeals declined to hear these arguments or to consider alternate choices available to the developer, such as use of a detached garage in the rear of the site.

The Ruling

In the end, the appellants' claim was denied. The Board of Appeals did not agree "that partial excavation of the terrace disqualifies it for the terrace credit," and therefore it found the terrace exception to have been appropriately granted and the permit to have been properly issued. The Board of Appeals felt that the language concerning terraces did not constitute an exception but rather a credit, despite the plain wording of the provision. It rejected the idea that the house exceeded the 35 foot maximum height allowance and accepted the view of DPS, which granted the Exfair project a "terrace credit."

The fact that the internal guidelines were not fairly or formally issued and that DPS failed to follow its own procedures for adopting or issuing guidelines was noted but not found to be significant. The ruling did, however, include the following statement: "The Board is concerned about the lack of formality and limited public notice with regard to the DPS criteria. The Board strongly advises that the terrace credit be formally reviewed and adopted in accordance with applicable provisions of the Administrative Procedures Act or through some other formal procedure, providing appropriate public notice."

Epilogue

The house on Exfair Road is now completed and occupied. The appellants, using their new knowledge of county interpretations and procedures, and with the help of a code specialist, have drafted a set of guidelines for defining the term "terrace." They are working with their elected County Council representative to get the proposal heard, and they hope to eventually see the county zoning ordinance amended to more clearly guide future development with respect to the issues raised by this case.

DISCUSSION QUESTIONS

1. Do you agree with the decision reached by the Board of Appeals? Why or why not? What arguments or other factors do you think motivated them the most in reaching their conclusion? Which of the arguments did you find most compelling?
2. How tightly defined are building regulations? How

much room do they contain for interpretation? Are tight or loose regulations better?

3. To what degree does a government have a fiduciary or agency responsibility to the public it is intended to serve? Should a government be able to make or enforce policies that help it in the conduct of its work without getting approval from, or informing, the public? Does the answer depend on whether the issue involves a generally applicable concept or an application that is project-specific?

4. What should an architect do when facing a regulation that is ill-defined? What are the consequences of failing to recognize ambiguity? Can or should regulatory ambiguities be seen as opportunities to push design?

5. What role can or should architects play in the development of good regulations or their enforcement? What, if anything, can or should architects do to increase their influence?

6. Who constitutes the public that the government is supposed to serve? Do residents (e.g., neighbors) have more or less legitimacy than businesses (e.g., developers) who like them, operate in, and pay taxes to the community?

Chapter 8

Risky Business

The concept that I've stressed over and over—*educate and communicate well with the client*—is applicable here in regard to risk management. Excellent, "giving" personal client relationships are so important on so many dimensions of architectural practice! Relations with contractors, subconsultants, and others with whom you work on a project are crucial as well. Being on good terms with all of these people will facilitate avoiding claims and resolving conflicts; it will help prevent any conflicts that do arise from escalating to the point where lawyers and insurance companies are compelled to get involved. The time and energy investment required to develop quality relationships pays dividends, not just in terms of reducing the likelihood of problems (or in enhancing the ability to deal with problems expeditiously) but in assuring genuine personal enrichment of projects and satisfaction for both client and architect.

Risk Management and Professional Liability Insurance

Practicing "safe architecture" in today's business climate is absolutely essential. "Protection" in the form of professional liability insurance, effective loss-prevention techniques, and, of course, risk-management tactics is available to the informed design professional. Insurance guru Bob Dean discusses the details of these strategies in the following.

ROBERT J. DEAN, Jr., is president of R. J. Dean & Associates, Rio Rancho, New Mexico, a licensed insurance agency specializing in professional liability insurance for architects and engineers since 1983. He is a frequent and highly respected guest lecturer at the University of New Mexico and has been in the commercial insurance business for over thirty years.

Risk is a part of everyday life, whether business or personal. How we deal with risk determines whether or not we ultimately succeed in life. In the practice of architecture, the professional also deals with risk on a daily basis. This is not just a matter of handling technical problems but of using appropriate business practices as well. It will be shown later that, perhaps surprisingly, business practices are a greater source of risks than technical plans and specifications.

The Elements of Risk Management

The process of risk management consists of several steps. First and foremost is to be able to identify those risks we face. Once they are determined, we can then deal with them. We can certainly avoid obvious risks that are not worth taking. Next, we can eliminate some risks by taking the appropriate steps ahead of time. For those that cannot be eliminated but are not so bad as to be avoided altogether, we can sometimes reduce or mitigate their impact on us. Another way to handle these risks is to transfer them to another party, most commonly accomplished through insurance. Finally, there are some risks that will persist no matter how hard we may try to alter their presence, and that is where we have to decide whether or not they are worth taking under the circumstances.

In the area of risk management, each firm must decide what is an acceptable level of risk. Obviously there are many considerations. Risk is not always a matter of finances but also of reputation. One of the best ways to identify and assess risk is to establish a procedure of evaluating clients and their projects. *Your relationship with your client has a great deal of influence on the likelihood of a lawsuit.* It may be impossible to have a good relationship if you have fundamental disagreements with your client about the way business should be conducted. If you sense your client does not measure up on the important issues, run, don't walk, to the next project. A client and project evaluator designed by the firm can be an important tool when deciding whether or not to pursue a particular project. The major professional liability insurance companies offer publications that can provide invaluable assistance in developing the criteria for client and project selection by the firm (refer to the note cited at the end of this essay).

Another area to emphasize is that of a sound written agreement between the design firm and the client. Certain onerous clauses commonly found in client-prepared contract forms are indemnities, certifications, guarantees and warranties, assignment, estimates of construction cost, stop-work authority, and insurance requirements, to name a few. These are what we might call "deal breakers." On the other hand, "deal makers," such as construction observation, delays, dispute resolution, environmental and health hazards, job-site safety, limitation of liability, scope of services, statutes of repose or limitation, and termination should be a part of every contract. Another critical area is that of attorney's fees. Although our legal system does not have a "loser pays" provision, this can be achieved in contract. Awarding attorneys' fees to the prevailing party can dissuade most people from filing frivolous lawsuits.

Another consideration in risk management is whether or not insurance can be purchased for the risks assumed by a design firm and the cost of that insurance. A stable, long-term player in the professional liability insurance marketplace can be a vital part of your business operation. *Architecture is more than just good design. Success also depends on your business acumen and your ability to manage risks.* If there is anything to be gained from my discussion of risk, it is the understanding that architects must be good business people to survive in the competitive society in which we live.

Professional Liability Insurance

The main discussion point of this section will be professional liability insurance and the use of effective loss prevention techniques. Insurance is not a panacea for the risks faced by a design professional. For one thing, with any insurance policy, there are exclusions (see the following section for examples of exclusions). Second, the marketplace imposes substantial deductibles on the policyholder in addition to limits that are usually inclusive of defense costs (legal expenses) and are finite in that there is an aggregate feature involved. Most policies have an aggregate limit equal to the per claim limit (i.e., $250,000 each claim and $250,000 in the aggregate). Policy limits may vary, and in some cases the aggregate limit can be a multiple of the per claim limit. Given the litigiousness of our society and the high cost of defense, one can see that a professional liability policy can easily be exhausted, even at limits of $1 million or more.

Insurance Exclusions

There are several reasons why insurance companies use exclusions. First, your professional liability carrier does not intend to cover something that is insured under a different policy. Worker's compensation, auto liability and physical damage, general liability, and property insurance are examples of coverages that are provided by other policies and excluded by the typical professional liability form.

Second, insurers can't possibly charge enough to cover certain kinds of extreme risks, such as work involving nuclear energy or hazards involving any type of asbestos product.

Third, professional liability insurance underwriters can't insure activities for which they are unable to measure and quantify risk. This includes activities that are not normally part of the standard professional design services—the assumption of another party's liability by contract for instance.

Fourth, insurers will not cover claims when doing so would be "contrary to public policy." In other words, if you do something illegal, good public policy says there should not be insurance to protect you. This usually includes claims for dishonest, fraudulent, or criminal acts, and claims for punitive damages.

There are other exclusions that eliminate coverage for certain high risk projects or services, but in some cases these can be deleted for an additional premium. Examples might include design–build work or design of such facilities as amusement parks, bridges, dams, and so on. Professional liability policies are *not* all alike so it is always best to review the policy form, and especially the exclusions, prior to purchasing such coverage.

Claims-Made Policy Form

Another key element of professional liability insurance for design professionals is the fact that, virtually without exception, these policies are written on what is known as a "claims-made" basis, in contrast to the customary "occurrence" basis of most other liability policies written for nonprofessional exposures. Also known sometimes as "claims-made and reported" policies, these policies cover only those claims made against you and reported to the insurance company during the policy term and any extended reporting periods that may be granted under certain circumstances. The implications should be clear: These policy forms require that you continually renew them to have coverage for claims made during the term, regardless of the date of occurrence. Once a policy expires, it is of no value to the policyholder for any new claims that might be reported. The renewal policy picks up the coverage of the expired policy and carries it forward for one more term, typically one year. Each policy then covers the prior acts of the previous policy term so that after a period of time, a single policy can be covering millions of dollars of construction work. All that, however, is subject to the retroactive date on the policy.

Prior Acts Coverage

The retroactive date on a policy is the starting point for coverage applicability. When a firm purchases its first professional liability policy, the retroactive date is ordinarily the inception date of the policy. As with virtually everything in this life, there are exceptions to this rule, but we will deal with the most common circumstances. This retroactive date is the point beyond which the insurer will not cover prior acts. In essence then, a new policy will not cover *any* acts prior to the retro date (as it is commonly known), which is the same as the inception date of coverage. One year later, the policy may be renewed but the retro date doesn't change. The policyholder now has one year of prior acts coverage. This process continues so that one additional year of prior acts coverage is added annually. Typically, most claims arise within two to three years after substantial completion of a project. Since claims arising before construction is completed are less likely, the most valuable part of your coverage is for prior acts. Let's illustrate this with an example.

During construction, the contractor requests a change order because a segment of the building does not meet applicable code. It is determined that the code was clear and existed at the time of design, and the architect clearly overlooked it. Assuming the cost to fix the problem is substantial enough to involve the architect's insurer, one of the first things the adjuster does in the analysis is to determine *when* the error or omission occurred. If it obviously fell outside the retro date, coverage is generally denied. The act, error, or omission must have occurred *after* the retroactive date.

Deciding on a Policy Limit

Insurance agents are often asked, "How much coverage should I buy?" This is like asking, "How high is up?" You may start by asking yourself, "How much (insurable) construction is out there and what can I afford?" but this really does not answer the question. For one thing, the policy will also respond to bodily injury claims made by injured construction workers seeking a remedy in addition to worker's compensation benefits or by individuals killed or injured on a project long after substantial completion. The number can literally be in the millions. Bear in mind that total building failures are extremely rare.

The problem then is that of many projects all vying for the same finite annual policy limits and our lotterylike legal system in which a few lucky individuals hope to strike it rich in litigation. In reality then, policy limits are based on economic considerations and sometimes on the requirements of owners who set minimum limits for design professionals hired to work on their projects. Insurance agents are also asked to provide cost estimates for this form of coverage, but the only accurate method is to go through the application process and have an insurance company quote a figure.

Premiums depend on a variety of factors such as professional discipline, type of projects, type of services provided, type of clients, and annual gross billings, to name a few variables. The competitive nature of the insurance market and financial cycles also have an impact on pricing. Amount of coverage and size of deductible are also factors. Typically the average mature firm pays about 2 to 3 percent of annual gross billings as an annual premium. Structural engineers are often double the average of architects and other building engineers.

Loss Prevention

Given the cost and somewhat restrictive nature of a professional liability policy, what is a design professional to do? Insurance certainly has its place and is recommended for most firms and even required for most public work and some private sector projects. *Insurance then is only one aspect of risk management. First and foremost is a sound system of active loss prevention within a firm.* Earlier it was stated that technical deficiencies are not the real problem. Yes, mistakes happen, and as Alexander Pope once said, "To err is human, to forgive divine." Unfortunately, a quality of forgiveness is not common in our world of business and commerce. To achieve a claim-free practice may be too idealistic, but significant strides can be made through good business practices that emphasize loss prevention. This involves education of your staff *and* clients. Communication is paramount. So is file documentation. Here then are the three basic tenets of loss prevention:

1. *Eliminate liability illiteracy in your firm.* Teach your employees the effect of everyday business practices on your exposure to litigation. Engineering and architectural schools don't teach much about the real-world problems of low bidding contractors, failed expectations, and lawsuits.
2. *Avoid unnecessary litigation by implementing alternative dispute resolution (ADR) provisions in contractual agreements.* Inserting ADR provisions in all of your contracts has enormous potential. Nonbinding mediation is an excellent first step.
3. *Refuse to accept unlimited liability for your services.* Work for a limitation of liability clause in your contracts that caps the amount of liability you assume if there is a problem on the project. This won't be easy. While our hope is that you can obtain such a clause in every contract, there is still resistance to the concept from some owners, contractors, and even design professionals. But the tide has turned. More architects and engineers are successfully negotiating such clauses.

Subconsultants

The complexity of many building projects often requires the services of consulting engineers and may include structural, mechanical, and electrical subcontractors. Customarily, the architect will act as the prime consultant and subcontract the engineering services as necessary. While it may be preferable for the architect to engage these consultants to coordinate their efforts and exercise more control over the design process, it is not without a certain amount of risk. That risk is due to something known as *vicarious liability*. Whenever you hire an independent contractor, for whatever purpose, you can become legally liable for their actions. For that reason, it is wise to choose competent subconsultants using a quality-based selection process and to require that they also carry professional liability insurance. The former is wise because it lessens the probability that the subconsultants will be the source of a claim, and the latter because it makes it less likely that you will become the "deep pocket." It goes without saying that subconsultants should be given the same scrutiny as clients and projects prior to engaging their services. Having a written agreement between the architect and engineer (as opposed to an oral agreement or "handshake") is just as important as having a contract between you and your client.

Not only should subconsultants carry professional liability insurance during the term of a contract but also afterward; hence the wisdom in using established consultants with a history of providing such insurance. A case in point: An architect retained a structural engineer to help design a school building. A couple of years after substantial completion, a major structural beam showed signs of severe deflection. It was determined that the engineer had made an error in his calculations, and the beam was undersized. The cost of the fix exceeded $20,000. The architect notified his engineer and was later shocked to learn that the engineer had been easing himself into retirement and decided he could no longer afford to purchase professional liability insurance. The school district turned to the architect for recompense. The architect's insurer paid the claim but only after the architect had satisfied the $5,000 deductible that he hoped to recover from the engineer. Whether or not the recovery is successful, the architect has to live with a claim on his otherwise spotless record.

Contracts

Finally, a word about contracts. Perhaps nothing else has such an impact on a firm's liability as the agreement between it and the client. That document probably has more implications than anything else. A good written agreement is therefore the foundation of sound loss prevention. One of the pitfalls of poorly written agreements, especially those offered by the client and/or the client's attorney, is the assumption of liability that would not otherwise be yours in the absence of such a contract. So severe is this exposure that insurance companies routinely exclude any liability assumed under contract. It behooves you, therefore, to have a sound, balanced agreement.

The professional societies—the American Institute of Architects and the Engineers Joint Council Documents Committee—have developed excellent forms that are fair to both parties. They are a good starting point and are widely accepted in most applications. Due to the complexity of some large-scale projects, however, and the huge amount of money involved, it is wise to have nonstandard or modified agreements reviewed by legal counsel and a competent insurance advisor. Many firms have adopted the best of the association forms and added other terms and conditions applicable to their practice or to the specifics involved in a particular project. It is preferable to control the contract process yourself. Where you can't, then strong negotiating skills and a sound knowledge of liability issues are a must.

Evaluating a client and a project before accepting the work is a critical component of loss prevention. Don't assume your client is knowledgeable in your business and that the project is adequately funded. Part of your role is to educate your client on your part of the process and in that way eliminate false expectations. It is amazing how many owners expect a perfect result, whether they admit it or not, and do not seem to understand the complexities with which you must deal. Good communication to all parties involved is critical to your success. The relatively small fee you earn on a given project is not sufficient to handle too many problems. Making a profit is predicated on not only turning out good work but being able to anticipate and respond to the myriad of problems that may occur. The more control you exert, the more successful you will be.[1]

Negotiating Strategies and Consensus Building

In spite of having little or no formal training in group dynamics, communications, or negotiating, the architect must become a hybrid of persuader, arbitrator, leader, creator, improviser, technical and legal expert, showman, patient listener, and, at times, therapist. Moreover, as Harvard Professor of Management Practice Michael Wheeler states, "People can feel possessive about an idea—or a bargaining position. Good negotiators recognize this and find ways to let people save face so that they don't feel that they've been stripped of their possessions, including their self-respect." What are some of these basic negotiating skills with which all architects should be intimately familiar?

An outstanding synopsis of negotiating strategies is provided in the following excerpts from a book review by Ruth V. Washington of the first edition of the classic text *Getting to Yes: Negotiating Agreement Without Giving In* (New York: Houghton Mifflin, 1981) by Roger Fisher and William Ury. Architects can apply these strategies to numerous situations, such as contract negotiations with an owner, persuading a stakeholder to embrace a design feature, or lobbying for consensus among building committee members.[2]

---

[1]*Note:* There are two major professional liability insurance companies for design firms: The Design Professional Group of XL Insurance, www.xldp.com, and CNA Insurance Companies/Victor O. Shinnerer & Company, Inc., www. Shinnerer.com. They both offer frequent seminars and workshops on risk management and loss prevention techniques and publish extensive and excellent resources on these topics.

[2]For more information and an excellent guide to negotiation principles, tools, and techniques that are specifically directed to design professionals, see *Architect's Essentials of Contract Negotiation*, Ava J. Abramowitz (Hoboken, N.J.: Wiley, 2002).

The book review from which the following material is quoted was published in *Brooklyn Law Review* 48: 647 (1982) and is excerpted with permission. Special thanks to Pamela Blumgart for editorial assistance.[3]

All of us are negotiators, whether we realize it or not, and we employ basic negotiating techniques in our everyday social and business interactions. Roger Fisher and William Ury, in [*Getting to Yes*], claim that negotiation is the "basic means of getting what you want from others." Their unique book provides, in compact form, a tested method for resolving disputes and settling conflicts.

The authors identify two traditional negotiating postures. The "soft negotiator" seeks to avoid personal conflict and is, therefore, willing to concede readily in order to reach agreement. Unfortunately, the soft negotiator "often ends up exploited and feeling bitter." In contrast, the "hard negotiator" views any given situation as a battle of wills with victory going to the side that adopts the most extreme position and holds out the longest. The hard negotiator often forces his adversary to adopt an equally hard position, which "exhausts him and his resources and harms his relationship with the other side."

Fisher and Ury propose an alternative method, which they term "principled negotiation." Their method suggests that issues be decided on their merits rather than through a "haggling" process in which each side comes to the bargaining table presenting unalterable positions. The authors suggest that negotiators look for mutual gains and that conflicts be resolved based on fair standards "independent of the will of either side."

Principled negotiation involves the application of certain basic concepts that remain constant even though any particular negotiating situation may, in fact, be different. From a substantive point of view, the book is written on the theory that the underlying principles of negotiation are based on well-known psychological factors and practical propositions. The reader is counseled to use his own knowledge and experience in a manner that will best secure an agreement beneficial to both sides.

The authors present four basic tenets of successful dispute resolution. *First, the authors counsel that the negotiator "separate people from the problem."* The point being made is that one must recognize that "negotiators are people first," and that one must be "committed and psychologically prepared" to deal with the personality of the negotiator separate and apart from the substance of the problem.

Second, the negotiator is counseled to focus on interests as opposed to positions. Fisher and Ury advise that amicable solutions can only be obtained if one focuses on the underlying interest of the parties instead of confining oneself to an examination of the parties' stated positions.

Third, the authors advocate that negotiators concentrate on inventing options for mutual gain. This technique is employed to avoid the typical "all or nothing" choice that people frequently feel faced with in a negotiating situation.

Finally, the negotiator is advised to "insist on objective criteria" rather than trying to settle differences on the basis of will. The solution suggested in *Getting to Yes* is to "negotiate on some basis *independent* of the will of either side."

[3]Ruth V. Washington, "Getting to Yes," 48 *Brooklyn Law Review* 647 (1982): 647–651.

Fisher and Ury acknowledge the potential difficulty inherent in a situation where there is an obvious inequality of bargaining strength . . . It is their suggestion that such an occasion calls for finding a best alternative to a negotiated agreement (BATNA), premised on the theory that the person who has alternatives can affect the relative strengths between the parties so as to weigh the outcome to that person's advantage.

The authors also recognize that while the principled negotiator will focus on interests and seek to develop reasonable options to maximize common goals, the other side might not be "playing the game." "You may attack the problem on its merits; they may attack you." The authors propose, somewhat optimistically, that the methods of principled negotiators are "contagious" and that one can influence the other side to play along by "hold[ing] open the prospect of success to those who will talk about interests, options and criteria." If that doesn't work, the student is cautioned against falling into a cycle of action and reaction.

> If the other side announces a firm position, you may be tempted to criticize and reject it. If they criticize your proposal, you may be tempted to defend it and dig yourself in. If they attack you, you may be tempted to defend yourself and counterattack. In short, if they push you hard, you will tend to push back.
>
> Yet if you do, you will end up playing the positional bargaining game. Rejecting their position only locks them in. Defending your proposal only locks you in. And defending yourself sidetracks the negotiation into a clash of personalities. You will find yourself in a vicious cycle of attack and defense, and you will waste a lot of time and energy in useless pushing and pulling.

Fisher and Ury suggest that the negotiator prevent this cycle of actions and reactions by adopting a strategy termed "negotiation jujitsu." This technique involves, in part, sidestepping your opponents' attack, not attacking their position, and recasting their attacks on you as an attack on the problem itself.

As noted previously, it should be kept in mind that the method of reaching a negotiated settlement illustrated in *Getting to Yes* at times seems to oversimplify the subject. The novice might not be able to employ this method with as much efficiency as a more experienced student and therefore should consult a more structured manual on this broad subject as well.

Top 10 Ways to Manage Risk and Prevent Losses[4]

1. Eliminate Liability Illiteracy

Make sure all employees learn how everyday business practices affect your exposure to risk. All must understand that claims not only arise from tech-

---

[4]Copyright © 2005, XL Specialty Insurance Company.

nical mistakes but from nontechnical issues such as client selection, contracts, project team selection, and communication issues. Make sure your employee training and risk management programs support your commitment to quality and address these critical practice management issues.

2. Select Projects and Clients Carefully

Certain projects (such as condominiums) and certain clients (such as developers) are higher risks than others. Check into the client's track record and finances before accepting any assignment. Don't accept projects that do not provide adequate fees for your services, that restrict your scope of services to an unacceptable level, or that are outside of your firm's area of expertise.

3. Set Realistic Expectations

Make sure the client understands that error-free projects simply don't exist. Discuss potential problem areas and changes that may be needed. Strive for a commitment from the owner and the contractor to identify and address the inevitable problems at the earliest opportunity and to work together to achieve win-win resolutions.

4. Draft a Comprehensive Written Contract

A fair, well-defined professional services agreement that precisely states the intent of both parties helps prevent misunderstandings and has terms easily understood by a mediator, judge, or jury. This alone may discourage a plaintiff from asserting an otherwise marginal claim.

5. Offer Comprehensive Design Services

A full scope of services that includes construction observation provides the design professional with the best opportunity to ensure a quality, claim-free project. You should also list in your contract those services you have explained and offered to the client, but that the client has declined.

6. Implement Dispute Resolution Provisions in Contracts

Make every effort to avoid litigation. Commit to a program of early problem identification and resolution. Agree that conflicts be resolved fairly, quickly, and inexpensively through mediation and other alternative dispute resolution techniques.

7. Refuse to Accept Unlimited Liability for Your Services

Work for a limitation of liability (LoL) clause in your contracts that makes the amount of liability you assume proportionate to your ability to control risk.

8. Identify "Deal-Breakers"

Some risks are so significant that you cannot possibly accept them. Let clients know that they must retain the liability for such risks (through indemnities) if you are to provide services.

9. Know the Warning Signs

During the course of a project, there are certain signs that should alert you that a claim may be forthcoming. Recognize and react appropriately to communication breakdowns, accusations, finger pointing, significant overruns on the budget or costs, work stoppage, and being excluded from important meetings.

10. Select the Right Insurance Program

By selecting the right insurance program, your firm gains a partner that focuses on the many risk management issues in your practice. Carefully consider the benefits that a professional liability insurance carrier can offer—strong financial ratings, broad coverage, relevant loss prevention education programs, and the proven technical expertise to resolve an incident or claim to your advantage quickly and efficiently.

Case Study | Capital Architects

Courtesy of ROBERT J. DEAN, Material is copyrighted by XL Design Professional f/k/a DPIC Companies.

Facts

Capital Architects, a large firm with extensive experience in school projects, was selected for a major remodel and expansion design on a school built some 25 years earlier. A Capital principal, Frederick Shepherd, negotiated an agreement with the school district that set Capital's fee as a percentage of the total construction cost, excluding change orders that resulted from negligent errors or omissions by the design team. The contract also stipulated that if the lowest bid exceeded the agreed-to budget, Capital would perform redesign at no cost to the school district in order to bring the project back into budget.

It was clear that mechanical and electrical (M & E) engineering would make up a larger-than-normal percentage of the design effort.

Capital contracted with an M & E subconsultant they had not used before, Acropolis Engineering. There was an Acropolis branch office in a neighboring state, and Capital had heard of the out-of-state branch's long track record and good reputation. Capital executed its standard subconsultant contract with the local Acropolis office, requiring Acropolis to carry professional liability insurance.

It quickly became obvious that the school district wanted everything in the toy store window—and a lot more than it could pay for. As the design phase progressed, the district asked for one embellishment after another. Instead of remodeling the old gymnasium, for instance, the district insisted on a budget-busting new facility. Nevertheless, after much discussion and countless program adjustments, the district finally agreed to a $9 million construction budget.

Because Acropolis had become increasingly unresponsive, Frederick Shepherd was not surprised when the subconsultant called him with the news that the mechanical and electrical bid documents would be late. When the M & E documents finally arrived, Capital hired a cost estimator who priced the construction at slightly less than $9 million, based on available plans and specifications. This was set as the budget figure. Capital went ahead and prepared the bid advertisement, even though Acropolis advised Capital to expect a rather large addendum to its bid package. While the documents were out to bid, Acropolis submitted a 100-page addendum for mechanical and electrical elements.

The lowest bid was for $10 million. Rather than reject all bids, the school district told Fred Shepherd that, although the district could not negotiate with the low bidder to lower the costs to conform to the budget, the architect could do so in the district's stead. Because the alternative was a schedule-busting redesign for which Capital would receive no compensation, Fred agreed.

Fred advised the school district that the most straightforward way to cut $1 million was to forego the new gymnasium altogether or to do an inexpensive renovation of the existing gym. The district refused. Instead, a forty-page list of more than 200 miscellaneous cost cuts was developed into a large change order that would, when totaled, reduce the construction costs by $1 million. Although approving the change order was against his better judgment, Fred Shepherd felt he could not object. He decided not to send a letter to the school board documenting his concerns and his alternative recommendations. The school district awarded the contract for the $10 million bid and the following day signed Change Order No. 1 that cut $1 million out of the contract. The project was now officially on budget.

Not a month had gone by before the contractor had submitted dozens of requests for clarification concerning aspects of the mechanical and electrical design. Just as Fred decided he had better deal with his problem subconsultant, he was notified that Acropolis was going out of business. Indeed, it was only a matter of weeks before the local branch closed its doors and filed for bankruptcy. When Fred contacted Acropolis' out-of-state branch, he was duly informed that the two branches were owned by the same

holding company but that the relationship ended there. The out-of-state branch had no intention of coming to Fred's aid.

Acropolis had left quite a mess in its wake; significant problems were evident in the M & E design. Determined to mitigate the damages as much as possible and continue his good working relationship with the school district and contractor, Fred Shepherd quickly notified his attorney, his insurer, the school district, and the contractor of the problem. He assigned an architect to work full-time on site and retained a well-respected mechanical and electrical consultant on a time and expense basis.

To the rescue came the replacement consultant firm, Gergen Consulting Engineers, which found itself faced with scores of requests for clarification from the contractor. After reviewing the mechanical and electrical design, Gergen insisted that major changes would be necessary. With little direction from Capital, and often dealing directly with the contractor, Gergen began authorizing change orders by the handful.

The school district and contractor began adding their share to the growing pile of change orders. The district's project manager and the contractor both saw the mechanical and electrical problems and the hundreds of change orders as a golden opportunity to add back into the project every bell and whistle otherwise unobtainable when confined to a tight budget. The district, finding the contractor amiable and easy to work with, also began using the contractor's employees to perform tasks usually left to the district's maintenance people. Each of these tasks required yet another change order. Although Capital was concerned about money being spent, it did not voice a concern.

By this time, it was clear that a claim against the design team was probably inevitable. But the contractor, the school district, and Capital were resolved to continue working together. Privately, the contractor and the district believed they could pass most of the change order costs through to Acropolis's and Capital's professional liability insurers. For the time being, however, they agreed that the most important thing was to get the school built and occupied as quickly as possible.

In the spirit of cooperation, the on-site architect and the contractor sifted through the mountain of change orders and determined which could be attributed to design error, design omission, owner request, hidden condition, or code requirement. All told, more than 700 change orders were processed. Gergen Consultants alone handled over 500 requests for clarification from the contractor and authorized well over $1.5 million in additive change orders on the mechanical and electrical systems, as both systems were virtually redesigned during construction. The contractor suffered delays, and some of the construction was not complete by the time the school year began, adding to the district's costs.

Two claims were made. The contractor made a claim against the school district for $1 million in delay damages. The district, in turn, made a claim against Capital for an additional $1.5 million for its own delay costs, extra construction costs, and a return of architectural fees paid on change orders.

DISCUSSION (PRIOR TO READING THE NEXT SECTION OF THE CASE)

1. State the central problem and other issues.
2. *Diagnosis:* List the factors that may have contributed to the problems.
3. *Remedies:* What actions would have mitigated the situation? Think in terms of quality assurance procedures, communications and relationships, business practices, contract language, initial response to the problems.

Sometimes a design professional believes he or she has done everything right in order to *avoid* a claim. In this instance, the architect did a lot that *was* right. There were, however, certain measures that might have prevented this claim.

Effective loss prevention also means taking the right steps *after* a loss occurs, too. Once the claim was inevitable, additional actions could have helped contain the loss.

Preclaim Measures

The Contract. Capital's first misstep was to agree by contract to perform unlimited redesign in the event the bids came in over budget. Although not an uncommon provision in client-written contracts, such an open-ended clause can be dangerous to the designer if the client's program and budget are not reasonable. A better approach is to use protective contract language that limits the design professional's obligation for such redesign.

Investigating Subconsultants. Perhaps more serious was Capital's retention of the mechanical and electrical subconsultant without first checking references and determining its financial stability. Although Acropolis's bankruptcy was certainly not Capital's fault, it was probably the most important factor in the eventual claim against the architect. Capital should also have looked into the connection between the two Acropolis offices. The good reputation of the out-of-state office had no bearing on the local office.

Supervising Subconsultants. Capital missed an important cue when Acropolis gave notification that they would be late with the complete mechanical and electrical package. A design review at this point would probably have been helpful. Certainly more decisive action was called for when Acropolis announced that a major addendum was forthcoming. It may be that Capital should have stopped the bid process then or at least discussed alternatives with the school district.

Retaining Subconsultants. There is a third factor relating to subconsultants here: the retention of the cost estimator. In spite of good references, his or her estimates were more than 10 percent lower than the lowest bid. This set in motion a search for budget cutting devices—the only alternative to Capital having to redesign without compensation. It is unclear why the estimator was so far off—sometimes such things just happen. Certainly the estimator was later able to claim that the estimate was low because he or she didn't have the 100-page M & E addendum in hand. The real issue, however, is who should have hired the estimator. In most cases it is much more desirable for the client to contract directly with an estimator—and assume the related risk.

Client Expectations. Far too many claims can be traced to a lack of understanding by the client as to what he or she can realistically achieve within a given budget. It is the role of the design professional to educate his or her clients on the realities of the design and construction process and guide them every step of the way. In this instance, it was clear from the start that the school district wanted more program than it had money. Given the budgetary restraints, Capital had a responsibility to bring its client's expectations back to reality.

Documentation. Unfortunately, on public projects where there is a limited budget, it is not unusual for the public entity to cut items out of the project during design and then add them back during construction. When the school district embarked on its dubious course of postbid negotiation, Capital Architects should have carefully documented every detail. For instance, when Capital recommended that a new gymnasium be omitted as the most obvious step in bringing the project back into budget, the district refused. Instead, the district insisted on a budget-cutting exercise that worried Capital. That worry, however, should have been put in writing—perhaps in a letter that voiced Capital's objections and documented Capital's alternative recommendations.

Limitation of Liability. Through little fault of its own, Capital was brought into a costly dispute and ultimately absorbed a loss far in excess of its degree of culpability. One potent way to lessen the impact of that claim would have been a Limitation of Liability clause in Capital's contract with the district that, at the very least, held Capital's total liability to its fee.

Postclaim Measures

Claim Notification. Capital Architects notified its insurer of a potential claim as soon as it was learned that the M & E was going to close its doors and walk away from the project—and was proud of its prompt action. But how timely was the notification? In fact, the potential for a claim was evident far earlier than that. The attorney and insurer should have been put on notice as soon as Acropolis announced it would be late with the bid package or, at the latest, when the 100-page addendum was delivered.

Retaining and Coordinating Replacement Subconsultants. Retaining Gergen, the supplanting mechanical and electrical consultant, was the architects decision. A highly regarded firm, Gergen was given what amounted to an open checkbook to redesign a Ford Falcon into a Cadillac. It appears there was a lack of coordination between the architect and the subconsultant. Here, it was the responsibility of the architect to keep the changes made by the subconsultant within reasonable budget and program parameters.

Damage Control. In an effort to mitigate the loss, Capital put a full-time architect in the job trailer. That was an admirable measure—but one person was not enough to handle the tidal wave of change orders. There are times when, in order to mitigate a loss, the wisest move is to allocate as many of the best people and resources as necessary to contain the damage.

Documentation. During most of the construction phase, the contractor was spending an incredible amount of money. Since a claim against the design team was a forgone conclusion, it was especially important that Capital stay on top of those expenditures and carefully document any objections. Instead, Capital failed to voice its objections to the district or the contractor over the expenditures.

Assuming Responsibility for Change Orders. In the spirit of cooperation, Capital's on-site architect and the contractor sat down to allocate change-order causation. They sorted through each of the 700+ change orders and decided on the cause: design error, design omission, owner request, hidden condition, or code requirement. On the face of it, this step made sense. From a loss prevention standpoint, however, it caused a lot of problems later on. By agreeing it had liability for a portion of the associated costs, Capital left its attorney and insurer little or no negotiating room in which to reach a settlement. The architect would have been better served by not allocating responsibility or fault during the change-order approval process.

Chapter 9

New Modes of Service and Project Delivery

Is the "right to stay in your pajamas"[1] (i.e., in a virtual office setting) the only significant by-product of new technology and innovative thinking for the future of architectural practice? Not to trivialize sleepwear, but real innovations in both architects' services and ways in which they are delivered to clients are necessary for the profession to respond to increasing client demands for buildings that are faster to design and construct, less expensive, and higher quality. We must also respond to the volatile economic climate so that there is *always* satisfying and challenging work available.

So, what are some of these innovations within the context of a broad definition of architectural practice? Thomas Fisher begins this chapter by identifying key practice issues, and proposing new strategies for successful implementation. In subsequent essays, a virtual architectural practice is described and success strategies in design-build partnerships are elaborated. Chuck Thomsen presents a brilliant discussion of the advantages and disadvantages of myriad nontraditional contracting arrangements for design and construction. Tim Castillo concludes the chapter with a case study profiling a digital practice that clearly demonstrates why the application of computers to architecture is not a matter of "easier and more rapid, but rather a case of different."

Models for the Architectural Profession

My interview with Thomas Fisher, Dean of the College of Architecture and Landscape Architecture at the University of Minnesota and former editorial director of *Progressive Architecture,* is very much a sociological treatise. Fisher is a keen observer of the great social currents and trends, and he understands how professions respond and adapt to changing times. Specifically, Fisher shares his views on what architects would do well to borrow from other professions, namely law and medicine. In addition, Fisher has really intriguing and important ideas on the continuing evolution of the architectural profession in terms of extending the scope of what we now

---

[1]Nicholas Negroponte, in Stewart Brand, *The Media Lab: Inventing the Future at MIT* (New York: Viking, 1987), 251.

call "alternative practice," not only by widening the horizons of architecture, but also by contributing to a better world. Simultaneously, Fisher takes the pressure off the student to be the solitary heroic form giver, and he proposes an entire new spectrum of roles that are just as significant and with greater likelihood of genuine social and economic impact. The interview follows.

AP: I was intrigued with the three models for the architectural profession that you detailed at Harvard several years ago and in one of the last issues of *Progressive Architecture*. Could you elaborate on this subject of professional practice, particularly for the student audience?

TF: I think we're at a point right now where practice issues are some of the most challenging that face the profession. In some sense, the architectural profession, like many of the professions, is in a place where we have to now start thinking about *designing* a practice. The practice is as much a design problem as doing a building.

What's interesting is that a lot of professions are going through similar kinds of self-scrutiny. This is in part the result of larger questioning within society about the role of professionals. The medical and legal professions are facing a situation in which they have been turning out too many specialists and are in fact looking at architecture as one of the few professions that has managed to maintain a kind of generalist stance.

As I've visited various architecture schools, I've heard deans (and Peter Rowe at Harvard has mentioned this to me) say that other departments are now coming to the Graduate School of Design to look at how architects learn. There is a lot of talk now about project-based and studio-based learning in other departments, in business schools, for example. When you begin to hear what they're talking about, it sounds remarkably like architectural education. So they're in a situation where other disciplines are starting to look to architecture as a model, and conversely, I think, there is some value in the architectural profession looking at what some of the other professions have done. For example when you look at the history of the medical profession a good book to read is *The Social Transformation of Medicine* (New York: Basic Books, 1984) by Paul Starr. In this book, he documents how the medical profession in the nineteenth century was in many ways structured similarly to the way architecture is now structured— where there were a lot of general practitioners (GPs) who had a kind of general knowledge but not a lot of specialized knowledge. They were not in fact particularly valued in society. They were turning too many doctors out of school for the demand. Louis Thomas talks about his life as a physician in comparison with his father's. In his father's day, doctors could do little more than hold the patients' hands and make them comfortable—and these patients either lived or died. What happened in the late nineteenth and early twentieth centuries is that medicine transformed itself into a more research-based discipline, allying itself with hospitals.

Implicit in my argument is that medicine, despite some of the problems it is facing with HMOs now, has been rather successful—certainly economically—in the twentieth-century, in part because of a model with a relatively small number of GPs who have a good deal of involvement with a lot of patients. Those GPs then can call in and put together a virtual team of specialists, depending on the patient's needs. This is a very effective structure.

AP: There will always be illness and accidents and physicians will mend you when you're torn apart, but in architecture is there a big enough client population?

TF: I believe so. Architects have said that their clients need major work (i.e., design a new building or large renovation). If we were to take the model of the medical profession, *our clients really should be everybody who owns a building*. GPs in medicine are essentially diagnosticians. An equivalent to that would be an architect who would make house calls. For example, an owner would say, "I've got some cracks; come and examine my building." Or, "It's too hot in one place and too cold in another—is this something I should worry about?" The architect would have enough diagnostics knowledge to say, "These two cracks are not important, but this one is—you've got to worry about this one," or, "You don't just have overheating and cooling, you've got severe indoor air quality problems here; I need to bring in an HVAC specialist."

I'm not arguing that everything should be a professional-level activity, but I do believe that the diagnostics of buildings has been a fundamental role that architects have let others begin to take over. Building inspectors are the obvious ones. They usually get involved only when there is a transfer, a sale. However, I believe implicit in this activity (and facilities management as well) lies an entire realm of work. What it suggests, for example, is that diagnostics would have to become a much more important aspect of architectural education as it became in medicine. Diagnostics is still the core set of courses early on in medical education. It has very low status in our profession.

This is just an idea—but when I hear architects say there are fewer clients and more architects competing for less work—one of the central questions is how can you expand the pie?

AP: Can you extend the analogy to health care even further regarding service delivery and economics? What would you think about an HMO-type organization for conducting a new form of architectural practice?

TF: Robert Gutman raises the point that we don't have an institution like the hospitals for us to ally ourselves with as doctors did in the nineteenth century. Yet it does raise a question—are there other, perhaps market-oriented, ways in which architects could team up in sort of HMO alliances?

AP: What about equating building diagnostics to managed care of patients?

TF: Exactly. Where, for example, there might be some percentage of graduates from architecture schools who are really oriented toward being generalist diagnosticians. They would be trained to take over or work in these architectural HMOs. And another group of people who would be more research based, specialized, who would be brought in to handle particular problems (i.e., technical, or building-type-related, like retail or hospital specialists). Such architects might be small, independent practitioners similar to specialist or consulting physicians.

The typical architectural firm—the model—has been more of a corporate one, ever since Daniel Burnham. The firms that get a lot of attention tend to be rather large with a few partners on top on a kind of pyramid of people. Within these firms are many people with specialized knowledge about curtain walls or detailing roofs, and so on, but they tend to be invisible to the client. They tend to be paid less than the generalist partner or principal. Physicians, on the other hand, completely invert this. The medical profession makes the specialists quite visible; physicians have discovered that people will in fact pay more for specialized knowledge than for generalized knowledge. Instead of having large corporate kinds of structures, they broke themselves down into very small operations; the doctor's office is comprised of one or only a few physicians. Doctors run small, autonomous operations, which can be brought together as a team to solve a patient's problem. This is in contrast to the large, bureaucratic corporate-type organization with high overhead that many architects have developed.

I think this is changing; I think the computer is rapidly undermining the large corporate architectural office. As Frank Stasiowski said, two people with a good computer system can do almost anything now. So this really creates a crisis for the big firms—how should they operate in this context? The creative big firms are breaking themselves down into smaller units that are entrepreneurial. This is not unlike what the big corporations are doing in this country. The units may even be financially independent; if a particular entrepreneurial group isn't hacking it, the firm will close it and perhaps open something else.

We're on the road to this fragmentation and that brings us closer to flexibility and the notion of a virtual team within which physicians have been operating.

AP: For young interns just entering the world of practice, as it stands today, how would you reconcile the cliché ivory tower with these economic realities of running a typical architectural firm?

TF: Despite all of the veneer of avant garde debate and discourse, the schools are incredibly conservative institutions. And our profession, as in all the professions, particularly in the last decade, they are a drag on change. We're in a period right now where market forces are changing so dramatically that the real cutting edge is with people out in the trenches who are responding to those radical shifts in the marketplace. The veneer of radicalism in the schools is disguising a very traditional structure of architectural education and traditional assumptions about the practice of architecture. This is why there's been not nearly enough theoretical debate about practice in the schools. It's an area that has economic, social, and political implications. This is what I was suggesting when I said that practice is really one of the most interesting design problems right now.

The legal profession offers other interesting parallels for us. They encountered a situation similar to ours, again roughly 75 to 100 years ago, with an educational system that was basically turning out trial lawyers. They really had too many lawyers for the demand. The history of the legal profession is in some ways parallel to what is now occurring in architecture. There is talk about too many architecture schools turning out too many graduates who want a traditional practice. What I find interesting about the legal profession is that instead of closing schools as some have proposed in our field, lawyers simply redefined what it was that they were doing. It wasn't so much that they restructured themselves the way the medical profession did, but they reconceived legal education as not so much training for a particular set of tasks but as a way of thinking; a kind of problem-solving analytical model. It was recognized that legal training could be useful in running corporations, becoming president, doing all sorts of things. They too, in their own way, have been incredibly successful in this century. In fact, the architectural profession has allowed lawyers to do things that architects should be doing. There are too many lawyers writing zoning codes and making decisions about the shape of the built environment, for example. There should be architecturally trained people at that table.

So, with lawyers I find a model for us in terms of what is it that architecturally trained people should or could be doing. Here too I think that the schools are behind the marketplace. What I believe has happened in the last few years is that students getting out of architecture school are realizing that there are too few opportunities in traditional practice; they have been making their own opportunities and going into what we all euphemistically call alternative practice. It may not be long before alternative practices become the mainstream practices. Just as in law, the number of trial lawyers is the minority of practicing lawyers, probably within our lifetime the number of architecturally trained people doing traditional practice may be in the minority. I find this condition largely positive, and I raise these issues to say that we shouldn't discourage this kind of broadening-out. The AIA and the schools should acknowledge it, and what it foreshadows is perhaps another shift in architectural education.

In law school, after about the first year and a half, law students start to concentrate on different tracks (i.e., corporate law, trial law, and so on). One could envision a similar structure in architectural education. There could be a core set of design courses, after which students would begin to specialize. Design of buildings might be one track; facilities management, construction management, and so on could constitute others. This also suggests that the profession needs to reembrace things that we have been allowing others to essentially walk away with; why have we let facilities management and construction management get out from under us? Wouldn't construction managers and construction itself be better if we at least had the large majority of these associated professions training in the first year courses along with architects?

AP: Just being informed with a real design sensitivity would make a world of difference.

TF: At least the language and the assumptions we all would be using would be understandable to each other. So there wouldn't be this cultural conflict that currently exists in the construction industry.

AP: Returning to building diagnostics and the analogy to the HMO mode of service delivery, there are people who can't afford health insurance, so how could they possibly afford architects?

TF: They can't, as traditionally defined. For example, people's investments in their buildings are one of the biggest investments they have. This is not only true for individuals and their own houses but for corporations. The ability to forestall a big problem by periodic checkups can lead to amazing savings, but that suggests not only that the profession be able to offer those kind of services but that we document the savings. It's true that people have a hard time affording health insurance; however, most people who can afford it are still going to see their doctor every so often because they know that cancer caught early is a lot easier to deal with than cancer not caught early. We as a profession have not really been interested in servicing building owners in a kind of precautionary diagnostics way. It's just not been part of our culture. I find it interesting that the few diagnostics firms that do exist in this country have been so busy that they've been turning work away all during the recession. To me there is a clear demand for this kind of activity in good times and bad.

AP: Do you think that it's crucial that these new services be performed by architects?

TF: Ideally, yes. I'm architecturally trained; I believe in the culture of architecture. I think we can do a better job if it's done under the aegis of architecture. There are no education requirements for contractors or building inspectors, for example. This kind of activity is too important to just allow it to be available to anybody who makes the claim that they know something. It would be far better if diagnostics was performed on a research base so that expertise is always linked to research going on *today* in architecture and engineering schools. In the preservation community, there is a lot of research concerned with how buildings change over time. There is exciting work going on in various related fields for which architecture could serve as a synthesizing and integrating entity.

AP: So what you're saying is that there's a place for design excellence even within all these subspecialties.

TF: Absolutely. There's also an art to diagnostics, as any generalist will tell you in medicine. The art is not just the making of objects; it's how you deal with people, problem analysis, and so on. It probably means we charge differently, that we charge on an hourly basis and be willing to see a building owner for an hour every six months. Certain buildings might not need a checkup any sooner than every few years.

AP: Or clients could pay an annual premium for services and have easy access to specialists, and so on?

TF: Some firms are working their way into this. Gensler, for example, maintains a three-dimensional model in their computer system when they do a building, regularly check-in with the building and update their model. So they, in essence, have the virtual building in their computers. They become the "internist" for the building: If any problems arise, the client is going to call his "doctor."

AP: I wonder how they get the clients to pay the extra fee for that.

TF: They don't charge the clients for the updating. They make themselves indispensable, as doctors have done.

Another thing I've been thinking about is where design stands as a process. There's a lot of questioning going on about scientific method and the limitations of science in many disciplines. When you look at various fields, the hard sciences and also the social sciences, the scientific model and data analysis have served as the foundation on which these disciplines have operated. More people in these fields are recognizing limits to these methods; there are certain kinds of questions that can't be addressed through this traditional model, and this awareness is coming to the fore at a time when universities are having to justify their existence in their communities and state governments. These entities are demanding solutions to the problems of drugs, crime, homelessness, and health in general that specialized departments in universities have not been particularly effective in addressing. To get at those kinds of wicked problems demands an interdisciplinary way of operating, a way of bringing different specialized groups together to analyze problems and develop synthetic solutions. In this regard, I would argue that design is an excellent model; unlike the scientific model, which is very good at analysis, design is very good at synthesizing cross-disciplinary activity. Yet, one of the things I'm finding as I dabble in various disciplines is that looking at design may lead to superior ways of examining global issues. Scientists seem to limit themselves to breaking things down in order to understand the particulars; design methodology helps to look at the overall relationship of all the parts. I think what's most important about what students learn in architecture school isn't necessarily how to design an elegant façade or how to hold a structure up; it's a way of operating, thinking, and looking at the world. And this brings us back to the legal model; just as lawyers recognized that their kind of legal analysis had application to many different disciplines, we're at the cusp of recognizing that design and design thinking also have tremendous implications for many different fields.

Instead of sleeping through your practice course (which is usually at the end of your formal education), recognize that it may be one of the most important courses. But also, practice courses need to be much better. They should not be just about AIA contracts; they should teach a theory of practice, and practice should be seen as a design problem. At the same level, I would argue that in design studio there should be more articulation of the thought process—so the focus isn't so much on the product (i.e., they should consider what's going on in the minds of students as they design). *Students should be made conscious of the design process in the way that scientists made themselves conscious of the scientific method.*

AP: Do you think there should be more of a linking of practice issues discussed in the course to what actually goes on in the studio?

TF: Yes, because once we become conscious of the design process, we'll recognize that design has applications to not just the overall form of a building but to the design of technologies and systems, the design of practice, and the delivery of the building. *We have defined design far too narrowly just as we've defined architecture far too narrowly.*

The Emergence of the Virtual Architectural Practice

In contemplating the establishment of his own firm, architect Craig Applegath was inspired by an early internship experience with O. M. Ungers in Germany. Ungers would set up office and living quarters in each city in which he had a building project and then assemble staff as needed for the particular job. Ungers was running, in a sense, a precursor to the "virtual office"—one that moved along the *vehicle* highway instead of the *information* highway.

Applegath was convinced that the only way he could open an office in the context of a severe economic downturn was to reconceptualize traditional small firm methods of practice. This was fundamentally a strategic vision of how maximum utilization of computer technology could support his work and give him the flexibility to expand, downsize, or associate with others as a function of market conditions. Management of his practice, therefore, is almost exclusively project-driven.

While the idea underlying a virtual practice is certainly not new—assembling a team appropriate for a specific project—it is very much relevant as a management strategy. Whether this mode is considered a "networked" practice, a virtual practice, or merely an assemblage of consultants, the firm description in the following essay is illuminating in the context of today's practice environment.

"Tele-everything" (a cute term coined by *Contract*) may not always be adequate for conducting practice. On occasion, there is *no* substitute for the face-to-face meeting—whether it is collaborating with a consultant on a design, discussing a change in the field with a contractor, or educating a client. Be certain not to lose sight of the fact that personal rapport is essential to building and maintaining a trusting alliance, and to unguarded and meaningful communication.

Craig Applegath demonstrates that the dream of owning a successful firm is not only alive and well but may be an ideal model for delivery of services well into this new millennium. William Mitchell, former Dean of MIT's School of Architecture and Planning, predicts the impact of design and information technology on architecture firms: "In a fast-changing world, the winners are likely to be smaller, more nimble organizations structured to form effective ad hoc alliances with other organizations, to aggregate expertise 'on-the-fly' as specific circumstances arise. The virtual design [office] establishes a new paradigm for CAD."[2]

J. CRAIG APPLEGATH, OAA, RAIC, is an architect practicing in Toronto, Ontario. He received his master's degree from the Harvard University Graduate School of Design and conducts an annual seminar on virtual offices at Harvard.

Every organization of today has to build into its very structure *the management of change*. It has to build in organized abandonment of everything it does. It has to learn to ask every few years of every process, every product, every procedure, every policy: "If we did not do this already, would we go into it now, knowing what we now know?" And if the answer is no, the organization has to ask: "And what do we do now?—Peter F. Drucker, *Post Capitalist Society,* page 59.

A
s we begin the twenty-first century, we are witnessing the rapid transformation of the practice of architecture in North America. Economic pressures and advances in digital information technologies are combining to force significant changes in the way architects practice. One such change is the emergence of the "virtual architectural practice." In this essay, I examine some of the reasons for the apparent decline of traditional architectural practice, explore the emergence of virtual architectural practice, and comment on how existing architectural practices can prepare to survive and thrive in the digital information world. As a practitioner experiencing and participating in these changes, I will also discuss how our practice has evolved as a virtual practice.

The Demise of the Traditional Architectural Practice

The traditional architectural practice still bears marks of its descent from the European guild system: a hierarchical structure with few masters and many apprentices. This type of practice is under significant pressure to reshape itself from many sources: The post–cold war recessionary economy, the baby boom bulge in demographics blocking upward mobility of younger architects, and now widespread use of the computer and other digital information technologies. The computer, digital networks, and other advances in digital and communication technologies are significantly transforming the way architects design and practice. (See the case study, "Digital Practice—Rethinking the Design Process, page 313.) In the recent past, many of these technological changes complemented and in many ways enhanced the traditional nature and structure of an architectural practice, without necessitating radical transformation. The drafting table has now been replaced by computer stations, the typewriter has given way to the word processor, and surface mail has to a great extent been supplanted by e-mail and the fax machine. These new technologies have been successfully

---

[2]William Mitchell, in B. J. Novitski, "Designing by Long Distance," *Architecture* February 83 (1994): 119.

Figure 9-1 Cartoon by Peter Kuttner, FAIA, of Cambridge Seven Associates, Inc.

incorporated into the management and production structures of architectural practice. But more recently, a new generation of digital networking technologies, combined with the pressures of the marketplace, and the profession's decreasing control over architectural fee rates and membership levels have significantly altered the environment. As a result, the architectural profession is beginning to see the emergence of new forms of practice. One of the more interesting and potentially important new forms of practice is the virtual architectural practice.

The Virtual Architectural Practice

The virtual architectural practice is based on alliances of experts and specialists coming together for individual projects or groups of projects, who are linked together by computers and online network systems. At its core, the virtual office is held together by both the common sense of purpose and the mutual trust and competence of its members. Common purpose and trust, more than any other qualities, serve to establish and maintain the bonds that will keep the virtual practice operating as a cohesive enterprise when the other physical realities of the typical practice are absent.

This new form of organization is, of course, not conceptually new or foreign to architects. Architects have always acted as prime consultants and put together teams of engineers, landscape architects, and numerous other consultants to carry out the requirements of the project brief. And generally this team continues on for the life of the project and is then disbanded when the project ends. As well, joint venture partnerships between architectural practices are not uncommon when projects call for expertise or staff size that cannot otherwise be accommodated by one firm on its own. Most of the architectural production, however, is done within and by members of the architecture practice itself and within the confines of the traditional place of practice.

It is becoming evident, however, that pressures of the marketplace, coupled with advances in information technologies, are providing the opportunity for low-overhead virtual practices formed from expert alliances and joint venture partnerings to compete with traditionally structured practices. Moreover, medium and larger sized traditional practices, weighted down with heavy real estate and employee overheads, are being forced to seriously examine their mode of practice or face possible decline as virtual and other new forms of digital practices emerge as viable competitors.

Virtual practices by their very nature are not constrained by physical, national, or geographic boundaries (although they do have to operate within the regulatory structures imposed by local authorities). A virtual practice exists by virtue of its phone, fax, modem, and video connections. A designer and project architect may be based in New York, the specifications writer in Chicago, and the contract documents production team in Kansas City. For that matter, team members can be located any place in the world so long as there is good access to phone lines, and team members have expertise relevant to the project at hand. Given the portability of digital information, a project is as accessible to the virtual practice team members scattered across the city or continent as it would be to the members of a traditional practice operating within the confines of one office space. Indeed, the selection of the virtual practice team members should be based more on the appropriateness of, and expertise of individual team members, then on their physical location. But there is also no reason why a successful virtual practice need be international or regional in scope, and virtual practices with participants located in the same geographic area have the advantage of meeting face-to-face on a regular basis. The need for good personal communication on both a professional and personal level is just as important in the virtual practice as in the traditional practice, if not more so.

Probably the most important force driving the formation of virtual practices is economic, and of the economic forces, the boom-bust pattern of the construction cycle plays a crucial role in defining the economic logic of the virtual practice. Because of their relatively low overhead in comparison with traditional practices, and more important, because of their ability to transform fixed overhead costs into variable costs, virtual practices are able to provide equivalent professional services for a lower fee, and most important, have a greater chance of riding out the ups and downs of the construction cycle. As virtual practices become more common, the traditional practice, burdened with proportionately higher fixed overheads and a higher ratio of fixed costs to variable costs, will find it more difficult to compete against the more nimble and expert virtual practice, and much more difficult to survive extended recession cycles.

Perhaps one of the most important aspects of the virtual practice is its ability to pair costs with revenue, and in effect change otherwise fixed costs into variable costs. Each member of the team forming the virtual office brings to the team some portion of both revenue generating potential and overhead costs of the project. In the traditional practice, however, overhead is for the most part independent of revenue production. For example, in the traditional practice, office space leasing costs, utility costs, and property taxes are independent of the amount of revenue produced by project consulting and production. The manager of a traditional practice has always had to rely on having enough cash flow to cover the costs of overhead or, at least, cover the financing costs of a line of credit used to cover overhead during slump periods. Covering the servicing costs of a line of credit in a slump period and then taking profits in a boom period is the typical mode for medium- to large-scale traditional firms. But in protracted recessionary periods, this strategy puts a practice under severe stress, and in many cases is the key reason for its failure when the period of downturn is extended beyond the capacity of the firm's savings or line of credit.

Our Experience as a Virtual Practice

Since the early 1990s our firm has operated as both a digital and a virtual practice—"digital" to the extent that all design, design development, construction documents, project administration, and office administration has been mediated by computers; and "virtual" to the extent that team members and project consultants have been linked by computers over phone lines using modem connections. Design and construction documents are done using CAD (computer assigned drawing programs); project administration is handled using software designed specifically for the purpose; and all office and client information is tracked and managed within a number of linked databases. From the outset, our firm has made an effort to explore various methods of bringing project team members together using digital communications techniques.

Ironically, the decision to go virtual was more evolutionary than revolutionary. It was influenced by both the restrictive nature of the economy at the time, such that we could not be sure of the frequency or size of commissions we would be dealing with in the first few years of practice, and also by the fact that developments in telecommunications networking technology made sharing project information over phone lines feasible. Thus we realized it was possible to handle almost any size of project—expanding or shrinking as required—and that we would not have to commit to real estate overhead, freeing us from the concern of whether the size or number of commissions were sufficient to cover a fixed real-estate overhead. More important, as a design-oriented practice, we were not overly fond of any organizational structure that was based on hierarchy and top-down control. So the move to a virtual practice seemed to be a way to gain greater size without giving up the spontaneity and character of the small design office.

Management Issues

Team Mission. If any one factor stands out as having been most critical in the overall success of our virtual teams to date, it is that our teams always had a clear idea of why we were doing a particular project and how we should accomplish it. The "why," a question of mission, took the form of a search for thoughtful and meaningful design, carefully thought out and skillfully executed. Part of the question of "how" was informed in many ways by our decision to practice as a virtual practice. Thus the virtual team was not simply just a means of *survival* in a tough and competitive market. It was a means to accomplish our mission of *good design* in a tough and competitive market. However, there was another mission operating in the background that was always implicit at the time of team formation and then during the course of the project: Team members had to respect and care about the other team members. A common sense of commitment to both the project and each other was implicit in all of the actions of the team.

Communication. It was apparent from the outset that the success of our virtual teams, and thus the success of any project, was very much dependent on the ability of the "virtual team" to function as well or better than a traditional project team. Coordination of information and individuals became a much more demanding and critical aspect of the project. Because there was no one office space where day-to-day interaction of team members could happen as a matter of course, communication between virtual team members was something that had to happen through our server, complemented by many phone calls. There seemed to be no more or less order to communication than in the traditional practice. However, the communication that involved messages sent over the server created an instant record and history of the evolution of the project. This came in handy when trying to dig out information from earlier stages of the project that might otherwise have been consigned to memory.

Leadership. In our virtual practice, the team leader has the responsibility to ensure that the team and project is coordinated and running close to schedule, but otherwise the team members are solely responsible for their own work. The team leader for the most part is responsible for making sure that everyone has the resources they need to carry out their tasks and finding solutions to coordination and scheduling problems. Probably one of the most important responsibilities of the virtual team leader, one that is critical to the success of the virtual team, is his or her ability to maintain team morale, which in many cases means keeping the team members feeling like they are part of a team. One of the great dangers that individual team members face is the feeling that they are isolated from the project and the decision-making process. This is the virtual team's Achilles' heel. Daily phone calls and regular pep talks seem to be as important a part of the team leader's responsibilities as the actual tracking and coordination of project information.

Proximity. In our experience as a virtual practice, most of the members of project teams have been located within the same city, which has facilitated face-to-face meetings and personal interaction as needed. Actual face-to-face meetings in the virtual practice do not happen as casually as they might in a traditional office setting so they tend to be more focused and energized. Conversely, the more casual chatting and brainstorming tends to happen over the phone on quite a regular basis. But ultimately the nature and quality of meetings and exchanges between members is determined as much by the chemistry of the team as by the setting or timing of the meeting. The nature of proximity and team interaction seems to vary depending on the team members involved and also the stage of the project.

Trust, Competence, and Responsibility. As in the traditional practice, the success of the virtual practice is determined by the abilities and competence of its members. However, because the virtual practice is always changing in composition, forming and reforming with new projects, the competence and abilities of team members are crucial to both its immediate and long-term success. Given that team members will be working with little direct supervision, the expectation for competence and individual responsibility is significantly higher than in the traditional practice. Concomitantly, the requirement for individual team members to trust one another becomes much greater as well. We have found that this mutual combination of trust and responsibility is a very powerful motivating force for team members. It is also very apparent to all involved that their participation in future teams is always contingent on successful participation in an ongoing project.

Core Skills and Knowledge. One of the requirements for the successful continuance of a virtual practice is its ability to put together teams of skilled and expert team members. This assumes that there are such individuals and that they are willing to be a part of the team. We have found that one of the most difficult aspects of running a virtual practice is finding team members who are both technically or professionally skilled and also capable of (and interested in) working in a virtual environment. One of the associated problems with the emergence of virtual practices is, of course, the competition for skilled team members by competing virtual (and traditional) practices.

Perception of the Virtual Practice by Potential Clients. One of the greatest hurdles for the virtual practice to overcome at each new request for proposal or project interview is the perception by potential clients that such a practice is not able to accomplish what a larger and more traditional practice can accomplish. Such perceptions are very difficult—in many cases, impossible—to change even when the logical arguments of services for fees and qualifications of the team are advanced. There is no way around this problem except to say that a practice must do what it believes in or it will not survive at all.

The Future

There is, of course, much room for debate on the relative merits of traditional versus the virtual architectural practice, and no doubt, as in all human activities, change is anathema. As times and technologies change, however, it is incumbent on the profession to examine and evolve new modes of practice that embody the goals of the profession and allow architects to prosper in the quickly evolving information economy. If the architecture profession is not proactive in ensuring that current and future transformations of the modes of practice reflect our aspirations and ideals, then these changes will be imposed from outside, and reflect goals and interests of others.

To conclude, listed below are steps architects should consider taking to make the most of the brave new worlds of the digital and virtual practice:

1. Every key person in the architectural practice—starting at the top (and this almost goes without saying)—should be comfortable using a computer for designing, drawing, word processing, and project management. These key people should not need any intermediaries, assistants, or juniors to help them use the various necessary technologies to do the job they are specialists in; it just adds to the overhead and reduces efficiency and flexibility. And in the end, your office should be made up of *only key persons.*

2. Determine the unique strengths of the best people in your practice and form a plan for the development and marketing of those strengths. Every person in your practice must be regarded as a consultant and potential profit center and be able to be a possible player in a transient alliance with other practices. Remember, the virtual architectural practice is a team of specialists, and your practice should be a stable of those specialists, whatever its size.

3. Look around at your peers and competitors. These people will be your new partners in the creation of the virtual architectural practice. Start thinking about strategic alliances with them. And remember, play fairly. Today's competitor is tomorrow's partner!

4. Map out one-, five-, and ten-year plans that outline the road your practice will take in transforming part or all of itself into a virtual practice.

5. Once the planning has been done and is being implemented, realize that the structures you implement and the new methods of practice that you embrace may themselves be only transitional and temporary. As Peter Drucker points out, you should be asking the question, "And what do we do now?"

Computers and Practice: The Digital Guerrilla

In 1992, Peter Rowe, then Dean of the Harvard University Graduate School of Design, stated that the "rapid deployment of new information technology within the realm of design fundamentally promises to alter the very way in which we perceive and therefore make physical environments. It is clearly not a matter of 'the same way but easier and more rapid,' but rather a case of 'different.' "[3] Dean Rowe could not have been more prophetic in describing the way in which architectural firms *must* function to survive and prosper in today's economic climate.

Geoffrey Adams describes below the application of these new technologies and concomitant ways of thinking about design. Equally important, he sets forth the context in which design and information technology

---

[3]Peter G. Rowe, *The Harvard Graduate School of Design: Directions for the Near Future,* Harvard University Graduate School of Design, October 24, 1992.

has evolved, and quite objectively, how it might be integrated into all phases of architectural design and construction processes.

GEOFFREY ADAMS is on the faculty of the University of New Mexico and maintains an independent practice in Albuquerque. He received a BA in studio art from the University of California at Davis, an MArch from the University of New Mexico, and completed his internship with Antoine Predock.

Différance comes very close to the Japanese word *ma*, a word that has had intermittent currency in architecture since the mid-sixties. *Ma* means "interval in space," "interval in time" and "moment/place/occasion" all at once. *Ma* is in the gaps between stepping stones, though we might walk smoothly, in the silence between the notes of a song, though we might sing *legato*, or in the moment a pendulum reaches the top of its arc and stops without stopping. *Ma* is born *of* juxtaposition the way *différance* is said to be conditional to juxtaposition. In this sense they are complements.

Computer science tells us that all information can be coded into a binary sequence of 0's and 1's. *Between* 0 and 1 lies *ma*. *Because* of *différance* there can be "0" and "1" in the first place.

—Michael Benedikt, *Deconstructing the Kimbell*
(New York: SITES/Lumen Books, 1991)

With the inception of relatively inexpensive desktop computational hardware and software a little more than two decades ago and the ensuing conflagration of processing speed, storage capabilities, and connectivity developed since then, architectural practice (along with almost everything else) has undergone a profound transformation at a dizzying pace. In every facet of contemporary architectural practice—design, documentation, management, marketing, etc.—the networked computer has become the digital hub. So ubiquitous is digital technology in today's office that it is hard to imagine practice without it, especially for new graduates now entering the field who have not only been educated in a digital world but have grown up in one. Yet, it is worth a reminder that just a generation (twenty-five years) ago, the vast majority of all tasks in architectural offices were done by hand. Only the largest firms could afford the mainframe computing systems whose computational capabilities are now easily outstripped by a laptop.

A paradigm shift of this magnitude and swiftness doesn't occur without discontinuity and dislocation, false starts, and excursions down blind alleys. The proprietary nature of both software and hardware developers presents the architectural practitioner with a myriad of conflicting claims. Promises of ever-expanding capabilities are tempered all too often by the experience of unnecessary complexities and incompatibilities. The inherent flexibility and deftness of the tool, at times, seems to be its own Achilles' heel. All this results in a digital landscape of ever-shifting modes of designing and making that are at once exhilarating, overwhelming, transcendent, and tedious. One of the challenges of writing about digital technology is the very real possibility that the information will be dated and useless before the work can make it to press. In an attempt to avoid such a fate, this discussion will endeavor to engage questions and issues of digital practice that have been, and promise to continue to be, central to a cogent and critical practice.

The fundamental difference between the way in which a human brain cognates and a digital device computes resides at the fulcrum of this discussion. This difference between associative thinking and algorithmic computation directs a bright light on how one might begin to meaningfully engage digital technology in a critical architectural practice. Tracking large amounts of data and manipulating this information algorithmically is the undisputed domain of digital technology. This strength has been put to work with resounding success alleviating any number of formerly mind-numbing tasks that architects used to endure. Anyone who developed a schedule or changed window types on endless pages of elevation drawings in a predigital practice can attest to the wonder of making global changes with the click of a mouse, as opposed to hours of repetitive labor. The temptation (one that a number of software developers have enthusiastically taken up) is to believe that by diligently describing all the interdependencies that make up a building project and creating software that allows the designer to model the building in its "entirety," much of the drudgery and cost of producing documents will be eliminated. While this complete model approach is very seductive and may ultimately be appropriate for the design of an aircraft (with its necessarily narrowly focused agenda and intolerance for error), it is flawed as a design tool for the architect because the vast set of dependencies that the designer must cognitively juggle effectively negates or at least radically impairs associative thinking. Associative thinking is the very strength of the human mind and the soul of design work. This situation is further complicated because design often doesn't fit neatly into pre-arranged categories, sometimes a wall will exhibit characteristics of a roof or vice versa, or it may simply want to exist as a plane devoid of any other attributes. Associative thinking, the ability to bring together disparate information from seemingly unrelated sources to create something new, lies at the heart of the human creative act and is easily short-circuited when the mind is required to navigate numerous contingencies in advance of their useful deployment.

Taking this tack a little further reveals another precept or at least a point of contemplation. In a lecture given a few years ago at a meeting of the Association for Computer Aided Design in Architecture, Greg Lynn observed that he could identify the software that designers had used to create different toothbrushes. The implication was that different software afforded or biased certain shapes based on the way the code was written. This notion of software bias has profound implications not only with regard to form but also in the way a building might be conceptualized, organized, and even built. In fact, the more complicated and layered a software tool is, the more likely it is to privilege certain methods of working and the more likely that the user will be oblivious to this (as all their effort is expended simply trying to learn the system). Tool bias can potentially produce positive as well as deleterious consequences. Regardless, as a designer, it seems of paramount importance that one always question both what the tool is doing to the design process as well as what it can do for it.

Becoming a registered architect is an arduous journey requiring years of education both in the academy and as an intern. A similar commitment in time and effort is required to develop the skills and knowledge necessary to deploy digital technology as a meaningful component of an architectural process. A basic dilemma in this passage is whether to choose the "Swiss Army Knife" package that promises to do everything or to develop a pallet of specialized software programs that form an ensemble. One solution is to do both, to become in a sense a digital "guerrilla," learning and using the best of what any software package has to offer and skipping out before a quagmire ensues. Developing a conceptual understanding of digital processes is an essential first step. A computational device stores and manipulates data with no regard as to whether the data represents a text, an image, a group of sounds, or whatever. For example, the same algorithm can be used to apply compression to an audio file (reduce the difference in volume between soft and loud) or contrast in a raster image (reduce the difference between the light and dark). With that understanding in place, it quickly becomes apparent that there is a lot of repetition of capabilities in different software packages, but some will do certain tasks that are more useful to a design process than others. Or, at times, just the act of working in a different context will create opportunity. Moving deftly in and out of different software to achieve a larger goal requires acclimation to a new mode of experimentation. The "guerrilla" process celebrates using tools in unintended ways, it revels in accident and seeks unintended paths of discovery, and it endeavors to reveal bias and eschew unnecessary complexity. Not a half-bad description of the application of associative thinking to inform a design process.

Project Delivery Strategy

Project delivery strategy can be complex and wide-ranging. One of the forces that may be driving alternatives to the traditional design-bid-build method was articulated by George Heery: "Architects have ceased to represent the cutting edge of construction technology and the most practical way of building buildings. That knowledge is not even found among contractors anymore. Construction technology today lies among specialty subcontractors and product manufacturers." Of course, there are other forces that strongly influence the project delivery approach, including the circumstances of the project (i.e., schedule, budget, and quality issues), and many public sector entities that procure design services, for example, now incorporate design-build or construction management into project requirements.

No discussion of project delivery would be complete without mentioning partnering. Developed by the Army Corps of Engineers (and used in both public and private sectors), partnering is an attempt to formalize a mechanism for cooperation, collaboration, and communication among project team members including architect, contractors, client, consultants, and regulatory bodies. Regular meetings and workshops with these members are arranged to facilitate close working relationships to clarify objectives and resolve disputes, and as the Corps defines it, "promote the achievement of mutually beneficial goals."

Finally, we must make sure clients know that, as architect Virgil Carter reminds us, "Without high-level design skills, the total design delivery system loses its very essence, and architecture simply ceases to be a design profession."

Chuck Thomsen has a talent for discussing contracting methods for design and construction in an incredibly clear and concise manner, and does so in the following.

CHARLES B. THOMSEN is Chairman and CEO of 3D/International (3D/I) of Houston, Texas, and formerly President and CEO of the CRS Group, Inc. He has worked on projects in most states and in twenty-two countries, directed over thirty branch offices and more than a dozen subsidiary companies, and participated in numerous acquisitions. He is also the author of *CM: Developing, Marketing and Delivering Construction Management Services* (New York: McGraw-Hill, 1982), and *Managing Brainpower: Organizing, Measuring Performance, and Selling in Architecture, Engineering, and Construction Management Companies* (Washington, D.C.: AIA Press, 1989). Courtesy of Charles B. Thomsen, President, 3D/International.

Introduction

Early in a project, a client must select a process for design and construction. The process will affect the financing, the selection of the project team, the schedule, and the cost.

We have experience with all the processes. We have worked as project managers, construction managers, and design-build contractors. We have worked with fast-track, bridging, and traditional processes. We have worked with guaranteed maximum price (GMP), cost-plus, target price, and lump-sum contracts.

All these processes are flawed, but they can all be made to work. The best choice is governed by the exigencies of the project. Pressures on schedule, budget, the symbolic role or practical functionality of the design, the experience of the client's management, the project's corporate or government oversight, or the regulation of procurement policy will influence strategy.

Tradition will also govern. Usually things are done a certain way simply because that's the way they have always been done. Strategy simply isn't considered.

Finally, the process only helps or hinders. The biggest issue is the quality of the people. The best way to get a good project is to get good people to do it, set the environment for collaboration, and make sure responsibilities are clear.

The Phases of Design and Construction

Design and construction can be divided into three distinct phases: project definition (PD), design, and construction.

These phases (and their subphases) are discrete because they typically employ different technology.

The phases can be overlapped, subdivided, or regrouped, but none can be eliminated. If one phase is done poorly, the following work is usually impaired.

1. Project Definition

At 3D/I, we subdivide this phase into two activities.

- *Discovery:* The identification and analysis of project requirements and constraints.
- *Integration:* The description of the project and the plan (including an estimate of cost and time for delivering it).

2. Design

Typically, design is divided into three phases.

- *Schematic design:* The basic appearance and plans.
- *Design development:* An evolution of design that defines the functional and aesthetic aspects of the project, and the building systems that satisfy them.
- *Construction drawings and specifications:* The details of assembly and construction technology.

3. Construction

Construction can also be divided into several basic activities.

- *Procurement:* The purchasing, negotiation or bid, and award of contracts to construct the project.[4]
- *Shop drawings:* The final fabrication drawings for building systems.[5]
- *Fabrication, delivery, and assembly:* The manufacture and installation of the manufactured components of the building.
- *Site construction:* The labor-intensive field construction and the installation of systems and equipment.

When to Contract for Construction

A construction contract may be awarded at any level of definition. Following are four standard techniques.

1. The Traditional Process

Common because many owners want to know exactly what they will get before they agree on the price or start construction. Projects aren't bid until construction drawings are complete. However, shop drawings are done by contractors, so it's correct to argue that in all standard processes, some design is done by the contractor.

---

[4]This activity occurs at many levels. The way the client buys construction affects the methods that may be used by construction managers, general contractors, subcontractors, and suppliers.

[5]One could easily argue that shop drawings are really the last phase of design—with considerable logic. They are included in the construction phase only because they are done by contractors after the selection of contractors.

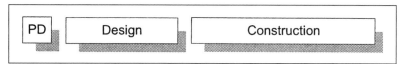

Figure 9-2 There are three classic phases of design and construction.
Courtesy of Charles B. Thomsen, President, 3D/International.

2. Bridging

A hybrid of design-build and the traditional process. The contract documents are prepared by the client's architect/engineer (AE). They specify the project's functional and aesthetic requirements but leave the details of construction technology up to the contractor. Construction technology is specified with performance specifications. Final design (the construction drawings) is done by a design-build contractor or a general contractor (GC) with an AE as a subcontractor (who is also the AE-of-Record).

3. Design-Build

Such contracts are typically negotiated before project definition, or just after. All design (including construction drawings) is done by the design-build contractor.

4. Fast-Track

This is jargon for overlapping design and construction to accelerate completion. It may be done with the traditional process, bridging, design-build, or any other process.

There is no technical reason not to overlap design and construction. The problem is cost control: construction begins before the final price is fixed.

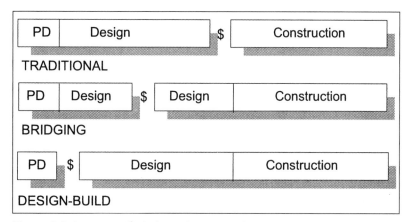

Figure 9-3 A contract ($ sign) may be awarded at any level of definition. The question is when you turn the design over to the contractor. Courtesy of Charles B. Thomsen, President, 3D/International.

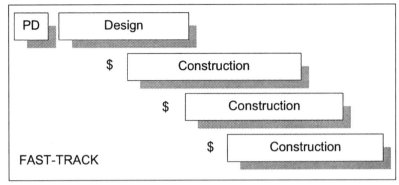

Figure 9-4 Fast-track may be applied to any process—traditional, bridging, or design-build. Courtesy of Charles B. Thomsen, President, 3D/International.

There are two basically different ways to fast-track a project. A single contract can be awarded to one contractor who may build the project under a cost-plus contract, perhaps with a guaranteed maximum price (GMP)[6] or the project may be bid in stages with complete contract documents for each stage. Site work, shell and core, and interiors may be bid separately, resulting in three contracts, or there may be forty or more prime trade contracts.

Contract Documents

A construction contract that includes a fixed price, a target price, or a GMP requires a description of the result that the contractor must produce. Different countries and different industries have different traditions (and convictions) about the detail required to describe the building. Typical documents are:

1. Construction Drawings and Specifications

Most AEs, working in the United States, believe that detailed construction drawings and specifications are required to enforce a contract. Construction documents show how the building is made and what it's made of. The drawings show details like the size and location of reinforcing rods, wiring runs, and duct sizes. The specifications typically define the construction by product or by prescription.

2. Bill of Quantities

In countries influenced by the British, licensed quantity surveyors measure drawings, calculate the amount of each required material, and prepare a Bill of Quantities. Contracts are based on the unit cost of each building material. Unit-price contracts are common for highway construction and tenant fit-out in office buildings in the United States.

---

[6]See the discussion of GMP contracts on page 297.

3. Design Development and Performance Specifications

In many countries, projects are bid with what we would call design-development drawings (35 to 50 percent of the level of detail that is contained in a full set of construction drawings and specifications). Performance specifications describe what systems must do rather than describe how they will do it. Construction drawings are completed by design-build contractors who maintain a staff of architects and engineers. In the United States, the petrochemical industry, GSA (General Services Administration), and the U.S. Air Force are using this process.

(There are three classic ways to specify something: By product, by prescription, or by performance. For instance, if you wanted heating, ventilating, and air-conditioning (HVAC) equipment you could specify the manufacturer's *product* that would do the job and say "or equal," or you could *prescribe* what it's made of and how it's made (i.e., the horsepower, duct size, metal thickness, and so on), or you could specify the *performance*—the air changes, temperature, and humidity results that you require. The latter method provides latitude to contractors to meet your requirements.)

Key Decisions

There are infinite variations in delivery strategy, but there are four basic decisions. They are:

1. Number of contracts
2. Selection criteria
3. Relationship of owner to contractor
4. Terms of payment

These decisions aren't either/or. There are shades of gray.

1. Number of Contracts

A project may be awarded to one contractor, as in design-build. In the traditional process, there are two contractors: An AE and a construction contractor. (There are three with a project manager.) With a construction manager, you may have contracts with forty prime subcontractors, or you may purchase building materials and equipment and arrange multiple labor contracts. There may be thousands of contracts.

With multiple contracts, you can fast-track a project (overlap design and construction). Direct purchase of labor and materials eliminates overhead markups. Unbundling design allows you to select specialists, and unbundling construction allows careful selection of specific manufacturers and trade contractors. So as the number of contracts increases, the opportunity to save time, money, and improve quality also increases.

So does risk. Owners who choose to manage multiple contracts must manage the contracts well or take the responsibility for management failures. Consequently, most owners choose a construction manager (CM) to help them if they use multiple contracts.

The term "construction manager" is frequently used synonymously with "project manager." Often the term "project manager" (PM) is used with the traditional process, and "construction manager" is used with multiple-contract fast-track. A general contractor may take the title of construction manager with a GMP contract. The same company may provide all three kinds of services for different clients.

2. Selection Criteria

A contractor may be selected on the basis of price or qualifications. Owners often consider both and require a proposal (which could be a management plan or a design) *and* a price.

Typically, AEs are selected with an emphasis on qualifications, and construction contractors are selected on the basis of price. But there are owners who select AEs on price and those who select GCs on qualifications.

The selection criteria are influenced by what is to be bought. If it's a common product, easily defined and easily evaluated, there is little reason not to choose on the basis of price. But if the product is unusual or proprietary, or if service is required, or if intellectual qualities (talent, creativity, wisdom, judgment, or experience) are required, selection is usually based on qualifications.

3. Relationship of Owner to Contractor

You may view contractors in one of two ways: as an agent or as a vendor. An agent represents the client's interest and has a fiduciary responsibility [see Sapers' discussion of professionalism in Chapter 1, page 4, for elaboration]. A vendor delivers a specified product for a price. Agents tend to work for a fee and are usually selected on the basis of qualifications. Vendors sell a product for a price and are usually selected on the basis of cost.

Typically, AEs are viewed at the agency end of the spectrum, and contractors are at the vendor end. But there are exceptions. Some owners ask contractors to act as their agents in procuring and managing construction, and treat AEs as vendors of plans and specifications.

When owners need guidance or advice, they typically choose an agent (a fiduciary) relationship. Owners who know exactly what is required typically form vendor relationships.

There can be a conflict of interest if a contractor is both agent and vendor or if a contractor changes from agent to vendor. For instance, an AE who designs a building for a professional is usually precluded from bidding on construction. Some owners don't worry about the conflict of interest and look for good reputations and continuity instead.

4. Terms of Payment

You can pay a contractor based on the contractor's cost. At the other end of the spectrum is a fixed lump sum. Contracts tend to be on a cost-plus basis when the scope is unknown, and lump-sum when the details of the work are well understood. There are variations between cost-plus and lump-sum contracts. The common arrangements are:

- *Cost-Plus Contract:* Contractor is paid actual costs plus a fixed or a percentage fee.

- *Cost-Plus Contract with Target Price:* Contractor is paid actual costs plus a fee. However, a target price is set, and the contractor will share in the savings or the overrun. The target price is modified by change orders as the project progresses.
- *Cost-Plus Contract with a Guaranteed Maximum Price:* Contractor is paid actual costs plus a fee. However, a maximum price is set, and the contractor will share in the savings but will pay all of the over-run. The GMP is modified by subsequent change orders.[7]
- *Unit Price Contract:* Contractor is paid a predetermined amount for each unit of material put in place (or removed).
- *Fixed Price Contract:* Contractor is paid a fixed sum for the work.

These payment terms may be combined in one contract. For instance, many contracts are fixed price lump sum with unit-price provisions for rock removal during excavation or tenant work during lease-up. Change orders may be based on a cost-plus arrangement.

Typical Project Delivery Methods

Variations are infinite, but the most common are as follows.

The Traditional Process

Most U.S. projects are design, bid, build. An AE defines the owner's needs, designs the building, prepares construction drawings and specifications, and administers construction. Drawings and specifications serve two purposes: they are guidelines for construction, and they are the contractual definition of what the contractor is to build. Contractors are prequalified and short-listed and usually provide a bond. Typically, the low bidder is awarded the work. The AE is at the agent end of the spectrum; the contractor is at the vendor end.

- *Pros:* The process is easy to manage. Roles are clear; the process is universally understood. Since the owner has a defined requirement and a fixed price, it appears prudent.
- *Cons:* Construction can't start until design is complete. There is not a fixed price for construction until much work has been done. If bids are over the budget, more time and money are lost to redesign. Design suffers from a lack of input from contractors and subcontractors. Procurement of subcontractors by the general contractor is typically unbusinesslike during the bid period.

---

[7]Many people use the term guaranteed maximum price (GMP) synonymously with fixed price. That is incorrect. A GMP is a lid on a cost-plus contract with a defined scope. It is one of the most difficult of all contracts to manage. It has the problems of both lump-sum and cost-plus contracts. It is *more* susceptible to change orders than a lump-sum contract, because it is typically given before construction drawings are complete. There will also be many issues over the definition of "cost," for example, rental rules on contractor-owned equipment, or ownership of workman's compensation refunds or penalties.

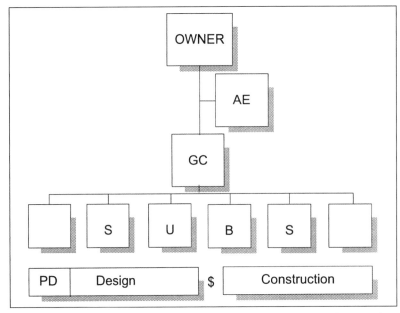

Figure 9-5 The traditional process: Design, bid, build, with the AE (architect/engineer) as agent of the owner, the GC (general contractor) as vendor. Courtesy of Charles B. Thomsen, President, 3D/International.

The Traditional Process with a Project Manager

Owners often add project management companies to the traditional process to mitigate the traditional flaws.

The idea is to select an organization with experience in construction to improve cost, schedule, and quality control; improve the constructibility of the design; develop risk management and claims protection programs; improve other management controls to smooth the process; and improve field management.[8]

Often, project managers (PMs) unbundle other contracts. Instead of a single AE, projects may have a planner, a design architect, a production architect, and separate architects for different aspects of the interiors. These firms may be selected by the owner and PM and assigned to the lead architect. The PM may also negotiate major items of manufactured equipment, and subcontracts, and assign them to the eventual general contractor. That maintains a single, bonded price for construction, but it allows direct negotiation (and useful collaboration) with specialty subcontractors and manufacturers. Procurement of subcontracts also provides cost feedback. That reduces the possibility of a bust on bid day.

Construction Management and Fast-track

Many owners look for ways to accelerate schedules. Fast-track—starting construction before finishing design—is a common technique.

---

[8]Although it is not yet common in the industry, 3D/I has also emphasized the project definition phase as an important project management service.

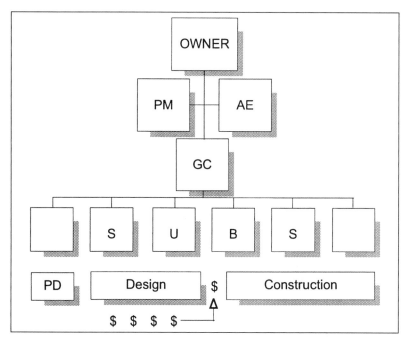

Figure 9-6 Project Manager (PM) with negotiation and assignment of subcontracts. Courtesy of Charles B. Thomsen, President, 3D/International.

- *Pros:* The process saves time.
- *Cons:* The problem with fast-track is intrinsic in its advantage. Since construction is started before design is complete, the owner lacks the security of a fixed price based on complete construction documents. There is no *contractual* assurance that the project will be completed within the budget. Two procedures are common with this problem.

1. Negotiated Cost-Plus General Construction Contract with a Guaranteed Maximum Price (GMP). The argument is simple: Since the project isn't fully designed when construction begins, the contract should be "cost-plus." But to give the owner security that the project will be built within the budget, the contractor provides a GMP.

- *Pros:* The process works for developers or small, experienced, private-sector owners who can select contractors on the basis of qualifications and integrity, reward them with repeat work, and manage them vigorously. The process also works best for simple office buildings that are well understood by all (the owner, the AE, and the contractor).
- *Cons:* The contract can be hard to enforce. The guaranteed maximum price is for a specific project that isn't completely defined. As design progresses there is an opportunity for a contentious or inept contractor to make claims for change orders that are "out of the original guaranteed scope." The GMP is a defined price for an undefined product.

Owners with complex buildings, the public sector, or large corporate or institutional clients should be circumspect about a cost-plus contract with a GMP. First, it's difficult for these kinds of owners to award and administer cost-plus contracts. Second, these owners are particularly vulnerable to claims and change orders. And, for owners with deep pockets, awarding a contract on the basis of incomplete documents increases vulnerability to claims and litigation.

2. Professional Construction Manager with Multiple Prime Contracts. The general contractor (GC) is eliminated and replaced with a construction manager (CM) who manages the project in an agency (fiduciary) capacity.

The CM bids construction to trade contractors just as a GC would, beginning with items critical to the schedule. One common strategy to avoid downstream overruns is to award only the shop drawing phase of the first trade contracts. The CM delays final notice to proceed with construction until most of the work is bid and the project cost is certain. On government work, the subcontracts are directly with the owner. In the private sector, the CM may hold the subcontracts as agent of the owner.

- *Pros:* You have a professional construction manager on your side of the table. The multiple trade construction contracts are fixed price based on complete documents with little room for change orders.

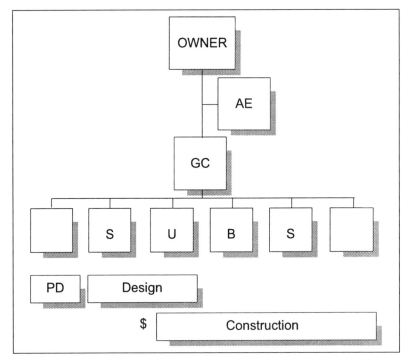

Figure 9-7 Construction Manager (CM) fast-track (negotiated contract with a guaranteed maximum price). Courtesy of Charles B. Thomsen, President, 3D/ International.

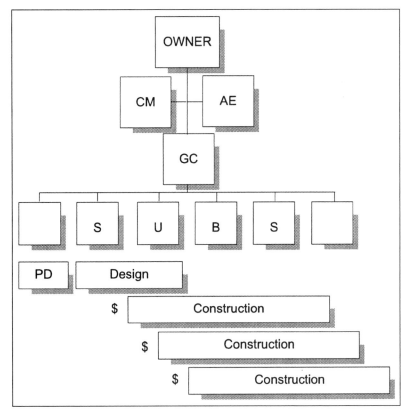

Figure 9-8 Construction Manager (CM) fast-track (with an agent CM). Courtesy of Charles B. Thomsen, President, 3D/International.

- *Cons:* Multiple contracts can make for administrative difficulties. If one prime trade contractor damages another by delay, the owner can get caught up in the fight.

The secret of a successful fast-track project isn't the legal security of a contract, nor does anyone believe it's risk-free. Success only comes from good management. The professional approach works better for the public sector because governments can select professionals on the basis of qualifications to replace the function of a general contractor. Even if source selection procedures (the term for federal government selection procedures that consider qualifications as well as price) are used to select construction contractors on the basis of qualifications, the government has difficulty exercising the management sanctions that are the necessary stick to make a cost-plus GMP contract work.

Design-Build

With design-build, one company provides both design and construction. Some owners like the design-build idea, but they want to cherry-pick specialized designers. In these cases, the AE is a subcontractor to a GC or a design-build contractor.

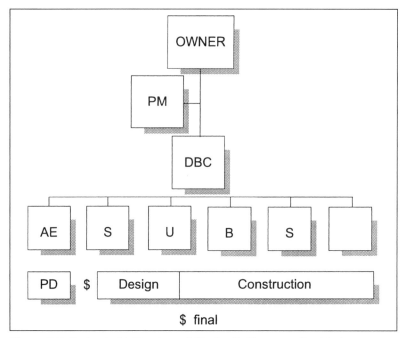

Figure 9-9 Design-build. Courtesy of Charles B. Thomsen, President, 3D/International.

- *Pros:* There is a single point of responsibility for both design and construction. You can influence design imagination with construction practicality. You get an enforceable price for construction sooner, and if you need to, you can fast-track the project. The contractor can negotiate subcontracts methodically so you benefit from good prices, reliable subcontractors, better technology, and tighter contracts.
- *Cons:* More projects would be design-build if they could be bid. But it's difficult to formulate an enforceable price before design begins. The paradox: It's hard to define the work to be done for an agreed upon price without design, but if design is done, then it's not design-build.

Some design-build companies work under an AE fee with a target price until the design is set. They then negotiate a final price. They agree that the owner may obtain prices from other contractors as well. The design-build contractor begins in an agent role and changes to a vendor role. Many do so with integrity. Many owners feel, however, that it's unwise to hire a contractor, as an agent, to define a product that they will then sell as a vendor.

Bridging

Bridging is the U.S. name for a design-build process common in Europe and Japan, and in the petrochemical industry.

In the bridging process, there are two AEs. The first AE is under contract with the owner. Bid documents define the functional and aesthetic characteristics of the project. They include drawings similar to design development in the traditional process. There is a combination of performance and traditional specifications. These documents define the parts of the building that the owner wants to control, typically the functional and aesthetic aspects. But the documents leave considerable latitude for contractors to look for economies in construction technology.

The project is bid by design-build contractors or by a GC with an AE as a subcontractor. The contractor's AE (the second AE) does the final construction drawings and specifications and is the architect-of-record. Typically, construction isn't begun until the final construction drawings are complete, and it's clear that there are no misunderstandings about what was intended by the bid documents. If there is disagreement, the owner owns the plans and may use them to take competitive bids.

- *Pros:* Bridging has the beneficial attributes of the traditional process: A bonded, enforceable lump-sum contract and complete contractual documentation before construction starts. It also has the beneficial attributes of design-build: Centralization of responsibility and integration of practical construction knowledge into final design and reduction of the time and cost required to obtain an enforceable lump sum price for construction. By centralizing responsibilities during construction, bridging minimizes the opportunity for contractor claims based on errors or omissions in the drawings or specifications. It also centralizes the responsibility for correction of postconstruction faults in the design or construction.

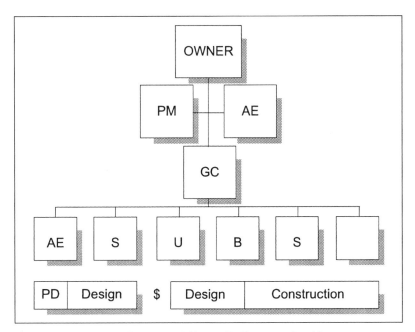

Figure 9-10 Bridging. Courtesy of Charles B. Thomsen, President, 3D/International.

- *Cons:* The biggest problem with bridging is that it's new in the United States. The construction industry is large and replete with many contractors, AEs, consultants, subcontractors, manufacturers, and suppliers. Tradition is the great facilitator. When you change the process, you must manage well.

Three Issues

The traditional process emerged a century ago. There was less bureaucracy among our clients and the agencies that constrain construction, and our world was less litigious. The changes in technology, bureaucracy, and law require responses in the process of design and construction.

1. Construction Technology

A century ago, buildings were custom-made of wood and masonry. Then AEs were masters of construction technology. Today, most of a building is built with technology developed and best understood by manufacturers and specialty subcontractors. Shop drawings guide construction. AEs are system integrators. The master builder is a team.

With the traditional process, collaboration and negotiation with industry are awkward. Dealings with specialty subcontractors and manufacturers must be at arm's length. Subcontractors and manufacturers can't disclose detailed cost information without losing competitive advantage on bid day. Even worse, many will understate costs to encourage AEs to specify their products. Thus it's hard to make decisions with confidence that the price quotes are accurate. Furthermore, AEs can't incorporate proprietary technology in their designs without losing competition on bid day.

Separated from contractors and manufacturers, AEs have their hands tied. It's hard for them to know the latest or most practical building technology and almost impossible to know what things really cost. They may design custom buildings that use yesterday's construction methods, are not detailed practically, and cost more than necessary.

The best way to buy construction is to influence design with procurement. It's a simple idea. You don't specify a system until you know its price. And you let the subcontractors and manufacturers tell you how best to save money and get better products. As design evolves, someone (a contractor, CM, or PM) negotiates. The AE may establish design directions for a window wall, but negotiations with a manufacturer and a fixed-price agreement are struck before the design is set. The same may be true for ceiling and lighting systems, raised floors, elevators, mechanical equipment, and so on.

This process can work with design-build, bridging, and construction management. It can also work with the traditional process if there is a project manager negotiating subcontracts and assigning them to the eventual GC.

2. Bureaucracy

Environmental issues vie with economics and defense as the main concern of Americans. Clean air, clean water, mobility, historic preservation, and urban design are common concerns. Fine arts commissions, historic preservation groups, zoning boards, and planning agencies restrict or deny construction—even on military bases. Ad hoc citizens' groups influence public affairs. America no longer accepts a priori that construction is good; a pervasive attitude persists that America is overbuilt. We have eliminated tax incentives for development, many states have no-growth movements, and major cities have restrictive development plans.

It's not only external bureaucracy that slows the project. Our clients are larger with more layers of oversight. Boards, executive management, project teams, and users can all contribute to, delay, or derail a project.

These barriers to construction are entrenched and multiplying. They delay and interrupt the momentum of design and construction. Yet the effect of this bureaucracy is good. With it we will have better buildings. Certainly the best projects come from effective collaboration between the owner and the AEs.

The best way to deal with these influences is with thorough project definition. If a deal is made for construction before all approvals and all definition is in hand, there are likely to be painful change orders.

Good project definition is possible (though often slighted) with any of the processes—with the probable exception of a fixed-cost design-build or a fast-track cost-plus GMP CM contract.

3. Litigation

All of us—owners, PMs, AEs, and contractors—operate in an increasingly litigious environment. Too many projects blow their budgets with litigation costs as the building nears completion.

The traditional process is based on the incorrect assumption that AEs can prepare flawless plans and specifications. That's impossible. Everyone makes mistakes. So AEs and their clients are exposed to claims during and after construction. Legal costs add to budget overruns for clients and increase overhead for architects, engineers, and contractors.[9] Errors and omissions insurance is now half of typical profit for most architects—a significant cost passed back to clients as overhead.

As construction is more complicated, contractors have more opportunity (and more cause) to pursue claims for errors and omissions in drawings and specifications. Indeed, there are more mistakes to pursue.

Furthermore, AEs' errors and omissions insurance doesn't completely protect clients. American courts don't hold AEs to a standard of perfection; the legal test of their liability is professional judgment, not craft. To defend themselves, AEs don't have to prove that they designed a perfect building, only that they acted with a standard of skill, knowledge, and judgment equivalent to that generally exhibited by members of other professions.

The result: Today's clients can't require contractors to correct defects that were caused by errors in the plans—without a change order—and may not have recourse to their AEs.

---

[9]In 1960, there were 12.5 claims per 100 AE firms; in 1988, there were 29.4. In 1976, the average claim paid by carriers was $60,000; in 1988 it was $183,000 according to CNA/Schinnerer.

The product of both the AEs' and the contractors' work is construction; hence with the traditional process it's often difficult to separate responsibility for problems. Often the problems have been contributed to by all so the responsibility for correction *is* murky.

Processes such as bridging and design-build centralize responsibility for the final result. Owners have the right to expect defect-free buildings and design-build contractors do not have the AE "standard of skill" to weasel out of responsibility.

Paradoxically, litigation with the professional CM approach is surprisingly low. On the surface, the multitude of contracts (perhaps as many as forty trade contracts) would appear to open forty cracks for litigation to slip in. Experience does not sustain the suspicion. There are probably two reasons.

1. Subcontractors are not as litigious as general contractors.
2. CMs on-site know the facts, develop risk management systems, maintain good files, and are on the owners' side of the table.

Keys to Quality: Success Strategies in Design-Build Partnerships

David Hinson crystallizes the critical issues related to design-build in the essay below. He discusses the circumstances in which this popular mode of project delivery can be successful in serving the best interests of clients in terms of design quality, cost, and schedule.

DAVID W. HINSON, AIA, is Associate Professor and Program Chair, School of Architecture, Auburn University. He leads *The Designhabitat Project,* an award-winning collaboration between the School of Architecture and Habitat for Humanity. David holds a Master of Architecture from the University of Pennsylvania and currently serves as Chair of the AIA's Educator/Practitioner Network. Courtesy of David W. Hinson, AIA, Professor, School of Architecture, Auburn University.

It seems clear that the design and construction services delivery method we have come to know as "design-build" is in use on a significant portion of projects initiated in the United States. Many suggest that it will soon vie for at least an equal share of the market alongside the traditional "design-bid-build" and "negotiated-bid/CM" methods.

Advocates of the process point to several key advantages of this method: a less adversarial relationship between the design and construction teams, single source responsibility for design and construction services, and shorter project-delivery schedules.

What is less clear is how this method will impact two significant aspects of practice: the integrity of the architect's role as advocate of the owner and the public, and the quality of design involved in buildings that result from a design-build delivery process.

With regard to design quality, the design-build process gets decidedly mixed reviews from architects. Those with design-build experience offer assessments, which range from enthusiasm to a cautious "it depends . . . " to "that's a great way to deliver bad design faster." To better understand these positions, we've turned to two firms with first-hand experience.

Lord, Aeck, and Sargent (LAS) is a 140-person practice based in Atlanta, Georgia, specializing in science and research, housing, higher education, and cultural facilities along with historic preservation. The Atlanta office of HOK, with a staff of sixty, gives this international multidisciplinary practice a presence in the southeast. HOK-Atlanta specializes in planning, higher education, and science and research facilities. Both practices have significant experience with design-build as well as design-bid-build and construction management delivery methods.

Their perspectives provide valuable insights into what it takes to address the key issues of the design-build process. Each firm has completed successful buildings via the design-build process for the Georgia Institute of Technology (Georgia Tech), and we used these projects as a context for discussing the challenges associated with this process.

Choose Your Partner (Carefully!)

Both HOK and LAS stressed the importance of choosing your design-build partners carefully. Howard Wertheimer, principal-in-charge for LAS on the Georgia Tech Student Health Center, credits a strong personal relationship with the project leader for Whiting-Turner, the builder on the project, as the foundation of their success on the project. According to Wertheimer, "This relationship was characterized by trust and respect for the special skills and expertise each of us brought to the team."

Mike Greer, project manager for HOK on the new Biomedical Engineering Building at Georgia Tech, described a similar relationship with their design-build partner, Archer Western Contractors. Mike credits prior collaborations with Archer Western on projects completed under a CM-based delivery process as instrumental to the development of this trust and respect. He noted that shared values between the architect and the builder are so critical to a successful experience that HOK prefers to "test-run" the relationship with a builder process before entering into a design-build collaboration. "Working together under another delivery method (such as a CM process) gives us a good idea of the builder's values and process," Greer observes.

Both architects noted that this collaborative climate required a big shift from the historically adversarial relationships between architects and builders commonly associated with other delivery approaches—especially design-bid-build.

Wertheimer noted that their collaboration with Whiting-Turner began with a full-day "partnering workshop" in which LAS, Whiting-Turner, and representatives of Georgia Tech hammered out communication protocols and a charter of shared goals for the project. Wertheimer said that the positive tone established in this session carried through to the end of the project and added, "We seldom experience this kind of collaborative atmosphere on design-bid-build projects."

Both firms noted that this climate of mutual trust and respect required substantial attitude shifts from both architect and builder. Rohit Saxena, design architect for HOK on the Biomedical Engineering Building, noted that, "Architecture students are weaned on the idea that builders are not to be trusted and that architects make all the key decisions on projects." In contrast, Saxena observes that in this approach, "The whole ivory tower syndrome must be left behind." Saxena stressed that "the paradigm of the builder (or the owner) waiting for the architect to tell them what to do has no place in this process. You have to listen to each other and work together from the very start."

When Is Design-Build the Best Choice?

In both of the projects discussed here, the driving consideration behind Georgia Tech's decision to use a design-build delivery process was the opportunity to shave time off the project schedule. Project funding constraints and sequencing of other campus projects framed these tight schedule demands, and Georgia Tech turned to the design-build process for a solution.

Both teams delivered impressive results.

The Student Health Center, a 40,000 square foot structure budgeted at $6.1 million, was completed 53 weeks after LAS and Whiting-Turner were awarded the project. The $19 million Biomedical Engineering Building was completed by HOK and Archer Western in 20 months.

In the case of both projects, Georgia Tech came to the table with the right ingredients for a successful design-build process—a clear understanding of what they needed and a clear set of quality standards to guide the project.

In the case of the Student Health Center, Georgia Tech provided a comprehensive program to LAS and Whiting-Turner, including a set of conceptual floor plan diagrams. These documents, along with Tech's "Yellow Book" of design and specification standards, allowed LAS and Whiting-Turner to jump directly into the project.

Both firms cited this clear understanding of the project objectives and quality expectations by the owner as critical criteria for success in a design-build process. Both also agreed that projects beginning without this clarity are better suited to another delivery method—one that allows more time for considering alternatives and establishing expectations.

The time pressure associated with design-build, like all other "fast-track" approaches, also places greater emphasis on the firm's experience and confidence with the building type—especially when schedule pressures demand they commit to key design decisions early in the process. Greer cautioned that "this pressure can be even more significant in design-build collaborations" and emphasized the distinction between making timely decisions and "just hurrying up."

Wertheimer echoed the importance of project-type experience and noted that, as with any fast-track project, design-build projects demand a different staffing strategy than design-bid-build projects and "this has an impact on the fees needed to do the work profitably." Wertheimer illustrates this point by noting that in a design-build project, "the project staff is designing, generating construction documents, and performing construction administration services simultaneously; you need a deeper team."

Balancing Acts

As design-build emerged as a delivery method in the 1980s, many in the profession voiced concerns that architects participating in design-build business relationships would have an insurmountable conflict between their duty to protect the public's health, safety, and welfare, and their financial interest in the profitability of the design-build venture.

These early concerns seem to have abated as experience with the design-build process has broadened. Since relatively few architects act as the prime contractor in design-build projects, they rarely have a direct financial interest in the profitability of the design-build business venture.

Registration boards have made it clear that architects will be held to the same standard relative to protection of the safety and welfare of the public regardless of who they work for. Both LAS and HOK noted that they don't view their duties to the public to be any different on design-build projects and noted that this position is consistently supported by the builders they partner with.

Relative to their duties to act as the owner's advocate, both Wertheimer and Greer agreed that balancing their (contractual) obligations to the builder and the owner's expectations relative to their role can present some dilemmas. The idea of the architect as an objective advisor to the owner— owing duty only to the owner (and the public)—is the foundation of the legal and ethical framework taught in architecture schools, and it is codified in the registration laws that govern practice in most every state. Regardless of the fact that in most design-build arrangements the architect is under contract to the builder, owners still expect architects to look out for their interests as well as those of the builder.

According to Greer of HOK, the key challenge in design-build projects relative to this issue comes in to play when evaluating alternative means of meeting the owner's expectations regarding performance and quality. In other delivery approaches, this discussion (or in some cases, debate) takes place in full view of the owner. But in design-build, the owner is often excluded from this process.

In the case of the Georgia Tech projects, the contract between the owner and the design-builder included a supplemental "tri-party agreement" that gave the architect specific authorization to reject work that did not comply with the contract documents and the design intent. Wertheimer noted that LAS never had to invoke this clause in their collaboration with Whiting-Turner, but it gave Georgia Tech the confidence that this potential conflict would not negatively impact their projects.

Greer points out that, regardless of the delivery method used, "the project is still an HOK project" and must stand alongside their other work in the eyes of the owner and other potential clients.

What About Design?

This brings us to the last question: How does design quality fare under the design-build approach?

While we might like to believe that the sole determinant of design quality is the talent of the architect, anyone involved in contemporary practice understands that design quality "hangs in the balance"[10] between the priorities and values of the owner and the values, talents, and expertise of the design and construction team. The way the goals and objectives of a project are developed, or more specifically the role of architects in this negotiation, can vary significantly depending on the delivery method in use.

In the design-bid-build method, design quality is negotiated between the owner and architect *prior* to builder involvement. The architect is the owner's principle advisor relative to the weight assigned to design quality, schedule, and cost of the project. While this delivery method is still in widespread use, it has been gradually edged aside by the construction management (or CM) delivery method.

In the CM process, the construction manager's relationship to the owner can take a variety of forms—from an independent advisor to an "at-risk" constructor. The most significant impact of this alternative delivery method on design quality is the introduction of a cost and schedule savvy "expert" in the formative stages of the project. In the ideal scenario, this delivery system provides the client with a "check and balance" benefit—the architect is expected to advocate for "quality" and the CM for "time and money." Despite shifts in reassigned responsibility for estimating project cost and schedule, the architects' ethical and legal relationship to the owner remains much the same as with the design-bid-build approach.

In the design-build method, however, the architect's position relative to the owner undergoes a profound shift. This shift reframes the ethical and legal relationship between the owner, architect, and builder, and has the potential to reshape the architect's influence on design quality.

The anxieties architects hold about the design-build process are rooted in the concern that design quality will suffer as architects are distanced from the owner (via their status a subconsultants to the builder). Architects are concerned that their legal duties to the design-build entity will force a change in client and public perceptions relative to the objectivity of architects' counsel and the motivations that drive the profession.

Both LAS and HOK agreed that the weight given to design in a design-build project is largely a factor of the owner's values. Where buildings are seen by owners as consumable, short-term tools, the choice of delivery method will be driven by the most efficient options the marketplace can produce. It is in this "strong-delivery"[11] end of the market where design-build earned its first foothold (and where it earned much of its reputation among architects for low design standards).

Despite architects' anxieties, it is becoming clearer that high-quality design is just as achievable under a design-build method as in any other approach—*provided the owner places a priority on quality* and *provides an adequate budget to support their quality objectives.*

This is born out by the experiences of both LAS and HOK on their design-build projects at Georgia Tech. Even within the context of the very ag-

---

[10]Dana Cuff, *Architecture: The Story of Practice* (Cambridge, Mass.: The MIT Press, 1993).

[11]Weld Cox, David Maister, et al., *Success Strategies for Design Professionals* (New York: McGraw-Hill, 1983).

gressive schedule constraints framing the design process, both the Biomedical Engineering Building and the Student Health Center had to earn approval from Georgia Tech's independent "Planning and Design Commission," and both projects incorporated Georgia Tech's newly developed goals for sustainable design. Wertheimer credits the close collaboration between LAS and Whiting-Turner with "giving Georgia Tech a better (and larger) building than they expected."

From the perspective of these two experienced practices, design-build delivery approaches have the potential to realize the advantages touted by its proponents and produce good buildings, provided these projects are framed by the right conditions. For Wertheimer, Greer, and Saxena the keys to a quality-driven design-build project rest with how you start it—with carefully chosen design-build partners and with owners who understand how and when to use the design-build delivery method to realize their goals. Get this right and the project is primed for successful results.

Small-Scale Commercial and Residential Projects

What is the architect's role in the small-scale project domain? I believe that there are creative solutions to forging a high quality and cost-effective niche for architects (one that has, for the most part, been nonexistent). Examining the scope of architect's services and the project delivery mode are worthwhile. *Perhaps a design consultation focusing on the schematic design, materials selection, or even an aspect of construction detailing—whatever the overarching idea is toward making poetic, magical space—could be the service.* And if the owner found a great builder at the beginning of the project—so that the architect could work with him or her during the "consultation"—that would ensure a degree of quality control through subsequent phases. This arrangement could be structured as a negotiated contract between the owner and the builder.

In other words, I'm proposing that architects can get creative in proposing and testing how projects may be delivered to clients in this realm without compromising strong ideas or integrity. Must architects have a $50,000 fee, for example, on a typical custom residential project to make a profit? Must architects perform comprehensive services to ensure high-quality design? Is there a way to raise the design bar, provide a needed service that is client-responsive, and make the fee affordable so many more prospective clients can hire architects for their residential additions, renovations, and new construction? And the same idea applies to small-scale commercial tenant build-outs in leased space. This is not unlike one approach to project delivery in Japan.

Leading to Project Delivery in Japan

The preceding essay on design-build is a great lead-in to the following discussion of the context of practice culture in Japan by Nancy Finley. According to Dana Buntrock, in her book, *Japanese Architecture as a Collab-*

orative Process: Opportunities in a Flexible Construction Culture (London: Spon Press, 2002), "Construction firms handle about 40 percent of all building design in Japan, from detached single-family homes to soaring office towers as part of design-build packages." Indeed, there are highly integrated design-build firms in Japan. Buntrock describes one (of several) delivery approaches as a process similar to bridging in which the "architect produces only a conceptual design and basic design drawings . . . . The contractor is responsible for producing all construction documents." On the opposite end of the spectrum, in another common approach, design development through construction administration occurs *at the construction site*. It is easy to speculate how coordination and collaboration are facilitated in this model. Hopefully the messages from Japan of sharing information and working as a team—to produce excellent architecture—will not be "lost in translation."

NANCY FINLEY is Associate Professor of Architecture and Urban Design at Tohoku University in Sendai, Japan. She is Principal of Factor N Associates, based in Tokyo, and holds a Doctorate in Architecture from the University of Tokyo. Finley is the recipient of numerous awards including the Japan Institute of Architects Award for the Best Young Architect in 1998. © 2005 Nancy Finley.

Education

A redefinition of architectural education in Japan is underway. Until around 2000, architecture departments in both public and private universities were under the auspices of faculties of engineering. Private institutions, the first to redefine their curriculum, emphasized the human, environmental, and communication aspects of design, which led to a relocation or expansion of architecture to faculties other than engineering. For instance, when Tokyo National University of Fine Arts and Music opened its second campus in 1999, Architecture (with a new name of Communications Design) was placed in the department of Inter Media Art. The shift gave social, environmental, and communication technologies equal status with building sciences and construction methodologies. Responding to the rise in popular interest in architecture among young people in the 1990s, institutions of higher education that were motivated to increase their student body acknowledged the incentives for curriculum innovations. It is too soon to tell whether these organizational shifts will benefit the profession by introducing a more entrepreneurial atmosphere among the faculty and student body.

Meanwhile, professors continue to work with their students through the laboratory. The laboratory, a system that is unlikely to change in the near future, provides a unique training ground for architectural design programs. Graduate programs at Japanese universities are organized by laboratories in which the professor directs group research and design projects that supplement the general design curriculum. The environment, much like an atelier-sized design firm, is composed of students ranking from fourth-year undergraduate to the PhD level. Collaboration, discussions concerning group projects, and social hierarchy are strengthened by this system of architectural education. It prepares young designers to learn how to practice by providing a trusting, collaborative yet competitive environment. *The lab establishes strong foundations for the collaborative and communicative style found in the Japanese professional architectural community.*

Fumihiko Maki taught at Tokyo University throughout the 1980s. After he retired in 1989, he returned full-time to his design office where today he continues to compete for and complete internationally acclaimed projects. At Tokyo University, Maki's lab concentrated on two areas: providing the chance for students (1) to join in international competitions and (2) to consider the nature of the city and architecture by researching Tokyo. During one competition in Vienna for the renovation of the Messepalast, Maki shared some observations with a foreign student on how in the West, at the initial stages of design, the concept seems to precede form, whereas in Japan, development of the concept is often generated along with and from the manipulation of form. Considering form and material in a scaled context allows the designer to feel the space more than to just think about it.

In the United States while one out of four people seek a career in law, in Japan one out of four seek work in engineering fields. Maki's observations explain how the Japanese tend to move empirically toward spatial resolution by giving precedence to material, form, and scale over that of pure thought, concept, and assumption. The nature of materiality affects the idea. Maki often names his buildings, and in a delightful way this naming gestures toward the form and captures the essence of his concept. Some names: beetle, helmet, wafer, and traditional tea set. By focusing on material innovation and spatial sequencing, a cultural context is defined, bringing his projects a subtler depth. It is fascinating how students approach design resolutions and developed ideas. One student submitted a prototype for a chair for Designer's Week in Tokyo in 2002. By studying the form of the soybean he came up with three types of beans for sitting: A lightweight polycarbonate bean for bathing and two variations for living—one out of foam and the other of wood. They were as charming as three peas in a pod.

Housing

Housing design warrants acknowledgment simply because for the majority of people architecture means housing, and in Japan, as in the United States, many dream of owning their own home. Prefabricated home companies dominate production and control the Japanese market. Carpenters and contractors are becoming assemblers. Atelier architects competing in this housing market can find opportunities by consulting for these corporations. For many Japanese, purchasing a "customized prefab" home rather than commissioning an architect makes sense, due to the high cost of purchasing land and houses. As a result, some architects are pursuing other ways to produce housing.

"Due to the rise of environmental sicknesses like asthma among the Japanese, more homebuyers are reconsidering wood homes over the plastic prefab varieties," says Yuzo Harada, an architect in the town of Kawasaki in Miyagi Prefecture. "It gives us the opportunity to renew our forests and reemploy the craftsman's skill in wood construction. The challenge is finding a way to produce a home under 500,000 yen/tsubo ($433/square foot) that meets or exceeds the same level in housing quality."

Harada, with others in Kawasaki (population 10,000), set up a nonprofit organization for promoting ideas about water purification, agriculture, leisure, forestry, and construction. The group aims for a 100-year vision and calls itself the Kawasaki Group for Restoring Nature. One of its first projects, the Miyagi Prefecture model home (2005), is officially certified by the Miyagi prefecture government as promoting and supporting the housing industry. It is Harada's response to the prefab housing market. The model home aims are to build affordable homes with the following criteria: houses made mainly from the local wood in Kawasaki, finished with unvarnished chemically untreated wood for ensuring the health of its residents, and created such that they foster the use of renewable local natural resources. The houses are to be designed and built by the local architects, construction companies, and carpenters with a goal of revitalizing the local economy.

Manabu Chiba finds inspiration in the urban form of Tokyo neighborhoods. Many of his projects are located in the suburban towns of western Tokyo, where potential clients and housing developers are more likely to commission architects. Vested with the interest of creating spatial fluidity between private interiors and public exteriors, he concentrates mainly on housing: both single-family dwellings and apartment complexes. A favorite choice among architects commissioned for the current trend of "designer apartments" in the rental apartment industry, Chiba recently completed the design for a three-story, six-unit apartment complex in Setagaya-ku, Tokyo. The project, called Mesh (2004), redefines living conditions through what he calls infrastructure by wrapping a space of specific functions around the core and using it as an interface between the inner dwelling and the exterior environment. The building, constructed of reinforced concrete with an exterior steel-frame façade of glass, mesh, and steel panels, is innovative both for its resolution of the maintenance of mechanical, electrical, and plumbing infrastructure, and for its degree of layered privacy given the spatial transparency.

The inner reinforced concrete wall of the building makes up the structure and the outer steel frame and panel system contains the infrastructure. The functions for kitchen, entry, terraces, and bath and toilets are placed between the narrow layer of space—one and a half meters wide—between the exterior steel frame and interior concrete wall, leaving the inner core of rooms for simply living.

An experienced developer usually tends to go with typical conservative housing resolutions, because there is always a need for housing in Japan. There is no reason for the developer to support innovations in urban housing, even if the architect thinks otherwise. "Today the typical plan of a 2-DLK (two-bedroom apartment with a dining, living, and kitchen space) doesn't fit the needs of the client or user," says Chiba. "In the case of Mesh, the client went directly to the architect for a design even though there was a developer on the project. After the developer refused the design, the client went ahead anyway, ignoring the developer. Now as it turns out it, with the building completed, the developer turned around to support the design and in fact wants to work together. This back and forth strengthens the potential of the project." The architect's ability to redefine living with an innovative spatial configuration and with the support of the client may be the first sign of change in the traditional urban housing market.

| Case Study | # Digital Practice—Rethinking the Design Process |

TIM B. CASTILLO joined the faculty at the University of New Mexico in fall 2002 after teaching at the University of Colorado and the University of Arizona. He is the principal of Hybrid Environments, a critical design office located in Albuquerque, London, and New York. His work was honored this year in an international competition sponsored by the Groupe e2 in Paris. The work was exhibited at Pavillon de l'Arsenal, Paris, and Ecole Polytechnique Fédérale de Lausanne. His primary interest lies within digital research and its impact on the environment. He holds a Master of Architecture from Columbia University.

The real is not opposed to the virtual but the possible, and the virtual is not opposed to the real, but to the actual.
—Gilles Deleuze, *Différence and Repetition,* translated by Paul Patton (New York: Columbia University Press, 1994).

As we continue to head forward into the next century, a profound transformation in the practice of architecture is occurring. The incorporation of digital technology into the design process has greatly affected the parameters of spatial development, time, and economics. Digital practice has become the current mode of architectural production in many offices in the profession.

The evolution of digital research has origins in many places around the globe. In the mid-1990s one of the most influential institutions to make a pedagogical shift that incorporated digital technology was Columbia University. Funded by a large grant, Dean Bernard Tschumi and the faculty began to incorporate Silicon Graphics workstations into the studio environment. Utilizing special effects software such as *SoftImage* and *Alias Wavefront,* they introduced a new tool for designing architecture. This had a profound effect in the academic and professional world. Many of the students that emerged from Columbia began to further research ways of incorporating this new technology into their practices. Perhaps one of the most influential groups to emerge from Columbia was the office of ShoP (Sharples, Holden and Pasquarelli) Architects.

ShoP began to realize that practicing digitally relied upon traditional methodologies for executing built work. While the computer was yielding spectacular potential for realizing new spatial languages, a weak translation between digital and analog formulations was occurring. They began a series of investigations into the realm of computer-aided modeling technology. Utilizing rapid prototyping, CNC (computer numeric control) milling, and 3D printing, they began to research a method of extraction that allowed for a more seamless connection between virtual simulation and analog production.

As ShoP's early work explored the realm of digital technology, they also began to see opportunities for restructuring the process by which architecture was being practiced. Optimizing the potential of material, structure, and technology through technique rather than digital imagery, they began to investigate an ideology they labeled *Versioning.* According to Gregg Pasquarelli, "It is a method of rethinking the design process through technology." *Versioning* rethinks the design process in terms of procedure and outcome in ways that common practice, the construction industry, and conventional design

Figure 9-11 Porter House, the twenty-two unit, ten-story residential addition and renovation, New York, NY. Courtesy of Greg Pasquarelli of ShoP Architects/ Sharples Holden Pasquarelli.

methodologies cannot conceive of. This, in turn, has had an equally profound impact on legal practices, insurance liabilities, and design and production partnerships, thereby initiating a restructuring of the traditional relationships of power, responsibility, and accounting in design (1, see References, page 317).

The opportunity to implement this new form of practice emerged in one of their larger commissions to date. The Porter House, a 10-story residential renovation and addition in Manhattan's Meatpacking District, allowed the

firm the opportunity to explore a partnership with developer Jeffery Brown (see Figure 9-11). Becoming simultaneously the client, developer-owner, and marketers, ShoP engaged in a more holistic design process than previously conceived. The $22 million renovation integrates into the fabric of the existing warehouse vernacular, yet distinguishes itself by utilizing a zinc-panel system that extrudes four stories above the existing building.

ShoP's unique approach to design on this project evolved through the restructuring of the architect's role in their relationship with the client and developer. Perhaps the most crucial difference in this restructuring was that ShoP would not be paid until all the apartments were purchased. This risk was a collective effort that the firm was willing to take in order to push design and implement an architecture that they felt was appropriate for the context. This opportunity of being both the architect and client afforded them the ability to explore other issues that they would not have pursued in a traditional client-architect relationship. In particular they were very interested in researching new materials and utilizing a palate that was more luxurious.

As the project evolved, zinc became a material they wanted to select as cladding on the exterior. ShoP began to research the cost of the material; in contacting various distributors domestically they realized it was very expensive. They decided to go to the source where the zinc was being produced in Europe and found it more economical to ship the material to the United States and customize the panels themselves. They felt like this was a great opportunity to continue working on economy of material customization through digital processes.

In producing an efficient scheme for the cladding of the façade, a customization system was produced that encoded the panels for fabrication. This conscious effort to explore construction execution is an area that the firm continues to redefine and refine. They believe that to create a better dialogue with the contractor you must simplify the process when developing complicated systems. "As an architect, all you can do is organize information and lay it out in an intelligent way, so complex things become simple," explains Pasquarelli (2). In creating construction documents that included isometric drawings, the zinc panel cladding system was communicated in a self-explanatory manner (see Figure 9-12). Every project is prototyped at large- or full-scale so that that the firm gains an understanding of how to best communicate with contractors. This builds confidence in the contractor's eyes that the architect is fully invested in the practice of building and therefore will aid in the construction process that many times is left to the contractor to figure out.

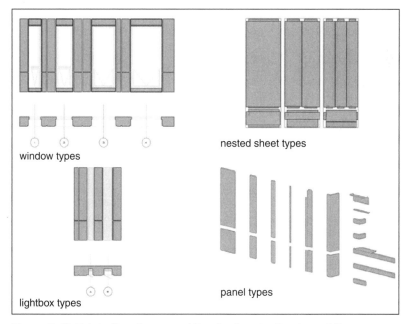

Figure 9-12 Fabrication diagrams of the zinc façade. Courtesy of Greg Pasquarelli of ShoP Architects / Sharples Holden Pasquarelli.

Figure 9-13 Construction progress photos bring the fabrication diagrams to life. Courtesy of Greg Pasquarelli of ShoP Architects / Sharples Holden Pasquarelli.

Communication is essential in the construction phase of a project, and Pasquarelli believes that getting input from contractors and subcontractors is a vital necessity. This interaction is crucial in optimizing a product that is cost effective and efficient in construction. The conventional model of owner, contractor, and architect can be problematic, many times setting up a confrontational dynamic. By creating a feedback loop in their design process, ShoP incorporates strategies for economic and logistical realities. By generating several options for a design, the computer allows them to visualize elements that are quickly analyzed and to formulate options for intelligent decision making. This system has been productive in setting their practice apart from other young architectural firms. As a result, they have received several commissions that, perhaps without this approach, they

would not have been as successful in the competitive New York market.

ShoP is not interested in the ability of the computer to render pixilated imagery, rather, they are more interested in performance analysis through vector application. The emergence of digital visualization has created a greater disconnect between design and fabrication. It really comes down to how you utilize the tool (digital technology) intelligently to create architecture. Pasquarelli encourages all young architects to "get dirty and really understand how something is built." Architectural practice recently has become enamored by image and not willing to really understand how architecture comes together. "We see great potential for the way the digital realm has allowed us to envision our future," explains Pasquarelli. Practice is a constantly evolving condition, and to stay ahead,

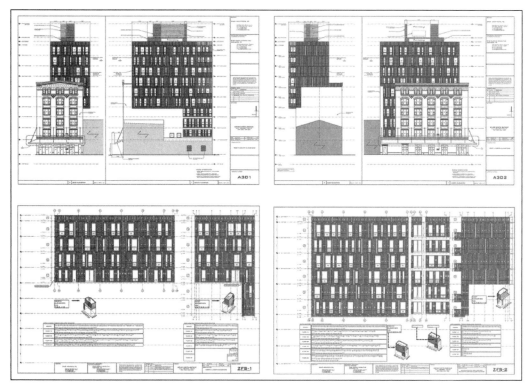

Figure 9-14 Elevation drawings highlighting the placement of the zinc-clad panels on the upper floors. Courtesy of Greg Pasquarelli of ShoP Architects/ Sharples Holden Pasquarelli.

you must be willing to take risks to be creative and financially productive. Many times architects complain that we don't make enough money. Pasquarelli believes that it is a matter of conviction and desire to rethink all aspects of design. The practice of architecture in the future will require architects to become experts beyond design. Gehry Partners has already taken steps in this direction. A recent spin-off company from the firm, Gehry Technologies, is formalizing the process of going from CATIA models to fabrication and providing the necessary training to contractors and fabricators in the use of this technology (3). This type of initiative is where the future of architectural practice will really emerge.

REFERENCES

1. Moss, Sara. "Calculated Risk: Porter House, SHoP Architects, New York City." *Architectural Design* 74: 1 (2004): 16–19.
2. Moss. "Calculated Risk," 16–19.
3. Khemlani, Lachmi. "Technology at Work at Gehry Partners: A Case Study." *Architectural, Engineering, Construction Bytes—Analysis, Research and Reviews of AEC Technologies* (2004), www.aecbytes.com/feature/Gehry_Study.htm.

Chapter 10

Nontraditional Practice

"You're not a real architect unless you've designed and drawn stair details." This old cliché, uttered with a touch of sarcasm by a senior associate on my first day of internship, still makes me twitch involuntarily. I soon discovered that this was an incredibly myopic view of our profession.

Private investigator, comic book illustrator, real estate developer, photographer, advertising executive, virtual reality imager, journalist, professor—this is just a small sampling of careers in which architects or architecturally trained individuals have achieved success. There is no question that nontraditional architectural career tracks are on the rise. It is therefore critical that we examine why this is so and illuminate a broad range of fascinating options that architecture graduates are very much qualified to pursue. Moreover, this trend should, at the very least spur redefinition of some aspects of the required professional practice course and ultimately inspire the genesis of a greater degree of flexibility within architectural curricula.

There are numerous practice settings in which a graduate with an architectural background can establish a special niche (with or without additional formal education or training) that is consistent with his or her goals, talent, experience, and motivation. The discussions and case studies in this chapter depict a number of nontraditional career options that have proven to be quite satisfying to those who have chosen them.

The Maverick Architects: Success in Nontraditional Careers

Several years ago over lunch at Harvard's faculty club in Cambridge, Massachusetts, Bob Douglass was animated in describing his doctoral dissertation on the "Mavericks." At that time, I was aware of the importance of his research and was hopeful it could be disseminated to all those who could be truly inspired by it. I am delighted that Bob agreed to present his findings here.

Bob told me that when he started his study in 1992, nearly *half* the architects in this country were employed "outside" architecture. His point was that the profession must reinvent itself and step back to a broader, more integrated social role. According to Bob, this is happening—this shedding of old skin is typified by the subjects in his study.

What Bob really thinks is important about his investigation is that almost none of the Mavericks had a clue that there was an interesting, creative, remunerative life beyond an architect's design office until they were several (or many) years out of school.

"The schools can never prescribe or prepare students for the serendipitous possibilities of professional life beyond the curriculum," says Bob. "They should, however, at least alert students in the early days of their formal study to the fact that there is a world of opportunity beyond the arbitrary limits of the curriculum, NAAB accreditation, NCARB internships, and so on."

ROBERT DOUGLASS, FAIA, holds a doctorate and master's degree in Design from the Harvard University Graduate School of Design. He was the founder of Robert Douglass Associates, Healthcare Consultants, which was sold to Deloitte & Touche, an international accounting and management consulting firm, in 1988. Prior to establishing his own practice, he was a vice president of CRSS in Houston and an associate professor at the Rice University School of Architecture. He has received numerous honors including the Presidential Silver Medal (awarded by the National Endowment for the Arts), a *Progressive Architecture* Design Award, and other state AIA Awards. (From *"Architectural Education and the Profession," Occasional Paper #2,* CRS Center, Texas A & M University. © 1995.)

I've been an architect for twenty-five years and have functioned in a variety of "maverick" offshoots. Still close enough to the field, I was nominated and elected for Fellowship in the AIA by other architects. But after about twenty-two years, my son reached college age, and I was greatly troubled because I found myself not able to encourage him to become *an architect* in the traditional sense. Allow me to expand. . . .

Although I had a great time in my work life, I did lots of worrying about whether or not what I was doing was architecture, whether or not I was an architect, and should I really be doing this. Should I be designing this dam? Or should I be negotiating this site for this hospital? Or should I be doing a systems analysis of some facility management branch of a university? Then my associates and I found ourselves competing, not with architects, but with accountants and management consultants in this hospital and health care planning field, and competing effectively enough so that some of them wanted to buy *us.* So, that's how my sabbatical to pursue research on the maverick architects was funded. We sold our firm to Deloitte & Touche in 1988, and after a couple of years of managing the transition, I was able to exercise an option to retire at a tender age. My wife and I decided that we could go back to school, and that's how this all started.

I studied a group of about seventy people who were professionally qualified by formal education or professional registration in architecture but who made their livings in other than design office settings, other than governmental architectural bureaus, and other regulatory settings. And they were quite a varied bunch.

I certainly had no background in research, yet I'd spent twenty-five years being paid by clients who thought that was what I was doing for them. I had to start from scratch and figure out what constituted academic research. I pulled my inspiration from the fields of sociology and human development, and under that broad umbrella I looked at the career development of architects who made their living doing something other than what they had envisioned at the outset of their training.

It's important that you know how I selected the people I talked to in this study. It's called a *snowball sample.* The "scientific method" behind the snowball sampling is that you identify an individual who is likely to provide some insight into the issue or question at hand. When you get through talking to him or her, you say, "Who else should I talk to?" And that person then provides you with another name, and so it goes.

I started this snowball by contacting thirty universities around the country, most of which made some kind of response. I asked them if they kept track of their graduates in terms of career directions and physical locations, and whether they could recommend any individuals in nontraditional careers who might be willing to participate in my study. Quite a few responded.

This sample took on very special characteristics because the deans and administrators to whom I talked wanted me to talk to people about whom they were especially proud. So they picked out some shining examples, and I talked to them, and those people referred me to other people with whom they were pleased to be identified. Thus there was a built-in bias for success stories in this sample. (I want to proclaim this right off before somebody else feels compelled to point out a "threat to validity.")

What I found is that people who contributed to this study, through this snowball sampling technique, were a dramatic contrast in satisfaction with the published indications about the dilemma of architecture as a profession today. One of the elder statesmen in the literature who led me into this area was Robert Gutman. I don't know if I dare say he is the foremost student of such things, but he certainly had the most publications on the state of the architecture profession when I was doing my work. And there was a statement in one of his books, *Architectural Practice: A Critical View* (New York: Princeton Architectural Press, 1988) that just sizzled. He wrote, "There are more disillusioned, alienated, disappointed men and women in architecture than in any other major profession." The only thing good about that is he called architecture a "major" profession.

I looked around, however, and I looked at my own life. I had a good life—and I am still having a good life, albeit idiosyncratically—in architecture, after all these different things I've done: management consulting; writing political speeches and legislation; and a partnership in a big-eight accounting firm. Whenever anybody asked me what I did, I said, "I'm an architect." It got so I'd say, "I'm an architect, but. . . . " Nevertheless, I'd start out with the architect idea. And I was always pleased with that mind-set. I thought, "Well, why am I so silly happy when most architects are so unhappy and disillusioned?" I began to consider the situation of those of my colleagues in various consulting fields, and I looked at others in emerging ambiguous fields like program management. There were still others who were involved in some very exotic things like managing race tracks and zoos, and everybody I talked to seemed to be having a good time. They seemed to be making quite a bit of money, comfortable, and happy that they had studied architecture.

With this kind of fuzzy foundation, I started a more formal investigation involving telephone interviews and questionnaires. The questionnaires weighted responses to several questions concerning the nature of the skills the respondents used, along with the skills that the National Council of Architectural Registration Boards used to define the core of traditional architecture practice, the skills on which they base their examinations. Then, in a second part of the interviews, I simply turned on a recorder and said to my subjects: "Tell me everything you are willing to say about your career and your life and what motivated you, what satisfactions you feel, and what you did, would do differently, how you feel about your education, and whatever you want to tell me. Please, let's have a conversation."

Those narratives were recorded with permission and transcribed verbatim, so there were two parts to the methodological set in this project. One was a quantitative part, the way the responses to these different skill sets and value motivation sets were examined through a process called factor analysis. This takes a whole lot of variables, and if there is any logic to follow, reduces them to smaller, more manageable, clumps of variables to which a label can be given, and then these clumps are further collapsed into a smaller set of variables.

What I discovered through this quantitative factor analysis was that there was a definite and strong pattern that emerged from this data without any sort of subjective assessment, without any kind of manipulation on my part. The data went into the hopper, was stirred around by the computer, and out came two cultures. I want to pay homage to Willie Peña because I chose to characterize these two cultures more or less in his words, as "Seekers" and "Solvers."

I could see that some people, by their nature, seemed oriented to seeking. They were reflective, they were intuitive, they were aesthetically oriented. Then there were others who were more task and results oriented.

I started to fill out one of my own questionnaires, and I just got self-conscious and puzzled because I kept thinking, "Do I want to be this kind, or do I want to be that kind?" I couldn't go through the exercise without distrusting myself too much. So, I quit . . . and I must qualify all this by noting that everybody has aspects of "Seeker" and "Solver." I also believe that there is such a clear break between the two poles that the data dramatically suggest that this is a reasonable construct to reflect upon when you consider architectural education. That was the quantitative part of the study, and it raised this question: Is it valid to suggest that there are these two cultures? And that question pointed back toward the essential investigation for an answer.

I used a technique called content analysis to survey the recorded, transcribed narratives to collect the evidence of orientation to this task, this motivation, and to see if the qualitative evidence would support this statistical suggestion. Numbers are often meaningful, but sometimes they are coincidental. That's the difference between the lower order statistical question and the higher order of analytical confirmation based on the content analysis. That's the academic part of it.

What all this has to do with architectural education really became clear after the study was completed. There was a thesis, and it was tested, and it was confirmed. Yes, indeed, there are two cultures, and they do have discrete characteristics. I went back into the interview data and tried to track down what these people felt their education contributed. Since they are not making their living as architects, did they wish they had gone to dental school or business school or something else? What about their architectural education had a pay off? What didn't? And as you can imagine, it was a pretty mixed bag. But again, the patterns reflected these cultural characteristics in a paradoxical way.

The Solvers primarily made their livings in circumstances that had something to do with construction. They might have been financing construction, they might have been real estate developers, construction managers, general contractors, or design-builders. But they all tended to hover around this business of construction and therefore seemed closest to the traditional set of architecture. And those people had the most things to say about architecture. They are the closest to it, and they are the most bitter toward it. In fact, many of them said that the reason that they went into that field, construction management or whatever, was because they were just so fed up with architects and architecture. The traditional ways just didn't deliver value.

On the other hand, the Seekers were the writers, artists, inventors of the group, much more diverse in their employment settings. Many of them were completely out of any association with architecture, building, or the construction industry. And they all said, "I'm an architect; I do experimental video art, but I'm an architect." They were the most removed from the field in their day-to-day activities, yet they felt the most allegiance to it as far as their self-definition.

When I say that they were well paid and that they were happy with their careers, let me give you some sense of dimension. I think the ball park average for, at least, AIA members in the country in the latest report I saw was about $35,000 a year. That's across all architects. The principals average somewhere around $50,000. There was a recent study that the AIA conducted of AIA members in nontraditional employments and those people, the principals within that group, averaged something on the order of $57,000 to $60,000. The average of the group that my snowball sample produced had a mean annual income of $140,000. The age of these people was almost precisely midcareer, between 40 and 45 years old. Women comprised $12^1/_2$ percent of the group, which happens to be, coincidentally, exactly the percentage of women in the AIA's nontraditional membership survey.

So how many of them were driven into these peripheral fields by the recession, the job market, or the difficulty in finding their way into appropriate careers? It turns out that less than 10 percent felt that their difficulties in architecture were due to lawsuits for such things as errors and omissions, or a collapsed job market. Nearly all of them electively chose the direction they took. Why did they make that choice? A substantial percentage, about 20 percent, expressed bitterness toward negative experiences in the design-jury process. That was really the major negative. Running a close second to it was, "Just couldn't make enough money." Running third was something close to, "I became convinced that . . . architectural design was almost trivial." One guy said, "I thought about telling my mother that I had been picking the paneling for the country club, and I just didn't think she would be too proud. Then I got to work on a hospital, and I felt a lot better about that." The same guy said, "I really wasn't happy with the way architecture treated me. And I discovered that by changing my title to consultant, I could do the same work for more money and a lot more respect." So there were stories. . . .

At the other end of this spectrum, I asked all of these people, "When somebody says what do you do, what do you tell them?" A great majority said, "I say I'm an architect." One guy said, "I say I'm a retired architect. That really gets them." I guess it's the idea that people would be shocked that an architect could actually retire.

Factors that represented the skill sets and the values that represented the shaping motives of these careers fell out of the statistical analysis in discrete clusters. The Solvers cluster only included one value and that value was financial gain. The Seekers cluster included only one value and that was creativity. So there it is. It certainly implies a cultural schism.

The Solvers were oriented toward nuts and bolts, environmental technology, issues of access, real estate law. But paradoxically I think on the Seekers side the largest single factor was business. But with it was design, writing, and ethics as a tiny role planted out at the edge of the solar system. Some of the occupations represented were: art and illustration, construction and program management, corporate real estate, design-build, digital photography, environment planning, exhibit design, environmental graphics, facility management, different varieties of facility planning consultants (such as my firm, which did health-care consulting), research labs, fire protection, energy management, materials handling, a surprising number in financial services (a lot of people in mortgage banking and a couple in investment banking), and forensic architecture. There was actually a private eye (that was one of the Seekers)! Other occupations included historic preservation and industrial design; there were several lawyers, a variety of management consultants, and several people in manufacturing. One fellow in manufacturing said, "I never did want to be an architect. I think it's the stupidest profession, and they are the stupidest people in the world. But they were sure fun to go to school with." He had invented a modular system of playground equipment that was manufactured and shipped all over the world. There were a lot of people in marketing, advertising, public relations and other aspects of communications, real estate development, theatrical scenic design, production design, and video animation. I can tell you that architecture is not the only insecure profession. One of the scenic designers I talked to won an Emmy for his soap opera two years ago and went into his boss's office the day after, expecting to be congratulated. Instead he was fired. So, the world isn't fair.

There are a lot of hot new visioning techniques, virtual reality and things associated with that. People are taking the sort of image-making skills that originated in their interest in architecture and are applying them in more dynamic settings such as advertising and television and movies.

I'm really not making a case against people learning to design buildings or to become good architectural technologists. What I am suggesting is that there is quite a bit of evidence that those kinds of skills are only going to be directly useful to something less than half of architectural graduates from now on. There are a flood of talented students coming through schools all

Exhibit 10–1
Implications for Architectural Careers

The "Maverick" careers in the study by Robert Douglass, FAIA, included:

Advertising
Art and Illustration
Construction and Program
  Management
Congressman, Deputy, Mayor
Design-Build
Digital Photography
Editors, Authors, and Critics
Environmental Graphics
Environmental Planning
Executive Search
Exhibit Design
Facility Management
Facility Planning Consultation
  (i.e., industry specializations
  such as health care, research labs,
  fire protection, energy management,
  materials handling, and so on)
Fashion Design
Financial Services*
Forensic Architecture and Investigations
Furniture Design

General Contracting
Historic Preservation
Imagineers
Industrial Light and Magic (Fx)
Law**
Management Consulting*
Manufacturing
Manufacturers' Representation
Marketing, Advertising, Public
  Relations
Photography
Private Investigator
Product Development and
  Marketing* (Nike)
Public Relations
Real Estate Development*
Theatrical, Scenic, and
  Production Design
Rock Tour Manager
Video Animation
Virtual Reality Imaging
Yacht and Cruise Liner Design

*These fields often involve additional degrees such as the MBA, although there are no formal requirements as such.
**Requires additional degree and admission to the Bar.

over the world. But concurrently the global inventory of new space is growing at a much slower rate than it used to, and there is a major conviction that more of what exists ought to be preserved and conserved. Corporations that were oriented to growth are now oriented to downsizing. That is a structural change with which our profession needs to learn to live.

One way we're going to learn to live with it is to look to these maverick architects, look to the example they are setting. What we are accustomed to thinking of as "Architecture: The art and science of building construction" really should, perhaps, be perceived differently, alternatively. The architectural profession should be seen as a source of unique problem-solving skills; architectural sensibility, combined with a humane commitment, should be able to address a broad spectrum of social and commercial and economic problems.

Architects can do this. The reason they can do it is that we are indoctrinated with this wonderful, grandiose impertinence. We learn from our first day in school that we can go into a factory that covers 30 acres and in a few days or weeks figure out a much better way to design it than they have been able to figure out in the last hundred years. That's what we architects believe; that's the faith that drives us. Otherwise how would we be able to go into a hospital or a computer center or some other complex setting and begin to preach, in our naiveté and our energy and our good intentions, to the people who invented the place? Though I am a little tongue-in-cheek here, I'm not kidding about this. *This is something.* This is a view that somehow architectural education allows people to discover in themselves. And some people discover and have it, and others don't. I think that is just one of the facts of life. So one of my recommendations from an educational standpoint is that educators begin to admit that there are going to be Seekers and there are going to be Solvers, and that these people by their nature are going to select different things and use them different ways. People who are supposed to know about such things tell us that a career in the future might be only one of a half dozen sequential careers that our children are going to experience. They might be pretty well trained for the first one or two of those careers, but down the line they are going to have to use their fundamental resources of intelligence and generic knowledge and skills to adapt to challenges that are unknowable right now.

So, if I am an advocate for a particular approach to education, it's for latitude that will permit discovery.

Choosing Multiple Career Paths

The following essay originally appeared in *Architect's Essentials of Professional Development* by Jean Valence (Hoboken, N.J.: John Wiley, 2003)—in "Mavericks and Sole Proprietors" and is reprinted with permission of John Wiley & Sons, Inc.

For mavericks and sole proprietors, implementation is actually the easiest element of the professional development cycle—provided you don't bite off more than you can chew, of course.

Insider Andy Pressman, FAIA: The Cyclone Approach

The implementation process for mavericks and sole proprietors reflects the individual's specific professional goals and unique personality. When architects' passions are unleashed, they can, and do accomplish a great deal. Andy Pressman, FAIA, has chosen multiple career paths within the profession of architecture. He has his own practice; he teaches in the Architecture Program at the University of New Mexico; and he has written five books, including *Architectural Design Portable Handbook: A Guide to Excellent Practices* (New York: McGraw-Hill, 2001) and *Curing the Fountainheadache: How Clients and Their Architects Communicate* (New York: Sterling Publishing, 2005). In the profile here, Pressman interviews himself to share his learning process and to . . . see what it would be like to be featured in one of those advertisement "personality profiles."

What phrase do you repeat too often?

"Everything's a design problem."

Favorite movie?

Joe versus the Volcano. That tropical island is my fantasy: Jewish natives who love Orange Crush and get massaged with dead fish slapped on their backs, drinking coconut milk and eating mangos.

Okay, back to reality. I'd love your perspective on professional development in the realms of teaching, writing, and practice. How do you do this? Better yet, why do you do this?

First and foremost, I'm an architect, and passionate about doing design. I discovered that teaching was incredibly stimulating and that the academic environment provided a venue for the discussion of ideas. It was difficult for me to find time to reflect and think while working exclusively in an office context. Writing presents an extraordinary challenge, with the possibility of failing miserably and making a great fool of myself. But, as the cliché goes, without risk, without failure, there is no growth, professional or otherwise. Writing has become another mode of creative expression, similar to other artistic endeavors, that helps me to discover and communicate meaning in design.

So, basically, you're implementing the "cyclone approach to lifelong learning."

Yes. All these activities are synergistic, inform each other, and infuse my work with excitement, energy, and passion for engaging new architectural challenges or for examining mundane architectural projects in new ways.

Let's get personal. Jean's readers want to know: What's your best suit?

Ermenegildo Zegna. It's mostly the material, but I like the cut.

Briefly describe yourself.

Reluctant sex symbol and sensitive male of the new millennium.

Which computer do you use?

Titanium Mac PowerBook G4.

Which car do you drive?

Titanium Honda Civic hatchback, 1996.

What else contributes to your professional development?

I think that design competitions are one of the most enlightening continuing education strategies, because they offer the freedom and luxury to push the design envelope. At best, a new commission or publicity can be secured; at worst, losing schemes can enhance a marketing portfolio. I'm batting .500. I won an open competition, lost an invited competition. My losing scheme is featured in my latest book, and I pity the fool who did not select it. I also discuss some of my design strategies with students and colleagues and see how it could have maybe evolved. You spend more time on something, it usually gets better.

Favorite ice cream?

Cookies 'n Cream. Here's a professional development and urban design lesson derived from dessert: The higher the Oreo-to-ice-cream ratio (O:IC), the better. Dense clusters of intense-flavored cookie, followed by minimalist vanilla, dramatize the contrast, yielding the most satisfaction. Also, the skillful use of these different materials coalesces in an artful composition that touches all the senses, and the soul.

What motivated you to teach and write?

I'd like to say it was intellectual curiosity, as well as the noble idea to give something back and help students. The real reason was I needed extra cash to augment income from my fledgling young firm. But, amazingly, in spite of myself, I've been extremely fortunate to structure a situation that is sometimes quite satisfying, always difficult, and provocative.

The cyclone approach is adopted by many mavericks, because learning opportunities are everywhere and often coincide with marketing opportunities. The jaws of public committees and boards yawn for design professionals. Slots open up on award juries and convention panels. And in corners, books and magazines pile up, waiting to be explored.

The Implementation Timeline still pertains, however, for individuals who want to balance long-term goals, such as writing a book, with immediate learning opportunities. When in doubt, map it out. Then select one or two long-term professional development initiatives for dedicated pursuit, as you reserve time along the way for unanticipated chances to grow. As Pressman suggests, satisfying plus difficult plus provocative is not a bad learning environment for a design professional.

Pursuing a Career in the Academy

This is such an accurate depiction of the stages—and expectations—of an academic career in architecture that if you don't get an anxiety attack reading it, then a tenure-track position is probably not for you.

STEPHEN D. DENT, AIA, IES, is a partner in Dent & Nordhaus, Architects, AIA, in Albuquerque, New Mexico, specializing in environmentally sensitive designs. The firm has received numerous awards and honors for their work. He is also an associate Professor of Architecture at the University of New Mexico School of Architecture and Planning. He has been teaching design studios, passive environmental controls, and lighting for over twenty years.

Assistant Professor, tenure-track, to teach design studio and an area of specialization in technology, theory, or practice issues. Teaching experience and registration preferred. Terminal degree required. Please send résumé, portfolio of representative design work, letter of intent, and three letters of recommendation to: Chair, Search Committee, School of Architecture, University X.

The above is fairly typical of, though less detailed than, most ads that architecture schools place in their required national searches for new faculty members. In rough numbers, there are about 100 accredited schools of architecture in the United States with about 2,000 full-time faculty members and about 100 open positions per year. There are a much larger number of part-time positions available, but no matter how you look at it, this is a pretty small profession. The few available full-time positions are highly prized and often receive up to several hundred applications from talented aspirants. Those doing the hiring are often amazed at the numbers of eager applicants when we think we are underpaid, underrecognized, and overworked. But when asked why we are still here, one hears comments about the intellectual stimulation, the chance to challenge oneself professionally, the rewards of working with young people who have endless potential and enthusiasm, and the love of the profession of architecture.

The student may see the job of a professor as simply that of a teacher, but the day-to-day responsibilities also include preparation for classes, meeting with and advising students, numerous meetings with other faculty and university committees, and finding time for one's own scholarly pursuits. The evaluation of a professor for tenure (i.e., a guaranteed continuing professorship at the university) is commonly in the sixth year as an assistant professor. It is typically based on two major areas (teaching and scholarship) and two areas of lesser importance (service and personal characteristics). The reality of most tenure reviews, however, is that the area of scholarship, including research, recognized creative works, and scholarly writings, is given much greater importance than the other areas. It is in this area of the tenure evaluation that your particular abilities and talents are shown as having real value relative to a peer group that extends beyond your department to a regional or national comparison. Remember, you will be hired in a national search and the university expects that you will perform at that level. You have undoubtedly heard of "publish or perish." It means that if you intend to pursue an academic career, then you will be expected to develop a recognized expertise and disseminate the results of your design, research, or theoretical explorations for peer evaluation. Accepted review or recognition may be in scholarly journals, books, conference presentations, research reports, design awards, and exhibitions. Additionally, your teaching is expected to be of high quality, you will have contributed to service in your school, the university, and the community, and you are of sound and ethical character. This is just a long and roundabout way of saying that there is more to the job than meets the eye. If you don't have the interest, inclination, or intention to develop skills beyond design studio teaching, then an academic career is an unlikely possibility.

If the real life of a Professor *still* appeals to you, how do you prepare for a career in academia? How do you make a good application when you see an appropriate opening? And how do you get started on the road to a successful career with a unique challenge six years ahead—your tenure review?

Preparation

First, you must acquire the appropriate terminal degree. This means the university will require a Master of Architecture degree for the more "general" positions such as described in the above ad. There are, of course, specialized positions in areas such as history, architectural research, environment and behavior, and structural or mechanical engineering that do not require design studio teaching. In many cases these positions require a PhD or doctorate, depending on university standards for similar subject areas in other departments. In the not-so-distant past, an advanced degree was not required of architecture faculty. Practical experience, especially professional prominence, was essential. Most universities today have taken the position that faculty must have at least the degree that they are offering in their program. Some exceptions are still made for extraordinary talents and special circumstances, but don't count on this.

So you are a great design student, do beautiful drawings, and get high grades. What else is needed in way of preparation? There are usually three additional concerns: teaching experience, practice (licensing is often required), and evidence of ability to teach in another specialized area. You should pursue any and all opportunities to be a teaching assistant while in school as well as part-time teaching positions after completing your degree. You will get much needed experience and find out if this is, indeed, your calling. Sometimes, the best designers aren't the best teachers, so don't be intimidated if this is what you really want to do.

By doing the best possible work you are capable of in school you will be much more likely to get a job with a quality architectural firm. No matter what school you are in—low cost state university or pricey private college—the work you do in design studio and present in your portfolio may be quickly evaluated by the person doing the hiring. When job hunting, the graduate from a more prestigious school may get the first interview, but the better skills and experience are easily recognized through reviewing a well-documented portfolio. (Interestingly, I think this simple fact has helped architecture schools avoid the extreme importance given to "brand name" schools that is evident in most professions.)

A quality firm may be defined in many ways. It may be one that is often recognized in local design award programs, one that has a good reputation among other architects for highly competent professional work, or one that does work that is exciting to you. Experience in the many firms that fit in this category is much more valuable in your professional growth than experience in firms that are complacent and care little about pushing their "edges."

If possible, get some experience in a "name" firm, as they often provide a unique outlook, get important commissions, and are participants in significant design competitions. All of this is a great learning experience and draws attention to your resume. And get your license! You cannot legally call yourself an architect unless you have passed the architectural licensing examination. Teaching architectural design without this validation (however one might question the test's relevance) puts one in a weak position in the academy and with your peers and students.

Perhaps of greatest difficulty and confusion for the aspiring professor is the need to develop an area of specialization. For some this is not an issue as they obtain specialized advanced degrees in history, engineering, psychology, landscape architecture, and so on, but for the future studio critic what are the options? Looking at our studio faculty I see the following specialties: programming, professional practice, beginning design, design applications for computing, energy and lighting, construction, technics, design theory, presentation graphics, urban design, and housing, among others. This additional expertise may come from a specialty in graduate work, by professional practice and employment, or by individual interest and study—or some combination of the above. In any case, having additional skills will greatly expand your employability either in practice or the academy.

Application for Teaching Positions

When you respond to an ad from a particular school you must meet all of the requirements and be on time. Many universities have quite specific procedures and are guided by detailed affirmative action policies. Make sure that you tailor your application to the needs of the school that you apply to. We receive numerous applications that are so general that we are not even sure the applicant has read our ad. For example, if the search is for a teacher of beginning design and you feel you are qualified, address your letter of intent to those issues specific to beginning students, your approach to teaching at that level, and expand your resume and portfolio so that your experience in that area is clear.

A few comments about portfolios are in order at this point. Make sure that for each project shown you state the title, give a succinct project description (especially if it is needed to understand more abstract assignments), where and when completed (which design studio or office and date), and, for professional work or team projects in studio, state your role in the development of the project. Without the above information, it is often difficult to deduce responsibility for work, development of skills over time, or even what the intentions were for the work—all of which is critical for its evaluation. I also suggest that you submit a portfolio that shows your full range of skills as they apply to the position at hand. You may want to include: slides of student work completed under your direction; samples of student assignments or programs you have written; examples of design sketches, concept diagrams, design details, construction drawings, and process sketches, and especially papers, research reports, or other evidence from your academic area of specialization.

The portfolio needn't be overly produced. Generally, the "precious" or overdone portfolios I have seen tend to obscure the work itself or attempt to hide the relative lack of experience of the applicant. Also, the portfolio should not be too long or too short. This is a little harder to define, but put yourself in the reviewers' shoes and think about going through a hundred or more portfolios. Maybe then you'll edit your portfolio to the essential information that conveys your strengths and abilities to best advantage.

Resumes should be clear, concise, and clearly state your experience and responsibilities. Give starting and ending dates (by month) of employment and education. Make it clear if you did or did not receive a degree. Have you completed your licensing exam? Or the internship? One would think that the need for such basic information would be obvious, but after reviewing hundreds of applications, I can tell you that I am often unable to ascertain such essential facts. I truly appreciate a beautiful graphic layout and the effort it took to create, but the information must be there first. (Come to think of it, that's a pretty good way to look at the design work, too.)

Letters of recommendation, when required, should come from people who can truly evaluate your abilities relative to the specific position for which you are applying. General letters are not nearly as effective as letters that address the nature of the advertised position and your capabilities to perform well in it. This also shows that you have talked to the recommender and discussed the position at hand.

Finally, a reminder: the completed package almost always has to be received on time or you application will be disqualified.

Getting Started

Now that you have been offered the position, how do get started on the road to success? As an administrator, maybe I shouldn't give away too much, but as a faculty member I must advise you that before you even start to work there is the critical issue of a contract. You must negotiate as good a deal for yourself as possible at this time. Once you are in the university system there are only two promotions (from Assistant Professor to Associate Professor and from Associate Professor to Professor) and seldom are any significant funds available for merit raises. So, where you start is where you will be for a while in financial terms relative to your fellow faculty members. If you have especially strong skills or experience, or if the school is pursuing you, then use these factors to negotiate from a position of strength. If you have taught for several years and move to another school, make sure you are given this credit in your initial contract. But be aware that your tenure review will come in your sixth year, and the tenure documentation will be required of you in the fall of that year. Therefore, you really only have five years to prepare and if you get credit for previous teaching, you will have even less time at your new school. Somehow that time flies and the numerous responsibilities of professorship will eat up that time like a rapacious Pacman.

The other major issue in the negotiation of a contract is the definition of your duties. You should be totally clear about the number of courses and credit hours that you will be responsible for, the expectations for your service and committee work, and understand fully the school's requirements relative to scholarly and creative work leading to tenure. This "package" must be reasonable and fair for both parties and must be negotiated to the benefit of both. If the expectations of either party are unrealistic, there is trouble ahead.

Once you have signed a contract and settle in your new position, I have several suggestions. First and foremost, be well prepared and thoroughly organized for your classes. I hope you kept notes, outlines, and syllabi from classes that you have taken or taught and don't be shy about requesting them from other faculty, as many will be very helpful. Don't, however, hesitate to incorporate your own ideas on the topic or on class organization or assignments. Remember, you are a *professor*, and it is expected that you have a viewpoint to *profess*.

Next, you should have a mentor. Many schools will assign a senior faculty member as an advisor or mentor to you; if not, you may choose to develop a mentorship relationship on your own. This voice of experience may advise you on everything from departmental politics (never have so many made such ado about so little), to grant writing, teaching evaluations, tenure strategies, and how to manage or control your ever-growing committee responsibilities.

Of most difficulty for the new professor is the need to develop a reasonable level of expertise and a publishing record in his or her specialty in five years. Grants may be difficult to obtain, research funds in architecture are less than plentiful, outside design work may be less available or more mundane in potential than you have been used to, and the time to complete your other tasks at the university is more than you estimated. No matter what the reasons, at the tenure review there is only the bottom line— so get started as early as possible. You must balance your efforts to be a good classroom teacher with your development of your academic specialty. These are the primary areas of evaluation at your tenure review, and you can't ignore one or the other. Your mentor can help you in preparing yourself in both areas. There will be a formal midtenure review in the third year of your contract. It is usually very tough and very useful. Listen, learn, and respond to it with help and advice from your mentor and fellow faculty members.

The last bit of advice I can give may be the most obvious and the most useful. You are there for the students and for the advancement of knowledge. The university expects both; you should demand no less of yourself.

Out of the Swamp, or the Evolution of a Career

I could not imagine a more appropriate, timely, and humorous addition to this chapter than Charles Linn's story of his trek from architect to editor of the top professional journal in the field.

CHARLES D. LINN, FAIA, is Senior Editor of *Architectural Record*. In addition to writing design features and essays, he occasionally pens cartoons and takes photographs for the magazine.

Evolutionary theory teaches that those creatures who can change, or adapt to change, are the most likely to survive. In modern times if a job is driving someone to extinction, changing careers may be the best path to thwarting evolutionary disaster, if the subject can stand it. After finding that I had become nearsighted after eight years of drawing architectural details and that my spine was taking on a permanent curve from being constantly hunched over the boards, I felt I had started evolving into a mole. I wasn't reproducing because I worked a lot of nights. My fingernails were dirtier than an auto mechanic's from spilled india ink, and not only was the mechanic stronger, but also he was better fed than me because he earned more—I still only made $24,000 a year five years after I'd earned my license; I decided it was time to evolve if I was not to perish. I applied for a new job.

Jim McCloskey was editorial director at the publishing company where I hoped to become the editor of a new architectural trade magazine. He picked me up at the airport for the last interview in a Subaru station wagon onto whose dashboard had been glued dozens of toy plastic dinosaurs, all locked in miniature mortal combat.

I don't blame myself for not realizing at the time that the prehistoric Waterloo just behind his steering wheel was sort of a permanent "things-to-do-today" memo, a diorama to remind himself he was taking a trip back to the Stone Age each morning and what would happen when he got there. How could I have known? I really thought this nice thin man, whose teen years on Venice Beach had left his face with deep happy lines, just liked dinosaurs.

McCloskey had a high jolly cartoon voice that sounded as if a Tootsie Roll had lodged in his throat. He used it to pep me up on the way to the restaurant where I would meet Ed, the publisher. I had it sewn up, he said. All I had to do was get through this one interview, and I would be editor of the new magazine, a trade for architects and engineers about lighting for buildings. "About the only way you won't get this job is if you stick a fork in Ed's forehead at lunch," he said, not knowing how vulnerable to suggestion I become when I'm provoked. There, for a second, I just barely felt that tiny spasm I get in my left eyelid when I feel threatened.

Jim had always been evasive about Ed, and I discovered why as soon as we entered the restaurant. The bald, bearded behemoth was threatening on sight and instantly dislikable. His beach-ball-sized rear end enveloped the circular pad on the bar stool, while the buttons of his rayon Hawaiian shirt strained across an equally large belly. At first, I hardly noticed the spikey scales that covered his arms or that Ed's eyes moved independently, allowing one to track a fly while the other watched Jim have a conversation with me. He breathed a few tongues of flame in our direction through a slot between his front teeth wide enough to dispense whole packages of Pez at a go. After a flourish of his clawed hand, his martini glass was instantly refilled by the bartender.

"Hello, I'm Charles," I murmured gingerly, offering a clammy palm. "Yeah," Ed growled in reply with a sarcastic tone I would come to loathe and fear. His tiny blue eyes rolled back into his great big dome of a head, and he shook it slowly from side to side as if to indicate "no." I thought I was in trouble and I was right. My identity was just the first of over thirty consecutive items on which we would disagree during the first half hour of our acquaintance.

I sat down in the middle of a huge horseshoe-shaped banquette, with my back against the wall, as Ed and Jim sat side-by-side in chairs stuck in the aisle across the table from me. As soon as we ordered, Ed started jabbering.

What in the hell do you think some architect could know about publishing? What is this arrogance that makes you think you can be the editor of a magazine? What do you know about architects that I can't learn from a survey? Obviously you know nothing about the lighting industry. I don't like your kind. You're making stupid assumptions. You don't know anything about advertising. I don't agree with that. You're wrong. You're overeducated and have no common sense. I hate that shirt you're wearing. Where can I get one?

Every so often, I managed a sort of "wha-wha-wha" sound between his questions, but he always interrupted me. Jim just watched.

When Ed finally wound down, I was staring in silence at my cioppino. I knew exactly how those fish had felt, getting chopped up into little pieces. Then, God help me, I blurted out,

Well, if you know all the answers to all of those questions and I don't, why do you need me? I didn't fly halfway across the country so you could talk to me like this. You just keep your crummy job, you asshole. You don't know the first thing about architects or architecture. This stupid magazine idea of yours doesn't have a chance the way you're doing it. It's doomed.

I wished with all my might McCloskey hadn't mentioned Ed's forehead, because after I'd smarted off, that "power of suggestion" impulse kicked in. Maybe it was rooted in some ancient, survival-instinct thing; all I know was that I could think of nothing but penetrating that ridge of bone between Ed's eyebrows with the stainless-steel tines of my salad fork. My left eyelid was whirring like a hummingbird's wing now as I started leaning forward, shifting my weight to my feet, my grip on the fork tightening until my knuckles turned yellow. Halfway to my feet, my arm suddenly flew toward Ed's forehead, perfectly duplicating the delivery of the Kansas City Royal's great sidearm-relief pitcher Dan Quisenberry. Damn! Just in the nick of time, Ed suddenly stood and headed for the door. My fork had just missed his forehead. Damn!

It all happened so quickly neither Jim nor Ed noticed I had attempted to murder the obnoxious man. For a second I had another chance, but I shook it off—I knew no defense attorney could prove I was in an insane state of mind while killing him. I bowed deeply at the brilliant green-and-orange beach ball with the palm trees printed over it bouncing toward the door. "So nice to meet you, Ed." He ignored me.

"Jim. Outside," he called over his shoulder. When they were gone, I suddenly noticed how hot the restaurant was. I wanted to smoke a Lucky until it burned my lips and drink something it might ignite, but I settled for simply smoldering. McCloskey was gone for about twenty minutes. When he finally returned, he threw his body into the chair across the table and just stared at me. I stared back for a time before finally summoning up the courage to ask, "Well. How did Ed like me trying to stick that fork into his forehead?"

"He liked it a lot. Said it felt very natural to him. Congratulations. You're our new editor."

I know now that it would have been just as accurate if Jim had said, "Congratulations. You're the newest lumbering member of my prehistoric-reptiles-doing-battle-set," because I found out later he did epoxy a Stone-Age representation of me to his dashboard. He didn't choose a mole, however, but one of the early apes as my icon, which I took as a compliment. But even with superior intelligence and a tiny salad fork, the plasticized early cousin of the orangutan was still clearly inferior to the dinosaur that attacked it: something massive, green and orange, with big rotating eyes, armor, impeccable combat instincts, and Pez falling out of its head on sharp turns.

Years later it came to me that Jim's dashboard was a pretty accurate depiction of what was going on at that company: the process of natural selection was in full swing there. The monkeylike editors, amoeba-minded sales managers, and slimy, arthropodan circulation gurus who came up with perfect adaptations for survival one month were extinct the next. Shortly after my arrival, Jim himself was permanently readapting to Venice Beach. I know his happy-lines never looked happier.

I was dumb not to realize when I accepted the job offer that I wouldn't evolve into an editor by my own efforts. I would evolve because I was forced into daily combat with a big fat dinosaur in a swampy pit of primordial corporate ooze. But I'd have headed right into it anyway, just like the plastic ape on Jim's dashboard did. In the end, we were the same: a couple of primates who needed new jobs. And I did successfully evolve from a mole into an editor. My magazine was extremely successful with readers and advertisers. It won a nice award, and sailed along with the easygoing times of the late 1980s until the construction market teetered on the brink of collapse, when Ed sold my magazine for a huge profit, handed me a pink slip, and threw me back into the evolutionary swamp.

Today I'm still an editor but with a much better magazine. The magazine I started has consumed three more publishers, and the editor who replaced me, and is now on its third generation of owners. Ed sold the rest of his publishing empire, and started over. I hear that his new company, between growls, is evolving.

Case Study | The Urban Design Jazz Ensemble

PROFESSOR MARK C. CHILDS is the author of *Squares: A Public Space Design Guide for Urbanists* (Albuquerque: UNM Press, 2004), *Parking Spaces* (New York: McGraw-Hill, 1999), and numerous articles. He is the creator and coordinator of the Town Design Certificate, and Director of the Design and Planning Assistance Center (DPAC) at the University of New Mexico. DPAC is a service-based learning center that works with communities and nonprofits in the region to improve the built environment. Mark has won awards for teaching, public art, heritage preservation, and poetry. He is a Fulbright Scholar studying public space in Cyprus.

Urbanists—those of us who wish to guide and shape the physical form of cities, neighborhoods, main streets, plaza districts, and other collectively made places—can play multiple roles. Architects, landscape architects, planners, artists, developers, traffic engineers, lawyers, bankers, and city officials all may work as urbanists. Great settlements emerge from the work of many professions.

To play jazz, it is necessary to master an instrument, but one must also learn to collaborate and improvise. To tend an ecosystem, one must understand not only single species but also the complex interactions of species over time. Similarly, to consciously compose the city, an urbanist must attend to the emergent character of towns and districts. A typical small town main street, for example, is not the creation of a single designer, but arises from the interactions of many players over time (Figure 10-1). Thus to revitalize or add to a main street, an urbanist must understand the relationships and assumptions that formed and will continue to shape the place. Why is it difficult to get a loan to refurbish an old main street business? Why does the zoning code require more parking than could possibly be accommodated? How have people revived the Friday evening stroll?

We are almost always playing in the context of previous and ongoing riffs, and even our wildest solos should add to the larger work.

Because the work of urbanists is the shaping of our human habitat, we seek to work not only across professional boundaries but also with the public for the public good. The art of shaping the *polis* is political. It is political not only in the sense of working with city hall but also in shaping the relationship between designers and users, defining the roles of public art, creating financial and physical structures to nurture small local businesses, and in influencing a myriad of other relationships.

Who are the members of this urban design jazz band? What roles do they play? Following is an outline, based on interviews of acclaimed practitioners, of four typical roles—the architect and landscape architect, the planner, the developer, and the public artist. Certainly many others participate. Lawyers, for example, may shape zoning and public policy, write law, structure real estate transactions, and facilitate negotiations to help shape the city. The engineers of the city water works may create works of beauty that teach us about water and provide public space (as did the engineers of the Roman aqueducts). Journalists, storytellers, and poets may tell the stories and myths of the city with an eye to inspiring the physical redesign of the city. Even in replanting my front yard, I may seek to create a coherent street and pleasant sidewalk, add habitat to the hummingbird flyway, or decrease the urban heat island effect. Urbanists seek to improve the built common wealth.

Architect and Landscape Architect as Urbanist

Architects have, at times, conceived of urban design as architecture writ large. Disneyland, master planned communities, and company towns are products of this approach in which the totality is designed by a single hand. Most settlements, however, are the result of many designers working over time. Rome was not built in a day. Working as an architect-urbanist in this complex multiple-designers environment requires a deep understanding of built form design and the values and motivations of other players.

The architect William Morrish founded and ran the applied urban design research center called the Design Center for American Urban Landscape at the University of Minnesota and was a central author of the Urban Design Plan for the Phoenix Public Arts Program. He describes his role as an urbanist:

> River Pilot—charting the course and flows of the political landscape's cultural ecology from its source and throughout its system. This metaphor represents my interest as an architect in how the terms of making architecture for a city are set, "up river" of when we typically get the problem to solve. A river pilot helps others read the changing river mosaic, so that they can navigate their own way in the city and its urban landscape.

The Design Center, for example, provided a "neutral ground" for political bodies to explore ideas on contested urban spaces and issues.

> We used the tools and methods of design to open up the questions, explore optional futures, and then begin the process of framing strategic design, policy, implementation, and finance strategies. We educated

Figure 10-1 The coherence of this street in a small town in southern France is not due to a single designer. Rather the designs of the different builders work together because of a shared set of building methods and conventions, such as building up to the edge of the street, creating two to three story buildings, and construction using a limited set of materials and techniques. Courtesy of Mark C. Childs.

the public and private civic leadership to be better urbanists and gave them the skills to demand great creativity from staff, citizens, professionals, and entrepreneurs. We did not propose defined plans, but frameworks for short-term needs and long-term efforts. (William Morrish)

According to Morrish, skills that are central to success of this role include the ability to:

- Cross disciplinary boundaries and creatively demonstrate common ground, connections, and gaps.
- Understand the depth of your own discipline's contributions to the issue.
- Research and synthesize complex multiprofessional data and terms—to become "multilingual."
- Format complicated issues in accessible language and images.
- Literally "draw out" data into spatial form and structure.
- Develop a wide range of design options.

Artist as Urbanist

Public art can be works of urban design. In concert with other built works, artworks can help create great public places by providing support for activities, giving excuses to play, and creating riddles, stories, and myths that engage people in exploring the sense of place. Public art may be classic sculptural objects or may recast the pavements, walls, street furniture, utility equipment, or signage of our squares and streets.

"Artists have the option to choose the approach which best exploits the gestalt of place. Our process is often protracted, convoluted, and layered, not a cost effective approach for those in the business of urban design, but, one that has been the basis of great cities," claims Buster Simpson, artist and honorary AIA member.

His work includes: "Growing Vine Street" (Seattle, 1997–ongoing) that involves the artistic and ecological redesign of an urban street; development and implementation of urban design concepts for Pike Place Market's Post Alley (1978–81); and the environmental artwork "Host Analog" at the Oregon Convention Center, Portland, Oregon (1991).

> I prefer working in public domains. The complexity of any site is its asset, to build upon, to distill, and to reveal its layers of meaning. Process becomes part and parcel. Site conditions, social and political realities, history, existing phenomena, and ecology are the armature. The challenge is to navigate along the edge between provocateur and pedestrian, art as gift and poetic utility.

Key to much of his work is Simpson's ability to engage other players in the urban design process. "We all need to affect the political and economic system which is creating dysfunctional urban and suburban landscapes. Projects need to be amortized over a much longer time . . . in that way, design will be more sustainable and spiritual. We all need to come to the same table at the same time as the developer and the banker start to envision a project (Buster Simpson)."

Planner as Urbanist

If architects, landscape architects, artists, and engineers are the musicians in the ensemble, urbanist planners are, perhaps, best compared to a combination of band and venue managers. Frequently, planners seek to create a good process for the design of the city by articulating goals, shaping regulations, directing public funds, and facilitating communication between players.

Patrick Doherty, former manager of Seattle's innovative Design Review Program and currently the Economic Development Director for the City of Federal Way, describes the skills critical for this role:

- *The ability to engage a diverse set of players in the process with sincerity and honesty.* That is, the ability to communicate with neighbors of a proposed project about important siting and design issues without coming off as "superior" or "ivory tower," while also being able to communicate with confidence to internationally respected architects and designers on complex issues that often include an undeniable amount of subjectivity. This requires both a vast knowledge of design-speak vocabulary, graphic tools, and urban design principles, as well as a lot of interaction with the public in order to understand how the layperson might view the issues.
- *In-the-trenches work to recognize key issues*—that is, sufficient analysis of the various parties' interests, the site's specific attributes, and the city's environmental/urban design/architectural context.

- *Knowledge and insight about municipal regulatory and financial practices.*
- *Political skill.* Nothing grand can be achieved without availing oneself of the political system—rather than bucking it.

Developer as Urbanist

"A city builder or urbanist assumes responsibility for his own projects *and* the context within which he or she builds," writes Chris Leinberger. New development should work within existing places to "create what I refer to as 'upward spirals' of pedestrian-oriented, mixed-use, multiple-transportation option places. This is opposed to the throw away development ('downward spiral') we practice today to the detriment of tax revenues and our public realm."

This concern for the specific case and its context is evident in Leinberger's twenty-five years of experience consulting on city redevelopment and his prolific and insightful writing about this work. The practice of writing, giving public speeches, teaching, participating in forums, and the like provides a means for urbanists to reflect on their projects, draw out lessons, and discuss theory. These are critical means to conduct what Donald Schön calls *reflective practice,* which is characterized by learning-by-doing, a willingness to reframe problems and see them in broader contexts, and publicly reflecting upon what one did (1983).

Currently, Chris Leinberger is redeveloping downtown Albuquerque: "This has allowed me to put my consulting experience to the test. In essence, I ran out of clients who were willing to try my concepts on the ground. If I wanted to continue my education about how we can best build our metropolitan areas from environmental, social, economic, and fiscal perspectives, I had to do it myself."

He recommends that students wishing to become city builders first ground themselves in a liberal arts degree that teaches one to think and challenge, then to gain business education and experience: "Always want to keep learning and do not automatically accept conventional wisdom. Finally, I would advise they eventually get into the development business directly some day

. . . not just be a consultant. We desperately need progressive developers."

The Drum Line: Underlying Metrics for Urbanists

In addition to the roles outlined above, traffic and civil engineers, lawyers, bankers, city officials, and others may also work as urbanists conscientiously guiding and shaping the physical form of our cities. Key, however, to any of these urbanist roles are:

- *A sense of jazz*—the ability to communicate clearly and act in concert with other players and the underlying context.
- *Deep knowledge of the value and values of one's particular profession*—the ability to represent these to others, and the willingness to engage in politics to balance them with other goals.
- *Engaging in public reflection*—the willingness to discuss and critique one's work with others both during and after a project.
- *Understanding, taking responsibility for, and working to improve the greater context of a project.* In William Morrish's words: "Before you decide what you need, know what you already have. Before you decide what will be, know what might be."

STUDY QUESTIONS

1. Find people in your community who either identify themselves as urbanists (i.e., people who through their professional activities help shape the physical form of cities and regions) or you believe acts as such, and interview them. Questions you might consider include:

   - What have been a few of your greatest successes in helping shape cities? What skills were central to your success?
   - What would you like people, who do not work in your profession but who act as urbanists in other roles, to know or be skilled in?
   - What makes a great city?
   - What is your professional and experiential educational background? What advice would you give to students who wished to work in a manner similar to your own?

- Are there other thoughts or issues you would like to add?

2. Find a place where design work was obviously not coordinated across property boundaries (i.e., a sidewalk that ends in nothing or is not aligned with the next segment of sidewalk; a subdivision that has no access to a regional trail next to it). Discover the planning and zoning regulations that governed the design. If possible, interview the designers, city planners, and others who worked on the project to discover the source of the problem.

3. Choose one of the best blocks of a street or town square and document all the designers (planners, architects, landscape architects, civil engineers, sign designers, lamppost manufacturers, etc. who contributed to the place). If possible, find historic photographs and maps of the place to help describe how the place has evolved.

REFERENCE

Schön, Donald A. *The Reflective Practitioner: How Professionals Think in Action*. London: Temple Smith, 1983.

Case Study | An Unusual Consulting Practice— Dyer + Dyer

What follows is the case study of the firm Dyer + Dyer Architecture/Urban Design, written by the two principals, Gene and Dorothy Dyer.*

Gene Dyer, a native New Mexican (from five generations of New Mexicans), graduated from a five-year architecture program at the University of New Mexico in 1968. He began work for one of the largest firms in the state, Flatow Moore Bryan & Fairburn. After two years, he and a fellow Flatow colleague left the firm and started Dyer/McClernon Architects in 1970. This practice lasted twelve years and was tagged as one of the bright and talented young firms in the state.

By 1978, Gene Dyer decided to take a sabbatical from the firm and go to Harvard's Graduate School of Design (GSD), studying in the Urban Design Program. The newly created program at the GSD was headed by world famous Israeli-Canadian Architect, Moshe Safdie, who moved his main office to Cambridge to take the Harvard position. Gene was ready for a change; he was interested to learn about urban design and large city context. So, soon after his wife Dorothy received her Master of Architecture degree from the University of New Mexico, the family, which included their two teenage daughters, headed for Boston. At thirty-seven, Gene was one of the oldest in his class.

*Courtesy of Dyer & Dyer Architecture/Urban Design.

Dorothy found her first job out of the masters program with Wallace, Floyd, Ellenzweig, Moore, a well-known Cambridge firm in the Boston area. Dorothy worked with the firm for two years on the relocation of the Orange Line Subway in Boston's South End, the largest urban design project in the United States at that time.

After Gene graduated from his design program, the Dyers returned to New Mexico where Gene continued his partnership practice with Dyer/McClernon. The opportunity arose in 1982 to work with Moshe Safdie on a large urban design project, Robina, a new town in Australia. It would require being gone for several years, working in both the Safdie Boston office and in Robina. This opportunity presented a dilemma requiring big decisions. It was not fair to the Albuquerque firm to be gone for so long, yet going with the Safdie urban design project was what Gene's Harvard Education was about. Another dilemma was that Gene was rooted in New Mexico and felt loyalty to his family and state. He knew he did not want to join the Safdie firm permanently, but he was seduced by the work. He would go to Boston if he knew that at the end of the job he could return to New Mexico. Safdie agreed to this arrangement, and a relationship that lasted over twenty-eight years began.

Meanwhile, Dorothy had taken a job as the Urban Designer for the city of Albuquerque, not knowing that the Robina job would become available to Gene. Even with this wonderful op-

Figure 10-2 and Figure 10-3 Views of the Damascus Gate project, Old City of Jerusalem. "No Man's Land" transformed into a vibrant public square. The design was a collaborative effort between Gene Dyer and Moshe Safdie. Drawings courtesy of Dyer + Dyer Architecture/Urban Design.

portunity for Dorothy, she and Gene decided to go to Boston. Gene left his local practice permanently to work on the Robina job with no assurance of projects beyond the one being offered. While Gene worked on the Robina project, Dorothy found a job in Lowell, Massachusetts, to work on a set of projects with a two-year timeline. Dorothy's work was a series of downtown

revitalization projects involving four northeastern Massachusetts towns surrounding Lowell.

Gene and Dorothy contracted at low hourly rates. They made enough money to live comfortably and expose themselves and their daughters to some of the amenities of New England and Boston culture. They also had income from real estate property in New Mexico. Gene worked for a year and a half on the Robina master plan, which became a new city designed around a series of canals—a kind of modern day Venice. The Dyers planned to return to New Mexico at the end of the Robina project, which coincided with the conclusion of Dorothy's Lowell work. However, Gene was offered a one-year fellowship, sponsored by Harvard University, to lead a team of designers to Jerusalem, Israel. The project was the design of the "No Man's Land" at the Damascus Gate, Old City of Jerusalem (see Figures 10-2 and 10-3).

This project was too good to pass up, however, there were drawbacks. The Dyers had two teenage daughters who did not want to go to Jerusalem. One would be a senior in high school who did not want to attend a new school for her senior year, and the other had a serious boyfriend and was refusing to leave. Compromises and promises were made, and they all went to Jerusalem. They discovered early-on that being flexible and not being stuck in one place offered opportunities that they could not get in a regular practice. They also found that working with other architects and firms proved to be very exciting and creative. It allowed them to retain some sense of independence, flexibility, and control of their lives (they began a series of new real estate investments as their retirement plan).

The year in Jerusalem was one of the best for the entire family. The Damascus Gate project won First Honor Award for Urban Design in *Progressive Architecture.* Even the girls were profoundly impressed with living and schooling in Israel. The Dyers loved the flexibility to work with others, to travel and *not* to have the overhead and financial burdens that are required to support a thriving office. It did mean, however, when they were on contracted jobs in Israel or elsewhere, they often worked fifteen- to eighteen-hour days. But there were rewards for working long hours; for example, they would stop off in Paris for a seven-day retreat on their way home when projects were completed.

After the Harvard Jerusalem Fellowship, they returned to Cambridge for Dorothy to complete a master's degree at Harvard, in joint study between the School of Education and the GSD. Gene worked in the Safdie office during this time. After Dorothy's graduation, they de-

cided to return to Albuquerque to continue real estate development on their land. Until then, they both worked for different architects, and contracted separately on jobs. Why not start a firm together, and consolidate expenses and taxes? They established the partnership firm of Dyer + Dyer Architecture/Urban Design.

From 1985 to 1988, the new firm worked with the city of Albuquerque on numerous large-scale urban design projects, while pursuing their own building projects. They also built a small warehouse with their office on the second level, as income property, in the Fairgrounds district of Albuquerque. During this period they turned down jobs that would require them to be out of Albuquerque. They were home to start a partnership firm, work locally, and pursue their retirement plan.

With this phase accomplished, they were free to travel and collaborate again. The Jerusalem/Safdie connection was rekindled, and they soon left for a project in Jerusalem on which Gene would work for almost five years: A new city in Israel—Modiin—located between Tel Aviv and Jerusalem. Dorothy contracted to work with the Rahamimoff Architectural Office, also in Jerusalem, on several urban design plans. These projects would take five years and required living in Jerusalem full-time.

The Dyers worked on these projects until the beginning of the Gulf War, when Israel was being targeted with scud missiles. Gene left Israel to go to Boston to continue the Modiin work. Dorothy returned to Albuquerque to teach the "Jerusalem Studio" with the Israeli architect Arie Rahamimoff at the University of New Mexico. He and Dorothy taught the studio on alternate years for eight years. Gene continued working with the Safdie office as well as the Israeli office of Uri Shetrit.

After the Gulf War, the Dyers returned to Israel where their work continued. Israel, like the United States in the 1990s, had an economy that was booming, and all the Israeli architectural offices were busy. In the mid-1990s they returned home to care for ill and dying parents but maintained ties with the Rahamimoff office, working on the Nazareth Project, in Albuquerque. Every three months they would spend a month in Israel with the project team there. This collaboration continued until the end of 1999, when the Nazareth Old City Plan was complete and was quickly implemented in time for the visit of the Pope to Nazareth during the millennium-year celebration.

Soon after this they returned to work in Boston with the Safdie team. Although they participated on one particular project, Yad Vashem Holocaust Museum and Memorial, the office was receiving many commissions and winning many competitions, and this phase of their collaboration lasted four years. Gene worked as design team leader on many architectural projects, including the Salt Lake City Public Library. The Dyers worked together on the Peace Institute in Washington, D.C., and the Children's Palace in Guangdong, China. Dorothy also collaborated with Moshe Safdie on a book on the building of the new city of Modiin. Dorothy, with her media, writing, and architectural background assisted Safdie in his publication writings, sketchbooks, scrapbooks, and public relations.

As Gene and Dorothy approached their early 60s, they deemed it time to head home to Albuquerque to finish their real estate development retirement plan. They had several pieces of land with old warehouses that were underutilized. Their travels and work had kept them so busy that they had no time since the 1980s to dedicate to their personal plans. In 2003, they came home, supposedly to stay. Only home for seven months, Gene was off to Budapest, Hungary, collaborating again with Uri Shetrit, now Architect and Planning Director for the city of Jerusalem, on a large mixed-use development plan, Dream Island, in the Danube River. Dorothy stayed in Albuquerque and finished teaching the urban design studio at the University of New Mexico that she and Gene had started teaching in the spring semester.

As of this writing, the firm is working on a warehouse conversion to live/work lofts in Albuquerque. Try as they would, the lure of exciting projects and travel just wouldn't bury its head. They wondered if age 65 was too soon to retire to Albuquerque? There is one thing they do know: theirs has been an unusual practice. Both Dyers attribute their practice success to several factors. Their education at Harvard University and the amazing connections made during those years of study. The decision to return to graduate study at Harvard was truly invaluable and the key ingredient in the direction their practice followed. Loving freedom, travel, the excitement of change, the ability to pick up and rearrange their lives, and the benefits of working long hours for long periods of time made this kind of practice especially well-suited to the Dyers. Both partners agree that this kind of work and life would not have been possible if they were not in the same profession and understood what was required to have such a practice.

"Your practice can be whatever you dream, or be wherever it takes you, but it is always good to have roots and a place to come home to," stated the partners. The Dyers say coming home to New Mexico with its incredible landscape, creative people, and diverse culture is every bit as exotic as any place in the world they have worked or lived.

DISCUSSION QUESTIONS

1. Can you claim credit for work done while consulting with other firms or architects?
2. Can this type of consulting practice be successful with a little less abandonment of a local practice or roots? How?
3. How would you build security for your retirement in a consulting practice? How would you deal with benefits such as health and disability insurance?
4. What are the advantages and disadvantages of a practice like the Dyers'?

Case Study | # Unexpected Opportunities of an Urbanist Practice

CHRISTOPHER CALOTT, AIA, is Professor-in-Practice at the University of New Mexico. Committed to forming a practice that fundamentally considers architecture a form of urbanism, CALOTT + GIFFORD Architecture / Urban Design was established in 2000 in

Albuquerque and Santa Fe, New Mexico. In a region rich with urban history, the principals perceived this to be a time and a place where several communities throughout the state were beginning to re-value their urban cores after decades of unplanned growth. As a firm comprised of two relative newcomers to this state, they strategically focused the practice on the provision of urban design and infill urban housing expertise and services that were not being offered by other local professional firms. Fueled by their experiences working in many other cities throughout the United States that were undergoing dramatic downtown revitalization and infill housing booms, CALOTT + GIFFORD envisioned that this trend might naturally take hold in Albuquerque and throughout the state, thus providing an opportunity for their unique talents and urbanist vision. After a series of award-winning local urban design and infill housing projects, the firm positioned itself to financially participate in the development of future award-winning projects and formed the innovative urban design and development entity, Infill Solutions, LLC. The following case study describes the trajectory of CALOTT + GIFFORD from a service-providing architecture and urban design firm to a partner in the design and development process.

A Collaborative Network: Building a Practice from Within the Community

I moved to Albuquerque in 1998 to accept a position as Professor-in-Practice in the School of Architecture at the University of New Mexico. There I met Thomas Gifford, a talented student in one of my graduate urban design studios. Tom was completing his masters degree in architecture and also had an active practice working with a local developer who was building many of Albuquerque's important early infill housing projects. At the University of New Mexico my design studios focused exclusively on infill housing and urban design issues. We worked closely with community and neighborhood groups, non-profit organizations, and local municipality planning staffs. Through this work, my students and I were introduced to a broad range of local and state

planning professionals and planning project opportunities. Recognizing a large market for urban design expertise that was not presently being professionally served in Albuquerque, CALOTT + GIFFORD was strategically formed in 2000 to team, on a consultant basis, with other local planning and architecture firms to provide infill housing feasibility, urban design, and physical planning design services. Though initial consultant contract amounts were small, CALOTT + GIFFORD viewed this early consultant work with other lead firms as a means to keep overhead low, quickly expose our design talent in the community, and to attract more significant urban design and infill housing commissions. This early collaborative professional network, which got CALOTT + GIFFORD started, remains intact today and serves as an important source for some of the most interesting work that we do.

A clear focus on urbanism as an operative design strategy displayed through many of our early consultant work collaborations distinguished our firm in the community and positioned CALOTT + GIFFORD to acquire our own clients. Several nonprofit housing pro-viders, municipalities, and private sector developers throughout the state sought our firm to design projects for them that presented unique urban design challenges. The Catholic Charities of Central New Mexico commissioned us to design a HUD-sponsored affordable senior housing project on a difficult half-block infill site in downtown Albuquerque. Subsequently, the City of Gallup, New Mexico, retained us to demolish and reconfigure four blocks of their downtown to create the design for a new Courthouse Square public space. Private developers in Albuquerque seeking unique new infill housing products for sale, built our designs for a nine-unit condominium courtyard building in a blighted neighborhood, and sixteen contemporary townhouses on the edge of downtown. In Santa Fe, CALOTT + GIFFORD was asked to design the 7.2-acre Plaza Contenta, an affordable mixed-use project with a new plaza conceived as "Santa Fe's second Plaza," (see Figure 10-4) and the 5-acre commercial and residential Village Center at Las Estrellas, which was master-planned with an office park designed by the renowned Mexican architect Ricardo Legorreta.

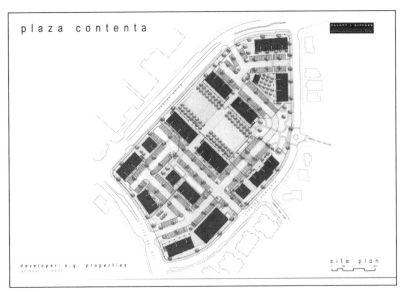

Figure 10–4 Plaza Contenta Master Plan: 7.2-acre infill housing and retail urban design and architecture project in Santa Fe, New Mexico. Courtesy of Christopher Calott, architect.

We were also successful competing in two City of Albuquerque-sponsored housing and urban design competitions along with our continued urban design consulting work with several local planning firms for projects throughout the state. Over the three-year period from the inception of our practice, our firm was recognized by four design awards from the American Planning Association, three from the American Institute of Architects, two from the City of Albuquerque, and one from the Congress of the New Urbanism.

In these early years of the practice, our ability to attract work in our community was primarily a function of three critical factors: (1) decisions to focus only on urban design and infill housing projects, (2) to work collaboratively with other "lead" professional firms as a means to develop a work source network within the community, and in all of our work, (3) to develop a consistent urbanist approach that reflected the roots and urban typologies of our rich region. Though other work opportunities were presented to us, we chose to only select projects, clients, or collaborative situations that would showcase our urban design and infill housing talents. We believed that there was a large unserved market relating to urbanism and infill housing in our community and

that we could benefit in the long-term by developing our firm's experience and portfolio in these areas. Additionally, as a young firm new to the area, we did not harbor hopes of pulling down a big first commission but pursued a collaborative strategy with other well-established local firms on a consultant basis. Specifically, we primarily targeted collaborations with professional planning firms, not architecture firms, who were usually unable to provide housing feasibility, physical, or urban design services but were often responsible for these in their contracts. From these consultant roles, which barely paid our initial bills, we might be retained in a later phase to design a larger housing component or to get referred to another client. Yet foremost as designers, we were interested in investigating an urban response in all of our projects that resonated with the history and climate of this place. To this end, we continuously worked with the fundamental urban typologies of New Mexico, which are variations of the courtyard, compound, and the plaza. In reinterpreting these hallmark regional elements in our urban design and infill housing projects, combined with an emphasis on local landscapes, CALOTT + GIFFORD's work became known for promoting shared communal open spaces and increased residential density within the City. In light of recent development trends that are expanding our cities' peripheries, our work provided a model for city officials, planners, and private developers who maintained local settlement patterns and populations while providing dense infill housing.

Generating Projects on Our Own: The Creation of Infill Solutions, LLC

The genius behind Infill Solutions, LLC, was a young, visionary commercial real estate broker named Jay Rembe who desired to meaningfully participate in downtown Albuquerque's revitalization boom, which started to gain momentum in 2001. From a prominent Albuquerque family, Jay was committed to make a significant and positive difference in his community through the development of high-quality, unique infill residential projects that he would be proud to put his name on. His method was to assemble his team first, and then look for land and projects to develop. He contacted CALOTT + GIFFORD based on our reputation for infill urban housing. In our initial discussions, he offered to identify several possible project sites for development of infill housing, however, he required us to convince him that we could design something on these sites that would work within city zoning constraints and also perform financially based upon his demanding pro formas. We would not get paid unless the project worked and went forward. In most instances, he had already determined requirements for the sites, and we needed to investigate appropriate designs. This back-and-forth proceeded for over a year, before we reviewed countless schemes and potential sites and found our first project, three infill bungalow houses in a downtown neighborhood. Infill Solutions was formed.

Moving forward in 2003, Infill Solutions, LLC, was conceived as an innovative urban design and development partnership between a creative real estate mind and an architecture firm focused on infill urbanism. Infill Solutions' mission statement states that "we are committed to quality infill development projects employing creative architectural and urban design solutions for urban lands throughout the Southwest." Our earliest work focused on land development where we would subdivide an underutilized parcel of land in an existing neighborhood into several lots and then select builders to speculatively build houses. Creatively working within City zoning requirements, these small urban design projects achieved admirable densities, employing New Mexico compound planning configurations with an emphasis on the provision of native landscapes. Infill Solutions was awarded the "Innovation in New Planning Techniques Award" from the American Planning Association in 2004 for a collection of five of these infill compound subdivisions. It soon became apparent that if we were to realize some of our more ambitious plans to build dense infill housing types that had not yet been introduced into the Albuquerque market, Infill Solutions was going to need to build these ourselves. This would greatly increase our risk and financial exposure, but we believed in the future of infill urbanism in downtown Albuquerque. Infill Solutions acquired a large historic building with a vacant half-block lot in downtown Albuquerque as the seed for a larger neighborhood revitalization program. Utilizing funds from a Federal Historic Tax Credit program, we renovated a 16,000 square foot building to house a popular Albuquerque restaurant, as well as Infill Solutions' offices and studio, which received a 2004 "Honor Award" from the American Institute of Architects (see Figure 10-5). We built eighteen new live and work lofts on the adjacent vacant block. We continued to acquire land around these properties and now have two more phases of high-density housing to construct in order to completely transform this neighborhood on the edge of downtown.

The structure of our practice as Infill Solutions is quite seamless with very little talent overlap. Jay finds the development opportunities, conceptualizes what might work from a real estate perspective, and financially handles most aspects of our deals while Tom and I primarily take care of the requisite city entitlements, project design, project consultants, and then oversee delivery of construction. As our practice has progressed and we learn from each other, these boundaries have become blurred. Jay now weighs in heavily on the design process and we critically participate in project selection. Each principal is also actively

Figure 10-5 Infill Solutions offices and studio: tax credit rehabilitation project of an historic building in downtown Albuquerque, New Mexico. Courtesy of Chrisopher Calott, architect.

participating on several nonprofit boards, city- and state-appointed task forces, and local initiative committees as an important means of keeping in touch with the community in which we live and work. Through this community network and the positive recognition we have gained through our completed projects, Infill Solutions is now frequently approached by the city, planning firms, and other potential development partners to participate in new urban infill project opportunities. This has led to new work in Albuquerque, Santa Fe, New Mexico, and Durango, Colorado, and as far away as San Diego, California, and Minneapolis, Minnesota. CALOTT + GIFFORD is still available on a limited basis to take on select housing and urban design commissions that fulfill our mission, but now primarily focus on generating our own projects through Infill Solutions. Collectively, in all that we do, we maintain our mission focus on innovative and quality urban infill projects, our trademark.

Conclusions: The Value of an Architect's Vision

The common wisdom is that the architect's vision creates the value while the developer client reaps all of the financial glory. The Infill Solutions business model combines these two operators into one entity, sharing both the considerable risks and rewards of development. One must develop a serious appetite for risk in this business as every project presents numerous unforeseen challenges. Significantly, all of our projects begin already fully financed from the bank, based solely on the strength of designs that must demonstrate a feasible concept in the marketplace. Therefore, it is architecture that lends value and inspires confidence, enough to spur financing. From a design standpoint, this model empowers architects to exercise much more control in the type and execution of projects designed, as they are owners. CALOTT + GIFFORD has found this formula extremely liberating as we are now in a position to generate our own projects, which conform to our urbanist design philosophies and objectives. Similarly, as partners in Infill Solutions, a healthy, newfound respect for the bottom line in each of our projects has challenged us to become better, more creative designers. CALOTT + GIFFORD started as a traditional fee-for-service architecture firm, but through a commitment to follow our design vision as an urbanist practice was unexpectedly invited to walk in the owner's shoes to create Infill Solutions.

DISCUSSION QUESTIONS

1. What unique talents, vision or expertise might your [future] firm possess or wish to develop?
2. What particular design, planning, or consulting services are not presently being served in your marketplace?
3. Describe a network of individuals, organizations, or professionals in your community that might promote your practice.
4. Conceive a project that your firm would wish to pursue and describe the steps that you would take to achieve this.
5. Identify an unconventional group or "partner" in your community with whom your firm might collaborate, and explain why.

Chapter 11

Social Responsibilities

Almost 40 percent of architecture students surveyed by the Carnegie Foundation (for their report *Building Community: A New Future for Architecture Education and Practice,* 1996) indicated that their primary motive for becoming architects was not salary or prestige but improving communities and the built environment. This drive toward civic activism through the vehicle of design is indeed inspiring. Directing talent to address basic social problems is an enormous challenge. But we must meet that challenge so that we are not practicing, as Paul Goldberger says, in the margins. Architecture must be elevated out of the exclusive, elitist realm of high art and high culture.

As architects, we must also be good citizens, which means *we must take social responsibility.* The report by the Carnegie Foundation referred to above concludes with this poignant statement by a young architecture student: "The larger purpose of architects is not necessarily to become a practitioner and just build but to become part of the community that enriches society." It is up to the profession (i.e., you and me) to create opportunities to plug into meaningful work in what amounts to the disadvantaged public domain.

That architects work in a vacuum of sorts may be part of the reason that we are so ineffectual. Our renaissance will involve making activist alliances in political and policy worlds.

Quality and excellence in our activism cannot be overstated. In general, any notion of quick fixes or impulsive actions is dangerous and must be avoided. Easy answers to complex and long-standing problems are usually bad solutions. The following essays and case studies offer inspiration, guidance, and examples of effective community engagement. How it is that we achieve genuine activism through clear communication and leadership is suggested in plain talk and with real wisdom.

Architects as Leaders

Chet Widom presents us with an inspiring wake-up call in the discussion below. He urges us to assert ourselves collaboratively and politically within the local community. He invites us to take some time to transcend disciplinary applications and bring our expertise and energy toward becoming a presence among our citizenry. Widom reminds us that we can be examples, role-models, facilitators, feathers on the arrow of progress; we can, and we *must,* be leaders. (See the case study later in this chapter, "Transformational Leadership in Architecture Firms," page 368. See also the inspiring book by Ambassador Richard N. Swett, FAIA, *Leadership by Design: Creating an Architecture of Trust* [Atlanta, GA: Greenway Communications, 2005].)

CHESTER A. WIDOM, FAIA, is the founding partner of Widom Wein Cohen, a forty-person Santa Monica, California firm, which specializes in health care, educational, institutional, commercial, and interiors projects. Mr. Widom served as the 1995 national president of the American Institute of Architects.

We are living in the midst of what are arguably the greatest, most concentrated changes in the history of humankind. The late Dr. Jonas Salk, who was a recent public member of the AIA's Board of Directors, spoke about what—from his perspective—was one of the most extraordinary realities of the world in which we find ourselves. He said that for the first time since the Earth was formed, nature has a coequal in deciding the fate of this planet. We are, he continued, increasingly dictating the path of evolution, deciding which species should live and die, and, for that matter, what the survivors should look like.

Whether or not you believe our power is this great, I think we can all agree that a new world is struggling to be born, a world that will be quite different from that into which we were born. Technology, in particular the technology of communication, is reshaping everything from entertainment to medicine, from finance to education. Consider the impact on our profession: the range of new products we specify; the potential use of virtual reality as a design tool; the shifting relationships within the construction industry. As citizens and as professionals our challenge would seem to be nothing less than to reinvent ourselves, almost on a daily basis!

This is a tall order. Not everyone opens their arms to change this profound, to a world in transition, on ground that is constantly shifting under our feet. In a world in which the old road maps no longer lead to predictable destinations, entire societies have lost their way. So have many of our colleagues. Far from being exhilarated by the challenge of reinventing how they learn and how they practice, many architects are frightened. They fear that their clients' appreciation of design is eroding even further. They fear competition from other members of the construction team who are questioning their own traditional roles.

While I understand and appreciate the stomach-churning nature of the changes transforming our society and our profession, the fact that there are few certainties these days should be good news—especially to architects. In fact, I would argue that the very fluidity of our world holds out great opportunity and that our training and talent should give us the opportunity to take a seat at any table where there is serious discussion about how our society should address the challenges of housing, transportation, education, land use, and sustainable design.

The architects we consider to have been the towering leaders during the first half of the twentieth century also faced a massive disruption in the fabric of their societies. They did not cling to traditional roles and design concepts. Whatever we may think of some of the solutions proposed by the then-new modernist movement, those architects deserve our respect and admiration because of the fearless way in which they confronted the changed circumstances. Where others lamented the breakdown of the old order, Wright, Gropius, Corbu, Mies, and other modernists saw clear sailing into a new and better future. Their ambitions, their optimism were of global proportions. They embraced and advocated new technologies, diversity, and new visual imagery. And they did bring about profound change.

I am not suggesting that we pick up the trampled banner of modernism for the sake of the styles associated with the movement. Instead, I would challenge architects to rediscover the modernist vision, which was to approach societal and technical change as an opportunity to enrich, enlighten, and improve the human condition.

Incidentally, where the modernists failed was not so much in their disregard for and disdain of the past, though that was a profound blind spot. They, as well as many of their generation, failed to appreciate how corrosive, how deadly was the *fear* of change. What happened then, and what I see happening now, is why I believe that fear, not change, carries the greatest threat to our profession and to our society.

There are many among us who fear that architects are losing their relevance within society. I believe we have the opportunity to *increase our relevance.* To accomplish this goal, I would suggest that we must become "architects who advocate," and we must produce "architecture that advocates."

Let me begin by addressing the issue of "architects who advocate." While there may have been a time when it was enough to have talent and training, to hang up a shingle, and to market our services, today that is not enough. Today we must come out of our professional closets and become leaders in both the construction industry and the community.

Dr. Sharon Sutton, FAIA, offers an arresting definition of leadership. Her definition rejects any thought of domination. Instead, it speaks of sharing authority and the dynamics that animate the special relationship between leadership and (her word) followership. During a series of focus sessions conducted by the AIA, a variety of clients who participated kept coming back to the same point: They wanted the architect to be a vital part of the leadership team, but they did not see us as the single, all-powerful leader.

In the face of the stresses and strains of a world being radically transformed—a world that cannot tolerate the divisive turf battles and mean-spirited struggles between design and construction professionals any more than we can tolerate the scorch-and-burn tactics that characterize so much of our nation's political life—we must create and embrace a new form of *collaborative leadership.* Many architects already work this way within their own practices: they creatively and appropriately shift the responsibility of both leadership and followership among their partners and their colleagues during various phases of a project. Come to think of it, the information deluge is so intense (and growing!) that, except for the smaller projects, it really is impossible to do the job by ourselves.

The collaborative leadership process is not only applicable to our individual practices, it works equally well in our relationship with our partners in the design/construction industry. As our collective voice, the AIA is developing and nurturing the concept of partnership among the design professionals, the contractors, and all those other entities that are so much a part of what we do today and what we will be doing tomorrow as architects.

Because our record to date has been so dismal, the concept of leadership in the community is even more challenging. We must become advocates within our society. *We must become political animals.* We must drop the reticence many of us feel about getting involved in the political process. It is arrogant to adopt a disengaged posture that suggests we are "above it all."

Yes, involvement has its risks. Yes, involvement takes up precious time. But I would suggest that the risks of not taking the time to become involved are even greater—no one will listen to us, which is another way of saying "you are not relevant."

The only way we can influence our society is to *assume a role as citizen-architects,* that is, as men and women who use their architectural talent and training to enhance the quality of life by engaging the community.

As professionals, we cannot ignore the second part of our responsibility, which is making "*architecture* that advocates." What is "architecture that advocates?" I believe Kevin Roche defined it best when, after receiving the AIA's Gold Medal, he said: Our mission as architects is "*to create a habitat that reflects the aspirations of our democracy.*"

I am suggesting that if we are to be successful leaders, if we are to be what Jonas Salk called "good ancestors for our children," then our design tools and vocabulary will not just include form, space, functional responsibility, and economic viability. *Our vocabulary will include the politics of community.* "Politics" as I use it is nonpartisan. It has little if anything to do with Republican or Democrat, Liberal or Conservative. In its original sense, "politics" is the art or science of community. When we think of community, we inevitably think of architecture, for without architecture, community or civilization is impossible.

The cities of the past we remember from images gained through remaining fragments of architecture. Through paintings and through literature we remember the Acropolis of Athens. We remember the Forum in Rome.

What we do not always remember, or maybe we wish to forget, are the social and human conditions associated with these cities. The slavery of both mind and spirit, the repression and intolerance, the lack of value for human life.

Our cities need not only buildings to house and shelter human beings, not only wonderful visual images, and not only exciting and interesting spaces. In this time of enormous, transformational change, what our communities are in desperate need of is *architecture that advocates the commitment of caring and involved people.*

The profession of architecture can bring success, honor, and respect, but it also carries great responsibilities: Responsibility to set an example in the way we work with clients, the way we work with our partners in the construction industry, and the way we work with the community.

A Situational Team Approach to Mentorship

Thom Lowther presents here a new, innovative strategy to mentorship that has potentially enormous benefits for all parties. There is implicit encouragement for the mentee to assume responsibility for finding appropriate mentorship for professional growth. The following offers one very effective way to take that responsibility.

THOM LOWTHER is the Director of the American Institute of Architects Continuing Education System (CES). Thom leads instruction at numerous CES events throughout the country, including AIA National Conventions.

As an alternate to the traditional mentorship format let me suggest a different approach, a situational approach. Instead of the traditional one-on-one approach, consider an approach that matches the mentee and mentors. Yes, mentors, more than one, a team of mentors. The traditional mentor approach assumes that the mentor has strengths in all vital areas of mentorship, when in truth, they most likely do not. The team approach to mentorship would most effectively match all four levels of Situational Leadership* as first identified by Dr. Ken Blanchard. This team approach would most effectively match the strengths of a mentor to needs of the mentee, and at the most appropriate time within the mentee's development. The basics of Situational Leadership identify four primary leadership styles. As applied to a mentorship role, it would look something like this:

- *M1–Directing:* Mentor defines many of the roles and tasks of the mentee and works with him or her closely. Suggestions, guidance, and instructions are made frequently by the mentor, so communication is largely one-way.
- *M2–Coaching:* Mentor still defines roles and tasks but seeks ideas and suggestions from the mentee. Decisions remain the mentor's prerogative, but communication is much more two-way.
- *M3–Supporting:* Mentor passes basic decisions, such as task allocation and processes, to the mentee. The mentor facilitates and takes part in exchanges and decisions, but control is with the mentee.
- *M4–Delegating:* Mentor is still involved in decisions and problem-solving, but control is with the mentee. The mentee decides when and how the mentor will be involved.

Traditionally, it is assumed that the individual mentor is at least good at all of the roles of mentoring. What is the reaction of the mentee when the mentor, a very experienced individual who is a good supportive manager, but is weak in directive behavior and lacks the desire to oversee fine details of a mentorship project? In such a scenario the mentee is likely to get frustrated with the lack of early, clear direction and not continue with the mentorship process long enough to reach the point where the mentor would be most effective in the supportive stage of the mentee's development.

---

*Situational Leadership is copyrighted by Dr. Ken Blanchard.

Or, the mentor may be very directive and detail oriented. A terrific start for both mentor and mentee! As the relationship progresses, however, and the mentee gains experience and confidence, what is likely to happen if the mentor continues to "micro-manage" the mentee? It is likely the relationship will deteriorate between the mentor and mentee. Frustration will build as the mentor wants to continue to give detailed advice while the mentee will want to expand and demonstrate newly developed skills and abilities.

How do you increase the probable success of both scenarios? First, look at the leadership strengths of the mentors and then the development level of the mentee as indicated in the box below.

D4	High Competence High Commitment	Experienced at the task, and comfortable with his or her own ability to do it well. May even be more skilled than the mentor.
D3	High Competence Variable Commitment	Experienced and capable, but may lack the confidence to go it alone or the motivation to do it well and quickly.
D2	Some Competence Low Commitment	May have some relevant skills, but won't be able to do the task without help. The task or the situation may be new to him or her.
D1	Low Competence Low Commitment	Generally lacking the specific skills required for the task in hand, and lacks any confidence and/or motivation to tackle it.

An individual mentor will be stronger in some mentorship styles than in others. Most mentees are likely to begin at the entry level or D1. Matching the correct mentor style for D1 would be the directive approach or M1 as described in the second example. The first example provided a mismatch where the mentor was at M3, while the mentee was at a D1 developmental level.

What is most important is to correctly match the mentoring level of the mentor and development level of the mentee. When using just one mentor, this may be difficult and in some situations it will be impossible. The alternate approach is to use a situational team or cadre of mentors. These mentors are assigned to the mentee as they progress in their development stages of a task. The advantage of this approach is that mentor "assignments" are designed to work well—with preferable matches.

The Potential of Pro Bono Practice

Pro bono publico means for the good of the public. One of the social responsibilities of an architect is to volunteer to help people or groups who might not otherwise afford architectural services—and really need them—such as organizations that deal with the sick, abused, and poor. Public service can take many forms from working on an individual basis on one particular phase of a project to collaborating with other firms and approaching projects in a comprehensive manner.

It should be clear that the motivation for doing pro bono work is fundamentally noble, and *not* an integral component of a marketing or promotional program. If the exposure and contacts happen to produce leads for future work, that is a *secondary* benefit. If you really don't care about the cause, don't do the work—it will be obvious, the quality of work will suffer, and in the end, nobody will benefit.

In writing about pro bono architecture (*Architecture*, September 1992), Michael Crosbie offers some important caveats. Pro bono projects should be executed with the same reasonable standard of care as any other projects; architects are just as liable for this type of work as for paid work. (The degree of risk increases with the degree of resolution, i.e., less with schematic design, more with construction documents.) Thus Crosbie recommends outlining the scope of services that you intend to perform so that all parties know what to expect.

The message: Keep your eyes open for worthy local projects to which you can contribute your special skills and energy.

JOHN CARY is executive director of Public Architecture, founded and hosted by Peterson Architects in San Francisco. He is also cofounder of *ArchVoices,* a nonprofit organization and think tank focused on emerging professionals and the future of the profession. John earned his Bachelor of Arts in architecture, *summa cum laude,* from the University of Minnesota and his Master of Architecture from the University of California, Berkeley. Visit www.publicarchitecture.org for more information about Public Architecture and www.theonepercent.org for more information about the 1% Solution program. Copyright 2005, John Cary.

Architecture firms and professionals alike regularly field requests to take on projects pro bono. Many of these inquiries come from churches, communities-in-need, and nonprofit organizations that genuinely cannot afford to pay market rates. Unfortunately, very few firms have institutionalized ways to respond to these requests, much less execute the projects at the same level of quality as their regular work.

Pro bono is defined generally as services rendered without the expectation of a fee, or with a significant reduction in fees for groups that could not otherwise afford professional services. While often thought of only as "for free," pro bono is as much about "for the public good." Such work includes the provision of architectural services to needy groups for actual projects leading to construction, and it also includes any activity that engages questions of public policy—service on volunteer boards and commissions, participation in community design charrettes, and advising public policy-making bodies. It can also include speculative work and other forms of research, provided that this work generates public discussion or otherwise engages the public policy realm.

Financial and liability concerns are but two of the most central issues that can make architects hesitant to take on pro bono work. It is important to understand upfront that architecture firms and professionals face significant liability issues, whether or not they are paid. Liability is a challenge that firms and professionals constantly face, but the perceived risk is heightened when work is being done with no promise of generating a fee. For this reason, many firms and professionals choose to limit their pro bono involvement to the early phases of projects, under the assumption that liability increases in the latter, more technical phases of a project. Most professional liability insurance plans cover pro bono work, but it is incumbent on the firm or professionals involved to fully understand their level of exposure as well as their coverage. This exposure can be limited or controlled, at least in part, through a waiver or limitation of liability, provided it is outlined in the contract. Whatever the case, these negotiations should be resolved as early as possible in the process.

For all its challenges, however, pro bono work can be attractive and beneficial from a number of standpoints. In firm settings, it can be used as a tool in the recruitment and retention of staff members; a professional development and mentoring opportunity for junior and senior staff members alike; and a way to gain exposure to new project types and markets. Along these same lines, pro bono work can be appealing to young architects and firms. Depending on the scale of the project, pro bono work—such as feasibility studies or small space renovations—can yield direct client interaction, valuable portfolio material, and even actual built work.

None of this is to say that architecture firms and professionals are not already generous with their time. Unfortunately, the architecture profession as a whole has never encouraged pro bono service as a fundamental obligation of professional standing—or as an integral component of a healthy business model.

Pro bono work is intended to account in part for the increased cost of professional services imposed as a result of the profession's monopoly over those services. If architecture were not a licensed profession, then architectural services would be cheaper and a much greater segment of society could more likely afford architectural services. By saying that professionals have an obligation to provide pro bono services, it is less a function of pure charity and more a result of the professional status itself. This is also why charitable activities like Canstruction and Habitat for Humanity are commendable, but they are not pro bono work. Unless the services provided are truly professional services, they do not contribute to rectifying the economic imbalances caused by the regulatory status of architecture as a licensed profession.

The vast majority of awards, press coverage, and practice resources are geared toward fee-based work. Pro bono work is mostly "catch-as-catch-can," slipped in between paying projects. The primary reason for this laissez-faire position is that there are no formal mechanisms supporting or recognizing public interest work in architecture. Contrast all this with the approach of the legal profession.

The Legal Precedent

For decades, the legal profession has distinguished itself through a systematic approach to pro bono work. Lawyers and law firms generally dedicate a significant portion of their practice to serving people in need and underrepresented segments of society.

While American Bar Association (ABA) guidelines specify 50 hours of carefully defined pro bono service per attorney per year (2.5 percent of the standard 2,080-hour work year), architects have only the vague suggestion of the *AIA Code of Ethics & Professional Conduct:* "Members should render public interest professional services and encourage their employees to render such services." This standard has had no measurable effect on the commitment of AIA members, and for nonmembers it has no effect at all. The same might be said about non-ABA members were it not for state bar associations, which are roughly equivalent to state licensing boards that register architects.

Led in large part by the ABA Center for Pro Bono, many state bar associations are actively exploring a requirement for attorneys to report on their pro bono service. This approach is distinct from mandating pro bono service, like continuing education, for example. In fact, many of the legal profession's most vocal advocates for pro bono service have spoken out against such a mandate. To date, a handful of state bar associations have implemented pro bono reporting requirements, although many others are considering it.

The legal profession's emphasis on pro bono service is supported by a cadre of public interest attorneys, as well as numerous groups that cater to all levels of the profession. The Pro Bono Institute, for example, supports major law firms, in-house corporate legal departments, as well as public interest organizations, providing management advice and strategy. It works most closely with partners and dedicated pro bono managers in private firms; the majority of the latter are full-time, working exclusively on coordinating the firm's pro bono activities. Other groups, such as Power of Attorney and Pro Bono Net, take a bottom-up approach by supporting the efforts of individual attorneys. One common trait is that all maintain a robust and inter-connected web presence.

Our Firm's Experience

Within our own firm, Peterson Architects, we discovered that our appetite for pro bono work was simply greater than what we could carry. As we thought about how to structure our own pro bono practice, we explored the various ways that other architects do so and how the profession as a whole supports this kind of work. That initially humble investigation inspired the establishment of Public Architecture, a nonprofit organization that puts the resources of architecture in the service of the public interest.

Public Architecture acts as a catalyst for public discourse through education, advocacy, and the design of public spaces and amenities. Rather than waiting for clients or funding, we identify and solve practical problems of human interaction in the built environment. Our first three pro bono design projects include an open-space strategy for former light industrial urban areas, design interventions for day-laborer gathering spots, and an initiative to transform single-family residence garages into accessory dwelling units. Each of these is being conceived as a prototype for adoption in other cities across the country, a criterion for every project that Public Architecture undertakes.

The 1% Solution

In an effort to engage other architecture professionals and develop a more pronounced culture of pro bono service within the profession, Public Architecture launched a national campaign called the "1% Solution," challenging architecture firms to contribute a minimum of one percent of their working hours to pro bono service. The 1% Solution focuses on firms rather than individuals in recognition of the fact that the policies and practices of firms are key to the ability and willingness of individual employees to undertake pro bono work.

One percent of the standard 2,080-hour work year equals twenty hours annually, which represents a modest, but not trivial, individual contribution to the public good. If all members of the architecture profession were to contribute twenty hours per year, the aggregate contribution would approach 5,000,000 hours—the equivalent of a 2,500-person firm working full-time for the public good.

Supported by a grant from the National Endowment for the Arts (NEA), the 1% Solution program focuses on commitment, support, and recognition. The goal is to significantly increase both the quantity and quality of architectural services in the public interest. By making public interest work a regular part of architectural practice, the 1% Solution will enhance the profession's engagement with the community, correcting a widely perceived gap between the two. By sharing guidelines and documenting model efforts of public interest practice, the program will increase the effectiveness of architects' contributions society. And by demonstrating the value of architectural services, the 1% Solution will increase popular awareness of design in the built environment.

Learning from the Law

The architecture profession has much to learn from the example and successes of the legal profession in pro bono service. Not all of those lessons will be immediately transferable, but many of the challenges the legal profession has tackled can provide insight into what it would take for architecture to truly engage a broader cross-section of society. Working together to mitigate the liability issues of design professions' engagement in pro bono work, the architecture and legal professions can help ensure a much more equitable distribution of professional services in places that need them most.

Selling Out or Selling Yourself?

There is a subtle but distinct line between "selling out" and appropriate, effective promotion. In other words, there is a "responsible" and "ethical" means of assuming a professional and public posture. This important and often overlooked art is clarified in this direct and humorous piece by Ray Novitske.

RAYMOND NOVITSKE, AIA, Principal of Novitske Architects, is an architect and real estate developer with over twenty years of design and construction documentation experience. His firm is based in Alexandria, Virginia.

"Always be presentable." These words were scrawled into the desk I claimed as home on the first day of the semester. Were these pearls of wisdom handed down by students from generation to generation? More likely I remember them today because they were out of place among the School of Architecture graffiti, which was considered to be some of the best on campus. However, they did force me to think about their meaning. Twenty years later I find the advice relevant to a small architectural firm as it relates to communications and image.

Everyone knows the importance of making a good first impression, since first impressions are difficult to change. A job seeker goes through great pains to be sure a resume is perfect because an employer often forms a first impression from it. A small architectural firm's graphic materials and brochure are very similar to a resume in that they precede the firm. These materials are often the only information the public has on which to form a first opinion. On several occasions, my business card was handed down from client to potential client before I had any personal contact. Decide what impression you want to make, and be sure your graphics and brochure materials clearly convey that image.

In addition to the basic information, my business card graphics had to communicate the fact that I was an architect providing architectural and professional design services, without explicitly stating so. I wanted clients immediately to differentiate me from nonarchitects against whom I was competing, such as contractors, home improvement stores, and self-proclaimed designers.

Business graphics also had to express my design philosophy and to relate to the market segment I was interested in (residential and small-scale commercial projects). My graphics had to make prospective clients feel comfortable and confident about retaining me. Designs that were too standard and constrained would not distinguish me from the masses. Something too avant-garde, on the other hand, would scare clients away.

Layout and style, fonts, and color speak volumes. You can say many different things just by manipulating these graphic elements. I know an architect who designed a firm logo incorporating a big black square with narrow white lettering inside of it. The white lettering looked like the text in 1960s vintage architectural magazines. It gave clients the impression of an old, dated firm, which in fact was the case. However, I doubt that the architect was trying to convey this image. *If you do not have the ability to design your own graphics, swallow your pride and hire a professional to do so.*

Always take the opportunity to present yourself as a designer. The greatest asset an architect has over nonarchitects competing for the same clients is design ability. Make the most of this distinction. I made sure the image projected through graphic design extended to everything sent out of my office. Fax cover sheets, transmittals, brochure pages, invoices, contracts, mailing labels, and even thank-you notes, sketch, and note pads were all coordinated and spoke the same language. Sometimes giving attention to the design of the smallest details that other professions never give a second thought to can help differentiate you from nonarchitects. Take survey notes with a slick-looking, colored clipboard; use a tape measure imprinted with your business graphics; or take notes with a tiny, chic tape recorder.

When visiting an expensive French restaurant, you expect superior service, fine wines, and great cuisine not available at national restaurant chains. If the restaurant's atmosphere resembles that found in the local fast-food place, expectations are not met. Suddenly, the quality of the food, service, and so on are all suspect. In the same way, clients expect architects to be capable of providing design services that other professions are incapable of. Continuously projecting the image of a designer in promotions as well as over the course of a project satisfies these expectations. If a client's expectations are not fulfilled, trust in you may be compromised.

In larger firms, which serve larger clients, a firm's reputation and image are usually already established. Architect selections tend to be based more on qualifications, past performance, or business contacts, and more often than not are made by committees. Smaller firms tend to be more of an unknown to clients. Having not been around as long to establish a solid image or reputation, they have less completed work on which clients can judge them. Usually the smaller the firm, the more important its image is in obtaining work.

On larger projects, the design and construction process is typically controlled by several people or by a committee or department. Clients with smaller projects insist on greater involvement in decision-making. This puts relationships with architects and smaller clients on a more personal level, since they involve fewer people working more closely together. Because of this more personal relationship, architects must be more aware of being presentable to clients. More contact with clients means more chances to reinforce your image, or to destroy it.

Graphics are not the only way to project image. Dress, language, and even the car you drive all send messages to clients. When considering an airline for your next vacation, would you select a large, established company, or a small carrier you never heard of? Clients want to hire the biggest architectural firm they can afford. Bigger is seen as more experienced, more capable, and safer. When I started my practice I took every opportunity to hide the fact that I was a sole proprietor working out of my extra bedroom. Try to convey an image that you are bigger than you are in everything you do. Use a telephone answering service while you are out. In lieu of this, my friend uses an answering machine with his wife's voice to give the impression of more than one person working in his home "office." In client conversations, be careful with your vocabulary. In my client conversations, my *office* was really that extra bedroom, my *staff, bookkeeper,* and *draftspeople* really meant me, and my *morning commute* meant the trip from the bathroom to the kitchen.

However, you are who you are. If you are more of a conservative, low-keyed professional, cultivate that image. If you are a wild, cutting edge individual, cultivate that edge. There are architectural markets for all types. However, do not try to build an image of what you are fundamentally not. Both you and your clients will be in for disappointment when expectations based on those images are not met and reality sets in. Above all, remember that you must maintain your image, so always be presentable!

Building Prose for Building Pros

> I am so frustrated that I have reached the point when I want to hire someone that their portfolio is almost secondary—I want a writing sample! Frequently, I have no idea what my staff is trying to say in reports and memos to clients even though I know the topic. The drawing and design parts are easy compared to the writing part.
> —Award-winning architect Carol Ross Barney

Here is a newsflash: *Architectural designs do not speak for themselves.* Architects can't affect policy or advocate the value of architecture, much less market their services, if they can't communicate well to nonarchitects. In *Building Community: A New Future for Architecture Education and Practice* (The Carnegie Foundation, 1996), Boyer and Mitgang acknowledge that "the ability to speak and write with clarity is *essential* [italics mine] if architects are to assume leadership in the social, political, and economic arenas where key decisions about the built environment are being made." They were disturbed at how undervalued speaking and writing are at many architecture programs—and had attended a class where the instructor gave a five-minute lecture on the difference between its and it's. (For an amusing—and quite educational—book on how to combat sloppy usage and poor punctuation, see the best-selling book, *Eats, Shoots and Leaves* by Lynne Truss [New York: Gotham Books, 2003].)

Excellent communication is a core skill in the professional practice of architecture. Bill Grover, a principal of Centerbrook Architects recently stated that "communication skills are essential to the profession because 90 percent of architecture is convincing people to do things." Jerry Shea's essay below is nothing less than a tour de force on the subject of the written word.

JERRY SHEA, PhD, is an Associate Professor in the Department of English at the University of New Mexico, where he teaches in the field of language and rhetoric (advanced expository writing, grammar, and rhetorical tropes). In 1991 he received the UNM Outstanding Undergraduate Teacher Award. He is a member of the professional writing faculty, and his publications include (coauthor) *Thought to Essay: A Process Approach,* along with various professional and occasional essays. Courtesy of Jerome L. Shea.

When Andy Pressman invited me to do a piece on writing for *Professional Practice 101*, I sent back a very tentative memo. Here are excerpts:

Are we still on for that book chapter you proposed back when? I'm still willing and able; here are some very preliminary ideas, observations, questions.

- "Good writing" covers so much that the term is almost meaningless. If you were in my Classical Rhetorical Tropes course, for example, we'd be beating the drum for chiasmus, anadiplosis, zeugma—all sorts of ornate things. But I'm sure that's not what you're after. I assume you want a sermon (with examples, etc.) celebrating workaday prose which is clear, efficient, and vigorous—the opposite of gobbledegook. Right? Have you any favorite models, favorite writers, incidentally?
- Some virtues off the top of my head: Verb-based prose, cutting out the deadwood; contra clichés (or "clichés will be the death of you"); at ease without being sweaty; sentence variety; diction variety; basically Strunk and White stuff but maybe a bit more sophisticated. Make sense to you?

So much for now. Do you check your e-mail regularly (I keep mine on all day)? Maybe we can arrange to meet soon, anyway.

This is hardly deathless prose (speaking of clichés), though I think it exhibits more relevant virtues than vices. More on that in a moment. The overarching fact to remember is that we see a certain writer addressing a certain reader, Jerry Shea addressing his colleague across campus, Andy Pressman. From that, everything else follows. Although I obviously didn't take great pains with that memo, I think Andy got the picture, the face, the "façade" if you will, of the Jerry Shea that I intended, and there are reasons for that.

Briefly, who is this fellow, Shea? Well in the best light, he's pleasant,[1] open, competent, fairly straightforward (note the lists of practical suggestions). In the worst light, he's a terminally chatty, breezy, somewhat dithery (note the sentence fragments and all the parenthetical asides). I hope the first impression carried the day; had this not been a rushed memo and had I not known that Andy was well disposed toward me to begin with, I'd have taken more pains to see that it did. On the traditional "high/middle/low" range of rhetorical style, I'd have taken pains to jack it up just a bit higher, toward the "middle."

The truth is, how you write becomes the face you present: Virtually all writing strategies flow from that truth. Another truth: In most cases, the best face appears in the middle style, the best amalgam of high and low, the best marriage of extremes, as Aristotle and Goldilocks have pointed out to us. My excerpts veer toward the low end, toward the colloquial, but at least they are not pretentiously periphrastic, not sedulously sesquipedalian—not, in another word, gobbledegook. Frankly, I'd rather look like a bit of a goof than like a stuffed shirt.

But let me put my skills where my mouth is. Here is that longest paragraph rewritten by a Jerry Shea who doesn't know Andy Pressman too well and who, therefore, wants consciously to make a good impression:

> "Good writing" covers so much that the term is almost meaningless. Good writing in a funeral oration follows a far different recipe than does good

---

[1]Pleasant, with a kick. Under cover of giving a helpful illustration ("chiasmus, anadiplosis, zeugma"), I make it clear that I have a black belt in the verbal arts. Sorry, Andy.

writing in a computer manual or good writing in an office memo. So I'm going to assume that you want to emphasize a kind of middle-of-the-road, utilitarian, workaday prose, a prose that is clear, efficient, and vigorous—the opposite of gobbledegook. Am I right? Incidentally, have you any favorite models, favorite writers? An example could give me some important clues.

How's that? I don't want to get bogged down in stylistic minutiae. Had we world enough and time we could discuss the real difference of effect between "have you any" and "do you have any." But we don't, so we won't. Instead, just notice that the writing here is more orthodox, less breezy and colloquial, still as direct and open as good speech but no longer slapdash. I blush to realize one clear improvement: There is less spotlighting of Jerry Shea here and more attention to Andy's project! (Even now I think I would take out the silly "Am I right?") The Jerry Shea that remains is, I hope, less goofy, less scatterbrained, though still trustworthy, loyal, helpful, friendly, courteous, and so forth.

Of course, this is not the only possible revision. Suppose I had written "Good writing for a funeral oration is a different animal than good writing for a computer manual or an office memo." Better or worse? More friendly or more flippant? Dropping the third "good writing" hustles the sentence along better, but have we lost a nice rhythm? I would split the difference, myself: I like the "animal" bit, but I also like the third beat of "good writing." The point (before they have to send tracker dogs into that paragraph to find me) is this: You do have a certain latitude, a certain "wiggle room," when working in that middle style. Practice and your innate good taste will help you find the boundaries.

The following version, by any measure, is out of bounds:

> The multiplicity inherent in such a term as "good writing" is such as to render it devoid of meaning. By way of example, given a certain academic milieu exemplified best, perhaps, by a course such as Classical Rhetorical Tropes, a student would be forgiven in linking "good writing" to terms such as "anadiplosis" and "chiasmus." Other things being equal, a strong suspicion arises that a style such as that is not germane to your needs. To the contrary, it is to be assumed that a high-level functionality is not least among the desiderata. . . .

All right, all right, I'll stop. You get the idea. This is gobbledegook, the "high style" run amok. If on the low end of the scale we have something like transcribed speech, with all the dithering, the meandering, the choppy self-editing, the slang—all the things so well parodied in "valley girl" talk—here we have the opposite: Not someone yammering inanely in our faces but someone droning on in the kind of technobaroque chant that is, alas, all too common in the professions.

So, middle style: Clean, straightforward, focused, vigorous, serious but not solemn, friendly but not flippant. These adjectives, however, represent value judgments, describing what the best style should be but not how one achieves it. Time, then, for some practical advice.

Favor Verb-based Prose

In verb-based prose, strong verbs do the bulk of the work rather than pushing that work off onto nouns and strings of prepositional phrases. Compare "There is a tendency on the part of many architects toward innovation at the expense of savings" with "Many architects tend toward. . . . " The very popular but very weak verb "to be" (i.e., "is") has been replaced by the more specific verb "tend" and the subject phrase "Many architects" is now where it belongs. Incidentally, a real tip-off to noun-based prose is a sentence beginning with "There is," "It is," or the like. (Oops. Notice the verb in that sentence? Would the sentence be stronger as "Noun-based prose often gives itself away by opening with 'There is,' 'It is,' and the like"? Rhetorician, edit thyself!) Try another: "It is evident that one of the traits of successful architects is their ability to form relationships of trust with their clients." How about "Successful architects inspire trust in their clients"? One more example: "One of the outcomes of any successful design process is, at least, a starting point for discussion." How about "A good beginning design will at least start a good discussion between architect and client." (And do you like the balance of "good = good"? You're welcome.) Is "is" always a bad choice? Of course not. Sometimes it's the best choice. But to be aware of how often we rely on it when we shouldn't, and to act on that awareness, is to fight sprawl and to make stronger, more vigorous sentences. Determine what the true subject of the sentence is and, then, what it is truly doing.

Don't Stop There

Take a hard look at your sentences and cut mercilessly, rewording if necessary. "Many architects tend toward innovation at the expense of savings" is an improvement (I hope), but "Many architects favor innovation over economy" cuts out four words, removes a seeming contradiction ("expense of savings"), and gives us the tidier balance of "innovation over economy." Much of what we write, especially at the beginning of sentences, is simply filler, throat-clearing, a desperate tap dance while we try to think. "It is evident that" is a good example of throat-clearing (why point out something that is evident?), so I rooted it out. If such extirpation is just too wrenching for you, perhaps you could compromise with "clearly." Learn to spot these big porous chunks of prose: "Among the many points I wish to make, the first and perhaps most important is . . . "; "The gist of my opponent's argument, if such can even be called an argument, is contained in a few ill-chosen words deep in the third . . . " (Aaargh! It's like the guy ahead of you who is doping off long after the light has turned green!); "What must be remembered in the foregoing discussion. . . . " Is there no place at all for graceful transitional phrases, introductory niceties? Yes, they do have their place. All I'm recommending is that you take a hard look, to separate the often helpful and graceful "consequently" or "in the long run" from pretentious professional harrumphing.

Combine Sentences and Vary Their Length

Look again at the middle style redo from my memo. Notice how the sentences vary—and why I'm glad, now, that I did keep in that quick phrase

"Am I right?" We have, in order, a medium length sentence, a long one, a very long one, a very short one, and at last, two medium ones again. Now: Add some short phrase to the first sentence, combine the last two, and take out "Am I right?" (No, do it yourself; I'll wait.) It begins to drone, doesn't it? We crave small surprises and nothing does that better than a short, strong sentence after the forced march of two or three long ones. Even a so-called "fragment" will do if the tone permits. Which it may. On the other hand, a string of very short and simple sentences will make you sound like Hemingway on a very bad morning. That is where sentence combining comes in, with the bonus that sophisticated combining into complex sentences will make the writer seem equally sophisticated, someone who literally knows how to think. Consider this admittedly simple-minded example: "The soil in your area varies quite a bit. Much of it is clay. We'll have to run tests to see how much weight the soil can bear. That will tell us just what size to make the concrete footings." Now put it all together: "Because the soil in your area varies quite a bit, much of it being clay, we had better run tests to see just how much weight it can support and, therefore, what size concrete footings we should pour." Better?

Write Sentence by Sentence and Listen to Your Meeyah

A "meeyah" is a mythical creature I grew up with whose nature is to whine and complain. Hence, my father would sometimes snap at me, "Don't be such a meeyah!" Years later, I put that meeyah to work for me: He sits on my shoulder and at the end of each sentence I write he chimes in nasally, "What's that mean? How come? I don't get it!" and so forth. An obnoxious little critter, but very helpful. He is, of course, the stand-in for the reader. So, having used the tricks outlined above to clean out your sentences and then to combine them, thus moving things along vigorously and briskly, you now have the time and space to put in important stuff, stuff that you think would be helpful. For example . . . well, precisely! Examples, for one thing, are what I'm talking about, as when (for example) I showed Andy, in the next sentence, what I meant when I said that "good writing" was such a broad term. Exploit what you've just said; help the reader out; listen to your meeyah.

Proofread as if Your Business Depended upon It

To a great extent your business does depend upon it. Correctness is as much a part of the face you present as are vigorous and graceful sentences. Fairly or not, many people will assume that an architect who doesn't take pains with words doesn't take pains with buildings, either. The design firm that trumpets, "Lientoux, Schaque, and Hovell—designing that leaves it's competitors in the dust" is not going to get my business. Proofread. Have someone else proofread. And do not rely on an automatic spelling checker: A sentence like "Your mistaken if you think this project is to costly" will strut right past any electronic sentinel, will walk, whistling, right through most spelling detectors.

A short chapter about anything has to stop somewhere, and that somewhere seems far short of any real help. I have given you just a few writing tips, a few suggestions about what seems to work. As to matters of grammar and correctness, I remind my students that a good and fairly current handbook of writing belongs in any educated person's desk library, right alongside a good dictionary. Some handbooks may differ in certain particulars from things I've said. Some, for example, will advise you never to use sentence fragments. If sentence fragments make you nervous, or if you are not sure of your audience, then by all means write more conservatively. The same goes for the flashier elements of punctuation, like dashes and gymnastic parentheses. To paraphrase Mark Twain, what works for me might be the death of you.

But those are particulars, and you are going to have to figure out for yourself what works for you and what doesn't (including, come to think of it, contractions), what you are comfortable with (including, come to think of it, ending sentences with prepositions). But if your writing is strong, vigorous, direct, and varied; if by whatever means you come across as intelligent and helpful; if you can read over your draft and honestly say, "Yes, I think I could do business with this person"—then you have the skills to keep teaching yourself how to write, and probably to design buildings. You can leave Jerry Shea and Andy Pressman far behind. Good luck.

Meeting the Minimums and Missing the Point

The following essay is an eloquent wake-up call regarding experiencing architecture. Inclusive design—whether codified or not—should be a formative consideration for each project we undertake.

KAREN J. KING is an architectural educator at the University of New Mexico School of Architecture and Planning where she currently teaches a master's studio and an introductory design studio/graphics seminar in the graduate program. She specializes in architectural design, believing that critical thinking leads to built environments that enrich all our lives—and that good design is inclusive, desiring the range of human experience. Prior to teaching at the University of New Mexico and beginning a collaborative practice, Ms. King practiced with design firms in Albuquerque, Phoenix and Austin. She holds a bachelor's degree in Mass Communication from the University of Denver and a Master of Architecture degree from the University of Virginia. This essay is the result of many conversations with fellow architect and access specialist, Rebecca Ingram. © 2005 Karen J. King.

Most architects design from the first person. The ability to use our bodies as a spatial measuring device and our personal experience as a gauge for design is a tremendous asset most architects utilize to full advantage. In general, however, architects don't design for other people except in the abstract. In serving clients, a fluid condition between the personal and the abstract is exceedingly important. We are hired in large part to look at design issues through a professional lens that couples acquired skills with personal experience to focus many complex components. Clients bring their own filters to a project. At their best, they trust us to balance their interests with our ideas of how to generate and express form and experience. But they are not always at their best, often being more concerned with the company's bottom line, the bank, the building as promotional brochure, the path of least resistance through the municipality's plan-check and inspection processes, etc. People tend to be obscured by all this, often being referred to as occupants, end-users, or inhabitants. And while it's important for architects to consider the collective, notably on projects with particular program imperatives (daycare centers for example), we must not lose track of the fact that any collective is made up of a range of individual people.

The fluid condition between personal and abstract must not preclude insight and empiricism, although the state of practice in this country, in this time, seems to. Firms tend to find their niche, establish a design position that establishes a market position that varies little after the first few years of practice. Suddenly the projects are being designed by code books and standards with an ostensibly pleasing wrapper. If the idea that budget + square footage + building code + ASTM + ADA + design guidelines = architecture seems an affront, look around the built environment you live in. How many buildings or places enhance the quality of your life? How many are even memorable? How many are designed to elevate the human condition?

Yet rate of return on investments can be balanced with architecture designed for people. It requires integrated thinking about the multitude of design issues in any given project and the development of insight, particularly around issues like accessibility. For reasons as varied as the approaches to practice and the humans involved, this is rarely the case. More than ten years have passed since the passage of the Americans with Disabilities Act, and many practices still don't make any attempt to grasp the principles illustrated by the diagrams in ANSI and ADAAG. In fact many firms grab the diagrams, choose the finishes and hardware, and call it designed. Designing in this manner invites disaster. These diagrams are intended to clarify spatial requirements and convey the ways in which many people who use assistive devices maneuver in certain settings. They are typically drawn to the minimum requirement. So when a firm chooses the method, diagram as design, it's comparable to a contractor entering a contract with no contingency fee in the numbers. Designing to the absolute minimums leaves no margin for error—and when was the last time anyone experienced an errorless project. CYA concerns alone should dictate the inclusion of a dimensional allowance, especially in the early stages of the project. Time may be money, but it's cheaper to get it right the first time.

Still other architects apply accessibility like a Band-Aid. They design the entire project, and then tack on ramps for wheelchair users (who are often identified in the architect's mind as the only people with disabilities). This approach is taken by some exceptional designers, sometimes with good intention and sometimes with an exhaustive number of hours of resistance to the requirements. Because people with disabilities do not have a common physical trait (they don't all use wheelchairs, are not all the same age, cross all ethnic and gender lines, and sometimes their disabilities have no readily apparent physical appearance), many architects (also being human) remain earnestly convinced that excluding what they believe are just a few individuals from their projects is not discrimination. But the law says it is, empiricism would reveal it to be so, and insight would disclose that demographics do not make for inclusive design. Inclusive design is both a matter of attitude and inches.

The key is a return to designing for people—all people, not just the "special" ones. Start with the idea that while we do not change our minds or our attitudes easily, our physical reality is in a constant state of change. When was the last time you as an architect, or your firm thought about the physical mechanics of human beings? How does the human hand work; what does the human gait tell us about the proportion of stairs; how does our physical envelope know hot vs. cold, damp vs. dry, comfort; how do legs work, short, tall, strong, weak, prosthetic, wheels? What changes as we age? When was the last time you thought about more than what can be seen? The practice of architecture must return to these questions, which are fundamental to why we do what we do. It must not only recognize but embrace the human condition.

This approach is called universal design and some very fine architects practice this way, whether they name it or not. It's an active approach to designing for people across lifetimes of experience and physical change. Sometimes it's confused with accessibility, which it is not. Scoping for accessibility relies on segregating people into identifiable groups, which are then translated into abstract percentages. Universal design doesn't seek to categorize people but to place individuals in the context of the full range of human experience. A rigorous understanding of how our physical vessels actually operate offers design opportunities beyond a human proportioning system based on one man (usually the architect). It's not about people with disabilities, although it aspires to include as many as possible in all their variation; it's not about people without disabilities, although it aspires to include as many as possible in all their variation. Universal design is not one size fits all, but designing for the continuum we are all a part of.

Practicing architects have the measuring device, they have the gauge, but most need to develop the necessary insight. A universal approach to design makes possible communities because it eliminates the attitudinal and physical barriers to participation. This can only happen, however, when human experience is design's object and not when architects meet the minimums and miss the point.

Case Study | Transformational Leadership in Architecture Firms

JACQUELINE N. HOOD, PhD, is a Professor of Organizational Behavior and Organizational Development at the University of New Mexico. She received her PhD from the University of Colorado at Boulder. Professor Hood has written numerous articles for management, entrepreneurship, and psychology journals. Her research interests include leadership, diversity in organizations, organizational culture, and business ethics. Professor Hood consults for profit and nonprofit organizations on team building, organizational development, conflict management, and enhancing communication effectiveness. Professor Hood previously held positions as Associate Dean at the Anderson Schools of Management and as Chair of the Department of Organizational Studies.

Background

Architects are varied in terms of their motivations, interests, and personal histories. The route by which an individual arrives at a career in architecture ranges from an interest in art and design to an interest in business and marketing. Architectural firms also differ in many ways, including their size, focus, and structure. Given this diversity in individuals and organizations, one would suspect that leadership styles must also vary according to the individual and the situation. However, successful leaders in architectural firms, especially larger firms, have much in common with successful leaders in other fields. They focus their attention on the needs of clients and employees and work to integrate those needs with the needs of the organization.

Leadership is a topic that has long been studied in the academic business literature and is a significant topic for the popular business press. Although there are numerous leadership theories, one perspective seems to provide a promising focus for architectural firms. This is known as transformational leadership, or leadership in which leaders arouse interest in others to view their work from new standpoints, produce awareness in others of the mission and vision of the group or organization, develop potential in colleagues, and motivate others to look beyond their individual interests to those that will benefit the group (Bass & Avolio, 1994). In architectural firms, individual skill level and competence is critical to organizational success, creativity is valued, and challenge is an expected part of the job. Professional architects have a great deal of choice in terms of which organization they might choose in comparison to many other workers in the job market. They will tend to choose those organizations that fit with their individual philosophy of architecture and can opt to work for managers that foster growth and positive interpersonal relationships.

Burns (1978) proposed that the leadership process occurs as either transactional or transformational. Transactional leadership is based on bureaucratic authority and legitimate power in the organization. Transactional leaders emphasize task assignments, work standards, and employee compliance. These leaders rely on rewards and punishment to influence employee performance. Transactional leaders are grounded in a world view of self-interest (Bass & Steidlmeier, 1999). Transformational leadership, on the other hand, is a process that motivates followers by appealing to higher ideals and moral values. Transformational leaders are able to define and articulate a vision for the group or organization and then inspire followers to carry it out.

Four dimensions to transformational leadership are often cited. The first is *charisma* or *idealized influence*. A charismatic leader provides a vision, instills pride in the follower, increases optimism, and gains respect and trust through his/her actions (Bass, 1985; Bass & Avolio, 1990). Followers' identify with the charismatic leaders characteristics and their objectives and attempt to emulate the leader. The second dimension of transformational leadership is *inspiration* or the capacity of the leader to act as a model for subordinates. The inspirational leader uses symbols and images to focus efforts (Bass, 1985). A third dimension is *individual consideration*. The considerate leader is part coach and mentor, provides continuous feedback, and links the individual's current needs to the organization's mission (Bass, 1985; Bass & Avolio, 1990). The fourth dimension of transformational leadership is *intellectual stimulation*. The intellectually stimulating leader provides followers with a flow of challenging new ideas that stimulate rethinking of old ways of doing things (Bass, 1985). This dimension of transformational leadership arouses recognition of their beliefs and values in colleagues.

Transformational leaders seek to stimulate interest in others to look at their work in new ways, generate awareness of the vision and mission of the organization, help others develop their abilities and reach their potential, and motivate others to see beyond their own self-interests to the interests of the group and organization. Transformational leaders are role models for others in the organization. They have referent power with others and are trusted, respected, and valued. Transformational leaders kindle team spirit in those around them. These leaders view the self as connected—to friends, family, co-workers, and community (Bass & Steidlmeier, 1999). They are grounded in a conceptual framework of individuals within community, which includes related social norms and cultural beliefs.

Most leaders have available a full range of leadership behaviors, including both transactional and transformational behaviors. Transformational leaders, however, use more of the transformational behaviors than the transactional in working with others. In contrast, transactional leaders tend to use transactional behaviors more frequently than transformational due to attitudes, values, and beliefs more in line with transactional leadership.

Given the difficulty of finding and keeping good architects (O'Connor, 2000), many firms are paying attention to factors related to employee satisfaction. Relationship with the manager is a key variable for keeping employees with an organization. Leadership style directly impacts employee satisfaction and their intent to stay with the firm. This is particularly important for architectural firms that manage a highly skilled professional workforce. The case below provides an example of the beliefs, values, and attitudes of the leaders of one major architectural firm in the southwestern United States.

Leadership at Dekker/Perich/Sabatini

Dekker/Perich/Sabatini, Ltd., is a large architectural firm located in Albuquerque, New Mexico. The firm has been in existence since 1959 and was founded by Art Dekker, one of the principal's fathers. Dekker/Perich/Sabatini notes on their website that they provide "comprehensive architecture, interiors, planning, landscape architecture, and structural engineering services to a variety of public and private clients." The firm has completed almost 3,000 projects during its history valued at over $1 billion and has received more than seventy-five design awards. The firm employs a staff of over 175 people, 78 licensed professionals, 45 of whom are registered architects, in three locations, including Albuquerque, New Mexico, Las Vegas, Nevada, and Amarillo, Texas.

The original firm of A.W. Dekker Architect & Engineer was started by Dale Dekker's father. Steve Perich joined the firm in 1987 when the organization employed 10 people. A downturn in the economy decreased the employee base over the next year to seven individuals. In 1989, Steve asked to become a partner and Dale agreed to a 25 percent ownership in the firm with an option to buy up to 50 percent ownership. Steve took that option in 1990 and they became equal partners. The firm had steady growth over the next eight years. Before joining Dekker/Perich in 1998, Bill Sabatini was an equal partner with Jess Holmes in Holmes Sabatini Associates, which had locations in Las Vegas, Nevada and Albuquerque, New Mexico. When Bill joined Dekker/Perich/Sabatini, he brought an additional twenty people from Albuquerque to the firm whose employees at the time numbered fifty-five. In 2001, the firm bought the Holmes Sabatini Associates office in Las Vegas, Nevada from Jess Holmes. The Amarillo, Texas office currently employs four individuals.

Dekker/Perich/Sabatini has achieved an annual growth rate in revenue approximating 25 percent per year since 1989. Last year's revenue was $24.8 million with net revenue that is better than the national average. Dekker/Perich/Sabatini has been ranked among the top 100 fastest-growing design and engineering consulting firms in the United States for four of the past five years (ZweigWhite Financial Performance Survey, 2004). The rankings are made by calculating a firm's dollar growth and percentage growth over a three year time span.

The firm is structured as a Subchapter S Corporation with eleven principals or shareholders. The Board consists of Steve Perich (President), Bill Sabatini (Secretary), Dale Dekker (Treasurer), and two other rotating Board members chosen from the principals. The other eight principals are listed as Vice-Presidents of the organization. The firm intends to add three more shareholders this year that will come from the current group of Associates. An associate is an individual who has been promoted within the firm to that position due to high levels of performance. Associates are in line to become principals.

Design is a key element to the success of Dekker/Perich/Sabatini. As Steve Perich stated, "The leadership here supports better design and constantly trying to do better design than we did five years ago." Bill Sabatini believes that the real challenge is to live by your value system and to not compromise your values for the sake of expediency or financial gain. As the box below indicates, design excellence and responsibility to the environment and context are key elements in the philosophy of the firm.

A SEARCH FOR DESIGN EXCELLENCE

Responds to Function: solving the problem logically, analytically, without preconception; and arranging space and building elements to promote use through clarity of organization.

Responds to the Environment: siting, orientation, and fenestration that mitigate or take advantage of the sun, the wind, and views.

Responds to Context:
appropriate to the culture, the People.
appropriate to the site and its surround, the Place.
appropriate for when it is built, the Time.

Relates Interior and Exterior Space: functionally, visually and by introducing natural light.

Is Simple: strong concepts supported by all elements, with simplicity of organization, circulation and form, as well as the restrained use of materials.

Provides High Standards of Building Technology: thoroughly detailed, high craftsmanship, simplified and integrated systems that seek the most for the budget and schedule.

Has spirit: unique, truthful, and uplifting.

An orientation towards people is also evident in the statements made by the principals, including both clients and employees. On the website, it is noted that "We focus on people—providing our clients the best design and function and our employees the best working environment." As Bill Sabatini said,

To run a successful architectural practice, you have to first know that it is a business, it's not just about doing cool buildings, it's about making money and doing it in such a way that you can sustain yourself as a business. And that's why this business we're in today is very successful. We pay attention to all the things we need to. You do good design and that's an important part of it, but we take care of business, too, we take care of finances, we take care of the money, we take care of the employees and the people. We treat them right so that we've been able to grow and I think we've been very successful because people like to work for us and we do the kind of work we want to do, the kind of work people like to do. They are challenged by the work and fulfilled as an architect or designer with the type of work we do. We deal with very interesting projects and very interesting people.

A comment by Dale Dekker provides further emphasis for the focus on people:

One of the reasons that this partnership works is that we respect each other and the people that work at this firm. We've all got egos, but we appreciate each other's talents for what they are and the diversity of those talents as they relate to the various facets of our practice, be it design, management, or marketing. We realize that it's not just the individual that creates the final end product; it is a team of people that works under the leadership of one of our principals or associates. For most leaders to be called a leader, they have to respect other people for who they are, what they do, and what they believe in. You might not agree with them, but you respect them. That's why this firm is as successful as it is. We do believe it's about people and we strive to include them in creating good solutions for our client's needs.

The leadership at Dekker/Perich/Sabatini has an emphasis on caring about the people. But how is this maintained and transmitted in this large architectural organization? According to Steve Perich:

> We have a principals meeting every month. We have associates and principals meetings every month. I make the day-to-day decisions, but I don't make the big financial, structural decisions without consulting everybody. We don't have formal votes. We pretty much go around the table and ask "is everybody comfortable with this?" If not, they tell us why and we change courses or tweak what we are going to do. We also do an annual retreat with the partners and about every third year we do [a retreat] with principals and associates. We have one formal Board meeting and all the principals are there.

Effective leadership involves developing trust with employees. Comments made by Bill Sabatini emphasize this point:

> You can't lead if you're not honest and people don't trust you . . . you can't. So you don't lie to people, you don't blow smoke; you don't always tell them what they want to hear. People won't follow someone that they don't trust. Trust is a big thing. . . . "He's not going to sell me out, he's not going to step on me to get above me," that kind of stuff. Those are the kind of behaviors that I talked about earlier that we don't tolerate here. We don't see that here. We try to put ourselves in others' places, we've been in others' places, we remember.

Architectural firms, such as Dekker/Perich/Sabatini are generally created as partnerships, which involve collaborative or distributed leadership. Highly skilled professionals in this firm want a say in the strategic direction of the organization as well as in the day-to-day operations. At Dekker/Perich/Sabatini, interacting and collaborating are seen as a key to the success of the firm. Steve Perich describes this collaborative leadership style:

> I solicit the opinion of all partners, primarily because it is collaborative. We don't just dictate it all. The three of us still control over 50 percent of the stock. So, everybody pretty much intuitively knows that what Dale, Steve, and Bill say is going to happen, is going to happen, but again we don't want to ram it down their throats. We try to make them understand where we're coming from because they're all bright people, too, which is why we made them partners, and we'd be stupid not to take advantage of it.

Bill Sabatini adds to this by noting:

> It's a collaborative leadership. We believe everyone has their strengths and everyone has their weaknesses. The collaborative team is how you make up for that. That is how this firm is organized. It is a very liberating and empowering attitude for our people. Because those people don't feel they have to know and do everything. You have a place in our workplace based on your strengths . . . we help people dwell on their strengths.

Ultimately, success for Dekker/Perich/Sabatini resides in growing the business through managing relationships with clients and employees. As Bill Sabatini states:

> Our success is driven by our ability to maintain and create relationships. Relationships with our people, relationships with our current clients, relationships with potential clients, relationships with allied professionals or industries or businesses. The firm has been able to grow as rapidly as it has in the last six years because of those relationships. And what we try to do is maintain those relationships; that's where our business grows.

What does the future hold for architecture? Dale Dekker predicted that architectural firms will have a greater influence on the quality of life in their communities and that the nature of the business of architecture is poised to change.

We're strategically positioned as a profession to have a major impact on the quality of life of our communities, the workforce and we do that through our projects, our community involvement, our creativity and we do that because we can visualize things as we want them to be not as they are and that is a characteristic in our business that is sorely needed. Our profession will be more of a leader in the future than in the past. Architects have greater impact and responsibility now than we used to have as master builders.

Furthermore:

We're in the real estate development business; we're in the land development business. Architects can apply their creativity and vision to real estate development to be the primary thought leader. There are a few pioneers now, but we will see a lot more of this. We'll be in demand as visionaries and designers but also to organize the process and break down complex processes into manageable pieces of work to get things done. We'll be in demand to participate more in the community.

Clearly, at Dekker/Perich/Sabatini, teamwork and distributed leadership is emphasized. The future of our communities could be well served by focusing on leadership that is collaborative and visionary. Given the nature of the profession of architecture and the distributed leadership styles exhibited by firms, such as Dekker/Perich/Sabatini, architects are poised to have significant impacts on the future of their

communities. As Steve Perich notes in discussing the future:

As the architect you are historically the one that manages the team. And I don't see that changing. I think we are well equipped to do that. We are trained to be generalists, to be problem solvers—that's what we learn in school whether we realize it or not is to solve problems.

DISCUSSION QUESTIONS

1. What are the features of leadership exhibited at Dekker/Perich/Sabatini?
2. What are the key aspects for effective in leadership in architectural firms in the future? Why?
3. If you were leading Dekker/Perich/Sabatini, what recommendations for improvement in leadership would you suggest?

REFERENCES

1. Bass, B. M. *Leadership and Performance Beyond Expectations.* New York: Free Press, 1985.
2. Bass, B. M., and B. J. Avolio. "The Implications of Transactional and Transformational Leadership for Individual, Team, and Organizational Development." Research in *Organizational Change and Development.* 4, 231–272, 1990.
3. Bass, B. M., and P. Steidlmeier. "Ethics, Character, and Authentic Transformational Leadership Behavior." *Leadership Quarterly.* 10 (2), 181–218, 1999.
4. Burns, J. M. *Leadership.* New York: Harper & Row, 1978.
5. O'Connor, M. *Architecture.* 89 (10), 60–65, 2000.
6. ZweigWhite Financial Performance Survey. "2004–2005 Small Firm Survey of A/E/P & Environmental Consulting Firms," 2004.

Case Study | Green Against the Grain

Why is a case study of an environmentally sensitive office/warehouse building included in the chapter on social responsibility in a book on professional practice? Because it goes to the heart of our social and environmental responsibilities as professionals. One

of the challenges that architects face is how to convince clients that excellent (or even good) performance at low cost should be a priority and an integral part of the design process from a project's inception. This case demonstrates how innovative "sustainable" design strategies—with low initial costs—can be applied to mainstream building design (i.e., those projects not limited to patrons with huge budgets).

STEPHEN D. DENT, AIA, IES, is a partner in Dent & Nordhaus, Architects, AIA, in Albuquerque, specializing in environmentally sensitive designs. The firm has received numerous awards and honors for their work. He is also an associate professor of architecture at the University of New Mexico School of Architecture and Planning. He has been teaching design studios, passive environmental controls, and lighting for over twenty years. © Stephen D. Dent.

Can an attractive, environmentally sensitive, highly energy efficient building be built at low cost? Yes! This case study explores the design and development process that led to the successful completion of the Keystone Building in Santa Fe, New Mexico in 2003.

Project Initiation

A development group was formed in 2001 to pursue the building of an office/warehouse in Santa Fe on a site purchased by the group. The leaders, and principal owners of the development group, were the managers of the business that would be the prime tenant and the contractor for the project. Our architectural firm, Dent & Nordhaus, Architects, AIA, was selected to design the project partly because of our willingness to invest half of our fee for partial ownership in the project and partly because of our background in energy efficient design. The biggest hurdle for many property developers is putting together the "upfront" dollars for design, planning, and engineering consultants. Consequently, participation by our firm and the landscape architect in ownership, in lieu of a standard service for fee contract, was highly beneficial for all parties. With no other employees in our firm, my partner Richard Nordhaus and I assumed all the risk and knew we would be working at a reduced rate on the project in hopes of greater long-term returns. With lower initial costs, the building financing

was eased and there was even the expectation (hope?) that a bit of that saving could be put into the quality of the final project.

Some have questioned whether there is a conflict of interest in an architect having an ownership position in a project he or she is designing. Is the architect looking at the financial bottom line rather than being an independent design professional that is obligated to produce the best possible product for the owner within the constraints of the particular project? What we found in this case was a challenge to our skills in designing a strong project that fit within extremely tight limitations on the project from the rental market, construction costs, and the generally restrictive regulatory environment in Santa Fe. I don't think our small ownership position changed anything about our process—other than heightening the need for creative solutions to the above issues. Being party to the financing, we also knew that the construction budget was not, in any way, "elastic."

The Design Brief

The developers of the Keystone Building originally asked for a building of approximately 18,000 square feet with office space on the upper floor and warehouse space on the lower floor. To be competitive in this market segment, construction costs had to be less than $65 per square foot. The conventional approach in this building type is either a series of warehouse bays with stairs to loft type offices within the warehouse volume or to have stairs at each bay entered from the exterior and connecting to the office floor above. Both of these building organizations require stairs for each bay and a toilet room or stubouts for possible future toilet rooms at each floor of each bay. It is rare that this building type responds to the local climate or energy performance criteria other than what is required in the building code.

If parking is needed for more than forty cars then Santa Fe requires much more costly site development standards—thus helping set the maximum allowable built area. The building was further constrained by requirements in the area of terrain management (drainage and runoff control), height limit, setbacks, landscaping areas, and especially by a tough point system for design controls. Although this project is not in the central historic district, there are detailed guidelines concerning building massing, rooflines, window placement, materials, and colors in an effort to keep new construction in rough conformance with the principles underlying the creation of the historic "pueblo"-styled architecture that makes Santa Fe a unique urban setting.

Energy and environmental issues were to be important criteria in the design from the very initiation of the project. In this aspect we were extremely fortunate in having a contractor, Bart Kaltenbach of R. C. Greene Construction and his partner Ren Greene, that have built a number of passive solar buildings, and were experienced with active solar collectors, photovoltaic systems, and water harvesting systems. In addition, the prime tenant is Dankoff Solar, a wholesaler of photovoltaic components including collector panels and PV powered pumps. Paul Benson, the business manager for Dankoff Solar, was the other principal owner and critical to organizing the financing and budgeting for the project. Their expertise and experience didn't lead to a let's do the "whole enchilada" and cost-be-dammed attitude. Instead, they became a highly informed and demanding client that kept our feet to the fire in making cost effective design decisions.

Design Response

The design brief appeared to be reasonable based on the owners and contractor's evaluation of the constraints, but it was worth a second look before we bought into their analysis. The site for the building was a rectangle with its short dimension on the street and its long dimension running east to west. The first thing that modified the initial analysis was the 9-foot drop in grade from south to north across the narrow dimension of the site. This would allow a mid-level entrance from the south to the offices on the upper level. We could then enter the offices from a lower scaled "public" side with the entrance to the 20-foot high warehouses coming from the north or "working" side. The recess into the slope would also be beneficial in reducing the visual bulk of the building, but also reduce exposure to the climatic extremes (see Figure 11-1). It then became apparent that we could add a mezzanine, entered at grade from the south that

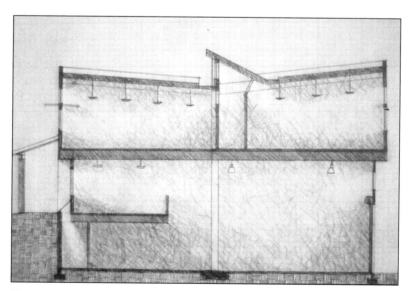

Figure 11-1 North/South cross-section of the Keystone Building (north is on the right). Courtesy of Stephen Dent, Dent & Nordhaus, Architects, AIA. © Stephen D. Dent

opened into the warehouses. By code, the mezzanine could be no more than 33 percent of the warehouse area below and had to open into it. Consequently, the mezzanine area added almost 3,000 square feet to the project for just the cost of the inserted floor, stairs, and railings and probably improved the marketability of the warehouse space. (We just paid for our fee in that one design move!) The building had now grown to 21,000 square feet and was organized into six structural bays 25 feet wide and 60 feet long.

The warehouse space was now well ordered and efficient so we took a fresh look at the office area on the upper level. We were concerned that the offices would be pretty inflexible in the original conception due to their fixed connection to the warehouse plan. By creating a loop hallway circulation system, office spaces could be flexible in area and as large as 4,000 contiguous square feet, but this required a costly elevator. However, having a common circulation system eliminated the need for individual stairs and toilet rooms for each office unit. It was a bit more expensive for the elevator, but it was a good trade-off for generating higher rental rates, easier movement of furniture and equipment, and especially for making the building fully accessible. The basic form was now a compact 60-foot × 150-foot rectangle elongated on the east west axis and partly recessed into the slope—a good start for an energy efficient building. We then cut in corner balconies at each end to break up the overwhelming visual simplicity, capture the distant mountain views, and, serendipitously, meet the design guidelines for "stepped massing." To make up for this lost square footage, we cantilevered the rest of the north side offices two feet at little cost for construction and great value in design richness on this previously flat façade.

The site plan was largely determined by: the parking requirements (40 cars); the delivery area (20 feet wide) for the warehouses; and an ease-

Figure 11-2 The arcade, showing a rich palette of materials (right), and innovative ways of capturing natural light (left). Courtesy of Stephen Dent, Dent & Nordhaus, Architects, AIA. © Stephen D. Dent

ment for a storm water ponding area (25 feet wide on north boundary of the site). In order to ease the movement of trucks around the west end of the site, the building was rotated 6 degrees counterclockwise. We then added an arcade to the south wall that tapers in width from five feet at the west end to ten feet at the east end at the main entry. The arcade moderates the scale, formalizes the mezzanine entries, and provides a shaded transition between the sunlit parking area and the building interior (see Figure 11-2).

Construction System

The basic construction system, because of costs, was to be a light steel frame, metal deck with concrete topping, steel studs, drywall interior, and stucco exterior. We had a preliminary design completed with a standard post and beam steel frame when we were asked by the contractor to have a price comparison made between it and a pre-engineered system. The pre-engineered frame would save about $150,000! However, using this system was not without coordination problems. In order to solve several issues that were important to us we made a major change to the standard long span frame with a center ridge. We inverted the ridgeline to create a "butterfly roof" and added columns on the centerline at each bay to reduce the span and girder depths. We then added a clerestory along the center that further complicated the basic frame. I'm sure the steel fabricators thought we were a bit crazy as they seemed to have a hard time incorporating these changes into the shop drawings. It took several extra iterations, but we finally got the frame design as intended.

Environmental Design Responses

It is important to note that at this scale of building with high internal loads, the primary energy cost issues are lighting and cooling, with heating third in importance. Santa Fe has a great climate for passive solar cooling (large diurnal temperature swings and mild summers), passive solar heating (sunny winters), daylighting (more than 70 percent possible sun for the year), and

natural ventilation (relatively steady breezes with mild temperatures). This is a climate that is driven by its 7,000 foot altitude in the high desert—and just begs to be exploited.

The aforementioned butterfly roof was a major feature of several environmentally responsive strategies. Being higher at the perimeter of the building, it allows daylight to penetrate deeper into the offices, and the low point in the roof collects the rain and snowmelt and directs it to 10,000 gallon storage tanks at each end of the building (see Figure 11-3). With the addition of outside and inside light shelves 8 feet above the floor and a 30-inch window above that, we could control overheating and reduce excessive brightness at the perimeter. The exterior light shelf/sunshade projects 30 inches and the interior light shelf projects 36 inches into the room. The exterior light shelf uses low cost corrugated galvanized sheets while the interior shelf incorporates easily curved flat galvanized sheeting. The clerestory over the center hallway was added to balance the light levels by introducing daylight into the heart of the floor plate and distributing it to the offices by way of high windows in the hall. The warehouses receive daylight from high north windows and fill light from the south where it passes through the mezzanines. This provides more than enough light for simple storage functions, but supplementary electric lighting is needed for more complex tasks.

The first line of defense against the temperature extremes is, of course, a well-insulated envelope. The steel studs are quickly installed and inexpensive and are typically made from recycled steel, but are great heat conductors. A steel stud wall that is fully insulated will have about half the R-value of a comparable wood framed wall. Consequently, $1^1/_2$ inches of rigid insulation was added to the exterior over the sheathing to compensate for the steel's conductivity. Though not a large cost, this is an example of an extra cost that is necessary for an energy efficient building. The roof is insulated to R-38 (and was included with the low slope metal roof in the cost for the pre-engineered steel frame!) The office windows are not the usual commercial windows but are high quality wood framed, alu-

Figure 11-3 The water harvesting feature is artfully expressed in the architecture. Courtesy of Stephen Dent, Dent & Nordhaus, Architects, AIA. © Stephen D. Dent.

minum clad residential windows with low-e glazing. It was actually cheaper to do this and have numerous operable windows than using the commercial windows that had limited options for operability. The warehouse windows use aluminum frames with a thermal break and low-e glazing and include one large operable unit in each bay. The large warehouse doors have 1 inch of rigid insulation and the concrete retaining walls at the lower level are insulated with 2 inches of rigid insulation.

The office heating system is an underfloor radiant system that is easy to control by zone and is extremely quiet and comfortable. In the taller than normal office spaces, the radiant system maintains comfort without heating the greater volume. Our thermal analysis shows that the *primary* heating source is the sun. Passive solar heat is collected and distributed during the winter from the windows and the clerestory when the sun drops below the sunshades and overhangs. An analysis was conducted to deter-

mine the costs of using solar thermal collectors for supplying preheated water to the boiler for the radiant system. This wasn't incorporated at this time but will be installed in the future. The mechanical cooling system for the offices is a series of evaporative coolers that are roof mounted and individually controlled from each office bay. Evaporative coolers function very well in the dry climate and are much less costly to install and operate than refrigeration units. We do, however, have semiannual maintenance costs for shutting them down for winter and cleaning and startup in the spring and they do use water for cooling in an arid environment. But they are not used for an extended period due to the sunshades, insulation, and natural ventilation. The warehouse space has no installed cooling systems, but there is a removable panel and water and power stubouts for possible future wall-mounted evaporative coolers. So far, no tenant has pursued this option.

The major power users are the plug loads and the electric lighting. We, as the architects, have little influence over the electric power requirements generated by the office equipment, computers, desk lamps, etc. We do influence the electric demands from the lighting and suggested an automatic dimming system be installed to maximize the "harvesting" of the daylight. The budget was invoked and this suggestion made a quick exit. Instead, the lighting is switched in rows that parallel the windows and, if used conscientiously, will provide significant savings. The installed fluorescent lighting uses electronic ballasts for both linear and compact lamps. In the public areas, to reduce costs, we designed very inexpensive diffusers for the linear T-8 lamps or have hidden industrial strip lights in coves or soffits.

Santa Fe and most of the mountain west is currently experiencing a major drought that is expected to be long-term. The two large tanks for collecting rain and snowmelt should provide for the entire drip irrigation needs of the native landscaping materials after they have been established for a year or two. If we didn't have the cisterns, the City would not have let us install the specified landscaping until the current water use restrictions are removed. The exposed and architecturally expressed cisterns were unique at the time, but with a continuing drought, the City of Santa Fe is now encouraging them for new construction. To help with runoff control (and reduce costs), we reduced the area of hard surface paving by using gravel for about one third of the parking area. Concerns about long-term maintenance in heavily used driveways, delivery, and parking areas prevented a larger area from being paved with porous materials.

Approval Process

We believed that we would have little demand for our time in getting approvals because the Keystone project was not asking for any variances and we just needed to meet code and regulatory requirements. We were, of course, wrong. The entire approval process took almost a year from initial submittals of the site plan to the receipt of the building permit. The project even had to go before the full City Council for a hearing for Development Plan Approval. In a highly politicized development process like Santa Fe's—and typical in many growing communities—the architect should budget for the extra time for neighborhood meetings, meeting with city officials, and for making required presentations to decision makers. If our Santa Fe-based contractor hadn't followed through with most of the approvals "legwork," we would have really been under-budgeted in this critical component. This is also the only project that we've been involved with that was delayed for several weeks until the site could be visited and cleared for construction by the Prairie Dog Inspector!

Construction Process

The construction process got off to a quick start with the foundations and retaining walls going up quickly and on budget. Then the steel erectors arrived: two workers and a forklift! This isn't a huge building, but progress dramatically slowed for three weeks until a full crew arrived after being diverted to another project. Then, as the frame took shape, we got a visit from the building inspector who had received a complaint from a "neighbor" who thought it was a three-story building when the zoning only allowed two story-buildings and wanted the project shut down. The inspector had to be mollified with a review of the drawings and shown that the "extra" floor was only the mezzanine.

As we got back on schedule we did have a problem with the concrete slab over the steel decking. We hadn't communicated to the steel frame fabricators the need for an extra inch of concrete to accommodate the installation of office partitions without puncturing the radiant heating tubes. They had not included that extra weight in their initial calculations and would charge a significant sum to recalculate and re-size the frame. The owners and contractor decided to avoid that cost and use a lightweight concrete with a fiberglass additive to minimize cracks. All was OK until the concrete was poured and it couldn't be smooth-finished to take concrete stain easily. We have stained the concrete in the common areas and for several tenants, but we are somewhat disappointed with its overall quality.

There were a small number of extra cost items that surfaced during the course of construction, but most were due to cost increases in materials. Since the budget was fixed, the result was a lack of full completion when the occupancy permit was issued. The unfinished items included the interior light shelves, site-built diffusers for some light fixtures, trellises for planting, and a number of smaller finish details. None of this was critical to occupying the building, but was a bit dismaying to the architects. We are used to doing a final punchlist and demanding its satisfactory completion before occupancy or shortly thereafter. As one of the owners, we knew that there simply wasn't the money to do this work at the time, and it is being completed as funds are made available.

Lessons

- The essential environmental responses *had* to be part of the initial design parti and be built into the basic form with little or no extra cost—or they would be cut to make the budget at a later date. This is a critical issue in designing buildings with great expectations and less than great budgets, and one that was successfully accomplished in the Keystone Building. Complex systems or forms are going to be value engineered right out of the project or may lead to abandoning the project altogether. For projects with tight and inflexible budgets—KISS—Keep It Simple, Stupid.

- Be inventive with the given program. Your design skills may lead to space planning efficiencies, innovative spatial or construction approaches, and make your contributions more valuable in the overall economics of the project than in just creating an attractive, functional building.
- During the approval process, keep your humor and patience—"work" the staff. Most plan reviewers and inspectors will be helpful if you don't try to overwhelm them with your knowledge or bully them. They have the power in this relationship and it's best to make friends here or at least develop mutual respect between fellow building professionals. It will pay off, maybe not immediately, but certainly in the long run. You, too, may encounter your very own "Prairie Dog Inspector" and you just have to roll with the punch.
- Ownership pros and cons. It took a separate monetary assessment of all owners to cover the costs of fully completing the project. Wow, when you have to personally help pay for the "architecture," you get a lesson in development economics that can't happen in any other way. This expenditure will be recovered over the next several years, but it has been a bit painful to both ego and pocketbook. We expect that the building will be a great long-term investment, but as architect-investors, we had to accept the discipline of definite budgets and their constraints on our design aspirations.
- Projected energy savings that justify greater initial expenditures must be recovered rather quickly. Life-cycle cost analysis may justify a twenty-year cost recovery, but few developers will let you go more than five years to recover the extra costs. A good approach to get more environmentally sensitive features included is to "bundle" a group together (much as you do with architectural elements) so as not to make any one factor stand out as too costly.
- Monitor your own design work. I suggest that you do post occupancy evaluations, whether formal or informal, to see how successful your project has been for your client. Satisfied clients that are happy to come to the building, enjoy being in it, and leave with some regret are your best advertisement.

Index